FRAMING EQUAL OPPORTUNITY

FRAMING EQUAL OPPORTUNITY

Law and the Politics

of School Finance Reform

Michael Paris

Stanford Law Books
An Imprint of Stanford University Press
Stanford, California

Stanford University Press
Stanford, California

Printed in the United States of America on acid-free, archival-quality paper

Library of Congress Cataloging-in-Publication Data

Paris, Michael, 1960–

Framing equal opportunity : law and the politics of school finance reform /
Michael Paris.

    p. cm.

Includes bibliographical references and index.

ISBN 978-0-8047-6353-0 (cloth : alk. paper) — ISBN 978-0-8047-6354-7
(pbk. : alk. paper)

1. Education—Finance—Law and legislation—New Jersey. 2. Education—
Finance—Law and legislation—Kentucky. 3. Educational equalization—Law
and legislation—New Jersey. 4. Educational equalization—Law and
legislation—Kentucky. I. Title. KFN2190.P375 2009

344.749'076—dc22

2009030099

Typeset by Thompson Type in 10.5/15 Adobe Garamond Pro

For Amy J. Higer

CONTENTS

FRAMING EQUAL OPPORTUNITY

INTRODUCTION

Almost twenty years ago now, Jonathan Kozol's *Savage Inequalities* offered the nation a disturbing portrait of unequal educational opportunities and stunted lives. Kozol took his readers on a journey through public schools in some of America's most impoverished cities and some of its wealthiest suburbs. In the poor cities, such as Camden, New Jersey, and East St. Louis, Illinois, the children were almost to the last one black or Latino, and most lived in poverty. The schools were old, broken down, and largely bereft of material resources. They were fearful places, places where danger lurked at every turn, and even the walls issued dire warnings about things like drug abuse and teen pregnancy. Many teachers and administrators were worn out and demoralized; they had given up hope. And the children, it seemed, knew what to make of all of this. They got the message: The larger society did not care about their education or their lives. In the wealthy suburbs, such as Cherry Hill, New Jersey, and Winnetka, Illinois, of course it was all the other way. Most of the children were white and well off. The schools were modern and clean. Resources were abundant and curricular offerings vast. The schools were cheerful places. Here, enthusiastic teachers were able to provide good teaching and high expectations for learning. And here too, Kozol revealed, the children absorbed messages, although of rather different sorts from those absorbed in the poor cities.[1]

Mr. Kozol's journalism brought us face-to-face with simple questions about basic rights and distributive justice: Why should some children have much less spent on their public education than other children? Does not simple justice demand that poorer, disadvantaged children receive more resources, and not less than or even the same as, their already advantaged peers? Should "education" or "equal educational opportunity" now be included as the pantheon of fundamental constitutional rights?[2]

As it turned out, Kozol wrote at what is now the midpoint of a national school finance reform movement. Like many social change efforts in the United States, this one has relied quite heavily on law and courts. Litigation marked its beginnings in the late 1960s, and litigation continued to drive it even after it suffered a major defeat at the hands of the U.S. Supreme Court in *San Antonio v. Rodriguez* (1973). After *Rodriguez*, litigation campaigns had to proceed in state courts under state constitutional law. Between 1973 and 2007, lawsuits challenging school finance policies reached the high courts of all but seven states.[3]

This book is about the role of "things legal"—lawyers, rights claims, litigation, courts—in struggles to produce more egalitarian school finance and education policies. Unlike most other research on school finance litigation, this book puts the spotlight on would-be reformers and their mobilization of law and courts. It chronicles reformers' use of law and courts in two leading school finance reform cases: New Jersey (1970–2009) and Kentucky (1983–2009). A comparison of reformers' efforts in these two cases provides a great window through which we can gain new insights about the interplay of law and politics in litigation-based reform projects generally.

LEGAL TRANSLATION AND WHY IT MATTERS

This book's central purpose is to highlight the crucial and often neglected role of legal translation in litigation-driven reform efforts. Toward this end, I develop a distinctive interpretive framework for studying the origins, mean-ings, and consequences of legal translation. This focus on legal translation is important because it gives us new purchase on how agents can use law and courts to bring about desired changes in public policies.

The metaphor of translation implies a "carrying over" from one language or domain to another. As I use the term, *legal translation* refers to the conceptual and rhetorical processes though which reformers translate their values and goals into plausible legal claims and arguments. Legal translation involves, simultaneously, an appeal to legal authority and the selection and representation of "facts" and evidence. This definition recognizes that the raw materials for legal translation are potentially quite diverse and that compelling representations of facts often drive the evolution of legal doctrines. It also gives rise to important questions.

What options do reformers have in the framing of legal challenges? What choices do they make about legal translation, and why? What is the relation-ship between legal translation, on the one hand, and reformers' thinking and action with respect to extrajudicial strategies, on the other? What difference does it make for the politics of reform struggles that would-be change agents embrace one kind of legal theory and rhetoric rather than another kind? The answers to these questions help show what legal translation is, how it gets done in context and in practice, and the many ways in which it matters.

Legal translation matters for three reasons. First, speaking one way rather than another within law can either help or hinder reformers in their efforts to mobilize supporters outside of court. Second, because the content of legal claims will have different meanings for different audiences, speaking one way rather than another within law can either neutralize or countermobilize inter-ested third parties and potential opponents. Third, speaking one way rather than another within law provides courts with specifically framed "opportuni-ties for decision." Legal translation can therefore shape the evolution of legal doctrine. In turn, legal doctrine often sets the agenda of contention in politics and defines the language of public debate.

In tracing legal translation's origins and mapping its consequences, I argue that reformers' legal translation processes are shaped by two kinds of ideologi-cal orientations that reformers will have or display.[4] First, reformers will have substantive ideology—that is, a vision encompassing values, perceptions, and goals. Second, reformers will also have a legal ideology—that is, an ideology about law, politics, and change. A substantive ideology provides direction to legal translation simply because reformers resorting to law and courts must render their vision in formal-legal terms. But a legal ideology also shapes translation because what reformers end up saying in court depends in part on how they see their litigation in relation to politics and change.

I offer a typology of three kinds of legal ideologies: legalism (or "the myth of rights"), realism (or "the politics of rights"), and culturalism. As views of law, politics, and change, legalism, realism, and culturalism each yield distinctive senses of what law is and how it relates to politics, how best to structure attorney–client relations, what courts are like and what they can and cannot do, and how social change actually occurs.

In both cases studied in this book, reform groups claimed that school finance policies violated state constitutions; in both, state supreme courts agreed. The two cases are dissimilar, however, in that the respective reform projects embraced different substantive visions of education and inequality, framed different legal arguments (legal translation), and took different approaches to combining litigation with broader political activities. In each case, reformers had to struggle to translate their visions into law. In neither case was the translation process simple or mechanical. In each case, translation mattered, for it influenced reformers' prospects in court and in politics, shaped the content of judicial opinions and the language of public debate, and produced distinctive policy processes and outcomes.

I find that legal strategies work best when used in conjunction with broader political mobilization and coalition building. This finding is consistent with much prior research on law and the politics of reform. However, I also argue that ideological coherence (or fit) across the legal and political prongs of reform projects has an important and overlooked connection to overall success. A focus on legal translation is required to apprehend the ideological content of legal claims and the key question of how that content fits with (or does not fit with) broader political arguments and mobilizing strategies. More generally, the focus on legal translation is intended to foster further reflection and research on how would-be change agents think about legal framing options in relation to political conflict and envisioned processes of change, and on how the content and character of legal arguments matter in politics.

CASE SELECTION AND THE CASES IN BRIEF:
TWO WORLDS OF EDUCATION REFORM

I develop the framework for understanding legal translation in conjunction with the examination of two leading school finance cases. Why school finance reform litigation, and why these two cases?

While working on another topic (known in political science as "the new judicial federalism"), I had occasion to read many school finance decisions. I soon came across two remarkable ones. In *Abbott v. Burke* (1990), the New Jersey Supreme Court mandated that poor children in the Garden State's urban ghettos receive "greater than equal" resources, compared to their already advantaged peers in the state's wealthiest suburbs. In *Rose v. Council for Better Education* (1989), the Kentucky Supreme Court invalidated every state law and regulation pertaining to education. But what struck me most about these two opinions were their radically different ideological content and rhetorical qualities. Although both opinions justified judicial interventions in school finance policy, they proceeded on the basis of different foundational assumptions about public education and inequality. It was as if they had come from two different worlds of meaning. My focus then shifted to understanding how these opinions came to be and to how they mattered in broader social and political contexts. I found their origins in reformers' different choices about legal translation and legal and political mobilization.

Each reform project emerged out of different historical conditions and personal experiences, and each had to make its way through different local political cultures and political-institutional channels. The story of each project is long and complicated. For now, I would just like to highlight the central features of legal translation and legal/political mobilization in each one.

New Jersey: Savage Inequalities In Law and Politics, 1970–2009

The New Jersey school finance controversy encompasses two related cases, *Robinson v. Cahill* (1970 through 1976) and *Abbott v. Burke* (from 1981 to date), and involves twenty-seven separate opinions by the New Jersey Supreme Court. In this effort, lawyers working out of a public interest law office in Newark (the Education Law Center, or ELC), took up the mantle of reform. These lawyers and their allies were steeped in an educational reform ideology that emerged in the mid-1960s in the wake of the civil rights movement. I will refer to this ideological orientation as a "compensatory vision" of education and inequality.

The New Jersey reformers saw racism and poverty as central, intertwined problems in American politics, and public education as a key arena in the struggle for solutions. On this view, as currently organized, public schooling reflects and reinforces "savage inequalities"—illegitimate advantages and disadvantages, systematically related to race and class. If it could be appropriately restructured, however, a system of public education could be a powerful remedial and equalizing force. The principle of distributive justice at the center of this view is compensatory: Educational resources should go disproportionately to the disadvantaged. The metaphor typically invoked for "equal educational opportunity" is that of a competitive but fair footrace for the good things in life.

At crucial turning points in this conflict, the ELC lawyers were remarkably creative in translating this vision into compelling legal claims and arguments. This was no easy task, and I show precisely how these reformers did it. Legal mobilization and judicial receptivity to their claims allowed them to project their vision onto the state's political agenda and to define the terms of public debate, even though many other actors continued to disagree with their views. And, ultimately, reformers won policy changes requiring a vast redistribution of state education aid to poor urban school districts.

In *Robinson v. Cahill* (1973) [*Robinson I*], the New Jersey Supreme Court invalidated the state's school finance system. It accepted the basic contours of reformers' innovative argument, holding that the state constitution's education clause implied an individual right to some substantive "minimum level" of equal educational opportunity. Reformers won an important legal victory in *Robinson* but then suffered a political defeat when they were unable to influence the legislative process thereafter. But the *Robinson* litigation taught reformers some valuable lessons and had other significant "feedback effects." It thus set the stage for the difficult task of translating the compensatory vision into plausible legal claims.

In 1981, the ELC filed its second challenge in a case styled *Abbott v. Burke*. After another decade of legal warfare, the New Jersey Supreme Court embraced reformers' vision and boldly fashioned its own remedial tests to implement this vision as policy. In *Abbott II* (1990), the court held that the state constitution required that children in twenty-eight poor urban districts receive at least as much money for regular education as did children in the state's wealthiest suburbs. Over and above this "parity mandate," the court also ordered the state to formulate and fund special compensatory programs and services in the poor urban districts. Widespread resistance to these judicial mandates then sent reformers back to court again and again. And, again and again, the New Jersey Supreme Court stayed the course. The mandated parity funding was finally achieved in 1997–1998. Since then, battles over the funding and implementation of additional programs and services have been ongoing. Between 1990 and 2005–2006, poor urban school districts received approximately $3 billion more in basic education aid than they would have received otherwise, absent the reformers' project and the favorable court decisions. In many ways, then, this is as success story about how a group of intrepid liberal reformers mobilized law and courts to transform educational policy in their state.

At the same time, I highlight two main criticisms of the New Jersey reform project. First, these reformers were often overly legalistic in their approach to litigation and social change. For a very long time, they acted as though legal pronouncements coming from courts would be sufficient to bring about desired changes. Eventually, they learned that this was not so, and that answers to puzzles of political change, if they are to be found at all, must be found through political action as well as litigation. Indeed, I argue that reformers rescued their entire project from constitutional obliteration in 1992 only by adroitly using their court victories for political mobilization, deal making, and coalition building. It was reformers' late turn to politics, and nothing else, that enabled the state high court to remain steadfast in its own commitment to redistributive change. Second, for strategic reasons not unrelated to their legalism, the New Jersey reformers frequently evaded and repressed legitimate questions about what else might have to change in poor school districts before additional resources could be used wisely. Questions about the wise use of resources have always haunted the New Jersey reform project, and they continue to haunt it to this day.[5]

Kentucky: The Common School and the Quest for Consensus, 1983–2009

In Kentucky, the reform project began in 1983 when a state-level administrator organized a group of school districts to back a legal challenge to the state's school finance system. This administrator put local school officials in contact with prominent local lawyers and policy experts. By mid-1985, the group included sixty-six of Kentucky's then existing 180 school districts. The group then incorporated as the Council for Better Education and filed suit. The Kentucky reform effort was also supported by a separate citizen's organization called the Prichard Committee for Academic Excellence. Founded in 1983, the Prichard Committee was initially much less concerned with school finance than with other educational policy issues. At the outset of the litigation, these two reform groups declined to work together. However, just before the case reached trial in 1987, they joined forces in support of the litigation.

After the trial court rendered a decision in reformers' favor in 1988, state defendants appealed directly to the Kentucky Supreme Court. In *Rose v. Council for Better Education* (1989), the state high court used the finance challenge as the occasion for striking down all laws and regulations pertaining to the state's entire public school system. Within a year after this sweeping decision, the legislature passed the Kentucky Education Reform Act of 1990 (KERA). KERA was an ambitious, multifaceted reform law. It included not only a new school finance system but also a welter of other substantive educational reforms. The finance reforms produced an infusion of funds for education from both state and local levels and a significant narrowing of the expenditure gap between rich and poor districts. The entire effort and its integrated set of "systemic" reforms soon made Kentucky, of all places, a nationally recognized leader in education reform.[6]

The Kentucky reformers championed what I will characterize as a common school vision of public education and equal opportunity. Unlike the educational reform ideology at work in New Jersey, the common school vision emphasizes education for common citizenship and social integration, and downplays the competitive, economic purposes and functions of schooling. When it comes to policy reform, proponents of this view tend to focus on the content of the curriculum, pedagogical style, and the culture and sense of mission in and around schools. The rhetorical emphasis is on what all children share (or should share) in common through public education, whatever their differences.

Moreover, unlike the New Jersey advocates, the Kentucky reformers took a realistic, pragmatic approach to litigation and change. Throughout, they coordinated their lawsuit with broader political strategies. Over time, this combination of litigation and political action created a favorable environment for bold judicial intervention and sweeping policy change. But there is more to this story than the mere fact of political efforts to complement litigation.

I argue that the Kentucky reformers' success can be explained not only by their sustained and coordinated use of legal and political strategies, but also by the ideological coherence of their overall project. In everything they said and did, in many different institutional locations and forums, they marched under the same banner of the common school. On this analysis, ideological coherence across legal and political prongs of reform efforts emerges as an important but generally overlooked factor in explaining the success or failure of litigation-involved reform projects.

In these two case studies, then, different patterns of legal and political mobilization, including significantly the nature of legal translation, shaped quite different local "cultures of argument" about education, inequality, and school finance policies. Each case represents a distinctive style of school finance litigation and reform. Each is in its own way a success story, and each has its particular problems, tensions, and unintended consequences, both positive and negative.

LEGAL MOBILIZATION THEORY
AND THE POLITICS OF REFORM

There is a long tradition of research in political science concerned with the role of things legal in struggles for social change. The umbrella term most often used to describe this tradition is *legal mobilization theory*.[7] The use of the word *mobilization* signals that agency and process are being studied. Whatever their differences, legal mobilization approaches typically shift the spotlight away from the more common focus on courts and judicial impact and shine it on the practical consciousness and strategic choices of would-be change agents. These approaches also typically conceptualize law as potentially "constitutive" of social relations and political understandings. On this view, specifically legal discourses are potentially powerful in the construction of cultural understandings and framing of politics.

I draw on this research tradition by provisionally adopting the standpoint of reformers and examining the interplay of law and politics from their perspective, by exploring the role of legal ideas and arguments in framing public debates and political conflicts, and by using a case study approach and interpretive methods in order to gain access to agents' practical consciousness and strategic thinking in relevant contexts.

But I go further, by offering a conceptual vocabulary and framework for a "closer-in" focus on legal translation, which, in turn, facilitates an exploration of the political implications of legal framing, both within reform organizations and in broader political contexts. In my view, existing research has not taken questions about legal framing options and choices seriously enough. Actors often have some measure of choice in how they project their claims into the legal system, and, I show, these choices are of great moment. Legal framing options ought to be regarded as a kind of political opportunity, and opportunities can be seized or missed. In addition, I think there is more to say about reformers' use of both legal and political strategies. Once we have a clear picture of legal translation, we can then examine how the content of legal claiming matches up with what reformers are saying and doing outside the courts. Again, I argue that ideological coherence across the legal and political prongs of reform projects is an important but overlooked factor that increases the likelihood of success.

PART I

IDEOLOGIES IN TRANSLATION

LEGAL MOBILIZATION THEORY AND LEGAL TRANSLATION: OLD TERRITORY AND NEW FRONTIERS

IN THE EARLY 1970S, STUART SCHEINGOLD SET OUT TO understand "the part that lawyers and litigation could play in altering the course of public policy" in favor of relatively disadvantaged groups. Gaining insight into this topic, he argued, depended on "abandon[ing] the conventional legal perspective and replac[ing] it with a political approach to law and change." He called the conventional perspective "the myth of rights," and the political perspective "the politics of rights."[1]

Scheingold's effort marked an important break from mainstream political science work on law and courts. Whereas mainstream approaches placed judges and courts at the center of analysis, Scheingold focused on the mindset and strategic thinking of would-be change agents. And whereas mainstream work adopted what purported to be a normatively disinterested stance, Scheingold acknowledged his practical interests in social change and his desire for engagement with his research subjects. He wanted better to understand the dynamics of law, politics, and change because better understanding might foster more informed and effective action in the world.[2]

The Politics of Rights thus staked out a new territory of inquiry. This territory has been for the most part populated by scholars "on the left" interested in the relationship between things legal and social movements or reform projects. In this chapter, I tell the story of the origins and development of legal mobilization approaches to the study of law and the politics of change. Like all stories, this one is highly selective and told with specific purposes in mind—three purposes, to be exact. The first purpose is to trace the trajectory of research from Scheingold's initial departure to current theorizing about law and change; the second is to sift out of this research tradition an account of three ideological orientations toward law, politics, and change; and the third is to address a few theoretical and methodological issues specific to my narrative case study approach and subject matter.

THE ORIGINS AND DEVELOPMENT
OF LEGAL MOBILIZATION THEORY

Scheingold's Argument

Scheingold described and criticized a broad ideological view of law, politics, and change that he labeled "the myth of rights." What Scheingold called the myth of rights is what I will be calling "legalism." Scheingold's book explicated and sought to debunk legalism and to replace it with a "politics of rights" perspective, which, he argued, gave us a more accurate account of "how law and politics actually work." What Scheingold called the politics of rights is the view that I will be calling realism.[3]

In his explication of the myth of rights, Scheingold relied on earlier work by political theorist Judith Shklar. Shklar had argued that legalism was an ideology that held that moral conduct was a matter of rule following. Legalists, she wrote, isolated law completely from its social contexts, treating it as "a single 'block' sealed off from general social history, from social theory, from politics and morality." Legalists believed "that law is not only separate from political life but a mode of social action superior to mere politics." They associated law with morality and high principle, and politics with mere self-interest and expediency.[4]

Scheingold retained Shklar's view as part of what he meant by the myth of rights. However, his myth of rights was broader than Shklar's legalism. It included not only beliefs about morality and law, but also more specific beliefs about American constitutionalism, law and politics in the United States, American courts, and the causal dynamics of social change. "Ideologists" (or law professors) and "strategists" (or reform lawyers) of rights, as Scheingold called them, tended to see things legal as things apart from, and over and above, mere politics—as a morally superior " 'block' sealed off," as Shklar put it.

Generally, the myth of rights began with reverence for the Constitution. On this view, the Constitution laid down timeless values to which wise judges could repair to restrain the erratic impulses of democracy. The long-noted American tendency to legalize conflicts, to turn political questions into judicial ones, made politics more coherent and rational. The myth of rights saw law as the realm of reason and courts as forums where reason could rule. Moreover, Scheingold argued, the myth of rights had tremendous cultural resonance in American politics and society. It provided a basic grammar for thinking about social organization and problem solving across a wide range of settings.[5]

In the specific context of efforts to use law and courts to bring about social change, Scheingold described the myth of rights and its import as follows:

Legal frames of reference tunnel the vision of both activists and analysts leading to an oversimplified approach to a complex social process—an approach that grossly exaggerates the role that lawyers and litigation can play in a strategy for change. The assumption is that litigation can evoke a declaration of rights from courts; that it can, further, be used to assure the realization of these rights; and, finally, that realization is tantamount to meaningful change. The *myth of rights* is, in other words, premised on a direct linking of litigation, rights, and remedies with social change.[6]

The myth of rights, then, was a distorted yet powerfully beguiling view of things legal and social change.

Why was the myth in fact myth? Scheingold gave four main reasons. First, the Constitution and laws embodied particular liberal values, such as individualism, faith in a market economy, and fear of state power. Causes posing challenges to these values would not easily be able to play the law game. Second, bench and bar were powerfully socialized to believe in the myth of rights. Even reform-oriented lawyers generally accepted the myth of rights as accurate description. They often distrusted democratic mobilization and protest, preferring instead to rely exclusively on litigation. Third, because the legal process was slow and costly, it could sap movements of energy and resources. Fourth, contrary to the myth, courts acting alone lacked the will, raw power, and/or technical capacity to produce the policy and social changes that reformers sought.

Therefore, Scheingold expressed "serious doubts about the capabilities of legal and constitutional processes for neutralizing power relationships." The "authoritative declaration of rights" was "usually only the beginning of a political process where power relationships loom rather large." However, even as his critique of the myth of rights implied pessimism about law and change, Scheingold's "politics of rights" perspective provided grounds for guarded optimism as well.[7]

The politics of rights was "a term to describe the forms of political activity made possible by the presence of rights in American society." Turning to law and courts could help change agents legitimize grievances and catalyze organization among relatively powerless groups. The politics of rights would involve the instrumental use of rights claims and litigation to produce positive, indirect effects. If activists and lawyers became more aware of the limitations of legal strategies in isolation and the potential of the political approach, then things legal could be vital, if ancillary, weapons in struggles of change. This analysis "underscore[d] the crucial importance of thinking about legal tactics in combination with other modes of political action."[8]

I want to note two central features of Scheingold's notion of the politics of rights. First, his implicit theory of social change held that certain forms of political action were more valuable and potent than other forms. This theory placed great faith in the transformative potential of democratic mobilization in political conflict. This is why, in his view, legal strategies are best conceptualized as ancillary weapons in broader, bottom-up struggles. Second, Scheingold's conception of law and politics was predominantly realistic. Its virtues notwithstanding, from our vantage point it is clear that one defect of realism is that it neglects the potential significance of legal arguments and legal doctrines. Thus, in *The Politics of Rights*, we find virtually no attention to the specific content of legal claims or judicial opinions. The notion that ideas in law might play a role in framing politics was outside Scheingold's realistic frame of reference.[9]

Yet, there was a "culturalist" undercurrent in Scheingold's analysis. His essentially anthropological insights about cultural resonance and symbolic power of rights pointed toward a cultural analysis of law—toward the role that ideas in law might play in politics, and to the need to examine various actors' consciousness about law and politics.[10]

Realism and Positivism/Culturalism and Interpretivism

The tension between legal realism and culturalism in Scheingold's analysis continued to mark research on the topic of law and social reform. Since the mid-1970s, these two conceptions of things legal and change have each been associated with two basic approaches to social inquiry and valid knowledge. Although there is no necessary relationship between these pairs, there is a strong affinity between realist conceptions of law and social-scientific positivism, on one hand, and culturalism and social-scientific interpretivism, on the other.

Positivism is an epistemological theory about how to obtain valid knowledge about the world, including the social world. Looking to the natural sciences for models, positivists "seek to explain social behavior through the formulation of causal laws . . . which allow reliable, probabilistic prediction."[11]

Realist analyses of law and policy change generally proceed through two steps. First, the realist observer provides an account of the legalistic story—the official version that sees law as a set of rules and commands that are to be obeyed simply because they are law. Second, the observer notes and investigates the frequent "gaps" between the official version and what really happened and why.[12]

On the topic of social reform litigation specifically, realist inquiry has examined both the determinants of rule change and the political logic of implementation and impact. On these views, legal reformers use litigation, either alone or in conjunction with other strategies, to seek favorable court decisions and policy change. Courts may then direct others to enact new policies or change their behaviors. Others then change their behaviors, or they do not. These inquiries seek to give us some purchase on the causal forces influencing outcomes at various points in the legal and political process. Law is seen as an instrumental tool, and the devil lives in the details of the gap. This conception of law lends itself to the specification of variables and the building of general models. Exposing the gap is what has long given realist scholarship its critical edge.

Leading examples of this affinity between legal realism and social-scientific positivism include Joel Handler's still-useful *Social Movements and the Legal System* (1978) and Gerald Rosenberg's widely debated and now classic *The Hollow Hope* (1991). Both works marry a hyperrealist conception of law to a positivistic outlook on social inquiry. Handler also asked whether litigation and court decisions produce social change. He then constructed a model of five variables about litigation and its contexts, with each one varying from unfavorable to favorable to change. He argued that in many situations one variable— "the bureaucratic contingency"—was both crucial and unfavorable. Rosenberg asked whether landmark Supreme Court decisions like *Brown* and *Roe* actually produced the changes for which many in the legal world give them full credit. After closely investigating hypothesized causal links between the decisions and measurable indicators of change, Rosenberg reached the general conclusion that courts alone had little power to produce either direct or indirect positive effects. The real causal forces driving change lay elsewhere.

These analyses are useful for puncturing the oversimplifications of legalism. For example, if reformers who turn to courts are unmindful of the wide gap that separates rule change and bureaucratic rationalities of action (Handler's bureaucratic contingency), then Handler's work teaches a valuable lesson. Or, more broadly, if reformers think that courts are powerful change agents, then Rosenberg's argument will certainly make them rethink that view.[13]

However, these realistic, positivistic approaches miss a great deal of relevant complexity by reading law simply as rules and policy commands. The commitment to social-scientific positivism means that the researcher is unconcerned with agents' practical consciousness. Therefore, this work does not tell us much about why people turn to litigation in the first place and what they expect to get out of it. Nor can it enlighten us about the content of legal arguments and their role in constructing the ideological terrain of conflict and social meanings. Understanding these important dimensions of law and politics requires a different approach.

An alternative approach—one that is interpretivist rather than positivist in its approach to social inquiry and culturalist rather than realist in its conception of law—emerged over the course of the 1980s and 1990s. It received its fullest elaboration in Michael McCann's work.[14]

Interpretivism is the view that the social sciences are distinct from the natural sciences because the social sciences "focus on thinking, interpreting, meaningfully oriented subjects, subjects who construct the world through shared meanings, in contrast to the insensate objects of the natural sciences." Interpretive accounts of social phenomena often proceed "in consideration of the understandings of the participants involved." As such, they involve interpretations of interpretations, as Geertz put it. Interpretivists generally agree that social action and events are shot through with complexity and indeterminacy. They argue that "thicker," more nuanced interpretive accounts may teach us things that we cannot learn from positivist approaches and models.[15] Over the past thirty years, there has been a general "interpretive turn" in inquiry across the social sciences. Interpretive legal mobilization theory reflects this broader trend.

Interpretive legal mobilization approaches drew on several strands of theory and research in the 1980s and 1990s. The critical legal studies movement in the legal academy focused new attention on law and legal discourses as potentially powerful (constitutive) sources of ideology and social meaning. The CLS critique of rights, in particular, gave rise to debates over the nature of rights and rights discourse, especially with respect to the claims and projects of subordinated groups. Around the same time, in law and society research, a focus on "disputes" and social processes of "naming, blaming, and claiming" pointed toward the cultural significance of legal language. In political science in the 1980s, several scholars built a bridge between realist and culturalist conceptions of law and social reform. Finally, in sociology, research on social movements turned from the rationalistic "resource mobilization approach" to a cognitive and political process approach centrally concerned with issue framing and symbolic dimensions of movement activity.[16]

In *Rights at Work* (1994), McCann drew on all of these trends in developing a general legal mobilization framework. First, McCann begins by endorsing a "standpoint shift," from law and courts to would-be change agents who mobilize the law. As a research strategy, the observer seeks to occupy the point of view of a specified set of individual and group actors. The goal is to understand meaning and action from the vantage point of these actors, given their history, experiences, goals, and sense of their environment.[17] Second, McCann embraced and further developed the culturalist conception of law, which he referred to as "law as social practice." This conception does not supplant realism but rather supplements and complicates it. Law is intertwined with politics, and things legal are nothing if not instrumental weapons. But things legal are not just that, for they embody and promote ideas and discourses that exist in complex relation with other cultural and political discourses.[18]

Third, McCann's theory placed legal mobilization within broader social and political contexts. Of course, the interpretive observer's sense of "relevant contexts" is itself a matter of interpretation; potentially relevant contexts are almost limitless. McCann constructed the relevant contexts for legal mobilization in social movement efforts mainly by placing legal claims and activities within a broader, process-based account of social movement goals and actions. He examined how law and rights worked at distinct phases of social movement activity. In turn, he also constructed contexts for action by placing the social movements themselves within broader economic and political contexts.[19]

McCann used this framework to study the role of legal mobilization in feminist/labor struggles for pay equity in the late 1970s and 1980s. He found that activists "derived substantial power from legal tactics despite only limited judicial support." Moreover, they were quite realistic about the potential utility and disutility of legal strategies. They understood and capitalized on litigation's "educating and mobilizing potential." From his culturalist perspective, then, McCann observed actors practicing a sophisticated, "politics of rights" approach.[20]

Legal Mobilization and Legal Translation

Legal mobilization is a complex process. It requires having and deploying particular resources, like money and legal knowledge; framing and marshalling evidence for legal claims; and contending with adversaries who have their own ideological commitments and resources. My interest in legal mobilization focuses with particular care on *legal translation* and how and why it matters. I offer a conceptual vocabulary for understanding legal framing processes and how legal framing can matter. Through a sharper, closer-in focus on legal practice, I seek to uncover how lawyer-reformers and their associates think about and rework the intellectual and ideological resources provided by law. The idea of legal translation anchors this inquiry. Legal translation should be seen as a central activity within legal mobilization.

Legal theorists like Martha Minow, James Boyd White, and Anthony Amsterdam and Jerome Bruner, among others, have shown what it means to pay attention to the narrative and rhetorical dimensions of legal claiming and argumentation. White has made the idea of translation central to his accounts of the "worlds of meaning" created within legal texts.[21] Amsterdam and Bruner define *rhetorics* as "the various linguistic processes by which a speaker can create, address, avoid, or shape issues that the speaker is called upon to contest . . . [S]etting the agenda of contention is crucial move for all rhetoricians." Categories and narratives are the building blocks of rhetoric in law. Categorization itself is an act of meaning making, with narratives forming larger wholes within which categories fit and work. Working the law involves "category-and-fact work," within broader contexts. The law, Amsterdam and Bruner say, is "awash in storytelling."[22]

In the context of reform struggles, legal translation is best viewed as a practical political activity infused with reformers' desires, calculations, and goals. Again, I define legal translation as the conceptual and rhetorical processes though which reformers translate their moral values and political goals into plausible legal claims and arguments. It involves both an appeal to legal authority and the selection and representation of "facts" and evidence. We can also distinguish between "framing" and "construction" in the legal translation process. Framing involves the mental road map through legal doctrine and factual representations, and construction involves the actual nuts and bolts of execution in court.

I view legal translation as a process proceeding from two basic, ideological starting points. First, we can give an account of reformers' substantive ideological vision and how they go about translating that vision into plausible legal terms. Second, and more to the point here, we can give an account of reformers' ideological orientation toward law, politics, and change (or, their "legal ideology," as distinguished from their "substantive reform ideology"). Legal translation and the use of legal strategies will depend in part on whether reformers are basically legalistic, realistic, or culturalist in their orientation toward things legal, politics, and change.

THREE IDEOLOGICAL ORIENTATIONS
TOWARD LAW, POLITICS, AND CHANGE:
LEGALISM, REALISM, AND CULTURALISM

These three ideologies about law and politics are oversimplified pictures that are nevertheless useful for examining how activists and lawyers think about things legal in reform struggles. Although each orientation may be embraced on either side of the observer/observed divide, my discussion here will focus on how actors in the world would think and act under each of the three orientations. While the terms *legalism*, *realism*, and *culturalism* focus on the conception of law and politics at the heart of each view, each also entails a different outlook on other key components of law and courts in reform projects. I suggest that each orientation gives us a different take on the following roughly linked *six elements of reform thinking and practice*:

1. How actors understand the nature of law and its relationship to politics;

2. How actors understand the primary audience for their legal claims;

3. How actors understand the nature of the attorney–client or attorney–constituent relationship;

4. How actors view the nature of judicial decision making, or why courts decide cases the way they do;

5. How actors see the implementation powers and capacities of courts and the likely impact of court decisions;

6. How actors understand the nature of social change processes (or how change actually occurs).

In practice, the three orientations and six elements are not neat boxes. Views in the real world are mixed. For example, reformers may be highly legalistic about some things, but basically realistic about others. Beliefs and practices also evolve and shift over time. Here, I provide a sketch of each view and note a few key manifestations of each in the case studies.[23]

Legalism

Legalism, or "the myth of rights," views law as an autonomous realm of ideas and practices that are superior to mere politics. Legalistic actors both believe in and trade on the broader optimistic hope in American politics that law has the capacity to rationalize (in the good sense) political debate and to render substantive justice. In law and courts, principled legal arguments matter. Whether legal doctrine is taken to be relatively determinate or indeterminate, legalists believe that well-formed doctrinal arguments shape judicial decision making. It takes talented lawyers immersed in the legal culture to make persuasive, principled arguments, perhaps with a supporting role for social scientific experts. When presented with such arguments, courts will "say the law," and then everyone else will do what the courts say, because the law is the law. In its pure form, legalism is unconcerned with questions of broader political mobilization to produce change and problems of implementation after a court victory is obtained.

In legalism, the logic of legal framing is heavily shaped by the fact that reform lawyers have their eyes exclusively on the courts. The courts are really the only audience, and winning the best possible court decision is really the only goal. How the legal translation process goes will depend on the reformers' particular substantive goals, the array of traditional doctrinal materials, and the particular constitution of, and conventional principles of elicitation within, particular judicial systems and courts. As we will see in the New Jersey case, legalism certainly does not preclude, and may sometimes even foster, creative legal translation. However, legalistic reform lawyers will worry almost exclusively about pleasing judges. Hence, in this tradition, lawyers and law reform groups are quite partial to the "big test case" strategy of legal change and quite concerned about maintaining the "control" that they think test case litigation requires. Legalists are therefore uncomfortable with broader political mobilization that might disrupt their felt need to control the legal process.

Legalism also entails distrust of ordinary citizens' involvement in the formulation of legal strategies. Clients are of little import, beyond their role as "nominal" or "phantom" plaintiffs. Legalistic lawyers typically cast about for and select the clients to play a predetermined role in a carefully stage-managed affair. The clients may be particularly admirable people, or their stories might offer particularly graphic examples of general problems, but they will disappear from view shortly after the initial press conference announcing the litigation. The "constituencies" other than the formal plaintiffs that matter the most are often those who provide the money to support litigation activity. Liberal foundations loom large in the history of legalistic social reform litigation. Given the legalistic view of law and politics and its concomitant view of lawyer–client relations, little thought is given to how litigation might foster political mobilization.

Legalism sees courts as powerful institutional and moral actors capable of purifying politics and righting wrongs. Courts are seen as unique forums in which elevated discussions take place and in which reason can rule. Judicial declarations of law are moral imperatives. Courts are much like E. F. Hutton in the famous advertisement of yesteryear: When they speak, everyone else listens. Those who disagree and disobey act immorally. Here, legal change may simply be assumed to be tantamount to real change. Legalists tend to overlook the wide gulf that often separates judicially articulated rights, on one hand, and the beliefs and practices of public officials or citizens, on the other.

Legalism in pure form seems to be increasingly rare in social reform practice. No one really buys this story as an accurate description of how things work anymore. However, as Shklar and Scheingold taught us, legalism does embody widespread hopes and aspirations, and these aspirations make legalism far more than just a sham. Because many of us want the official story to be true, legalism matters. Historical conventions and deeply embedded practices give us legalism. It can work as either an ideal horizon or a negative reference point. We cannot very well think about realism or culturalism without reference to legalism first. Moreover, as the cause lawyering literature has shown, actors can trade on the aspirational side of legalism without fully buying it. Actors may appear to be talking the talk and walking the walk, but they may well be making eyes-open strategic calculations about the best path to their goals.[24]

Realism

Realism views law as not much separate from politics. Rather, law is simply one form of politics. What happens within law and courts has much to do with what happens elsewhere. Realistic activists and lawyers are therefore more likely to see litigation as one weapon that can serve broader and more important political purposes. Realists view the legal system with skepticism. They know that the myth of rights is in fact myth—a badly oversimplified and distorted picture of how law and politics really works—but they know also that legal challenges can be newsworthy, that groups sometimes do rally around the lawsuit, and that courts can leverage gains in other institutional settings. The calculus of legal action involves whether, on balance, it will do more harm than good in helping one get things done in politics. A realist has a clear sense of the potential financial and political costs of litigation, as well as the potential benefits.

When it comes to framing legal actions, the courts are regarded as but one potential audience. Under certain conditions, realists will pursue legal claims that they know the courts will likely reject. Losing cases can sometimes help set the political agenda. Even the mere threat of litigation can sometimes provide leverage in political battles. Realism holds that legal doctrine is malleable. Its specific content is important only insofar as it has to be taken seriously in calculations about what courts might do, and this calculation sits within a broader calculus of law and politics. The specific content of legal arguments is much less important than the strategic benefits of using law to mobilize constituencies and enlisting courts as allies.

Compared to legalism, the realistic outlook posits a far different ideal relationship between lawyers and clients. Because the broader configuration of interests and raw distribution of political power will be dispositive in any conflict, the realist wants and seeks active group participation, both in the formulation of litigation strategies and in other forums. On this view, activists understand the mobilizing potential of litigation and self-consciously seek to use it accordingly.

Realism holds that judges are political animals who got to be judges for just that reason. Judges make political decisions for the same reasons that other political officials do. Judges do have understandings of law and the role of courts, and these understandings matter. But judges are also open to political pressures, even if legalism denies it. Courts can be "lobbied" in various ways. What judges think can sometimes be shifted by the human dramas unfolding before them in the courtroom. Realism also holds that the battle for real change often only begins with a favorable court decision. Implementation will require political power and sustained attention. Changes often do not come directly from courts, but require a series of complex interactions, moves, and countermoves, among many players.

Culturalism

The culturalist orientation builds on, modifies, and complicates the realist one. Like realism, culturalism sees legal doctrine as indeterminate and malleable. Unlike realism, however, culturalism does not see the content of legal doctrine as merely derived from, or a cover for, the harder stuff of material interests and raw power. In culturalism, the indeterminacy and malleability of legal doctrine do not mean that it is unimportant. Legal discourses are "part of our culturally conditioned ways of making sense of things." Legal ideas and doctrines can structure politics in first place by setting the terms of political debate and parameters of action, and they can provide discursive resources for reshaping meanings.[25]

Once we say that legal doctrine is relatively indeterminate but often of great moment, we go beyond legalism's and realism's respective ways of thinking about the significance what is said in law in struggles for social change. Legalism tends to wall off legal doctrine and institutions from broader politics and culture. Doctrinal arguments are focused on courts and winning favorable decisions from them. Realism distrusts but trades on the ideas of legal autonomy and the rule of law. However, it does so without much concern about the specific content of doctrinal claims and arguments. Culturalism retains realism's politics of rights approach but makes the content of legal arguments far more important in many social locations outside of courts.

Culturalism is not typically an elaborated position to which actors in the world subscribe, at least not in the terms used by academic observers. However, culturalism does often seem to be intuitively grasped and made part of reform practice.[26] Culturalism guides practice whenever we can say of an agent that she or he adds culturalist sensibilities to realism's concern with using law to foster political mobilization and the redistribution of power. A change agent's thinking about the attorney-client relationship would still value active client participation, but now the content and meaningfulness of legal claims would come into view for their potential effects on political mobilization. Legal translation options, and the content and power of the story told in law, would now be part of the calculus. Like realism, culturalism does not necessarily view courts as the primary audience or forum for claiming, although in culturalism the content of judicially articulated doctrine is given more weight as a force that can define the terrain of conflict. Legal argument embodies certain highly stylized and abstract forms, and these forms certainly can be confining and distorting. But law is widely regarded as authoritative. Ideas embodied in law can themselves be part of what constitutes the language of public debate. In any prospective assessment of likely difficulties in the implementation of policy change, a culturalist actor will think about the importance of ideas in law in shaping the discourse within which policy conflict takes place. While culturalist sensibilities yield no determinate answers about what to do, they do counsel mindfulness about the content and significance of legal claims, *in conjunction with* the mobilization of political action outside of the courts.[27]

From Legalism to Realism: The New Jersey Reform Project

Legalism was the predominant legal ideology of the New Jersey school finance reform project for about twenty years, from the early 1970s until the early 1990s. Legalism did not preclude highly creative legal translation. Legal reformers worked with legal doctrine to frame claims that projected their substantive vision of educational reform in the courts and through the courts onto the political agenda. But the audience for their claims was exclusively the courts. They opted for phantom plaintiffs and eschewed all forms of political mobilization until political necessity became the mother of invention. That is, until unbending political realities proved them wrong, they believed that once the courts rendered justice, all would bow down before the courts. The law is the law, after all. The New Jersey project thus has valuable lessons to teach us. It teaches us much about creative legal translation, and much about why creative legal translation is not enough.

Eventually, the New Jersey reformers became adept at coordinating legal and political strategies. They became much more realistic about law, politics, and change, with some considerable help from the political insights of the nonlawyers among them. It helped too that the courts were willing and able to offer ongoing support. But twenty years of legalism left a legacy of political and policy problems that haunt them to this day, notwithstanding their stunning success in bringing about egalitarian change.

Realism-cum-Culturalism: The Kentucky Reform Project

The Kentucky reform project offers a great case study of what culturalism would mean in practice. Here, the reformers, some of whom were politicians by trade, grasped realism's critique of legalism. Realism can explain much of what they did. However, many of them realized that their legal challenge was integral to a much larger public education campaign designed to change the way most people thought about public education. They knew that people had to act in politics in order to convey their particular "common school" message about education reform, and that it was important that that particular message got projected in court too. Although they were not entirely self-conscious about it all, and although different organizational actors made different contributions, overall the Kentucky reform project evidenced a deep awareness of law's cultural power. There was a great deal of ideological coherence between reformers' legal challenge and their arguments in political forums. These reformers also engaged in sustained, concerted action consistent with their overall vision. That is, they "enacted" this vision not only by what they said, but also by how they conducted themselves, in both law and politics. Ideological coherence and consistent actions demonstrated their commitment to their vision and their faith in democratic politics.

PARTICULAR THEORETICAL ISSUES AND ADAPTATIONS

A Brief Case for the Narrative Case Study

The goal of understanding the consciousness and action of would-be change agents "in context" has led me to take a narrative case study approach. The focus on legal translation has led me to pay particular attention to what political scientists sometimes deride as "legal doctrine" or "lawyer's law." The goal is to situate ourselves with the relevant actors as they contemplated their situation and made their choices. That cannot be done unless the narrative presentation is a relatively thick one replete with events unfolding over time and the details of legal doctrine and public policies.

Of course, no narrative presentation, however detailed, can hope to capture agency and action in the fullness of space and time. All narrative accounts proceed from and impose categories for classifying and observing events. All select out a few salient facts and events from an overwhelming number of possible ones.[28] The difference between an analytic approach that reorganizes reality under social scientific categories and a thick narrative approach focused on lived senses of agency, action, trouble and drama, is simply that the latter makes some attempt to represent consciousness and agency as situated and the former does not. The narrative approach is particularly well suited to portraying the meaning of problems and actions for the actors themselves at specific moments. It works out from and in dialogue with the actors' understandings, taking cognizance first of matters within their purview. This would seem to be the only way that an observer can fairly say of some choice that it made sense or that it did not, or of some performance that it was well done or not, or of some road not taken that it was both possible and desirable.

The sociologists Joe Feagin, Anthony Orum, and Gideon Sjoberg argue for the narrative case study through an appeal to "holism"—that is, the notion that (some) whole is greater than the sum of its parts. Narrative case studies uniquely provide a sense of motives and meanings, of definitions of situations, of decisions taken in context. They quote historian Simon Schama: "As artificial as written narratives might be, they often correspond to the ways in which historical actors construct events."[29] Narratives have the added advantages of grounding social scientific concepts and theories in the lived experience of social actors and thereby checking the researcher's interpretations against the understandings of those same actors. Narratives often suggest new relationships and theoretical possibilities, even if propositions asserted through "the enchainment of events" will not be subjected to rigorous formal testing.[30]

Narrative case study research also has its characteristic defects. Stories can be told in many ways, from many points of view. The question of why a story is being told is therefore a crucial one. My stories place reformers who mobilized the law at the center of things. One danger here is that "a focused study often attributes more influence to the subjects of the study than is warranted."[31] Following particular people and trying to see the world as they saw it risks limiting the observer's vision by tying it too closely to the particular actors. It risks vicarious involvement in things that we human beings do all the time—such as attributing great, if not heroic, significance to what it is that *we* do in broader webs of relations and events. Another danger here is that what is a gain in terms of complexity and contingency entails a loss in terms of analytical precision. Interpretivism does not deny the importance of argument and empirical evidence. It does hold that there are potentially many valid paths to truth.[32] In any event, this study is an interpretive one that relies heavily on the device of storytelling to make the argument.

Law, Politics, and Contexts

The legal mobilization approach that I take is a culturalist one focused on legal translation. Any culturalist view must grapple with the conceptual difficulty of marking the boundary between law and politics. The culturalist view holds that law is seamlessly part of politics and culture. The problem is that this notion of "seamlessly part of" undermines the ability to specify and verify causal claims about the constitutive capacity of law. Consider the common locution "law constitutes x." The statement would seem to assume some way to mark a boundary between what is "law" and what is "not law," as well as some specification of the processes or mechanisms through which law had the claimed causal relation to something that is not law.[33]

The problem cannot be avoided, but the sting is lessened somewhat by the fact that the case studies in this book involve a relatively small number of actors proceeding within a well-defined and limited policy domain. We do not deal here with the amorphousness and variation that characterizes most social movements or with movement activities ranging across many social locations and policy domains. This relatively narrow compass comports with a conventionalist way of marking the law/politics boundary. By "legal," as opposed to "political," I mean, first, propositions or claims invoking and interpreting authoritative sources conventionally recognized as legal (constitutions, case law, statutes, regulations) and, second, the activities and processes conventionally associated with the specialized personnel and institutions of "the legal system."

In my argument, the "law" in "law constitutes" begins with reformers' legal claims and judicial opinions reflecting and reshaping those claims. What "law constituted," I argue, was (1) discernible kinds of public conversations about education, inequality, and school finance policies; (2) discernible ways that actors defined their interests and aligned themselves with or against other groups; and (3) different kinds of policy processes and outcomes. The central purpose of this analysis is to bring into view the constitutive significance of legal translation and thereby to foster further reflection about legal translation and its significance among observers and activists alike.

The indisputable fact that the school finance reform projects proceeded "in contexts" calls for some judgments about defining the most relevant ones. I draw my sense of relevant contexts from my decision to adopt the standpoint of reformers and the practical intentions driving my inquiry. "Context" here becomes mostly a matter of the perspectives of would-be change agents and their particular angles of vision. I begin with the ways the actors themselves understood the relevant contexts. This choice on my part involves certain trade-offs. Like anyone trying to do something, school finance reformers did not think much about many relevant possible features of their historical and political situations. Like anyone, they took much for granted. An observer committed to standing with them and rendering an account of their actions in context will take much for granted as well.

Working out from reformers' perspectives, it makes sense for me to define *context* mainly in terms of the state-level interest group and political-institutional environments. Reformers seeking to change education policies will find an array of powerful interest groups occupying the field, and they will have a range of options for dealing with established interests. In the American political system, states retain a measure of sovereignty. They are bounded geographical spaces that contain their own social geographies and evolving political cultures and institutions. Within this broader matrix of "context" so defined, a study of legal translation and legal and political mobilization at the state level should pay particular attention to state law and courts as relevant institutional channels for thought and action. My goal in this regard is not to undertake an analysis of judicial decision making or state courts as institutions in their own right. Rather, it is to treat state law and courts as central to the context for legal mobilization and to do so with some degree of care about formal-legal doctrine and the independent doctrinal influence of state courts as institutions.

Assessing Consequences: Outcomes, Successes, and Failures

Another important theoretical issue involves conceptualizing consequences, both those that reformers intend and those they do not, and reckoning up "successes" and "failures." There are many plausible ways to think about the "effects" of political projects and/or judicial decisions, and assessing the "success" or "failure" of law reform activity "is always a very complex matter."[34]

An inquiry grounded in a practical intention to critically evaluate reform efforts relying on law and courts cannot very well avoid talking about successes and failures. However, before we get to the inherently normative activity of characterizing outcomes, we must specify the relevant universe of things for which we are looking, and the relevant evidence that would link reformers' actions to outcomes, whether that link is direct or indirect.

My central argument in this book is distinct from reformers' assessments of outcomes and quite distinct from the kinds of assessments of outcomes generally offered by most observers of school finance battles. My claim is that legal translation played a central role in shaping the language of public debate, the organization of education politics, and policy processes and outcomes. This claim is not amenable to precise measurement. Interpretations are required at both ends: The content of legal arguments and judicial opinions and the "language of public debate and so on," must be rendered. Explicating the content of things like legal briefs and judicial opinions is a straightforward enough task, but what evidence can support a claim that "legal translation" shaped (was causally related to) something as amorphous as "the language of public debate" about education and inequality? There might be many ways to make the argument, using both quantitative and qualitative data. I have chosen to make the case for the connection through narrative case studies making use of relevant sources, such as interviews, newspaper coverage, and documents that provide evidence of how various actors were thinking, speaking, and acting. The narrative case study relies on relatively thick representation of actions and events unfolding over time. For better and worse, thick description and temporal ordering do much of the argumentative work.

One kind of assessment that I explicitly bracket involves evaluating the normative attractiveness of each reform vision. Here, I wish to neither to endorse nor condemn but only to describe, to the extent that that is possible.

Beyond the central argument, I will also be concerned with the assessment of other more obvious outcomes, such as new political groups or alignments, shifts in how resources for education are raised and allocated, and what resource changes in education might mean in practice. Here, my commitment to taking the self-understandings of reformers into account makes some difference. One good way to begin the assessment of political and policy outcomes is to ask what reformers themselves expected and hoped for. This basic question can provide a sense of goals and criteria for the evaluation of whether they have been achieved. Reformers' subjective assessments are themselves interpretations, of course. Moreover, they have a tendency to shift over time as situations shift and as people learn from and reevaluate experiences. Nevertheless, a plausible approach is to say that each case gives rise to standards and criteria for success that are internal to each, simply because the reform visions, and therefore goals, varied.

In addition to evaluations under criteria internal to each reform effort, I will also make use of existing policy research to assess educational outcomes and results. School finance systems determine who pays and who gets what. Dollars are not hard to follow, at least at the state and school district levels of school governance. Tracking changes in the absolute level of resources for education and different kinds of measurements of the relative degree of resource inequality across districts is fairly standard practice in school finance research. More complicated questions involve the much longer, tangled causal chains from policy to educational process and outcomes, after we are done tracking the level and distribution of money. Obviously, a study like mine cannot have all that much to say about how resources are used and what educational results they produce at school district and school levels.

Still, as all reformers studied in this book would agree, changing the level or relative distribution of material resources for education is but a means to other ends. If "reform" is simply a matter of tinkering a bit with dollars and pronouncing new policies that don't change things on the ground, then reform could be mostly symbolism, all "myth and ceremony" that comforts some people by telling them that something is being done while leaving the intended beneficiaries pretty much where they were. Reformers would say that either more resources, or changes in practices facilitated by new resources and programs, should improve educational practices for intended beneficiaries, and not leave them where they were.

However, evaluating educational policies and practices involves competing ideologies about good education. One knows that education has improved when one sees better educational outcomes for children, somehow defined and measured. Participants in educational policy conflicts typically disagree about what "improvement" means. This is a study of legal mobilization and relatively elite processes of policy change. While I will rely on some existing policy research to address some effects on the ground, of necessity, questions about educational policy implementation and impact will be given somewhat short shrift.

The stories I tell are stories about how reformers turned to law and courts to project their own visions and stories about education and inequality onto the political agenda. The next chapter takes up the topic of what they were fighting about.

CHAPTER TWO

SCHOOL FINANCE REFORM AND EDUCATIONAL IDEOLOGY: A GUIDE TO LAW, POLITICS, AND POLICY

PUBLIC EDUCATION IN THE UNITED STATES IS A VAST undertaking. About 7 million people hold full- or part-time jobs in some 94,000 elementary and secondary schools, located in some 15,000 school districts. Forty-seven million children, or about 90 percent of the U.S. school-aged population, attend these public schools. On average, public schooling accounts for 25 percent of all state-level expenditures, and no other government program absorbs a larger share of state and local resources.[1] Measured in *real dollars*, moreover, education spending has increased threefold since 1960. In 1960, governments spent on average roughly the current equivalent of $2,331 per pupil; in 2001 that figure was $7,524. Even in the 1980s and 1990s, a period of general retrenchment in most other areas of social provision, education spending climbed steadily.[2] As Hochschild and Scovronick note, although the United States is generally regarded as a "welfare state laggard" compared to European countries, "education is the only issue in the arena of social welfare policies for which Americans are more supportive than residents of other welfare states."[3]

These authors argue that the peculiarly American ardor for public schooling owes a great deal to its exalted status within a much broader and widely shared American political ideology. Whether we call this ideology "the liberal tradition," "the American Creed," or, as Hochschild does, "the American Dream," there is a rough consensus on its basic contours. Individualism—the deep yearning for individual freedom from constraints, for "independence," for "self-possession"— stands at the heart of the American Dream. Each individual should be as free as possible to pursue the good life, as he or she defines it, provided that all others have an "equal opportunity" to do so. Individual freedom to pursue "success" is best protected by a political democracy that gives economic markets a large role in the production and allocation of things and experiences people want. If all are to have the opportunity to pursue the American Dream, then government must define and protect a set of basic rights to autonomy and nondiscrimination. In this ideology, the role of government is often analogized to that of an umpire ensuring a fair game to make "the pursuit of success possible for everyone." Within this view, public education easily becomes a primary vehicle for bringing each individual up to the starting line in the race for the good things in life and for securing the conditions of fair competition.[4]

In the lofty clouds of this pleasant ideological haze, sharp political differences over the basic purposes and functions of public schooling have the odd quality of being ever present and at the same time a bit hard to find. In school finance battles in particular, observers and actors alike have tended to overlook the bedrock ideological resting places from which claimants for change and defenders of the status quo proceed.

This chapter provides a guide to the historical evolution of school finance policies and reform litigation campaigns and then discusses educational ideologies and their role in the New Jersey and Kentucky reform conflicts.

THE EVOLUTION OF SCHOOL FINANCE
POLICIES AND REFORM LITIGATION

Struggles to produce change, it has often been said, are not conducted on the models of the philosophy or policy seminar. Like all would-be change agents, when they took action in pursuit of their visions, the school finance reformers in New Jersey and Kentucky faced a welter of specific constraints and shifting strategic questions. Believing that litigation and court decisions would be needed to succeed, they had to decide how to present claims and arguments to the legal system. In turning to courts, they turned to institutions that were relatively open to hearing their claims but also not particularly likely to be able to unsettle entrenched ways of doing things in politics. Thus, these reformers had decide whether to combine political strategies with legal ones and, if so, how. More broadly, they also had to decide how to situate themselves in relation to the very thick field of interests and institutions in educational policy. Although they could stride confidently against the backdrop of the American faith in education, in front of them lay the hard realities of a honeycombed system and its entrenched interests.[5]

School Finance Policy

In education, decentralization and localism were present at the creation, as it were. As a matter of both American constitutionalism and political practice, education has always been primarily a state and local function. Common school systems emerged bit by bit over the course of the nineteenth century. As the nineteenth century progressed, states increasingly embraced legal responsibility for schooling. Revised state constitutions included clauses mandating the provision of a "basic" or an "adequate" or a "thorough and efficient" education. States also took their first halting steps toward providing some financial support to local districts.[6]

Notwithstanding these state-level legal norms and policies, education finance and governance remained intensely local right through the early 1970s. Revenue for education has always come mainly from local taxes levied on the value of real property. In 1920, 83 percent of all expenditures for education originated in revenues raised locally. In 1940, this figure was 68 percent, and in 1960 it was 56 percent. In 1970, at 52 percent, it was still over half of all revenues. Since 1980, the average local share of revenues has hovered around 44 percent.[7] Another measure of the history of localism is simply the sheer number of school districts. While this number has declined dramatically over the years, from 127,531 in 1932 to just under 15,000 today, it still remains quite large.[8] Until the last forty years, state governments had little to do with the substance of education provided in districts and schools.

Against this historical backdrop, the problem of school finance policy is readily apparent. In such a system, the resources available to each student depend largely on the happenstance of where the child lives. Local district property wealth, combined with the willingness of residents to tax themselves for education, have largely determined spending levels. As the Texas Supreme Court once put it, the problem here is that "the property rich districts can tax low and spend high while the property poor districts must tax high merely to spend low."[9]

Over the course of the twentieth century, states developed school finance policies in response to this basic problem.[10] State policies addressed both inadequate levels of support in some districts and, to a lesser extent, inequalities across districts. The first state aid took the form of flat grants. The state simply gave all districts the same small amount of money for each pupil. Flat grants are not "equalizing" in that they do not disturb the preexisting, locally determined distribution of resources; they simply raise the absolute level of spending by the same amount for everyone.

Starting in the 1920s, some states began to use "minimum foundation programs." Here, the state mandates that all districts must spend some specified minimum amount per pupil (the foundation amount). It then makes reaching the foundation amount a joint state and local fiscal responsibility. States typically required a minimum local tax rate before a district could qualify for "foundation aid." If the local tax applied to the local base did not yield the foundation amount, then the state would make up the difference. Thus, unlike the flat grants, foundation programs were equalizing up to the minimum spending level.

Prior to the late 1960s, states relied on some combination of flat grants and minimum foundation aid programs. However, several new policy ideas grew out of the reform efforts of the late 1960s and early 1970s. Setting their sites on severing the link between the property tax and funding for schools, several policy observers argued for "full state assumption." On this view, the state government should take over taxing and spending for schools, even though it would continue to make use of local school districts as administrative units for the delivery of education. Full state assumption turned out to be way beyond the reach of politics.[11]

Another key policy idea in school finance arising out of reform litigation came from law professors John Coons, William Clune, and Stephen Sugarman ("the Coons team"). The Coons team developed the notion of "fiscal" or "wealth neutrality," which, in turn, led to a policy approach called the "guaranteed tax base" (or GTB). Wealth neutrality was the legal theory, and the GTB was the main, although not the only, policy approach that could comport with the legal theory once a court accepted it. Under a GTB policy, the state guarantees the same amount of tax yield for every increment of local tax effort. A GTB approach still relies on local decisions about the property tax rate and still relies on local property tax revenues, except now each district acts as though it had a hypothetical, specified tax base. Tax rates and spending levels can still vary, except now they will not vary in relation to local property wealth. In other words, the principle behind a pure GTB approach is "equal tax yield for equal tax effort." Coons and his colleagues argued that this approach was consonant with local control because it left taxing and spending decisions at the local school district level.[12]

Today, states typically use a mid- to high-level foundation approach. Sometimes states add a GTB tax base component on top of the foundation mechanism, thereby giving localities the option of taxing local wealth at a higher rate with some guaranteed additional yield. Only three states now rely exclusively on the GTB approach. State categorical aid and various forms of federal aid (most of it categorical as well) fill out state school finance systems.[13]

Nested Inequalities

School finance arrangements have long reflected and fostered a set of "nested inequalities."[14] The growth of public education in the United States was part and parcel of this country's broader pattern of political development. The framers used political fragmentation and decentralization as devices to divide and diffuse power and filter the popular will. Federalism meant that states would retain some measure of sovereignty. The power to govern, it turned out, could easily be delegated from states to local subdivisions. "Localism" is to each state what "federalism" is to the nation as a whole: a contested space comprised of attachments to place and political arguments about the relationship between political-institutional structures and the achievement of certain ultimate political ends, such as democratic participation, liberty and freedom of choice, efficient use of public resources, political experimentation, and social equality.

In capitalist democracies, class (and often caste) structures find their reflection in residential separation. The United States is far from unique in this respect. What is distinctive about the United States, however, is the melding of social and economic stratification with severe political fragmentation. Differences in economic power and social status are thus tightly linked with local political entities that generally crosscut economically integrated regions. The local political entities give rise to localist political identities and attachments to place. The seismic economic and demographic shifts of the latter two-thirds of the twentieth century—the great migration of some 4.5 million African Americans out of the rural South and into the urban centers between 1940 and 1970, the acceleration of the ex-urban movement of whites into politically separated suburbs, the shift from an industrial to a postindustrial economy and what this has meant for the nature and location of job opportunities, and the general suburbanization of American national politics—all of these poured into and reinforced the nexus between socioeconomic stratification and fragmented political geography.[15]

School finance reform projects thus face a twin set of "nested inequalities" and some rather difficult political terrain. First, educational arrangements and policies are nested within a broader set of institutional arrangements. The historical reliance on the property tax in a setting of political fragmentation has meant that taxing and spending for schools and the quality of schooling in communities are linked to property values and the operation of housing markets. A school district's reputation is often an important factor in the determination of housing prices. The fact that a relatively wealthy community has a "low tax rate on a high tax base" is not one that can be viewed in isolation from the prior choices of housing consumers and the prior actions of local governing bodies. Moreover, it is not just the typical better-off family's largest financial investment for themselves and their posterity that is at stake when school finance reform is on the agenda, but also their sense of place and belonging. Change can threaten the affective bonds of community. Indeed, many suburban governments routinely forego the economic benefits of commercial development precisely to maintain what they regard as the distinctive "character," "quality," or "look" of their community.[16]

Second, education funding arrangements and policies themselves contain a set of nested inequalities. As Hochschild and Scovronick point out, inequalities are nested one within the next, from state to state, district to district, school to school, and classroom to classroom, and they often correlate closely with race and class. States vary a great deal in average per pupil expenditures; in 1998–1999, expenditures in the highest-spending states were double those in the lowest-spending ones.[17] Within states, school districts typically have significantly different revenue raising capacities and expenditures. Just before the Texas Supreme Court's decision in *Edgewood v. Kirby* (1989), for example, the lowest-spending district spent $2,112 per pupil, whereas the highest-spending district spent $19,333. In Illinois, a state with 881 school districts and much residential racial segregation, the lowest-spending district spends under $5,000 per pupil, while the highest-spending one spends approximately $23,000. In New Jersey, just before the court's 1990 decision in *Abbott II*, impoverished urban districts like Camden, Jersey City, and Newark spent between $1,000 and $2,000 less per pupil than wealthier suburbs just a few miles away.[18] Even schools within districts can have different expenditure patterns because teaching assignment practices have typically meant that better-off neighborhoods have more experienced and better-paid teachers.[19]

School finance reformers have taken aim at one important "target" in this overall structure—state school finance policies. In doing so, they have had to confront difficult political terrain. School finance policies touch people where they live, for they impinge on "two basic issues that concern most American voters: the resources available for their children's education and their state and local taxes."[20] At least in the first instance, proposed changes will tend to be evaluated against the baseline of the current tax burden and expenditure numbers within school districts. And the key revenue source at issue here is not just any tax, but the tax most directly felt and despised—the property tax.

In addition, reformers must confront a vast array of organized interest groups in education. These too are diverse and geographically all pervasive. Teachers' unions, school boards and their associations, other professional associations, parent groups, educational reformers and advocates—all organize at each level of government and vie for influence. No change agent trying to get something done can safely ignore them. Finally, unlike in other policy domains, in school finance matters every legislator answers to a wide range of interested constituents, since legislative districts typically encompass many school districts. The aggregation of interests will be difficult at best.

School Finance Reform Litigation:
History, Arguments, and Counterarguments

Legal and policy observers typically divide the history of school finance litigation into three distinct "waves" or "phases." The first phase runs from the mid-1960s to the U.S. Supreme Court's decision in *San Antonio v. Rodriguez* in 1973. The second phase runs from 1973 until 1989 and the third from 1989 to date. The principles of division among these three waves involve the fluctuating fortunes of litigation efforts and, more importantly, what most observers characterize as the transition from "equity" to "adequacy" in litigation theories and policy approaches.[21]

School finance litigation's first phase really began with *Brown v. Board of Education* (1954), which forged a tight bond between the American faith in the redemptive power of public education and broader questions of racial justice.[22] Whatever else it did or did not do, *Brown* ensured that public education would be a central arena in the broader struggle for racial justice. Around 1965, many reformers turned their attention to new dimensions of "equal educational opportunity." The period saw rising criticisms of liberal integrationism and a creeping skepticism about prospects for school desegregation in the North. Many community activists embraced the turn to "black power" within the civil rights movement, while many liberals were newly attracted to arguments for "compensatory education." School finance policy became an object of inquiry just when, for the first time in American history, the courts constituted an inviting forum for claims on behalf of those who lacked economic and political power. Given this social context, and given the intractable, majoritarian nature of state-level politics, it is not surprising that school finance reformers turned first to law and courts for help.

As they considered litigation, reformers could draw on some remarkable developments in federal equal protection doctrine.[23] In 1968, advocates filed several lawsuits, including *Serrano v. Priest* in the California state courts, *Rodriguez v. San Antonio* in federal district court in Texas and *McInnis v. Shapiro* in federal district court in Illinois. *McInnis* is little known outside school finance circles. It was the first case in this area to reach the U.S. Supreme Court. Its abject failure there became Exhibit *A* for the Coons team's wealth-neutrality approach. Its failure also serves as useful reminder that the later achievements of the New Jersey reformers are indeed impressive.

In *McInnis*, legal aid lawyers in Chicago unabashedly argued that Illinois's failure to allocate educational resources "according to need" deprived poor children of their right to equal educational opportunity under the equal protection clause. The district court promptly dismissed the case for failure to state a cause of action. In lawyers' parlance, the case was "nonjusticeable." The court wrote that there were no "judicially discoverable and manageable standards" for the adjudication of such a claim. In 1969, the U.S. Supreme Court affirmed this decision without writing an opinion. The prospects for the nascent finance reform movement looked rather bleak.[24]

It was at this point that the Coons team's novel legal theory came to the fore. The Coons team members urged reform advocates and courts to endorse "wealth neutrality" as a constitutional constraint on a valid state school finance system. Wealth neutrality holds that a valid system, whatever else it does, may not allow the level of spending for education to be a function of local school district wealth. Wealth neutrality, they argued, was a simple "negative" nondiscrimination principle about relative local tax effort and expenditures. Wealth neutrality was an argument about "what equality did not mean." What it did not mean was "wealth discrimination." Education spending could "not be a function of wealth other than the wealth of the state as a whole."[25]

At the time, the theory was amenable to projection through federal equal protection doctrine. For federal equal protection purposes, reformers claimed that "education," like the right to vote, should be deemed a "fundamental right," even though neither one finds explicit textual expression in the Constitution. They also claimed that "wealth," like race, should be deemed a "suspect classification" when used in legislation. If courts accepted either of these propositions, then, under existing equal protection doctrine, states would bear a very heavy burden in trying to justify their school finance arrangements. Moreover, in theory, the judicial endorsement of wealth neutrality still left the legislative branch with numerous permissible policy options. Wealth neutrality thus provided a strong argument that other courts could use to distinguish their rulings from *McInnis*.

In *Serrano v. Preist* (1971), the California Supreme Court held that wealth neutrality was what the federal equal protection clause required. Education was a fundamental right, and wealth was a suspect classification.[26] *Serrano* was national news. It marked the beginnings of sustained nationwide communication among reform lawyers, and it provided other courts with a model opinion endorsing wealth neutrality. Other major trial court decisions soon followed. Just a few months after *Serrano I*, a federal district court in San Antonio struck down the Texas school finance system. Its opinion "was little more than a scaled-down rewrite of *Serrano I*."[27]

The state of Texas appealed directly to the U.S. Supreme Court. In its 5 to 4 decision in *San Antonio v. Rodriguez*, the Court rejected the Coons team's theory. With Justice Powell writing for the majority, the Court held that wealth was not a suspect classification and that education was not a fundamental right either explicitly or implicitly guaranteed by the Constitution. Texas therefore had to show only that its current school finance system was founded on some minimally rational basis—in other words, that it was rationally related to some permissible government objective. The nexus between local financing and local control easily met that standard. On the day it came down in March 1973, some might have thought that *Rodriguez* meant the end of school finance litigation. As it turned out, this decision did not end litigation, but merely redirected it to state law and courts. The first phase had ended and the second one had begun.

Reform lawyers in New Jersey filed *Robinson v. Cahill* in state court in 1970. The lawyer representing the named plaintiffs grounded his argument primarily in wealth neutrality. However, at the trial phase, Rutgers-Newark Law Professor Paul Tractenberg entered the case as the representative of the state chapters of the National Association for the Advancement of Colored People (NAACP) and the American Civil Liberties Union (ACLU), organizations that participated as amici curiae. Tractenberg did not like the wealth-neutrality theory, and his dissatisfaction with it drove him to search for alternatives. Although the difficulty of translating his views into law loomed large, he nevertheless argued that the education clause of the state constitution guaranteed each child a substantive right to access to "the best possible" education. This claim invited the courts to wade into the briar patch of substantive educational reform. In 1972, a trial court endorsed wealth neutrality and struck down the New Jersey school finance system. The state appealed.[28]

While *Robinson* was pending before the New Jersey high court, the U.S. Supreme Court handed down its decision in *Rodriguez*. Twelve days later, the New Jersey Supreme Court handed down its own landmark decision. Following Tractenberg's lead to some extent, it rejected wealth neutrality but held that the state education clause did guarantee each child the equal opportunity to receive an adequate education. It struck down the state's school finance system in light of this "standard."

With *Serrano* still pending in the California state courts, and with the New Jersey high court's decision in *Robinson*, reform-oriented lawyers and policy analysts were back in business. The first inklings of national communication and coordination that arose after *Serrano I* now took on organizational form and garnered foundation funding. A national "equity network" developed, with much support from the Ford Foundation.[29]

After 1973, and up until 1989, reform litigation succeeded in producing state high court victories in six states, in addition to New Jersey: California, Connecticut, Washington, West Virginia, Wyoming, and Arkansas. The presence of education clauses in all state constitutions could be invoked to say that education was a "fundamental" right under state law for equal protection purposes. State courts could also find some sort of right to educational equality or adequacy in their state constitutions' education clauses, standing on their own. However, over this period, state high courts in thirteen states rejected challenges. Even when important victories were won, as in New Jersey and California, judicial decisions produced long, drawn-out legislative processes, which in turn produced policies that reformers ultimately found disappointing. The bulk of the litigation during the second phase focused on equal protection arguments. Many state high courts simply appealed to the *Rodriguez* majority's arguments to turn back challenges.[30]

The third phase runs from 1989 to date. It is marked by far more success in court and more innovation in court decisions and remedies. The year 1989 is singled out because it saw state high court victories in Kentucky, Montana, and Texas. Observers point to "the Kentucky landmark" in particular as the key moment in ushering in a new era of "educational adequacy litigation."[31] One year later, the New Jersey Supreme Court handed down its central decision in *Abbott v. Burke*. In a new twist, the New Jersey Court held that what was "adequate" for poor, minority children had to be judged against what already advantaged children received in the state's wealthiest districts.

In response to new adequacy claims, many state high courts soon struck down school finance systems, with several explicitly modeling their opinions on the Kentucky Supreme Court's opinion in *Rose v. Council for Better Education*.[32] Many observers also explain the new success of adequacy arguments as an unintended consequence of the "standards movement" in state education policy. The widespread enactment of educational content standards and statewide tests to measure performance helped finance reformers by giving them state-endorsed norms for "adequacy" and concrete evidence of educational failure.[33]

Since its redirection to state law and courts in 1973, school finance litigation has been sustained, widespread, and ongoing. As of 2007, lawsuits challenging state school finance systems had reached the high courts of all but seven states. Plaintiffs have prevailed in court in twenty-six states, and they have failed in seventeen.[34]

Throughout the history of school finance litigation, there has been a common set of arguments and counterarguments in play. The reformers' opening move is quite simple and powerful. Americans believe that public schooling is the great equalizer, the one thing that gives every child a substantially equal chance to succeed in life. Yet, governments typically spend more money on the education of children who are already relatively advantaged, and they do so through systems dependent on something as morally irrelevant as the property tax wealth in the community in which children happen to live. How can this gross departure from shared ideals be justified?

Defenders of current arrangements in court have responded with *three big claims*: (1) *local control*, (2) *money without more won't matter*, and (3) *judicial restraint*.[35]

(1) Defenders argue that reformers' proposed policy changes will undermine local control of education, and local control protects many other things we hold dear. But what is local control, and what is so valuable about it? Is the appeal to local control anything more than a cover for unjust privileges?

Law professor Richard Briffault has unpacked the competing arguments swirling around "localism."[36] Briffault discerns two kinds of arguments in favor of local control of education as now practiced in the United States. One argument appeals to participatory democracy and self-government. This case for local control begins with the proposition that the existence of small geographic units with real decision-making power fosters both participation and accountability. This vision conjures up images of the New England town meeting. All citizens may be heard, and every voice counts. Localism as participatory democracy posits a synergy between a high level of citizen involvement in the political process and better educational governance and outcomes. Moreover, in a nation as diverse as the United States, federalism and localism ensure that local communities have room to define and pursue their own values and goals. These local control defenses hinge on the purported connection between local fiscal control, on one hand, and local political participation and administrative control, on the other.[37]

The second argument for local control appeals to the satisfaction of consumer preferences and economic efficiency. It holds that localism is valuable because the existence of many small governmental units provides a second-best substitute for a market where no real market exists. The existence of many school districts with local fiscal responsibility allows each consumer to choose his or her desired mix of tax burden and services. Here local school districts stand in for the firm, competing with each other to offer the most attractive product at the lowest price. This interlocal competition enhances efficiency and fosters experimentation.[38]

In turn, challengers have responded to the local control defenses in two basic ways. One response fully embraces the desirability of local control but simply adds that everyone should be able to enjoy it equally. If taxing and spending decisions are highly constrained—if, for example, they are demonstrably a function of the local tax base and not local tax effort—then local control is but a cruel illusion. Another response is less inclined to concede that local control is an ultimate end or that it serves any other ultimate ends. This response tends to counterpose other important values to localism, such as equality or the state's important interests in controlling public education in order to foster democratic citizenship. Local control may be a good thing, but it is very far from the only good thing.

(2) Another common response by defenders of existing school finance systems is that spending more money on schools without worrying about changing educational governance structures and performance incentives is highly unlikely to produce better educational outcomes. Spending more money, without more, is simply bad public policy. In public debates, this defender claim is often rendered as "money doesn't matter." The real claim is not that "money doesn't matter," but that empirical, scientific research has failed to demonstrate any *systematic* relationship between expenditures (or the particular inputs money buys) and improved student performance. Money matters, but if we do not know precisely when, how, or why money matters, then throwing money at

the schools will not help, and it could hurt. Moreover, the lack of a *systematic* relationship between inputs and outcomes indicates that there is a good deal of inefficiency in the educational delivery system now. Defenders have often used this implication of inefficiency to bolster factual claims about the existence of mismanagement, waste, and corruption in the administration of complaining school districts, especially urban ones. If districts used existing resources wisely, they would have enough money to provide the required level of education.[39]

Without doubt, the leading modern skeptic of the relationship between higher expenditures and better outcomes has been economist Eric Hanushek. Hanushek's reviews of the results of a vast body of production-function research led him to conclude that variations in several school inputs do not now have any systematic relationship to measurable student performance or outcomes. The punch line of Hanushek's argument is that current institutional arrangements will not provide the necessary incentives to encourage better academic performance. What is needed is a market or marketlike mechanisms.[40]

School finance reformers have met this production-function challenge in two ways. The first involves the presentation of research pursued within the production-function framework but reaching different conclusions, and the second involves an external critique of the framework itself. Several studies, and one prominent actual experiment, have found significant positive relationships between important inputs and student achievement or labor market outcomes. Specifically, these researchers say, smart teachers and smaller class sizes do seem to be related to enhanced student achievement.[41] Moving outside the production-function mindset, reformers point out that it embodies a set of very narrow assumptions about the purposes and valued outcomes of schooling. Reformers note that we have to talk about what money means. Expenditures are way up to a large extent because we now want schools to do many things that we had not asked them to do before, such as providing an appropriate education to disabled children.[42] Attention to the social meaning of money would include some attention to differential needs and costs across districts. If the defenders' charge is waste and mismanagement in local school districts, the reformers' response is often that some localities and districts are clearly "overburdened": They face higher costs and must respond to greater needs, both in education and in the provision of other important government services. Similarly, on the "output" side, reformers point out that we want schools to pursue a variety of goals; outcomes should not be reduced to only those that can be measured. The quality of educational experiences matters a lot too, especially if we care about training competent citizens in a constitutional democracy. In court, reformers have common sense on their side. We know that spending more money alone does not guarantee success, but we also know that more money can help.[43]

(3) Finally, defenders of current arrangements argue that courts lack the legitimacy and capacity needed to play a positive role in school finance policy. They thereby appeal to the popular sentiment that there is something wrong with "judicial activism" in a democratic society. Activism is especially troubling when courts are called on to recognize new rights claims and/or to involve themselves in complex matters of social policy. The case for judicial restraint, defined here as "deference" to the authority and decisions of the legislative and executive branches of government, has two basic dimensions. One dimension is normative, and it has to do with the democratic legitimacy of judicial review. The other is largely empirical, and it has to do with the policy-making capacities of courts as institutions. Considered together, the two dimensions of the judicial restraintist response hold that we ought not to be governed by courts, and that when we are governed by courts, we are not well governed.

On this view, reformers who run to court to get what they want are engaged in a cynical "end run" around the normal democratic process. When courts succumb to reformers' self-interested sob stories, they enervate democracy by removing responsibility from electorally accountable institutions. Moreover, as institutions, courts simply lack the access to information and expertise needed to evaluate competing claims about complex social policies. Finally, when it comes to remedies, courts must rely on binary rights arguments and coercive mandates alone, whereas legislatures have a much bigger tool kit of available policy mechanism, such as tax incentives and conditions on grants.[44]

School finance reformers respond to the appeal to judicial restraint with all of the argument that political projects in the United States have always used to move courts to action. Under state constitutional law, children clearly have some sort of "right" to education, and in our society rights cannot be held hostage to ordinary majoritarian politics. All legal doctrines that first recognize and then elaborate on the meaning of rights must begin somewhere. Courts sit to protect minority interests that often get short shrift in the ordinary political process. Reform lawyers also draw heavily on legalism, a professional ideology that they share with judges, and legalism posits a sharp separation of law and politics. Legalism holds that the supposedly unique institutional features of courts are a distinct asset in a constitutional democracy. A court is a "forum of principle," the one place in the system where an elevated conversation about justice and fairness can take place. Even reluctant judges are often enticed to act once they witness compelling factual presentations of unjust harms. Courts need not dictate specific solutions to the other branches. Rather, they can offer normative visions and side constraints on politics, thereby engaging in a dialogue with the other branches and the citizenry. In recent school finance cases in particular, a focus on "educational adequacy" invites an expanded role for education policy experts, and experts can help courts master the technical knowledge needed to superintend a reform process. Courts often do as well as or better than other institutions.[45]

Courts act or do not act for a variety of reasons. The arguments in play both define the terms of legal and policy debate and give courts wide latitude to chart their own course in school finance disputes. But when courts do intervene, as we will see, their judicial opinions often play a larger role in defining the terms of public debate and the policy agenda than in dictating specific policy outcomes. To gain an understanding of this important cognitive and political role of legal arguments, we must first pay some attention to educational ideologies.

EDUCATIONAL IDEOLOGIES

As I use the concept here, *ideology* is a nonpejorative term roughly equivalent to *vision*, in the dual sense of "perceiving reality" and "envisioning" a changed and better state of affairs. Ideologies are values, beliefs, and conceptual frameworks held by people in social contexts, about something in particular. Ideologies typically combine norms, concepts, and empirical propositions. They are at once diagnostic and prognostic. They are particular ways of seeing, which in turn presupposes that they are also ways of *not* seeing. Ideologies are not fully elaborated and rigorously tested theories. Rather, ideologies are rough and ready for political use. They structure thought through concepts and categories, provide justifications, draw boundaries, and motivate people to action.[46]

As I use the term here, *educational ideologies* are broad visions of the central purposes and functions of public schooling in the United States.

As noted at the outset of this chapter, the repression of ideological conflicts over education is fairly common. Nevertheless, several books over the past ten or fifteen years have offered discussions of such visions of education and the tensions among them.[47] These works offer us a useful set of ideas for perceiving educational ideologies in action. All of them suggest that much recent specific policy talk in education has downplayed the social fact that Americans value a wide plurality of values in education. Although each one uses different terminology, all of them organize their treatment of ideological visions around a set of linked distinctions—between the individual and collective goals of education; between education as a private good and education as a public good; between education as preparation for work or getting ahead and education as training for democratic citizenship; between education in service to what exists and education as an engine propelling us toward a better future.

Hochschild and Scovronick place the conflict "between what is (or seems to be) good for the individual and what is good for the whole" at the heart of their analyses of several specific policies. They use the notion of the American Dream and the pursuit of success to cover all individual goals. One basic individual goal for schools is the creation of individuals capable of defining success for themselves and then pursuing it. The individual goals are secured primarily by emphasizing knowledge and cognitive capacities, of course, but they also include some mix of social skills, moral or character development, and emotional coping skills conducive to psychological health. But, the authors note, Americans also want schools to embody and promote values and goals held in common, such as securing equality of opportunity and instilling a common core of knowledge and a set of liberal-democratic values.

For Hochschild and Scovronick, it is the conflict between individual and collective goals that defines several more specific battlegrounds. "Efforts to promote collective goals . . . through public schooling," they write, "have run up against almost insurmountable barriers when enough people believe (rightly or wrongly, with evidence or without) that those efforts will endanger the comparative advantage of their children."[48] In issue area after issue area, the collective good of fair equality of opportunity loses out to the power of individual success, defined comparatively and competitively. Relative position is key. Hochschild and Scovronick argue that the educational tournament could be conducted on fairer terms, to our collective benefit. However, the work of a few other observers leads us to notice the possibility of questioning of the allure and necessity of the footrace metaphor itself.[49]

Educational sociologist and historian David Labaree certainly agrees that education and getting ahead "are inseparable in the minds of most Americans." Social mobility is at the heart of the American dream, and education is central to social mobility. The observation that education is linked to social mobility naturally leads to the general argument, like Hochschild and Scovronick's, that the competition should be fairer and to specific reform proposals aimed at realizing "a purer model of individual competitive achievement." However, Labaree makes the normative argument that "we need to back away from the whole idea that getting ahead should be the central goal of education." He writes that the "connection between social mobility and schooling is doing more harm than good," for it encourages a general sensibility about schools that treats education primarily as a private good for individual consumption. In turn, understanding education as a private good, and hence as one that one needs *relatively* "more and better of" to get ahead, fosters rampant "credentialism" and the elaborate systems of differentiation, marking, and marketing that come with it. The mere badges of merit—test scores, institutional reputations, more and more advanced degrees—come to replace the teaching and learning of socially useful knowledge and the promotion of genuine human development.[50]

In making this case, Labaree distinguishes among three broad purposes and goals for public education: democratic equality, social efficiency, and social mobility. All three are real and operative. However, he contends, the third one has come to predominate over the other two, to our great collective detriment.

A focus on democratic equality highlights "schools as an expression of democratic political ideals and as a mechanism for preparing citizens to play constructive roles in a democratic society." Training vigorous citizens with a sense of civic virtue has been central to this tradition of thought, going back to Horace Mann's arguments for the common school. Since Mann, we have hoped that a common school experience for all children could maintain democracy by "balancing against" social inequalities arising out of the political economy. This self-same rhetoric of political equality and fostering the creation of citizens who can tend to the Great Republic still stands behind many modern claims for equal access and equal treatment. It also explains the continuing pull of "general education" and "liberal arts education" on our imaginations and, sometimes, our choices about what is taught.

A focus on social efficiency links schooling to the sorting and screening needed to prepare students for, and to adapt them to, "a hierarchical social structure and demands of the occupational marketplace." Like democratic equality, social efficiency sees education as a public good, but now the accent is on investment in human capital, preparing students to fit into occupational roles, and promoting overall economic growth.[51]

A focus on social mobility is similar to social efficiency in that it emphasizes the link between education and future places in social and economic hierarchies, except now the vantage point shifts from society to the individual. Here, the individual confronts a system in which education and educational credentials are well nigh essential if she or he want to get ahead, for "[t]he benefits or education are understood to be selective and differential rather than collective and equal."[52] Labaree sees our educational system as overly intricate and stratified, with far too much attention devoted to marking distinctions within and between institutions and levels. The historically growing predominance of social mobility explains an overall structure and many practices that otherwise makes little sense.

Social mobility fosters a general endorsement of "meritocracy," with debate centered on the fairness of the competitive, zero-sum game of getting ahead.[53] Ideologically, it mediates between democratic equality and social efficiency, for it puts a democratic face on social inequalities and radically unequal outcomes. The undeniable fact that some always do climb up the ladder through education supports this ideological edifice, even if getting ahead is not very likely for anyone, and even if it is less and less likely the farther one goes down the class structure.[54]

Educational Ideologies in the Case Studies

Both of the reform projects chronicled in this book began from distinctive ideological positions about the central purposes and functions of public schooling.

The New Jersey reformers were racial liberals who cut their teeth in the struggles of the 1960s. They fully embraced the American dream and the centrality of the social mobility goal within it. On their view, dire poverty, racial segregation, and inadequately funded schools combined to turn the American dream into a cruel nightmare for poor minority children locked within the Garden State's urban ghettos. These children bore the "scars" of racial and class oppression, and the schools only scarred them further. On their compensatory view, schools could and should do a lot more to "wipe out" the multiple disadvantages of poor minority children. The successful translation of this vision into legal terms was no easy matter, for it required the courts to recognize an affirmative right to the reallocation of resources based on need. Although much has been written about the New Jersey cases, the story of how the New Jersey reformers managed to negotiate this problem of legal translation has not yet been told.

Over the course of the 1980s, the crucial decade in their forty-year (and counting) struggle, the New Jersey reformers became locked in a long clench with powerful adversaries in government who had their own strong ideological beliefs about education. Interestingly, their adversaries' vision also had social mobility at its center. However, in this version of the protean concept of equal opportunity to get ahead, schooling was a neutral proving ground on which the talented could distinguish themselves and thereby earn the right to compete at the next, higher level. Everyone was to come to roughly the same basic set of instructional opportunities and challenges in the classroom (the starting line). But after that schools had to be part of a footrace, not prior to it. Reformers' adversaries defined getting ahead in school traditionally; getting ahead meant measuring up under well-defined, high standards. This was essentially a meritocratic version of equal opportunity and social mobility.[55]

What was shared across the gulf that separated the egalitarians from the traditionalists was as important as what divided them. As the conflict unfolded, the metaphor and associated language of the footrace came to pervade the whole of educational politics and policy in New Jersey, affecting the very definition and organization of interests.

In Kentucky, reformers embraced and pursued democratic equality as the central purpose of public schooling. A modern version of the common school vision became the order of the day. The Kentucky reformers did not believe that schools could or should be used as instruments to make up for past wrongs or to redress patterns of group inequality. Schools might have to take on new tasks, such as social service provision, but they should do so only as a means to the core end of improving the conditions of teaching and learning for everyone in schools and classrooms. The Kentucky reformers' rhetoric and goals never set one group off against another, but always put the accent on "better education" for all. The central purpose of education was to equip each child with the broad liberal knowledge and training required to be active citizens in a political democracy and to live "a larger life."[56]

Interestingly, as filed in 1985, the Kentucky reformers' legal complaint endorsed wealth neutrality as a viable theory of state constitutional meaning. However, in Kentucky, what was initially just a convenient legal hook to shake things up quickly became the conduit for the amplification and projection of the democratic common school vision. We will see how legal translation processes transformed wealth neutrality into a more broadly framed argument about educational adequacy. As the result of reformers' broader political efforts and the courts' endorsement of their rhetorical approach, the common school vision came to saturate the language of educational politics in the state.

The Kentucky reformers' adversaries in court were state-level elected officials. Unlike the New Jersey officials, the defenders of the status quo in Kentucky had no large educational vision that they sought to defend. They made a simple appeal to antigovernment and antitax sentiments and, to a lesser extent, to judicial restraint. However, the antitax appeal had great resonance in the state. Before Vice President and presidential candidate George H. W. Bush asked Americans to "read his lips" about taxes during the 1988 campaign, the successful candidate for governor in Kentucky in 1987 traversed his state screaming "no new taxes." The battle lines were thus drawn between dogged reformers with a vision about what was good for the whole commonwealth and right-populist officials opposed to government and taxes.

In each case, the distinctive ideological positions endorsed by key reform actors arose out of their life experiences at particular times in particular places, each one reflective of local social conditions and perceptions of problems. There came a time when these key actors joined together with like-minded persons to take up the mantle of reform. Through legal and political action aimed at changing school finance and education policies, they sought to bring public schooling as it then existed somewhat more into line with their visions of public schooling as it should be. We now turn to these reform projects, what they wrought, and the lessons they have to teach us about law and the politics of reform.

PART II

SAVAGE INEQUALITIES
IN LAW AND POLITICS

ON JUNE 6, 1990, THE NEW JERSEY SUPREME COURT handed down its landmark decision on the merits in *Abbott v. Burke* [*Abbott II*]. The Court held that the education clause of the state constitution required the state to spend as much on the education of poor minority children in its urban centers as it spent on children in its wealthiest suburbs. Beyond this mandate for spending parity between rich and poor, the Court also required additional spending on children in urban districts to compensate for their "extreme disadvantage." Fair equality of opportunity required no less, for "[u]nder the present system," the Court wrote, "the evidence compels but on conclusion: the poorer the district and the greater its need, the less the money available, and the worse the education." The Court did not mince words:

The students of Newark and Trenton are no less citizens than their friends in Millburn or Princeton. They are entitled to be treated equally, to begin at the same starting line. Today the disadvantaged are doubly mistreated: first, by the accident of their environment and, second, by the disadvantage added by inadequate education. The State has compounded the wrong and must right it.[1]

The Court's decision was a watershed moment in what was then already a two-decades-long struggle waged by a small group of intrepid liberal reformers. For two decades, they had repeatedly brought the claims of New Jersey's poor minority students before the courts. *Abbott II* was the result of a complex interaction between legal mobilization, on one hand, and judicial interventions and evolving legal doctrines, on the other. Throughout, the New Jersey reformers remained committed to making law embody their substantive vision of public education. As it turned out, after *Abbott II*, it would take two more trips back to court, some adroit political maneuvers, and seven more years, before they would actually win implementation of the judicial mandate for spending parity between rich and poor. And, after that, there would be still more conflict over additional compensatory programs and services. Nevertheless, *Abbott II* was a stunning achievement. The egalitarian, redistributive vision of *Abbott* is seldom seen in American law. The vision of *Abbott* was reformers' vision; they had prevailed. What follows is the story of the New Jersey reformers' project.

As part of the first wave of school finance litigation nationwide, reformers filed their initial challenge in 1970 in *Robinson v. Cahill*. In *Robinson I* (1973), the New Jersey Supreme Court sided with the reformers. It interpreted the state constitution's education clause as embodying a right to an "adequate" education and struck down the existing school finance system. When the political process produced a new school finance law that was unresponsive to the needs of poor students in the cities, reformers returned to court to challenge it. In *Robinson V* (1976), the Court reluctantly upheld the new law, but also noted that it might entertain future challenges if gross resource disparities persisted across school districts. Thus, in the *Robinson* litigation, reformers won an important legal victory but then suffered a political defeat. But *Robinson* taught reformers certain lessons and had important feedback effects. Most importantly, *Robinson* left a dense and potentially open-textured legacy of authoritative legal materials. Reformers would soon return to fight another day.

After they filed *Abbott v. Burke* in 1981, reformers faced a very long march to get to a trial and an ultimate appellate decision. In 1983, a trial judge dismissed their case, and reformers appealed. The court battle at this point was over procedural issues and legal standards. In *Abbott I* (1985), the Court addressed the question of legal standards and remanded the case to an administrative law judge (ALJ) for trial. In 1988, in a 607-page decision, the ALJ sided with reformers and struck down the school finance system. The state education commissioner and state board of education disagreed, thereby setting up the showdown before the New Jersey high court in 1990 in *Abbott*.

Abbott II evoked a new finance law (the Quality Education Act of 1990) that raised state taxes and redistributed state resources from better-off to worse-off school districts. The new measures produced a firestorm of controversy. A general tax revolt and opposition from wealthy school districts led to the unraveling of the new law before it even went into effect. In 1991, the Republican Party captured veto-proof majorities in both houses of the state legislature, and in 1993 New Jersey elected antitax candidate Christine Todd Whitman as its governor. Reformers returned to court in 1991. In *Abbott III* (1994), the Court reaffirmed its ruling in *Abbott II*, struck down the current finance system, and gave the state two additional years to comply with its mandates.

In 1996, the state passed the Comprehensive Educational Improvement and Financing Act (CEIFA), which sought to redefine "educational adequacy" so as to obviate the need to comply with the Court's *Abbott* decisions. Reformers returned to court once again. In *Abbott IV* (1997), the Court struck down CEIFA as applied to poor urban districts. This time, the Court specifically ordered the state to meet its spending parity mandate in the 1997–1998 school year and to maintain it thereafter. It also remanded the case to a trial judge for a hearing to formulate additional compensatory education programs for the urban districts. Finally, it added the improvement of urban school facilities to its list of remedies. In 1998, a trial judge ruled on compensatory program and facilities issues, and in *Abbott V* the Court upheld that order. Over the past eleven years, reformers and state officials have squabbled constantly over implementation issues, such as the provision of early childhood education and funding for capital improvements, and the case has been back in the courts many times.[2]

Whatever else is true of *Abbott*—and many things are—reformers succeeded in winning a massive increase in the level of educational resources for poor minority students in the Garden State's urban ghettos.

The following account of the New Jersey conflict emphasizes four main themes. The first is legal translation. In framing *Abbott*, reformers faced and brilliantly solved a very difficult problem of legal translation. Their substantive ideological vision of education was compensatory. As one of reformers' lead attorneys put it, it required law to take into account "relative needs and the resources available to meet those needs."[3] Yet law and courts are notoriously inhospitable places for egalitarian sociological arguments about "relative needs." How was it that reformers' compensatory vision ended up winning the day? The key legal translation moment came between 1979 and 1981 as reformers went about framing *Abbott* in light of *Robinson*.

The second theme is reformers' legalism and late turn to coalition politics. Until the early 1990s, the lawyers at the center of this effort distrusted community involvement in their case; they made no effort to use litigation to mobilize potential constituents for action in politics. As a result, they repressed or evaded serious questions about administrative capacities in the poorer urban districts. Their avoidance of political engagement also left their judicial victory in *Abbott* vulnerable to a political backlash. However, in 1991–1992, they adopted a more realistic political approach that helped to rescue their project.

The third theme involves the connection between legal translation and the agenda of contention in politics. This shaping of politics by law goes not only to the terms and language of debate, but also to how people understand their interests and organize themselves for action in politics.

The fourth theme is the paradoxes of reformers' compensatory vision and their implications for strategic action. One paradox was that reformers' vision ran headlong into what legal theorist Martha Minow called "the dilemma of difference." The dilemma "is how to overcome past hostilities and degradations . . . on the basis of group difference without employing and, in that sense, legitimating those very differences." Although it was undeniably grounded in social reality, reformers' vision risked reinforcing race and class divisions.[4] Another paradox was that the compensatory vision fully embraced the footrace metaphor that makes education largely a positional, private good in the competitive race for social advantage. In other words, it endorsed the very conception of education that undergirds defensive localism in the wealthy suburbs in the first place. The point that I will make here is not that the New Jersey reformers should have championed some other vision. Rather, the question is whether, *given* this vision and its rendition in law, these reformers were mindful of its political-strategic implications. I will suggest that, for a long time, their strategic thinking left something to be desired.

CHAPTER THREE

EGALITARIANISM MADE LEGAL: FROM *ROBINSON* TO *ABBOTT*

To study legal mobilization is to study the self-understandings of particular actors, with particular values and goals, acting in particular social and political contexts.

The key New Jersey school finance reformers were postwar racial liberals. While their parents had known economic depression and total war, they knew material abundance and the heady days of the civil rights movement. They had imbibed not only the optimistic spirit of that age—the hope that the American dream of freedom and prosperity could be extended to those who had always been excluded by racism and poverty—but also the conviction that law and courts could be the engines of social change. After all, had it not been *Brown v. Board of Education* and the activism of the Warren Court that had poked and prodded a sluggish nation to eradicate a virtual apartheid system within its borders?

When these reformers' acted, they acted in "the quintessential postwar suburban state."[1] As they surveyed New Jersey's social geography in the late 1960s, what they saw deeply disturbed them. What they saw was a hardening of lines separating people by race and class. Increasingly, and quite contrary to the great postwar promise of greater inclusion, they saw that rich and poor, white and black, lived in separate political communities, attended separate schools, and, consequently, had radically unequal educational opportunities and life chances.

Early on, these reformers' embraced a compensatory vision of education reform. Educational resources, they believed, should go disproportionately to the least advantaged. Throughout their long struggle, they remained committed to making law and policy embody their vision. This chapter and the next one describe how they eventually succeeded. It is in large part a story about successful legal translation—about egalitarianism made legal.

However, even ultimate success in court would not produce automatic results in politics. For a long time, most observers of reform litigation have understood that the implementation of favorable court decisions depends on some form of political mobilization in support of them. Yet, right through the early 1990s, the New Jersey reformers were strangely unmindful of the political uses of litigation and the broader need to mobilize political support for their effort.

This chapter covers the period from origins of the reform effort in the late 1960s through the New Jersey Supreme Court's 1985 decision in *Abbott I.* In the sections which follow, I highlight relevant features of the social and political environment, chart the emergence and evolution of litigation, and describe reformers' educational vision and its bold translation into law in the framing of *Abbott.*

CONTEXTS FOR ACTION: LOCALISM, SUBURBAN POWER,
RACIAL SEGREGATION, AND AN ACTIVIST SUPREME COURT

Localism and local control of education typically constitute the bedrock in most defenses of traditional school finance arrangements, and nowhere is localism more embedded than in New Jersey. What distinguishes Garden State localism from localism elsewhere is New Jersey's degree of political fragmentation and its long-standing identity as a suburban state, sandwiched as it is between New York City and Philadelphia. The increasing spatial and social isolation of racial minorities in small, poor cities has also been part and parcel of localism and suburbanization in the postwar era. Along with Connecticut, New Jersey is now one of the two most suburban states in the country, in an era in which "suburban politics has come of age."[2] Localism, segmented suburbs, and racial segregation gave rise to reformers' efforts in *Robinson* and *Abbott*, and these forces constrain their efforts still.

New Jersey is a geographically small and densely populated. As of 1990, among the fifty states, it ranked forty-fifth in size, ninth in population (with about 8.5 million people), and first in population density (with 1,130 persons per square mile). With its 567 separate municipalities, New Jersey also has more local government per square mile than any other state. It also has over 600 school districts, only 211 of which are K–12 and a third of which have fewer than 500 students.[3]

Historically, the state's political tradition of "extreme localism" has been reflected in the weakness of state-level political institutions. Until World War II, the legislative branch dominated state government, and local political machines and business interests dominated the legislature. Consequently, New Jersey has always been a comparative laggard when it comes to broad-based, state-level taxation. New Jerseyans have always insisted on the primacy of local property taxes, and they still do.[4]

In the postwar era, national elites and the federal policies they championed produced what historian Lizabeth Cohen has called a "consumer's republic." Cohen's consumer's republic signals "an economy, culture, and politics built around the promises of mass consumption, both in terms of material life and the more idealistic goals of greater freedom, democracy, and equality." On Cohen's account, New Jersey was something of the prototype of the new order—a "landscape of mass consumption," of vast suburban expansion linked by limited access highways and dotted with shopping malls, on one hand, and of small, poor, declining cities, on the other.[5] Between 1940 and 1960, New Jersey's "overall population grew by almost 2 million" (a 50 percent increase over two decades), yet almost all of its major cities lost population.[6] In 1930, New Jersey's six largest cities ("the Big Six")—Camden, Elizabeth, Jersey City, Newark, Paterson, and Trenton—were home to 30 percent of the state's total population; in 1950, they still housed 25 percent. However, by 1980, only 13 percent of the state's population lived in the Big Six cities.[7]

Race and racism were intrinsic to the processes of mass suburbanization, as the expansion of virtually all-white suburbs went hand-in-hand with the influx and isolation of poor minority people in the urban centers. As blacks and, later, Hispanic groups moved in, manufacturing jobs and whites moved out. The urban rebellions that rocked northern New Jersey in 1967 only accelerated the exodus of whites from the cities.[8]

The population shifts and situation in Newark were typical of the state's other cities. At twenty-three square miles, Newark is among the geographically smallest "large" cities in the country (Boston, by contrast, is forty-one square miles). African Americans comprised 11 percent of Newark's population in 1940, 17 percent in 1950, 34 percent in 1960, and 56 percent in 1970—"an overall increase of 466 percent during a period in which the city's white population declined by 56 percent."[9] By 2000, although blacks made up only 13 percent of New Jersey's total population, and Hispanics likewise 13 percent (for a total of 26 percent), combined they made up 83 percent of Newark residents.[10]

Residential segregation in the cities produced urban school districts that were highly segregated. By 1970, African Americans and Hispanics made up 72 percent of Newark students, while the percentage of minority students in Camden was 68 percent and in East Orange 83 percent. In 2000, the percentage of minority students in the Big Six school districts were as follows: Newark (91 percent), Jersey City (76 percent), Paterson (91 percent), Elizabeth (86 percent), Trenton (95 percent), and Camden (97 percent). In East Orange (total population 69,000), an old inner-ring "suburb" of Newark, 99.8 percent of the students were nonwhite.[11] Students in these districts, moreover, are overwhelmingly poor. By one commonly used measure, the percentage of poor students in the Big Six school districts were as follows: Newark (76 percent), Jersey City (72 percent), Paterson (80 percent), Elizabeth (72 percent), Trenton (55 percent), and Camden (80 percent). In East Orange, 68 percent of the students were poor.[12]

As the New Jersey reformers set their face against the massive economic and demographic shifts of the postwar era, they could at least look to some new developments in the state's constitutional and political order for signs of hope. During World War II, progressive elites spearheaded an effort to modernize the state constitution. The result was a new state charter, adopted in 1947. The good-government reformers hoped that this new constitution could provide the institutional basis for enlightened management of public problems. Two of the new constitution's central features were the strengthening of the executive and judicial branches of government.[13]

On the judicial front, Arthur T. Vanderbilt was the leading reformer. Vanderbilt designed the new judicial system and then served as the state's chief justice until 1957. The 1947 constitution established a seven-member Supreme Court, along with an intermediate appellate court to handle routine appeals, thereby allowing the high court to control its docket. It also provided that popular elections would play no role in judicial selection. In New Jersey, all justice and judges are appointed for seven-year terms, after which they may be (and almost always are) reappointed with life tenure until a mandatory retirement age of 70.

Vanderbilt's judicial philosophy combined the Hamiltonian view of judicial independence with a penchant for the sociological jurisprudence of the Progressive Era.[14] In his opinions and extrajudicial writings, Vanderbilt "categorically rejected the standard canons of judicial restraint." Vanderbilt founded and personified a tradition of progressive activism in the state judiciary. Reflecting on Vanderbilt's legacy in 1982, liberal Chief Justice Robert N. Wilentz (1979–1996) stated that "the experience still moves us" in that "it produced a refusal to accept rules that bear no present relationship to the needs of society." A tradition of judicial activism was already well established when the New Jersey school finance reform effort got off the ground.[15]

WINNING IN COURT, LOSING IN POLITICS

Viewed from a legal-realist perspective, the New Jersey reform effort had rather inauspicious beginnings. Armed with nothing but the tools of their trade, a few lone-ranger attorneys would seek to produce social change by judicial decree. As a realist would predict, the immediate results would be disappointing. However, as the transition from *Robinson* to *Abbott* will show us, judicial opinions and even modest policy reforms can sometimes have profound radiating effects over the longer term.

Robinson v. Cahill *and the Public School Education Act of 1975*

New Jersey's school finance conflict began with an attorney in private practice in Jersey City named Harold Ruvoldt Jr. In the late 1960s, Ruvoldt had been following the emergence of school finance cases in other states. In 1969, he penned and circulated an article on the subject to be published in the state bar journal. The corporation counsel for Jersey City had seen the piece and thought that his political bosses might be interested in backing a school finance lawsuit. After a few meetings, Ruvoldt and the local elected officials decided to go forward. They recruited officials from other municipalities to join them as plaintiffs, as well as eleven-year-old Kenneth Robinson of Jersey City.[16]

In February 1970, they sued Governor William T. Cahill and other state officials in state court. Ruvoldt framed his complaint primarily in the equal protection and wealth neutrality terms then recently developed by the Coons team. Aside from pretrial discovery and a few conferences with the judge, Ruvoldt's case did not move forward until after the California Supreme Court's 1971 decision in *Serrano v. Priest*. After a brief evidentiary hearing involving school finance data, a Rutgers law professor entered the fray as counsel for the Newark chapters of the ACLU and NAACP.

Paul Tractenberg was born and raised in Newark, New Jersey. After graduating from the University of Michigan Law School in 1960, he spent the next decade alternating between working at prestigious New York law firms and government jobs. In 1970, he joined the faculty at Rutgers-Newark Law School. Immediately after he arrived, Tractenberg began teaching a "clinically-oriented Public Education Law seminar" in which he and his students explored developments in education reform litigation.[17]

When it came to school finance, Tractenberg was troubled by the reigning legal approach of wealth neutrality. He understood the appeal of the theory to sitting judges, but could not accept its implications in terms of protected rights and education policy. As he put it in a 1974 law review article explaining his views, wealth neutrality "assured neither minimum levels of education funding nor funding commensurate with educational needs." Moreover, Tractenberg worried that Ruvoldt's focus on wealth neutrality dovetailed too well with the real interests of the local elected officials standing behind the suit. On his view, they were concerned mainly with local property tax burdens and "taxpayer equity," and not so much with the educational opportunities of poor urban children.[18]

Tractenberg's alternative view was that state constitutional law could and should recognize a substantive right to equal educational opportunity. Since 1875, the state constitution contained a provision specifically addressed to education. This "T&E" clause, as it is known, stated, "The Legislature shall provide for the maintenance and support of a thorough and efficient system of free public schools for the instruction of all children between the ages of five and eighteen."[19] Tractenberg had been using his law school seminars to trace out the history of this provision and to interpret its meaning.

Tractenberg solved his problem with Ruvoldt by securing the participation of the Newark chapters of the NAACP and ACLU, which he successfully projected into the case as amicus participants. As counsel for these advocacy groups, Tractenberg participated fully in the appeal and subsequent remedial processes in *Robinson*.[20]

In January 1972, the trial court ruled in favor of plaintiffs. Judge Theodore Botter's opinion held that the finance system violated (1) the equal protection of the laws under both federal and state constitutions, (2) the state education clause, and (3) the uniform taxation provisions of the state constitution. To meet federal and state constitutional standards, Judge Botter wrote, "the state must finance . . . education out of state revenues raised by levies imposed uniformly on taxpayers of the same class."[21] The trial court's decision thus rested principally on the idea of unlawful discrimination. The current finance system discriminated against both students and taxpayers in property-poor districts.

After the state appealed, plaintiffs successfully petitioned the New Jersey Supreme Court to hear the case immediately. The high court heard oral arguments in *Robinson* in January 1973 and rendered its decision on April 3, just twelve days after the U.S. Supreme Court handed down its decision in *Rodriguez*.

Legal doctrine channels thought and action in certain directions, but it rarely dictates behavior or outcomes. The New Jersey Supreme Court's decision in *Robinson I* did much to define the broad terms of debate over school finance policy for the next twenty-five years. The Court's opinion embraced certain terms and concepts and made those authoritative in a limited sense. After *Robinson I*, anyone who wished to act in the domain of education policy had to situate arguments within the framework of the Court's opinion. More specifically, *Robinson I* created and left unresolved a central tension over whether the state constitutional right to an adequate education should be defined primarily in terms of spending inequality, on one hand, or in terms of substantive programs and educational content, on the other. That tension would continue to matter right through the first decade of the twenty first-century.

Writing for a unanimous Court, Chief Justice Joseph Weintraub did not pause over Judge Botter's findings of fact. There were vast disparities in tax bases, tax rates, and educational expenditures across districts; these disparities were largely a function of local district wealth; and, although money was not all that mattered, "the quality of educational opportunity" did "depend in substantial measure on the number of dollars invested." The Court, however, did "not accept the constitutional thesis expounded by the trial court." Following Tractenberg's lead, the high court rested its decision squarely and solely on the state constitution's education clause.[22]

Chief Justice Weintraub began his explication of the meaning of the T & E clause with an account of its nineteenth-century origins. Although the state framers did not intend to require equal expenditures per pupil, he wrote, "we do not doubt that an equal educational opportunity for children was precisely in mind" (p. 294). But if equal educational opportunity did not mean equal expenditures, then what could it possibly mean?

To answer that question, Weintraub turned to *Landis v. Ashworth*, an 1895 case interpreting the T & E clause. In *Landis*, the New Jersey Supreme Court had held that this provision "required equality within the intended range of that amendment, permitting local decisions only above and beyond that mandated education."[23] Weintraub has now taken us from the phrase *equal educational opportunity* to the idea that all must get some adequate level of opportunity before others might get more. But of what could this adequate education consist? How could that be defined?

Although the Court gave no clear answer, we must note the nature of such explication and guidance that it did offer. Three points are pertinent. First, looking again to *Landis* and aided by Tractenberg's reading of it, Chief Justice Weintraub wrote that the content of the right to an adequate education had to be understood as one that evolved over time. What was adequate in 1895 would not be adequate today, and what was adequate today might not be adequate tomorrow. Weintraub then tied this concept of evolution to more modern, functional language about education: "The Constitution's guarantee must be understood to embrace that educational opportunity which is needed in the contemporary setting to equip a child for his role as a citizen and as a competitor in the labor market" (p. 295).

Second, Weintraub emphasized that it was the state's duty to ensure that all students received a constitutionally adequate education: "Whether the state acts directly or imposes the role on local government, the end product must be what the Constitution commands" (pp. 294, 297). While this might seem an obvious thing to say about a provision in a state constitution—whom else does it bind, if not the state?—it matters because it strikes a blow (at least in law) against local control. Although widely valued and institutionally entrenched, local control does not have constitutional status. Rather, it is but one means to a more important, constitutionally mandated end.

Third, when he turned finally to the question at hand—did the current finance system meet the constitutional standard?—Weintraub pointed in two seemingly different directions. On one hand, much of the opinion focused on "discrepancies in dollar input per pupil." Dollar inputs were "plainly relevant," and the current funding law had "no apparent relation to the mandate for equal educational opportunity" (p. 296). On the other hand, the opinion also expressed the Court's reservations about using money as the sole standard. It complained that "the State has never spelled out the content of educational opportunity the Constitution requires" (p. 295). The State's job was to "define . . . the educational obligation" and "compel raising of money necessary to meet it" (p. 297).[24]

The Court's opinion, then, was not exactly a model of clarity. It was hard to tell what the Court had in mind when it spoke of "what the Constitution mandated." Would compliance require more equal expenditures across districts? If so, how much more? Or was compliance simply a matter of raising the spending floor, without regard to the gap between rich and poor? If so, by how much? Or did the Court expect to see some combination of these two things? Or perhaps the focus on money missed the central point altogether. Maybe the main problem was the state's failure to define the substantive content of a constitutionally adequate education and then to regulate to ensure its provision to all. In that event, the future funding scheme would have to be evaluated in these substantive, and as yet undefined, terms.[25]

Soon after its April 1973 decision, the Court gave the other branches of state government until December 31, 1974, to come up with a new finance system.[26]

Over the next three years, *Robinson* "involved all of the state's institutions in a protracted minuet of pronouncements, proposals, and rejections."[27] For the most part, in politics the reform attorneys who initiated the process were consigned to the role of wallflower as the dance progressed.

The year 1974 came and went without any new legislation. Early that year, newly elected Governor Brendan Byrne proposed a new guaranteed tax base (GTB) finance plan and new revenue measures. However, legislators rejected the governor's plan as too costly and too much of a threat to localism.[28] In 1975, Governor Byrne aligned himself with the plaintiffs in *Robinson* and turned directly to the Court for help. A lawyer himself, Byrne not only filed a "motion in aid of judgment" but actually appeared before the Court to argue his cause. The Court declined to intervene, but it did set a new deadline for legislative action (October 1, 1975). This time, however, the Court included a "provisional remedy" to take effect in the event of the legislature's failure to act. If there was no legislation, the Court would reallocate state education monies itself.[29] After more intense wrangling and compromises, the legislature finally passed the Public School Education Act of 1975 (PSEA). The governor promptly signed the law and submitted to the high court for review.

Given its origins in *Robinson I* and the politics of localism, it is not surprising that the PSEA was a complicated piece of legislation. The high court's hand could be seen in the law's basic structure, if not in its overall spirit. Introductory language followed the Court by acknowledging that "the sufficiency of education" was "a growing and evolving concept." The law then contained two basic components, which in their separation mirrored the tension in *Robinson I* between a focus on spending disparities, on one hand, and a focus on the substantive content of education, on the other.

Article II of the PSEA stated "goals" and set forth "standards" and "guidelines" for state-level administrative evaluation. The general goal of a thorough and efficient (or T & E) system was to provide "all children . . . , regardless of socioeconomic status or geographic location, [with] the educational opportunity which will prepare them to function politically, economically, and socially in a democratic society." Article II then set forth ten elements of this T & E system, including such things as "a breadth of program offerings," "programs and supportive services for all pupils, especially those who are educationally disadvantaged," and "adequately equipped, sanitary and secure physical facilities and adequate materials and supplies." Article II included a sweeping delegation of power to the state department of education to further define and implement these provisions.

With its use of so many imprecise terms, terms like adequate, qualified, encouragement, and efficient, we might be tempted to dismiss Article II's language as so much meaningless verbiage. This would be a mistake. Even vague statutory language expresses and affirms certain normative ideals. As we will see later in this chapter, in *Abbott*, the New Jersey reformers would make liberal and creative use of this language in building and presenting their case.

Article III of the PSEA set up a new school finance system. It endorsed a modified version of the GTB approach. The new apparatus was a "modified" GTB system because it incorporated various devices for limiting the cost and redistributive potential of equalizing access to higher tax bases. In essence, the PSEA guaranteed all districts a tax base per pupil somewhat above the statewide average tax base. It would be equalizing up to that point. Beyond that point, wealthy districts would be free to tax and spend as they wished, and they would still be receiving other forms of state aid.[30]

Another major component of the state school finance system existed entirely outside of the PSEA. Under the Teacher's Pension and Annuity Fund (TPAF), since 1958, the state government has paid the full costs of teachers' pensions and the employer's (the school districts') share of Social Security taxes. TPAF was counterequalizing in that it went disproportionately to wealthier districts with better-compensated staff. Over the next two decades, TPAF would account for a growing share of state educational aid, reaching 22 percent of all state aid by the late 1980s. In response to *Abbott II* (1990), the state proposed to shift responsibility for the costs of teachers' pensions to local school districts. The proposal for this TPAF shift would be one great source of controversy in the broader political backlash against *Abbott*. It would also be at the center of the New Jersey's reformers' adroit political maneuvers in response to that upheaval.[31]

At the end of 1975, Tractenberg and a few other "urban reformers" who had by then joined him "objected strenuously to the program the legislature had just enacted." They argued "that the new financial provisions were unrelated to the educational needs of students; and they protested that the hard-pressed urban areas . . . were not notably better off under this plan than under the one that had been declared unconstitutional in 1973."[32] With Tractenberg attacking the PSEA and Governor Byrne and legislative leaders defending it, a badly divided New Jersey Supreme Court upheld the new law as "facially valid."[33] However, the Court punctuated its per curiam opinion in *Robinson V* with doubts, reservations, and expressions of openness to future litigation. The protracted interbranch battle that followed its 1973 decision, the opinion notes, made a "speedy decision" ending the conflict "desirable." "Parenthetically," the court quickly added, "whether [the Act] may or may not pass muster as applied in the future to any individual school district at a particular time, must quite obviously await the event. Only in the factual context then presented and in light of circumstances as they then appear could such a determination be made" (p. 131). These themes of reluctance and lack of closure set the terms for the rest of the opinion.

Why, then, was the PSEA constitutional? The Court gave two related reasons. First, the legislature had followed the Court by declaring that the sufficiency of education was an evolving concept. It had acknowledged "that what seems sufficient today may be proved inadequate tomorrow." (p. 133). Second, the Court noted the potential for educational improvement under the regulatory provisions of Article II of the Act: "The fiscal provisions of the Act are to judged as adequate or inadequate depending upon whether they do or do not afford sufficient financial support for the system of public education that will emerge from implementation [of Article II]" (p. 136). While plaintiffs' objections were not without merit, the new law "had taken a positive step to more nearly equalize per pupil tax resources" and "to eliminate gross disparities in per pupil expenditures" (p. 137).

Even with the Court's reluctant blessing of the PSEA, the Robinson saga was not quite over. In passing the new measure in 1975, the legislature had deferred action on a revenue measure needed to fund it. After the legislature balked once again by failing to find the tax revenues, the Court issued an order closing the schools. Finally, in July 1976, the legislature approved a new state income tax to fund the PSEA, thereby bringing the Robinson case to an uneasy close.[34]

A few reform-oriented lawyers initiated *Robinson* to redirect educational resources to New Jersey's beleaguered cities. In the end, they had little to show for their efforts. Throughout the legislative process, they lacked the resources needed for effective participation in the political arena. They were forced to watch from the sidelines as Governor Byrne took up the mantle of reform only to be beaten back by legislators responsive to local, suburban interests. As one reform attorney put it, "in *Robinson*, we won a ticket to the game, but we hadn't played much."[35] On the other hand, *Robinson V* threw open the courthouse doors for another legal challenge, albeit after some time elapsed to see how the new law would work. Tractenberg and some new colleagues started thinking about their next case the day after *Robinson V* came down. Their deliberations over the next few years would proceed in an interest group and political-institutional context remade by the Robinson cases and the PSEA.

After Robinson *and the PSEA: Feedback Effects*

For the past forty years, political scientists have been taken with the idea that political institutions and public policies are productive of political understandings, interests, and relationships and not merely the reflective outcome of these things. This was certainly true of the *Robinson* cases and the PSEA. *Robinson* and the PSEA created conditions and set other processes in motion that would allow the New Jersey reformers to deploy expanded resources in the future. These changes, in turn, facilitated a deeper, more sustained kind of legal mobilization in *Abbott v. Burke*, compared to the *Robinson* effort. They set the stage for reformers' creative translation of their compensatory educational vision into legal terms. Four interrelated developments are worth noting.

The Education Law Center. In 1973, Tractenberg secured funding from the Ford Foundation to establish the Education Law Center (ELC) in Newark, New Jersey. At the time, Ford was pouring money into burgeoning public interest law movement. *Robinson I*'s national prominence as the next frontier of school finance litigation facilitated Tractenberg's solicitation of funding from Ford. The ELC would become the hub of school finance reform in New Jersey.[36]

Tractenberg took a leave of absence from Rutgers Law School to serve as the ELC's executive direction for three years. In 1975, he hired a young Harvard Law graduate named Steve Eisdorfer. Eisdorfer had just completed a year as the law clerk to Morris Pashman, the most liberal New Jersey Supreme Court justice in the 1970s. Tractenberg and Eisdorfer established linkages between the ELC and other organizations in the national school finance reform network, such as the National Urban Coalition and the Lawyers' Committee for Civil Rights Under Law. After *Robinson* ended in 1976, the ELC lawyers held ongoing meetings with other attorneys, both national and local, and citizens' groups in order to coordinate monitoring activities under the new law and to brainstorm about their next legal challenge. I will return to these deliberations below.[37]

A Local School Finance Research Community. The ELC attorneys strongly suspected that the PSEA's finance provisions would do nothing to reduce educational spending disparities across rich and poor districts. But of course the actual operation of the new law would have to be followed. The reformers would have to know not only how the law operated, but also why it operated the way that it did. While following the money may sound simple, we must bear in mind that a school finance system involves a great deal of complexity. Money comes from every level of government, via various policy mechanisms. Policies and formulas interact with broader economic developments, especially in housing and real estate markets, and work their consequences through a bevy of individual choices made by both public officials and private citizens.

Fortunately for the ELC attorneys, the PSEA gave rise to a small, local research community devoted to studying the finance law's actual operation. Within a few years, the research confirmed the reform attorneys' claims about how the new law would in fact work. Two of the school finance researchers, Margaret ("Peg") Goertz and Ernest Reock, would go on to serve as consultants to the ELC and as plaintiffs' expert witnesses on finance policy throughout the *Abbott* litigation.

In March 1978, a report written by Goertz concluded that, under the PSEA, "[t]he basic distribution pattern for [state] aid was unchanged." The new law "had no impact on disparities among districts in per pupil expenditures," and, in fact, disparities between very rich and very poor districts had actually widened. A year later a separate analysis by Reock concluded that the PSEA's "impact on fiscal equity" had "run its course." The wealthier districts could still outpace others in the amount of expenditure increases, a trend being exacerbated by shifting property values in favor of the already better-off districts.[38]

State Regulation and Citizens' Participation. Just as the PSEA's finance provisions attracted attention, so too did its regulatory language and processes. The law's delegation of substantial power to the State Department of Education made administrative implementation into a battleground.

In 1977, a local foundation called the Fund for New Jersey organized a coalition of business and religious leaders into a group called Schoolwatch, Inc. The impetus for Schoolwatch came from Gordon MacInnis, the Fund for New Jersey's executive director. MacInnis had been a state assemblyman from wealthy Morris County during the *Robinson* conflict. He had been dissatisfied with the dilution of the regulatory language and standards in the PSEA as the legislative process went forward. MacInnis secured foundation support to provide Schoolwatch with an office and a small staff. Schoolwatch then hired Herbert Green, an education activist from Plainfield, as its director. Schoolwatch's mission was to foster citizens' participation in state-level education politics and to monitor the state board of education's implementation of the new law. The ELC attorneys became active participants in this coalition. Over the next several years, Green and Tractenberg religiously attended state board of education meetings.[39]

Allies within the State Education Department. The PSEA thus created a new bureaucratic arena for conflict over the substance of state education policy. Within the bureaucracy itself, a conflict soon developed over the nature of the new regulatory system. Some of the officials on the losing side of that conflict would soon ally themselves with the ELC's reform project and one in particular, Tom Corcoran, would provide valuable support for the *Abbott* litigation as a consultant and expert witness.[40]

By the late 1970s, then, there was an expanded network of advocates and policy experts orbiting around the new set of institutions and policies formed by the *Robinson* cases and the PSEA. The new environment was in part a product of reformers' own efforts. The environment offered a delimited set of opportunities and constraints. The next section situates us with reformers immediately after *Robinson* as they licked their wounds and contemplated their next steps.

LEGAL MOBILIZATION AND LEGAL TRANSLATION IN *ABBOTT V. BURKE*

In this new context, the lawyers at the center of finance reform—Tractenberg, Eisdorfer, and, later, Marilyn Morheuser—asked themselves two general questions. First, why had the *Robinson* litigation failed to produce their desired policy outcomes? The central beneficiaries under the PSEA were poorer and middle-income suburban school districts and taxpayers, and not poor minority children in the cities.[41] What had gone wrong? What lessons did reformers draw from this experience? Second, in light of these lessons, what kind of approach should they take the next time around? How should they frame their next legal challenge? What broader process of change did they envision?

Reformers' responses to these two questions reflected two central features of their substantive and legal ideologies. First, they were strongly committed to making the law embody their compensatory vision of education. Second, they were highly legalistic in their approach to law, politics, and social change. Their substantive ideological commitments and their legalism went hand-in-hand. One constantly informed and reinforced the other.

When they thought about *Robinson*, they thought in terms of law and reform litigation, which they conceptualized in a legalistic way. The bad outcome in *Robinson* was a function of how the case was framed, litigated, and decided. It was not a function of a lack of supportive political organizations and alliances. The solution involved bringing better reform litigation that would make the law say what they wanted it to say.

The portrait that emerges is of a reform effort with a particular mix of virtues and defects. The New Jersey reformers did eventually succeed in making law say what they wanted it to say. Given the egalitarian content of their vision, and given the doctrinal legacy of *Robinson*, this success on the legal translation front was no small feat. However, at the same time, legalism had its particular manifestations and likely costs. Reformers, perhaps, missed many opportunities to build a political support structure for the litigation and the realization of their ultimate goals.

Bare Statistics and Basket Cases

After *Robinson* ended in 1976, Tractenberg returned to Rutgers Law School, and Steve Eisdorfer took over as acting director at the ELC. The two lawyers and their colleagues and allies drew some lessons from their recent experience. For one thing, as Eisdorfer put it, "We all agreed that the next case would have to be much more fact specific." He continued: "The record in *Robinson* consisted entirely of statistical data and expert testimony. It was OK as far as it went, but between 1972 and 1975, this record had gotten very cold and dry indeed . . . There were bare statistics without any sense of the meaning for teachers and students in the classroom." Another concern was that "some way had to be found to keep the spotlight on the needs and interests of the urban, minority, poor children." They had "faded into the background" as *Robinson* progressed.[42]

Eisdorfer and Tractenberg mulled over two possible kinds of cases, or some combination of them. Both followed logically from *Robinson*, but neither was entirely satisfactory. Ultimately, the ELC rejected both options in favor of a third approach.

The first option promised to zero in on the poor urban centers. In *Robinson*, the Court had held that the state constitution's education clause guaranteed all children an "adequate level of education," even if the Court was not quite sure about what adequacy meant. The Court had also said that, whatever adequacy was, it was the state's responsibility to ensure its provision. Reformers considered bringing a case focused solely on one or more urban districts. Such a case could make vivid the meaning of inadequate resources for teachers and students in classrooms. Reformers called this first option "the basket case case." Some districts were simply basket cases. Children were not learning there, in large part due to a lack of funds and other resources. Whatever the cause of the problems, moreover, it was already the law of the state that it was the state's responsibility to fix them. It was exceedingly difficult to say what "adequacy" was, but surely judges could be convinced that what was happening in the poor urban districts was not it; they would know it when they didn't see it.

However, reformers worried that this case featuring the plight of poor urban children might instead put the spotlights on the poor administrative practices of adults in the urban districts. The poorer urban districts qua districts were big and messy, marked by a fair amount of political intrusion of the bad kind. The state could defend against such a case by claiming that there would be more than enough money, if only it were wisely spent. Even if reformers could keep this case from getting bogged down in the mud of school district politics, they still worried that it would not focus enough attention of relative disparities. Relative inequality was in itself an injustice.

All of these concerns led reformers to consider a second option, which they called "a traditional school finance case." Although it had not required the absolute equalization of resources, in *Robinson V* the Court had said that it expected to see the elimination of gross disparities in tax rates and expenditures. The PSEA had reduced disparities for some districts to a small extent, but disparities between the poor urban districts and the wealthiest districts had actually widened. Thus, a traditional school finance cases could begin with the betrayal of *Robinson*'s promise of more relative equality. It could then go on to make the usual claims about the link between a lack of money and constitutionally inadequate education. However, to reformers, this felt too much like a replica of *Robinson*. While it highlighted systemic inequalities, it might offer nothing special for the poor urban children.

In 1979, Eisdorfer left the ELC to take a position in the state's Office of Public Advocate.[43] The ELC then hired Marilyn J. Morheuser as its executive director.

Marilyn Morheuser and the Compensatory Vision in Translation

Although born in 1924, Marilyn Morheuser was decidedly a child of the 1960s. For roughly the first half of her adult life, Morheuser was a Catholic nun in a teaching order called the Sisters of Loretto. In the early 1960s, her work took her to Milwaukee, Wisconsin. In 1963, she left her religious order and became a civil rights activist. Morheuser, who was white, edited a black newspaper, worked at a settlement house running a Head Start program, and, finally, signed on as a researcher and political organizer for the local chapter of the NAACP. At the NAACP, she worked closely with lawyers on the Milwaukee school desegregation case. In 1970, at the age of forty-six, taken with law's role in struggles for change, Morheuser entered Rutgers-Newark Law School. After graduating, she held jobs at a public defenders' office, at the ACLU, and at the state's Office of Public Advocate.[44]

When she took over the reins at the ELC, Morheuser joined a reform network that already embraced an ideological vision, which she shared and to which she was totally committed. This vision emerged out of the evolution of school desegregation conflicts in the mid-1960s. Around that time, it became clear that school desegregation would falter unless its pursuit was combined with the upgrading of urban schools increasingly marked by de facto segregation. For many of its proponents, school desegregation was a means to the end of equal educational opportunity, which in turn was one main building block in the battle to end racial subordination. The upgrading of poor urban schools would be needed before desegregation in Northern cities would be politically feasible and, in any event, a high-quality education for poor minority children was a pressing matter of justice in itself.[45]

The compensatory vision begins at the core of nested inequalities in American society and its public schools. Racial segregation combined with poverty stigmatize and degrade their victims, doing particular harm to the psyches and self-development of poor minority children. The social conditions of the urban poor—a lack of good jobs and high unemployment; substandard housing; poor nutrition and health care; teenage childbearing, mother-only families, and family instability; neighborhoods marked by crime and violence—grind them down.

Public schools should compensate for these societal disadvantages and their attendant harms. Ideally, the school should "wipe out" disadvantages. However, schools for the urban poor are typically dreadful places that only "compound the harm." At the root of educational failure is a lack of the extensive resources needed to give poor minority children a fighting chance to compete with relatively advantaged children. Compared to the rich, the poor need much, much more, but what they get is much, much less.[46]

The problem of the precise legal theory of the next case remained when Morheuser arrived at the ELC in 1979. Reformers had resisted both the basket case and traditional school finance cases because neither really did the work they wanted their next case to do. They wanted their case to be about "relative needs, and resources available to meet those needs." However, the seemingly unavoidable message of *Robinson* was that the constitution's education clause guaranteed only some floor, some sufficient level of educational opportunity, beyond which local districts were free to tax and spend as they wished and could afford. Morheuser responded to this problem by letting her compensatory vision structure her approach to the authoritative discursive materials available from *Robinson* and the PSEA.

Morheuser's logic began with a first step clearly authorized by *Robinson*. As noted above, the Court had expressed a concern about what it referred to as "gross disparities," and the gap between the poorest and richest districts had actually widened. The first part of the case would be a traditional school finance analysis of tax bases, tax rates, and expenditures per pupil, statewide, with more detail and focus at the top and bottom of the distribution of districts. But it was not at all clear from *Robinson* that tax and expenditure disparities alone would be a sufficient legal basis to invalidate the new finance system. Any case would have to take the difficult second step of linking resource levels or disparities to a denial of something called a "constitutionally adequate education." This adequate education was one that equipped the child for citizenship and participation in the labor market. The ELC's other two options had foundered over this second step. "Adequacy" was free-floating and up for grabs. Moreover, adequacy's imprecision only reinforced the sense that it was something for legislators and educators to define, and not for courts.

Morheuser's bold stroke of legal translation involved pursuing this second step (linking finance to adequacy) through the lenses of the compensatory vision and its emphasis on relative needs. She paired selected poor urban school districts with nearby wealthy suburban ones and then gathered massive evidence to construct detailed, point-by-point comparisons between them. In this way, the central legal notion of "adequacy" could be individualized and pinned down. The meaning of an adequate education for poor minority children in the urban districts could be explicated in two ways: first, against the backdrop of their impoverished social environment; and, second, by reference to the background social conditions of and educational resources provided to already advantaged children in the state's wealthiest suburbs.

The regulatory norms in the PSEA could then be invoked and given meaning within this broader comparative social and educational frame. For example, in the abstract, one might wonder what it would mean for a school district's to offer "a breadth of programs" or "adequately equipped, sanitary, and secure facilities." But if we hold these terms in mind and then take a tour of schools in, say, Camden and its wealthy suburb of Cherry Hill, or Newark and its wealthy suburb of Millburn, then the vague normative standards can take on rather concrete meanings.[47] Morheuser's strategy, in other words, involved burrowing into *Robinson* and the PSEA and coming out with a "representation" of "facts" ordered by her vision. The hope was that one could thereby emerge from the doctrinal materials with new meanings attached to the old authoritative legal terms.

This fact-driven strategy was risky. Risk taking is a crucial and often overlooked factor in bold legal mobilization and legal translation. It would take a great deal of time and money to execute such a fact-heavy case. More importantly, a plausible response to the whole argument—and one that the state did in fact make, again and again—was that Morheuser's key comparisons and evidence at the extremes were irrelevant. For state officials, the constitutional standard was about ensuring minimal adequacy, and the fact that some districts had more and better than other districts was entirely beside the point. On the constitutional standard, the Court had spoken. All that was required was a constitutionally adequate education.

The early part of the *Abbott* litigation would be taken up with this crucial battle over the proper constitutional standard and whether Morheuser would even be allowed to present her case as she had framed it.

The ELC's Legalism and Its Manifestations

Throughout this book, I have claimed that the ELC lawyers took a legalistic approach to law, politics, and change. Of what exactly did their legalism consist? What were its manifestations and implications? Their legalism can be observed in three main ways.

First, until the early 1990s, the ELC never sought to use its litigation to organize new groups or to otherwise mobilize potential constituents in politics. Legal mobilization is not just about the mental roadmaps involved in legal claiming. It also involves a good deal of doing. In *Abbott*, the ELC had to engage in all of the communications and actions needed to build a massive factual case about the meaning of vast resource disparities at the district, school, and classroom levels. By the time the case was ready for trial in 1983, the ELC had interviewed some 500 people—teachers and administrators from twenty-five school districts as well as scores of policy experts.

The question that a realistic perspective on law and change poses for the ELC's legalism is a counterfactual one about political mobilization and its consequences: Would it have made sense to build into all of this activity an effort to found a citizen's group or to form some sort of coalition to promote and stand behind the litigation as it proceeded? How would things have gone if citizens had interacted in the process of promoting reformers' substantive vision in politics?[48] As it happened, reformers strongly believed that they were in court in the first place because democratic politics had nothing to offer them. Indeed, political engagement and political conflict would only jeopardize their litigation project. Winning the right kind of court victory would have to be prior to any political engagement.[49]

Second, the ELC's legalism can be seen in the fact that it affirmatively wanted nominal, or phantom, clients. Morheuser secured authorization from their parents to represent twenty school children from four poor urban school districts (Camden, East Orange, Irvington, and Jersey City). She and the ELC would speak for the poor children and not for any adults capable of articulating their own views and acting in politics. The poor children would be the plaintiffs. Of course, the poor children themselves disappeared from view soon after the initial press conference announcing the litigation. The ELC thereby enjoyed the moral authority of speaking for poor victimized children without having to answer to any live political organizations or formations about its litigation strategy and that strategy's relationship to politics. Conceivably, poor urban school districts qua districts and/or other advocacy groups could have been made plaintiffs in the litigation and thereby mobilized to inform the legal strategies and to act in politics. But the ELC's legalism placed a premium on a pristine legal case controlled by the reform lawyers. Of school districts and other advocacy groups, Morheuser said: "We wanted their help [with the litigation], but we did not want them in as parties."[50]

Third (and related to the desire for nominal child plaintiffs), the ELC's legalism drove its strategic evasion of questions about administrative capacities and practices in poor urban school districts. I will refer to this evasion as the ELC's "dance on the urban school districts." It is undeniable that, by and large, these districts were troubled. Anyone who knew anything about their administrative and teaching practices would at least reasonably wonder whether any amount of additional money could make any difference, in the absence of long and potentially painful local processes of capacity building and administrative reform.[51] Now, presumably, advocates for the poor children would have to be honest about these administrative problems. Indeed, one would think that they would have to make these problems their own, that they would have to acknowledge, analyze, and somehow try to mitigate or solve them.

However, Morheuser and her ELC colleagues had a big strategic problem when it came to the question of urban school districts' administrative capacities. Morheuser knew very well that "mismanagement, waste, and corruption" would be the key theme of the state's defense in *Abbott*. There was more than enough money for adequacy, the state officials would say, but for the fact that local urban officials routinely squandered it. In any event, there was no point in increasing funding for dysfunctional districts; the additional money would only be wasted. Moreover, with considerable justification, Morheuser viewed the projection of this argument by state officials as done in bad faith. State officials did not really care about helping urban districts do a better job of teaching poor minority children. And their mantra of waste and corruption was not without its racist overtones. The districts that were uniquely guilty of incompetence and corruption were always and only the minority-controlled ones. Many financially strapped suburban districts managed to produce good results with an average level of resources. Poor urban districts could do the same, the state argued, if only they were run and staffed by people with different moral and cultural values.[52]

In light of this racially charged dimension to her legal case, Morheuser determined to remain steadfastly "agnostic" (her term) on the administrative capacity and competence issue. Rather than openly acknowledging and engaging in the debate about the causes of the problem and its possible solutions, she and the entire ELC support network remained silent on it, both in court and in politics. In court, Morheuser simply answered the state's mismanagement defense with the legalistic claim that it was the state government's "mandated constitutional responsibility" to fix any problems, if indeed there were any. In politics, Morheuser put the word out that the reform network should not criticize urban districts for their policies and practices or otherwise highlight the issue. To do so would jeopardize the lawsuit's prospects for success. When it came to problems of district-level management, she would say, "That's the state's case. Let them make it."[53]

This strategic evasion in service of the lawsuit made some sense. Not only did it serve the cause in court, but, going forward in *Abbott*, it also helped Morheuser establish herself as a spokesperson for all the poorer urban districts. One reformer described the ELC's relationship to urban districts as "uneasy and ambivalent" during the early 1980s.[54] After all, the ELC did not want to be too closely identified with the districts qua districts. But over the course of the litigation, the adults involved in the urban districts did come to recognize Morheuser and the ELC as their representative. In establishing her legitimacy as someone entitled to speak for these districts, it could not have hurt that Morheuser took a hands-off approach to the question of local district responsibility for spending funds wisely. The strategic evasion thus had both legal and political benefits.[55]

On the other hand, the ELC's hands-off approach on urban districts' administrative capacities entailed an abandonment of the field of debate over the issue by the friends of a more egalitarian and better system. State defendants were then free to define it and to project their interpretation of it. And they did that through actions as well as words, through how they defended against *Abbott* and how they intensified state monitoring and regulation of urban school districts. The problem of making sure that additional funds could be wisely spent, and that they would be widely perceived to be wisely spent, haunts the ELC's project to this day.[56]

In the Kentucky case, we will see that reformers faced this same charge. Poor, rural (and virtually all-white) school districts in Eastern Kentucky, critics said, were rife with incompetence and corruption. And, in Kentucky as in New Jersey, there was at least some truth to the charge. However, the Kentucky reformers responded not by evading or minimizing the issue, but by taking it up head-on; they made the need for administrative reform part of their own cause.

Abbott v. Burke: *Stiff Opposition and Procedural Tribulations*

In February 1981, the ELC filed its complaint in *Abbott v. Burke*. It represented twenty schoolchildren from the poor urban districts of Camden, East Orange, Irvington, and Jersey City. Thirteen were black, six were Hispanic, and one, Raymond Arthur Abbott, was white.[57] Plaintiffs sought class certification to represent all children in the four school districts. In *Robinson,* the complaint said, the New Jersey Supreme Court had held the quality of education did depend on the level of financial resources and that gross disparities were impermissible. It continued:

In 1980 the situation has not changed . . . In financial resources available for educational facilities, services, and programs, disparities between plaintiffs' districts and districts having high property values and high expenditures are even greater in 1980 than they were under the prior unconstitutional scheme. As compared to children in wealthier districts, children in the plaintiff class attend school in older, poorly equipped facilities, frequently in disrepair; they have fewer and lower paid teachers; they have less adequate program offerings. Yet, plaintiff children have demonstrably greater educational needs, as evidenced by large numbers in need of compensatory and bi-lingual education, and by low test scores, high dropout rates, and low college attendance . . .

Those children deprived of equal educational opportunity under New Jersey's school finance scheme are the neediest children in the State. Plaintiff children are predominantly minority and poor. They live in urban centers where unemployment is high and many families are on welfare. Their personal poverty coincides with the poverty of their school districts.[58]

When the ELC initiated *Abbott*, Ronald Reagan had just been sworn in as president. In New Jersey in 1981, eight years of Democratic rule would soon come to an end. In the gubernatorial election that year, Republican Thomas Kean eked out a narrow victory over Democrat James Florio. Kean, the scion of a wealthy New Jersey political family, came into office with his own highly

developed ideas about education reform. He wanted to be known as "the education governor." In 1982, Kean appointed Saul Cooperman as his commissioner of education. Kean and Cooperman were early and vigorous supporters
of the "educational excellence" movement of the 1980s, and they constructed
the state's defense in *Abbott* accordingly.[59]

For Kean and Cooperman, money was not the central problem for urban education, and it was a grave mistake to regard increasing spending as
the central solution. In their view, the ELC's lawsuit sought more money so
that incompetent people could spend it doing the same old things that had
not worked. They argued that spending more money in poor cities was not
merely futile but actually perverse. It would make things worse, not better.
More broadly, the ELC's effort smacked of the academic permissiveness of
the 1960s and 1970s, the very vision they were committed to overthrowing.
It simply diverted everyone's attention from the true building blocks of excellent education: high expectation and standards, high quality teaching of core
academic knowledge and values, respect for authority and strict discipline,
and administrative accountability secured through testing. For their part,
they believed that their reform agenda was a morally superior path for poor
children in the cities.[60]

Christopher Jencks has called this traditional view a "moralistic" or "meritocratic" approach to equality of educational opportunity. Everyone plays by
the same "high standards" rules. Achievement is to be rewarded, and failure
punished. The schools are part of the competition in a competitive society,
not prior to it; they are judges of academic performance, not coaches bringing
everyone up to the starting line to run the footrace.[61]

Thus, in the *Abbott* case, two diametrically opposed educational ideologies
squared off against each other. Kean and Cooperman would fight *Abbott* tooth
and nail. Kean, an adroit politician, went on to win reelection easily in 1985.
Over their eight-year reign, he and Cooperman pursued their own vision of
"excellence," enacting many standards-based and regulatory reforms.[62]

The first battle in *Abbott* involved competing interpretations of *Robinson*'s
ambiguous legacy, as well as a related conflict over the proper institutional
process for hearing and resolving reformers' challenge.

The state's answer in *Abbott* challenged reformers' effort to reframe the
meaning of a constitutionally adequate education. *Robinson V* had upheld the

facial validity of the PSEA. It did not require the equalization of resources, provided that all students had access to a constitutionally adequate education. Finance arrangements were to be evaluated in terms of whether they met this standard. Moreover, the regulatory norms and oversight in the PSEA were the primary mechanism for the solution of any problems. The state's strategy was to put the spotlight on the urban districts standing alone, in isolation from the rest of the system.

As a legal matter, the state argued, a logical sequence of questions followed. Was education in any given urban district really inadequate? If so, why? If the answer to this "why" question at least in part involved administrative incompetence, then perhaps targeted administrative interventions could provide a remedy, thereby making education in that particular district adequate. Even if the answer was a lack of resources, the PSEA already empowered the commissioner of education to order local districts to increase their budgets to meet constitutional standards. This legal analysis eventually gave rise to a claim that the reformers should seek administrative remedies under the PSEA before they should be heard to challenge it writ large.

The state supported this legal analysis with two empirically driven arguments. First, it appealed to cost–quality studies for the proposition that money was not systematically linked to better outcomes. Second, as noted above, it claimed that mismanagement, waste, and corruption accounted for any deficiencies in urban education. It also undertook regulatory investigations and audits in the four urban districts from which the ELC drew plaintiffs.[63]

The ELC and the state spent all of 1982 and most of 1983 engaged in pre-trial motions and discovery. With a trial date finally set for December 1983, the state moved the trial court for summary judgment and to dismiss the case. The state's central argument here was that the PSEA already empowered the commissioner of education to hear complaints arising under the school laws. Because the ELC's complaint was one such, it being essentially a claim that education in certain districts was constitutionally deficient, reformers should have gone first to the State Department of Education for relief. In other words, the plaintiffs had failed to exhaust their administrative remedies.

In November 1983, trial judge Virginia Long granted the state's motion to dismiss. The "plaintiffs' claim that there is no administrative remedy," she held, "puts the cart before the horse."[64] The ELC viewed this dismissal as fatal to its entire project. In rejecting as premature its facial attack on the finance system and relegating it to an administrative proceeding that would focus solely on particular urban districts, the trial judge had placed them squarely on the ideological terrain they had worked so hard to avoid. The judge had, in effect, made the urban school district qua districts parties to the litigation. Moreover, as a practical matter, the ELC would face a proceeding in which their adversaries would control the conduct of the trial. Morheuser appealed the trial judge's order, of course, and she did so with an extensively developed factual case that was trial ready when it got bounced out of court.

In May 1984, the state's intermediate appellate court reversed the trial court's decision. It held that *Robinson V* had indeed contemplated just this sort of legal challenge to the PSEA and that the case should be heard in the first instance by the courts.[65] State defendants then appealed to the New Jersey Supreme Court.

"Relative Needs" Gains a Strong Foothold: The Court's Opinion in Abbott I

The New Jersey Supreme Court heard oral arguments in *Abbott I* in November 1984. By then, the Court had emerged as the boldest and most intellectually formidable liberal high court in the United States. In fact, at that very moment, it was embroiled in a pitched battle with elected officials and a majority of New Jersey's populace over the issue of exclusionary zoning.

Near the end of his second term in 1979, Democratic Governor Brendan Byrne nominated Robert N. Wilentz to serve as chief justice. Wilentz had deeply held liberal convictions and, by all accounts, a charismatic personality combined with extraordinary intellectual abilities. Wilentz joined a court that was already quite liberal. Justice Alan Handler shared Wilentz's values and was also a first-rate legal thinker and scholar. Together, Justices Wilentz and Handler would lead the court in its effort to create public policies that would mitigate the harsh inequalities embedded in the Garden State's landscape of mass consumption.[66]

Shortly after his appointment as chief justice, Wilentz thrust his court into a firestorm of controversy with its decision in a case known as *Mount Laurel II* (1983). *Mount Laurel II* threatened to open up the suburbs to low-income housing. Governor Kean and legislators from both parties denounced the court "in the language of the Cold War." *Mount Laurel II* led to a new reform statute (the Fair Housing Act of 1985) that blunted the force of the Court's *Mount Laurel* doctrine and effectively wrested control of zoning policies away from the courts. As *Abbott I* came up on appeal, all eyes were on the Court to see whether it would accept the tepid zoning reform law or risk more conflict and reprisals from elected officials by striking it down. In the end, the Court ended up retreating in *Mount Laurel* in a 1986 decision upholding the new law.[67]

However, one imagines that in 1985 the justices probably felt that they did not need to add fuel to the fires encircling them with a forceful ruling in the school finance case. In any event, what the Court did in *Abbott I* was give the ELC reformers a crucial legal-doctrinal victory cleverly disguised as a procedural defeat.

On the surface of things, the Court seemed to agree with state defendants in *Abbott I* (1985). Just as the trial judge had said, plaintiffs would have to pursue their case through a more cumbersome administrative process. However, at the heart of Justice Alan Handler's opinion for the Court was a doctrinal transformation. This reworking of *Robinson* was precisely what the reformers were hoping for, and it would be highly productive in shaping the future course of the litigation.[68]

Justice Handler's opinion begins by stating a broad definition of the Court's task in deciding the case. Although it is true that the appeal presents "only one narrow issue" and that "the ultimate merits of the constitutional claims and defenses are not before" the Court, Handler notes, "the merits . . . cannot be ignored, because the nature and scope of the necessary factual inquiry and legal analysis influence the procedural course to be taken by this litigation" (pp. 380–381). We can restate Handler's opening move here as follows: The narrow issue for decision is, Which tribunal shall hear this case? To answer that question, however, we cannot avoid looking into "the merits" (that is, the factual and legal claims on both sides) because we must determine what it is that the chosen tribunal will be asked to do ("the nature and scope of the factual inquiry") and how it should do it ("the legal analysis").

These elements—facts, law, and the future course of the litigation—set the terms for a long excursion in which Handler would swing back and forth between prior law and current factual and legal claims on both sides. At the end of the journey, Justice Handler and the law arrive at point very far from where they began.

Justice Handler states the Court's basic holding early on. The parties' claims should initially be presented to an administrative tribunal. However, in the very next line, he rejects the trial court's rationale for this conclusion and substitutes another. The administrative route is preferred not because plaintiffs' claims lack "constitutional dimension," but because the case presents the need for "the creation of an administrative record sufficient to guide the adjudication of the constitutional issues on any future appeal" (p. 381).

Justice Handler then reviewed the history of *Robinson* and the PSEA. Insofar as the PSEA defined goals and standards, it was concededly "constitutional on its face." But the broad question in this litigation was "whether the operative terms of the 1975 Act in fact assure that all of the state's children receive their due" (p. 383). Instead of turning directly to what it would mean for all children to "receive their due," Justice Handler then rendered fourteen consecutive paragraphs going over the factual claims on both sides. The discussions of the ELC's claims were punctuated with language indicating that reformers should be allowed to present their case as they had framed it (pp. 383-387).

Although Justice Handler disclaimed resolution of constitutional issues, he opined that they "must be gauged in light of the facts that the parties are prepared to marshal." In 1975, the legislature itself established that "the sufficiency of education" was "a growing and evolving concept." This "evolving standard," Handler continued,

will influence judicial evaluation of documented differences in either educational achievement or program offerings. If, for example, significant numbers of students in plaintiffs' school districts fail to receive an effective secondary education by reason of the 1975 Act's operation, then the Act fails to provide equal educational opportunity . . . Similarly, [the Act] may fail to provide equal educational opportunity by allowing equivalently qualified students to attend schools providing significantly disparate program offerings. (p. 388)

From this passage, it seems the constitutional standard is evolving as Justice Handler writes. Handler seems to know this, for he immediately moves to qualify the quoted passage by acknowledging that *Robinson* did allow that some districts could "go further" by taxing and spending above the "constitutionally adequate" level. But Handler then turns away from *Robinson* again by emphasizing a qualifier that we find there: State authorization for local districts to do more was permissible, "provided that such authorization does not become a device for diluting the state's mandated responsibility." The rest of the opinion substitutes "the state's responsibility" for the idea of "minimum adequacy" as the primary focal point.

"In evaluating whether the 1975 Act satisfies the State's responsibility," Handler wrote, unequal expenditures were clearly very important. Money mattered, and different districts had different costs and different needs. Indeed, differences in "qualities of students may result in different levels of spending required to achieve the same level of educational opportunity in different districts." In some cases, "for disadvantaged students to receive a thorough and efficient education, the students will require above-average access to educational resources" (p. 388). Plaintiffs' education clause claim called "for proofs that after comparing the education received by children in property-poor districts, it appears that the disadvantaged children will not be able to compete in, and contribute to, the society entered by the relatively advantaged children" (p. 390).

In the end, Justice Handler embraced the ELC's comparative method. As his language makes clear, deciding what's fair will involve an inquiry into relative needs and the resources available to meet those needs. In remanding the case for an administrative hearing, the Court also alleviated the ELC's concern about Education Commissioner Cooperman controlling the trial. It ordered the commissioner to transfer the case to the state's Office of Administrative Law (OAL).[69]

Abbott I was not big news. To the extent that the press covered it, the message was what the justices probably wanted it to be. According to the Newark-based *Star-Ledger*, the opinion "took no position on the underlying dispute regarding educational opportunities." A *New York Times* article a month later even described *Abbott I* as "a blow to New Jersey's urban school districts" because "the case must first be heard by the Commissioner of Education rather than the courts." The doctrinal significance of the Court's opinion was not lost on Marilyn Morheuser. For her, she said, the opinion "followed from the whole thrust of our claims and evidence . . . the Court adopted our basic framework. So, procedurally, of course, it was a bit of a setback. But when I saw what they gave us, I was delighted."[70]

CONCLUSION: THE ROAD AHEAD

Morheuser and her ELC colleagues had good reason to be delighted. The road from *Robinson* to *Abbott I* had been long and treacherous. *Abbott I* meant that Morheuser would be permitted to present her case as she had framed it. As we will see in the next chapter, the compensatory vision's comparative method would do prodigious intellectual and emotional work at trial. *Abbott I* also meant that the high court was, at the very least, open to the prospect of taking relative social positions and educational needs into account in its future reckonings of educational adequacy. Although it would be another five years before reformers could gain another audience with the justices, they were now well on the way to having their vision translated into law. They would win a compelling victory at trial and an even more stunning one on appeal in *Abbott II*. While reformers continued to tend the garden they had planted in law, they would continue to neglect the surrounding landscape of politics. The next chapter to turns to this phase of the conflict.

CHAPTER FOUR

THE FRUITS OF THEIR LABORS: THE COMPENSATORY VISION ASCENDANT

B ETWEEN *ABBOTT I* IN 1985 AND *ABBOTT II* IN 1990, THE New Jersey reformers would follow through on their legal strategy with perseverance and great skill. This chapter tells the story of their climb from foothold to the legal mountaintop. The narrative is dense and complicated, with three major threads through it.

The first thread is specifically legal. It involves the nature of reformers' court victories at trial and on appeal. A review of the trial court decision will show us how the ELC worked the compensatory vision. In a legal translation process, framing is one thing, and construction is another. Framing is the mental roadmap through legal doctrine, and construction is the nuts and bolts of getting it done. A review of the judicial decisions will also reveal the emergence and evolution of an internal logic to the court battle. As the state raised its arguments in defending against *Abbott*, the courts increasingly responded by shining the spotlight solely on the poor urban school districts.

This internal logic helps explain why in *Abbott II* the high court decided to limit its remedial mandates to these poor urban districts.

The second thread is about elite politics and policy making. It has to do with the role of Democratic Governor Jim Florio, viewed in a triangular relationship with the high court and the ELC. In November 1989, Florio won an open-seat gubernatorial election by a handsome margin. Although the high court had heard oral arguments in *Abbott II* in September of that year, it would not issue its decision until June 1990. In the interim, Florio and a small group of advisors designed a package of tax hikes and a new school finance law, called the Quality Education Act (QEA).

The executive policy-making process proceeded in the shadow of the Court's expected decision in *Abbott*. This process was secretive and technocratic. The Florio administration quickly sprung its plan on the state and rapidly pushed it through the legislature. In the end, the QEA and *Abbott II* would be different but complexly interrelated things. The QEA was not directly responsive to *Abbott II* because it was completed in anticipation of, and not in response to, that decision. In some ways, the QEA went well beyond the Court's *Abbott* mandates. Yet, conversely, when it finally came in June 1990, *Abbott II* demanded more of the QEA than it initially offered, and the law then had to be changed in an effort to conform it to the Court's ruling.

In their legalistic pursuit of just the right court victory, reformers had eschewed democratic politics. In its technocratic approach to liberal policy reform, the Florio administration officials also eschewed democratic politics. They thought that if they designed policies to benefit the majority, the majority would naturally rejoice. They were simply dumbfounded when, in the latter half of 1990, the majority vociferously rejected their plan. Reformers' legalism and Florio's technocratic style of governance would prove to be a volatile combination.

The third thread of the story tells how the legal endorsement of reformers' compensatory vision began to define the terms of public debate. In a sense, this third thread connects the first two by helping to explain how public perceptions and reactions related to the legal and policy process. As the internal logic of *Abbott* increasingly put the spotlight exclusively on the urban poor, the case became a case about "rich and poor, separate and unequal," in the media and in politics, as well as in court. That would be the frame within which the Florio plan would be understood, debated, and rejected.

From the perspective of the culturalist legal mobilization approach, the questions for reformers are questions about the connections between legal strategies and some broader, envisioned politics of reform—that is, about how to get from here to there. Reformers must be mindful of the need for some live political constituency or alliances that will march under their banner. Who will act to somehow make a reform vision real in politics and culture, as well as in the courts? The ELC's legalistic approach to change meant that it had not taken the problems of political realization very seriously. As we will see in Chapter Five, those problems would be particularly acute, given the content of the reform vision itself. For a time after the backlash emerged, the ELC network would not be central political players; the only political resource they had was a judicial decree that could not be enforced. The backlash and how reformers handled it politically is the subject of the next chapter. In this one, I explain how and why the backlash emerged. The fruits of reformers' labors would be sweet in court but bitter in politics.

TRIAL COURT VICTORY: THE LEFELT DECISION

Procedurally, *Abbott I* was "a bit of a setback" for reformers, as Morheuser put it. They had resisted an administrative process in part because it promised to be more cumbersome and time consuming. They were not wrong about this. On remand, the OAL assigned *Abbott* to Administrative Law Judge (ALJ) Steven Lefelt. Pretrial motions and haggling delayed the start of the trial to September 1986. Once it began, the trial was a truly massive undertaking. There were ninety-five actual trial days. ALJ Lefelt heard ninety-nine witnesses and accepted approximately 700 documents into evidence. After the trial ended in July 1987, the parties filed some 1,500 pages of proposed factual findings and 400 pages of legal briefs. The submissions continued until May 1988. Finally, in August 1988, Lefelt issued a 607-page decision in *Abbott*. Education was failing poor urban students, he held. The existing school finance law would have to go.[1]

The Lefelt Decision, as it came to be known in the state, was remarkable for its attention to detail, nuanced arguments, and, in several places, moving eloquence. After Lefelt ruled and ruled as he did, it was truly a foregone conclusion that the high court would side with the ELC. The only questions were "exactly when and by how much."[2] The Lefelt Decision is long and dense, and only a summary is possible here. For my purposes, two things about it are noteworthy.

First, the opinion provides a good window through which we can view the nuts and bolts of the ELC's translation of its compensatory vision into legal terms. The execution of the case capitalizes on the trial as a dramatic form and on the trial court as a uniquely hospitable forum for the articulation of narratives and the reconstruction of meanings. In *Abbott I*, the ELC won the opportunity to present its case as it had framed it. What did that case look like? How did Morheuser and her colleagues actually go about getting it done?

Second, as Lefelt worked back and forth between claims and arguments on both sides, the internal logic of the case, mentioned in Chapter Three above, began to take shape. In a nutshell, throughout the trial and on various specific points, the state objected that the ELC was not saying very much at all about school finance and educational adequacy for the vast majority of students and districts in the middle of the distribution. The ELC's focus on poor urban districts compared to wealthy suburban ones, the state argued, was legally irrelevant and factually distorting. Pointing to *Abbott I* several times, Lefelt held that the comparisons were indeed legally relevant. However, he conceded that reformers factual proofs did not go to adequacy for most ("ordinary") districts. Viewing reformers' factual presentations through their compensatory frame, Lefelt could and did make findings only about particular places. The urban centers were a world apart. Of course, this was precisely as reformers wished it to be. The legal endorsement of their position put the spotlight on the urban poor. However, later on, that legally enhanced spotlight would have some unanticipated political consequences, as well as the intended legal ones.[3]

The ELC's Case: Working the Compensatory Vision

In making out a case pursuing its compensatory vision and ordered by comparisons between the very rich and very poor districts, the ELC creatively made use of the state's own bureaucratic methods for classifying and ranking school districts by socioeconomic status and degree of urbanization. In 1974, the State Department of Education (SDE) developed a construct it called District Factor Groups (DFGs). DFGs classified school districts by socioeconomic status and ranked them in ten groups from lowest (DFG A) to highest (DFG J).[4] Another arm of the state government, the Department of Community Affairs, had designated certain municipalities as "urban" for purposes of distributing certain categories of state aid. In the early 1980s, the SDE adopted this designation to identify "urban school districts." There were fifty-six urban school districts in all.

By cross-referencing these two bureaucratic categorizations, reformers arrived at a list of twenty-nine "poorer, urban districts." Poorer urban districts were those districts within DFGs A and B and also classified as "urban." They were then able to compare the major poorer urban districts with a selected group of wealthy white suburban districts in DFGs I and J.[5]

The legal endorsement of these DFG/urban–suburban constructs in Lefelt's opinion and in *Abbott II* (1990) would make them a central part of the lexicon of political conflict over education in New Jersey. After *Abbott II*, poorer urban districts became "special-needs districts," and they would be singled out for particular attention, both sympathetic and hostile, in law, politics, and policy, specifically in relation to the wealthy I and J Districts. Law would frame politics.

The first third of Lefelt's opinion (pp. 15–228) tracks the ELC's theory of the case. We begin the journey with a statistical portrait of social conditions in the four "plaintiff-districts" (Camden, East Orange, Irvington, and Jersey City), as well as Newark, Paterson, and Trenton. These seven cities were marked by racial segregation and high unemployment and poverty. Patterns of racial isolation and poverty were only magnified in the school systems in these cities. In 1986–1987, of the 159,584 students who attended schools in these poor urban districts, 145,213 were members of racial minority groups. Lefelt blends statistics on high dropout rates and low test scores with graphic descriptions of school buildings set in urban ruins and lacking in basic services. The data and testimony pointed up "the unique educational challenges presented by . . . pupils residing . . . in property poor urban school districts" (p. 15).

After describing the finance provisions of the PSEA and how they worked (pp. 44–93), Lefelt turned to ELC's case in chief. Recall that the ELC's first step, and its hook back to *Robinson*, involved a traditional school finance analysis of tax and expenditure disparities. The Court in *Robinson V* had expressed its expectation that the PSEA would reduce what it called "gross disparities." Had it?

Morheuser relied on school finance experts Margaret Goertz and Ernest Reock for systemwide data analysis that showed that disparities at the extremes had actually widened. Spending differences between the poorer urban districts and nearby wealthy suburban ones were particularly jarring. In current expenditures per pupil in 1984–1985, Camden spent $3,318 and Cherry Hill $4,645; Trenton spent $3,888 and Princeton $5,320; East Orange spent $3,270 and South Orange/Maplewood $4,354; Newark spent $3,879 and Millburn $4,981; Paterson spent $2,976 and Paramus $5,375. Reock's analysis focused on tax bases and tax rates over time and across districts. In relation to the state average school district level of property wealth, poorer urban districts had shrinking tax bases. They were making greater tax effort, compared to the wealthy districts and compared to state average tax effort, and they had less, relatively, to show for it. Overall, spending still seemed to be in significant part a function of local district wealth (pp. 93–115).[6]

As noted above, the state objected that comparisons at the extremes were legally irrelevant and factually distorting. *Robinson* had said that wealthier districts could do more if they wanted to, and so they did. The PSEA was supposed to be equalizing for only the bottom two-thirds of the distribution. Although the ELC did present tax and expenditure data for all school districts, it had not sought to link that data to the conditions of education or to educational "adequacy" for the vast majority in the middle. If one turned one's gaze to the middle (to DFGs C through H), the state argued, things were more complicated. Many districts had below-average property wealth but managed to spend above the state average. Still other districts had below-average expenditures but managed to produce above-average educational outcomes.

In response, Lefelt happily acknowledged that the determinants of tax rates, expenditures, and outcomes were both many and complexly interrelated. However, to him, *Abbott I* meant that comparisons at the extremes were vital, for in that case the high court had held that "all children must be offered an education which if successfully completed would render them reasonably competitive in society" (pp. 545–546; see also pp. 27–28, 366, 418). If there were unmet needs that impaired schooling and learning, then those needs had to be met. The whole finance system would fall, but it would fall because of the way it particularly disadvantaged poorer urban districts and students.

Lefelt then turned to the ELC's "second step"—detailed, point-by-point comparisons among social conditions, resources, educational programs or experiences, and outcomes in very poor and very rich districts, often just a ten-minute car ride away from each other (pp. 140–228). Here, the ELC repeatedly invoked legal norms from the PSEA and its implementing regulations to order its presentation of testimony and documents. These comparisons did prodigious intellectual work for the ELC. In its laws, the state itself had endorsed a rather capacious vision of the appropriate goals and desired outcomes of education. The authoritative legal norms were not anything like Kean and Cooperman's vision, with its narrow, remorseless focus on "the basics" and standardized test scores. Things like art, music, and physical education also mattered a lot to children's educational development, as their obvious significance in the rich suburban districts made abundantly clear.

After this presentation, it was virtually impossible to say that, as a general matter, money was not the central problem. One could only say, as the state did, that more money would not help in certain places because it would be wasted there.[7] Not surprisingly, Lefelt would find that the presence of mismanagement and corruption might be a good reason for more state oversight or intervention, but it was not a good reason for depriving poor minority children of the level of resources that wealthy suburbanites routinely took for granted.

The ELC's case about what it called "program disparities" across rich and poor districts was highly detailed; it proceeded under fully eighteen subheadings, including such things as "science education," "guidance and counseling," and "class size." The ELC's main purpose was to fix the standard of "adequacy" in two ways: first in relation to the needs of urban students and second in relation to the resources available to already advantaged suburban students. Moreover, it was here that the ELC sought to make vivid and lifelike the conditions of education and their social meaning for administrators, teachers, and students in the ghettos. A few illustrations of the ELC's approach will provide a sense of its emotional appeal.

State regulations defined "artistic expression and appreciation" as a "state education goal." However, art education received rather short shrift in poorer urban districts. Whereas elementary school children in the wealthy districts of Montclair, Princeton, and Scotch Plains/Fanwood received "art instruction at every elementary school with certified art teachers," Camden did not even employ any art teachers at the elementary level (pp. 156, 160).

The ELC produced Anthony Guardadiello, the supervisor of art instruction for the Jersey City School District. Mr. Guardadiello testified movingly about a special program he had established to provide qualified urban high school students with what he called "full instruction" in art. The program included mentoring by professional artists and the involvement of students as artists in the life of their communities. One hundred and eighty students applied and could have been served, but resources were available to accept only forty; 140 students had to be turned away. In an interview, Morheuser mentioned that in her view ALJ Lefelt was "visibly shaken" by this testimony. The emotional effect must have been something like seeing a poor child's face pressed up against the glass of a storefront window (pp. 157–159). We could recount similar graphic portrayals of disparities in science, music, and physical education programs.

Woven throughout these point-by-point contrasts were references to the cultural deprivation suffered by poor urban students. The footrace metaphor was pervasive.

State regulations required districts to provide "comprehensive guidance facilities and services for each pupil." Poor urban children, Lefelt wrote, had "greater guidance needs than children in middle-class or affluent districts . . . They entered school less prepared . . . because they are not exposed to an environment in which stable work patterns are common. Their goals and values may not match what is expected in school or the workforce" (p. 168). School libraries were "particularly important to urban children who do not have many books in the home." Yet, budget constraints had led Camden to eliminate libraries altogether at sixteen out of twenty-four elementary schools. Paterson "had no libraries in any of its 30 elementary schools" (pp. 182–186). Poor children were in dire need of preschool and early intervention programs because they often did "not acquire skills and experiences at home which prepare them for school, they begin school developmentally behind middle-class children and have difficulty catching up." Yet, in East Orange, although testing revealed 700 students who were developmentally delayed and therefore in need of full-day kindergarten, the district had resources to serve only 100 of these students. By contrast, wealthy Paramus, Montclair, and Princeton all offered full-day kindergarten as a matter of course (pp. 214–219).

The State's Case: The Problem Is Immorality, Not Money

The state's case-in-chief raised a number of points, but nothing it said could overcome the force of the ELC's presentation. It made four main factual claims, each framed by its insistence that the constitution required only the provision of a minimally adequate education. It argued that: (1) Local choices about taxing and spending accounted for the observed inadequacies and disparities; (2) poorer urban districts were rife with mismanagement and corruption; (3) the existing finance system served other values associated with "local control"; and (4) the existing state regulatory and district monitoring system was sufficient to correct any existing deficiencies the urban districts. Lefelt took up and dispatched each of these claims in turn (pp. 229–513).

Lefelt was not much troubled by claims (1), (3) and (4). It was only theoretically true that poorer urban districts could decide to raise taxes to spend more on education. In reality, urban fiscal stress and the politics of municipal and school district budgeting made increasing taxes virtually impossible. Local control sounded nice, but the Court had repudiated it as a constitutional value in *Robinson*. Moreover, the Kean administration's educational policies had already "embraced a major departure from the tradition of local control" (p. 386). Local control implied fiscal capacity, and the poorer urban districts did not have that. The state's existing regulatory and monitoring system, it was true, had already resulted in some interventions and improvement in poorer urban districts. However, the problem with this argument was that the entire regulatory apparatus was "district and school specific." It took no account of "the adequacy of resources and comparability of programs statewide" (pp. 415–417). In Lefelt's view, *Abbott I* had held that a statewide perspective was in order (p. 418).

The mismanagement defense (claim 2) was really at the heart of the state's case. Plaintiffs' districts and other major urban centers were said to be rife with "mismanagement, political maneuvering and illegality" (p. 274). But for incompetence, waste, and chicanery, these districts would have enough money. In addition to putting the ELC's arguments about program disparities in a different light, the state's mismanagement defense also sought to make a future-oriented case against spending more money. Money was not tightly linked to the most prized educational outcomes, as the cost–quality research showed; but, even if it were, it would be wasted in these particular urban districts in any event. The state folded a general appeal to cost–quality research, as well as a cost–quality study of New Jersey that it had commissioned for the litigation, into this prong of its case. Just throwing money at these urban districts was well-nigh the worst thing one could do for the poor children who had to go to school there.[8]

The state persuaded Lefelt that there were indeed some serious problems in the poor urban districts, especially in East Orange and Jersey City.[9] However, he concluded that even shocking mismanagement could not account for much money. Fiscal stress was a contributing factor in mismanagement and political intrusion (p. 351). And even with good administrative practices, these districts would still be faced with the vast educational needs of their children and inadequate resources. The state's mismanagement defense did mean that money alone could not be the solution, but this was not an argument against providing more resources when they were so clearly needed (pp. 363–364).

Here, again, the ELC's comparative frame seemed to make a crucial difference, for it allowed vivid testimony from many teachers and administrators in both poor urban and wealthy suburban districts about the importance of money. For example, the ELC produced a Dr. Kimple, the superintendent of schools in a wealthy suburban district. He testified enthusiastically about his work and the high quality of the education that his students received. Morheuser asked Kimple "to compare his current expenses per pupil of $4,772 with Trenton's . . . $3,888 and to assess the impact on his district were it to be funded at Trenton's level." The lower per pupil amount would entail an overall budget cut of $1.5 million in his small district. Kimple stated that he would resign before he would preside over the program cuts needed to spend within this hypothetical budget cut (p. 537).

ALJ Lefelt's Conclusions

When he turned finally to the operative legal standards in the case and to what should be done, Lefelt purported to adopt a middle ground between the ELC's exclusive focus on "inputs" and the state's exclusive focus on adequate "outcomes" (pp. 518–521). But in the end, Lefelt's interpretation of "what the constitution commands" and his recommended solutions amounted to a full endorsement of the ELC's vision.

The standard was "educational adequacy." The constitution did not require absolute equalization but only a system "which meaningfully addresses the actual educational needs of all of the State's public school children so that children are offered the programs and other educational experiences necessary to assume whatever type of societal participation they are capable of achieving" (p. 545). If "social and economic disadvantage impairs learning," Lefelt wrote, "I do not see how schools can avoid attempting to ameliorate or eliminate this impairment" (p. 540). The constitutional goal was broad enough to allow some program flexibility from district to district, but "flexibility is not the same thing as inequality based on geographic location." One had to compare inputs across districts in order to assess "whether the system is providing students with equal opportunity, regardless of socioeconomic status or geographic location." No matter how great an effort she or he made, a pole vaulter with a bamboo pole could not compete against one with an aluminum pole. All children with similar needs should receive similar programs and services. All had to have the opportunity "to compete fairly for a place in our society" (pp. 545–548).

The current finance system failed this test. There should be a new finance system better tailored to the needs and hopes of the truly disadvantaged. Having reached the end of a very long journey, ALJ Lefelt offered this concluding remark:

Some fear was expressed by the defense that alteration of our financing system would present a risk of causing damage to other social values and to the system itself. I do not believe in fixing what is not broken. However, plaintiffs have proven that the system is broken . . .

I believe the case comes down to whether this State desires to enhance the educational opportunity of students living in poor urban areas . . . If we do not wish to spend monies easing these students' entry into contemporary society, then there are those who argue that we will have to spend the funds later on welfare, Medicaid, job training and prisons. They argue, therefore, that a thorough and efficient education system would be cost efficient.

I do not believe this question should be answered only on a cost–benefit basis. Some of the costs are relatively easy to calculate, but the benefits are not. How do you evaluate retaining a few students who would have dropped out? How do you weight the one student who becomes a successful artist and creates works that provide enjoyment for thousands of people? How do you cost-out the student who learns to enjoy reading and thereby adds excitement to what otherwise would be a rather ordinary existence? How important to society are flexible, imaginative, and inventive citizens? I cannot even guess. Suffice it to say that I opt for providing equal opportunity to all our children, no matter where they may live. (pp. 606–607).

With this powerful legal victory, reformers' compensatory language started seeping into media coverage and elite policy conversations. The Lefelt Decision would be the first of several occasions when events in court evoked media representations framed in the vision and language of the ELC's case. According to the *New York Times*, Lefelt had declared the funding system "constitutionally flawed" because "it failed to eliminate finance disparities between affluent suburban and poor urban communities." That same day, a front-page banner headline in the *Star-Ledger* read "School Funding Formula Found Inequitable and Unworkable." The lift-quote from Lefelt's decision conveyed the article's central message: "There are . . . vast program and expenditure disparities between property-rich suburban districts and property-poor urban districts."[10]

TO THE SUPREME COURT: PROCESS, VISION, REMEDY, AND TEACHERS' PENSIONS

Technically, Lefelt's massive opinion was merely "advisory." In the language of administrative law, it was an "initial decision" subject to review at higher levels of the agency. In this case, that meant review first by Education Commissioner Cooperman and then by the State Board of Education (SBE). In reality, everyone understood that the case was now bound for the Supreme Court and that the Court would surely hold Lefelt's decision in high regard.

In October 1988, Morheuser petitioned the high court to dispense with further delays and formalities and to take the case directly. Although the Court denied this motion, it did issue an unusually detailed order specifying a timetable and rules for further administrative review. Commissioner Cooperman would have until the end of February 1989 to issue his decision, after which the SBE would have until mid-April to rule. At that point, the Court added, plaintiffs might well want to renew their motion for direct review. It is likely that the justices calculated that they would like to be deciding *Abbott* right around the time of the open-seat gubernatorial election that year because that would allow them to gauge how things were shaping up in politics.[11]

As expected, in February 1989, Cooperman issued a strongly worded opinion rejecting ALJ Lefelt's decision.[12] In April 1989, the SBE upheld the commissioner. In railing against the SBE decision, Morheuser invoked the ghost of *Plessy*. "The tragedy," she said, was "that with this decision we have the highest education officials in the state condoning a separate and unequal education for hundreds of thousands of poor minority children in New Jersey's poor urban districts."[13] The ELC again petitioned the Supreme Court to take the case directly. This time, the Court granted the motion. Briefs were to be filed by July, and oral arguments would be heard at the end of September, just a little over a month before the election.

With 160 pages of facts and seventy-five pages of fact-laden legal argument, Morheuser's appellate brief in *Abbott II* was rather Brandesian. The brief pressed the compensatory view at every turn. Racial isolation and ghetto poverty gave rise to cultural deprivation. Cultural deprivation meant dire educational needs. Poor urban children were not like other children. They "commonly [had] single parents" with "low education levels and few job skills." They lived in poor, overcrowded housing located in crime-ridden neighborhoods. They were not exposed to "books and magazines" or otherwise exposed to "the world of ideas." Unlike other children, whatever education they got would have to come entirely from the public schools, for they "[had] nothing else." Under the current finance system, the dire needs of poor children could not be met.[14]

Morheuser's brief is interesting also for what it tells us about the reformers' approach to what we can call "the remedy problem." The remedy problem is always present in reform litigation. In politics, an old adage has it that it helps to be "for" something as well as "against" something. In reform litigation, however, the converse often seems true, at least to legalistic reform lawyers. In court, they think, one typically wants to avoid getting too specific about remedies and policy changes. Evading the discussion about remedies is often seen as part of a broader, necessary evasion of majoritarian politics. Specificity about remedies makes winners and losers clearer and gives opponents targets at which to shoot. It is far better to focus on the "constitutional violation" and then let the courts take the heat on remedies.

Morheuser's approach to the remedy problem fits this pattern. In a nutshell, she pretended to be in favor of a remedy that would not threaten anyone with losing anything, all the while knowing that such a result was not possible. Like her "dance on the districts," this too was an evasion undertaken for strategic reasons, with "strategy" understood as doing whatever was necessary to win the right kind of court decision. In other words, her approach to the remedy problem would be good public relations in support of her legalistic strategy, or so she thought.

In law, remedy follows violation. Morheuser's approach to remedy reflected a big problem with her legal theory of violation. She was arguing that education was constitutionally inadequate in poorer urban districts. That argument hinged on using the socioeconomic conditions, resources, and programs in the wealthiest districts as the key benchmark, and herein lies the dilemma. The argument implicitly endorses the notion that there is indeed an affirmative constitutional standard for educational adequacy; to find it one need only look at expenditures and programs in, say, Princeton. However, it would be an odd constitutional standard about an affirmative right to educational adequacy that varied according to the identity or status of the child. If what the constitution commanded could be readily found in Princeton, then logically that would be so for every child in the state, bar none. Otherwise, the constitution would mean one thing for the poor and something else for everyone else. The practical problem with the logical remedy was that it was outrageously cost prohibitive. Leveling up all districts to the level of Princeton would have cost about an additional $2.5 billion, at a time when total state aid for public education was about $3.5 billion.[15]

Morheuser's proposed remedy evaded the practical problems and followed the legal logic to its impractical conclusion. Her brief asked the Court to order that spending in all school districts be brought up the level of the wealthiest districts. The standard had to be "a funding equality standard." There were, she wrote, "no technical impediments to such equalization."[16] We can understand this plea simply as a case of a reform lawyer asking for everything to increase the size of the proverbial half a loaf, as well as a standard strategic evasion of policy complexities. But there is a bit more to it than that. Morheuser also believed that her position on the remedy would be good public relations, and this belief on her part reflects her larger, legalistic distrust of democratic politics.[17]

In public, Morheuser wanted to say that she favored "leveling up," not "leveling down." She did not want a decision that required anyone to spend less on education. She did not "want to take anything away from anybody." She was not "playing Robin Hood."[18] Morheuser and her colleagues would maintain this position in public long after the Court fashioned its own remedy focused on the urban poor.

However, obviously, if the poor are to have what the rich now enjoy, the money will have to come from somewhere. There are only three basic options. The money can come from new state and/or local taxes, other state policy domains, or a redistribution of state and/or local funds now spent on education. As a practical matter, it was unlikely that the poor could have what the rich enjoyed without some reshuffling of existing state aid.[19] If the better-off districts were to lose state aid, and most assuredly they would have to, then local school people in these districts would be faced with the prospects of convincing their local taxpayers to pay more in taxes or cutting educational programs. Finally, we should note, if education is only about the competitive race for social mobility, then even "leveling up" is still leveling, for it still might threaten current perceptions of relative advantage.

How, then, could Morheuser claim that she did not want to take anything away from anyone? The claim makes sense only if the only outcome that matters to anybody is the *theoretical* ability to maintain existing levels of per pupil expenditures, even if some taxpayers will have to pay more (and perhaps a lot more) to do so. But the claim rings hollow if people also care about how much they pay, compared to what they pay now. Because people obviously do care about taxes, the claim rings hollow. It may well be that some citizens can afford to and should pay more to support the education of "other people's children," but the ELC reformers were not saying that. They were trying to say that nobody would lose anything and that everyone would win.

When it came to existing categories of state aid under the PSEA, Morheuser's brief revealed a certain awareness of the policy difficulties below the surface simplicity of her call to "level up." One small category of state aid ("minimum aid") went to better-off districts for no particular reason. Morheuser singled it out, and policy elites assumed that the Court would strike it down. But at a total of $163 million in 1989–1990, minimum aid paled in comparison to the amount of money the state paid to cover the cost of teachers' pensions under its Teachers' Pension and Annuity Fund (TPAF). That amount had reached almost $1 billion. Morheuser's brief attacked that as well. TPAF, she wrote, had "a strongly counter-equalizing effect" because it went disproportionately to better-off districts.[20]

Anyone striking at state funding for the teachers' pensions would be striking at the heart of entrenched interest groups in the state. Both the powerful state teachers' union (the New Jersey Education Association, or NJEA) and

the School Boards' Association, (NJSBA) were active players in state politics. Both had substantial resources and active members dispersed across the
state. Shifting the costs of pensions from the state to local level was not likely
to make either group happy, for pension costs would then be a new bone of
contention at the collective bargaining table. Neither the ELC nor the Florio
administration appears to have given much thought to the political repercus-
sions of this policy question. [21]

Now, an egalitarian taking all of these remedy or policy questions into
view might well say, contrary to Morheuser's public stance, that Robin Hood
was not such a bad fellow. Redistribution from rich to poor is often a very
good thing, especially in the area of education. The point I am making here
is not about the moral attractiveness of redistribution. Rather, it is a point
about getting from here to there. The New Jersey reformers used law and
courts to frame a claim about compensatory justice that carried the implication of a vast redistribution of resources, and they did so without a political
prong that would make them players in politics. A Robin Hood solution may
well have been the most morally attractive one. But Robin Hood did not rely
on courts. He always went into battle thinking strategically about raw power
and reasonably well armed.

For her part, Morheuser was content to submit her well-crafted legal case
to the Supreme Court and hope for the best. The political difficulties that
might arise after the Court delivered the anticipated judicial victory did not,
at that moment, detain her.

TECHNOCRATS TO THE RESCUE: JIM FLORIO
AND THE QUALITY EDUCATION ACT

Before the Court, the outgoing Kean administration had stuck to its guns. *Robinson V*, it argued, was the sum and substance of the law. While reformers were
urging the Court to require the legislature to write a blank check, legislators
were "entitled to believe that easy money without hard responsibility would inevitably denigrate from rather than further thoroughness and efficiency."[22] The
Court, of course, would take a different view. However, it would not do so until
some nine months later. In the interim, newly elected Governor Jim Florio and a
small group of his policy advisors would take charge of school finance reform.

By 1989, a good deal of the luster had finally worn off the Kean administration. Kean had wanted to be known as "the education governor," but now
press accounts and policy discussion pointed to the "unresolved crisis in urban education" and the "woefully inequitable system of school finance" as the
main things that Kean would leave behind him.[23] As liberal Democrat Jim
Florio emerged as the frontrunner in the race for governor, the political winds
seemed to be shifting in favor of the ELC's project. In 1981, Florio had lost
to Kean in a virtual tie. By 1985, Kean was unbeatable, and Florio decided to
bide his time. Now, in 1989, Florio's time had come.

The 1989 campaign for governor was typical of New Jersey politics; it was
devoid of serious debate and deep in mud. Both Florio and his Republican
opponent (U.S. Rep. Jim Courter) promised that, if elected, they would not
raise taxes. Florio's most common locution on this question was that he "saw
no need to raise taxes." On education, neither candidate said much of anything. Thus, on taxes and education, the campaign provided no clues about
the profound changes to come. Florio received a strong endorsement from the
teachers' union (the NJEA). NJEA President Betty Kraemer called Florio "the
crystal clear choice of the educators." By July 1990, Kraemer and her union
would be single-mindedly devoted to the complete political destruction of
Florio and Democratic state legislators.[24]

With name recognition and character central to the campaign, "New Jersey
voters . . . warmed to Florio's plucky story: a high school dropout who got his
diploma in the Navy, worked his way through college, earned a law degree,"
and then went on to topple the Camden political machine and win a seat in
Congress. One journalist aptly described Florio as "a peculiar blend of working class Democrat and good government technocrat." This dualism in Florio
had its functional manifestations. The hardscrabble Democrat prevailed when
it came to getting elected, while the technocratic policy wonk held sway when
it came to governing.[25]

On election day, Florio outpolled Courter by 541,000 votes, garnering 61
percent of all votes cast. It was a landslide. Democrats did well riding Florio's coattails. They retained control of the forty-member State Senate (with a
margin of twenty-four to sixteen) and regained control of the eighty-member
State Assembly (by a margin of forty-four to thirty-six).[26]

Although elected with overwhelming popular support, Florio faced a political landscape that even the most adroit politician would have trouble negotiating. There were two big problems. First, the Kean administration had dropped a real financial crisis in Florio's lap. Overly optimistic revenue projections combined with an unexpected economic downturn produced an immediate budget deficit of $600 million and a projected shortfall for the next year of $1 billion. Second, of course, there was *Abbott* and the expectation that the Supreme Court would strike down the current school finance system. Florio's advisors assumed that a response to the Court would require an increase in state revenues of between $500 million and $1 billion, on top of the amount needed to handle the budget deficit.

In making his transition into office, Florio surrounded himself with a small group of advisors who shared his liberal values and technocratic policy proclivities. The liberal technocrats shared the goal of remaking the state's regressive tax system by eliminating its longstanding overreliance on the property tax. That goal was initially independent of the goal of school finance reform but quickly became bound up with it. The Florio administration's tax policy agenda structured and drove its approach to school finance reform.

The Florio administration worked out its response to its twin problems between January and March 1990. The whole process was tightly controlled and highly secretive. The fact that there would even be a tax increase, let alone the largest one in the state's history, was not formally announced until the governor's budget address on March 15, and the details of the Quality Education Act were not made public until the bill was formally introduced in the legislature in late May.

On the tax policy front, the Florio administration saw opportunity in the crisis. Now was the time to do something about the regressive tax system and to provide property tax relief to what Florio called "the beleaguered middle class." The solution to the budget deficit would come from an increase in the state sales tax from 6 to 7 percent and an extension of its coverage to some new items. The sales tax hike would produce roughly an additional $1 billion per year. To cover the anticipated costs of school finance reform, there would also be a state income tax increase targeted to hit "the wealthy"—that is, single individuals with incomes over $35,000 and families with incomes over $70,000. The highest marginal income tax rates would increase from 3.5 to 7 percent.

The income tax hike would bring in an additional $1.4 billion per year. Along with some other minor excise tax increases, in the end the total tax package amounted to an increase of $2.8 billion.[27]

The Florio administration developed its Quality Education Act (QEA) in the shadow of *Abbott*. "Without *Abbott*," said Tom Corcoran, "we probably would have just modified [the PSEA]." While generally sympathetic to the ELC's goals, the administration did not see itself as carrying out the ELC's agenda. Like virtually everyone else, Morheuser would learn about the content of the new law only when the Florio administration unveiled its plan in May.[28]

The QEA as enacted and signed into law in July 1990 was supposed to take effect in the fall of 1991. However, this law would never actually go into effect. In response to the upheaval over taxes and education that followed its adoption, the law would be amended—"gutted," Morheuser would say—in March 1991.

Florio's policy advisors began their policy reasoning by reviewing the Lefelt decision and the appellate briefs in *Abbott II*. For them, *Abbott* was a case about "educational program adequacy" not for some, but for everyone. The problem with the existing system was that school finance had no discernable relationship to providing the resources needed to purchase an adequate education. The Court, they thought, would surely reject the guaranteed tax base (GTB) framework, which left it up to local districts to decide how much to tax and spend. More specifically, the Court would also strike down minimum aid and, probably, state funding of the teachers' pensions.[29]

Therefore, the QEA shifted the basic structure of the state school finance system from the GTB framework to a "high-foundation" program. Under a high-foundation program, the state specifies a (relatively high) per pupil spending amount that each district must provide and then (somehow) specifies how much of that amount will come from the state and how much will come from the local level, for each district. Most state aid is typically doled out in inverse proportion to local district wealth. To arrive at the raw dollar amount per pupil for regular education, the Florio advisors simply looked to current expenditures in districts spending at between the sixtieth and sixty-fifth percentile of all districts. Here, Corcoran said, one could find "the conditions sought by the middle class—class sizes under 25, a range of course offerings, special services, and the like." This per pupil spending amount would be called "the foundation amount," and the general state education aid that got each district there would be called "foundation aid."[30]

The QEA, then, sought to level up all school districts to around the sixtieth percentile of districts, and to shift the burden of paying for education from worse-off to better-off citizens. To realize these goals, the policy architects devised a complicated method for determining how much of the foundation amount each local district could afford to cover on its own, and then determined to channel about 75 percent of all state education dollars (or $3 billion out of $4.6 billion) through this "wealth-equalizing" formula. Here, the poorer the district, the greater the state aid. In order to channel this much money through the wealth-equalizing formula, both minimum aid and state funding for teachers' pensions "had to end." Shifting the pension costs in particular would enhance equity and control costs in one fell swoop. All of the money now dedicated to these categories (over $1 billion), much of it going to wealthier districts, could now be used to level everyone up to a very good level.[31]

Under the QEA, there were 362 districts entitled to state foundation aid, and every one of these districts would see a significant increase in its overall state education aid. These districts encompassed some 70 percent of the state's students. For the remaining, wealthier districts, the "local fair share" was the full foundation amount. They could afford to pay for general education themselves, even though they would be losing minimum aid and funding for teachers' pensions. Still, the Florio advisors reasoned, their new law placed no limits on how much local districts could spend. Local districts could spend as far above the foundation level as they wanted, provided that their wealthy local taxpayers were willing to foot the bill. Moreover, to ease the burden on the rich, under the QEA, the loss of state aid would be phased in over four years.

Florio conceived of his package of tax changes and education finance reform as perfectly designed to provide substantial property tax relief to what he called "the beleaguered middle class." The vast majority would benefit on taxes and education, while the privileged few would now contribute their fair share. Majoritarian support, they thought, would follow readily from this elegant policy design. Why was it, then, that Florio's beleaguered middle class ended up rejecting Florio and his program with both hands?

The answer comes in two parts. For one thing, Florio's entire plan was developed out of the light of day and presented to the state as a fait accompli. Groups that would be profoundly affected by the QEA were not let in on the process. Even many legislators in the governor's own party were not consulted until late April. Democratic legislators introduced the QEA on May 25, and the Court handed down its decision in *Abbott II* on June 5. For another thing, with policy deliberation and design going on in private, the public discussion of reform continued to be framed by the ELC's pending litigation and the anticipation of the Court decision. The Court too viewed *Abbott* as a case about "educational program adequacy." However, its view of adequacy would be the ELC's, and not the Florio administration's.

While Florio's minions labored away in private, *Abbott* continued to foster increasing public attention to education, in terms framed by the compensatory vision.

Interestingly, for a few brief months, Governor Florio himself seemed caught up in the zeitgeist of *Abbott*. In his inaugural address in January 1990, Florio did not discuss taxes or school finance formulas, but he did boldly set his face against the existence of what he called "two New Jerseys." He would not tolerate one New Jersey "where youngsters go off to college, and another where youngsters go off on a road to despair." In early March, Florio told the *Star-Ledger* that "urban education would be his highest priority." He wanted "one New Jersey as opposed to multiple New Jersey's . . . We don't have one New Jersey in terms of its education system."[32]

A March headline in the *New York Times* read "New Jersey Schools: Rich, Poor, Unequal." Under the headline, two photographs appear. One shows black students in Scott High School in East Orange "taking a history class in a music room." The room looks to be in rather dismal shape, and the students are slouching in their chairs. The other shows a racially diverse group of students eagerly working away in a well-equipped computer science lab at Millburn High School in Millburn. The article then goes on to give detailed description of expenditure and program disparities across these two districts, districts "separated by only six miles," but "worlds apart." In May, another *New York Times* headline, this one on the paper's front page, read: "Florio Shifts Policy from School Testing to More Aid to Poor." The Florio plan, the article said, would "change the financing formula to shift state aid for public education from wealthy districts to poorer ones." The motivation for the change, we are told, was a pending "bias suit" against the current finance law. After comparing tax rates and expenditures in Princeton and Camden, this article states that "many of the suits goals have now become Mr. Florio's policies."[33]

Morheuser's legal frame had a certain resonance in media portrayals. Public debate and media attention proceeded in terms defined by *Abbott*. When the Court finally weighed in, the complicated QEA had been public for only one week. The Court's decision would only solidify the public's association of the QEA with *Abbott*, and its sense that together they represented a "Robin Hood solution" that would steal from the rich (white) people to give to the poor (black) people.[34]

THE SUPREME COURT MAKES ITS MARK:
JUDICIAL STRATEGY AND RHETORIC IN *ABBOTT II*

When it handed down its decision in *Abbott II* on June 5, the New Jersey Supreme Court was widely known for its reformist zeal. Typically, its major decisions on civil rights and social policy combined liberal values; a moralistic, sermonizing tone; and the kind of specific policy mandates from which most other courts tend to shy away, lest their decision be seen as "policy" and not "law."[35] The Court's decision in *Abbott II* was true to form.

Chief Justice Robert Wilentz wrote the lone opinion for a unanimous court in *Abbott II*.[36] Rhetorically, the opinion fully embraces the ELC's compensatory vision and amplifies it for public consumption. Not content to strike down the PSEA and let the pending legislative process run its course, the justice decided to place an indelible stamp on the entire conflict by writing a rule book to secure their vision of reform. The Court couched its rule book, or "*Abbott* remedy," as it would be called, in terms of, of all things, judicial modesty.

The internal logic of the case that we saw in the Lefelt decision reached its endpoint in *Abbott II*. Wilentz begins his argument with the notion that he is charting a pragmatic middle course between the ELC's proffered remedy and the state's defense of the current system, and in the opinion he repairs often to this trope. The Court could not strike down the PSEA as it operated in all districts, for neither party had given a precise account of "what is necessary for a thorough and efficient education" (p. 375). When it came to remedies, the ELC was indeed arguing from the part to the whole. Based on a case about urban education, it was asking the Court to strike down the finance system in toto and to mandate the equalization of spending for all at the highest levels. If the Court went along with the ELC, Wilentz wrote, "radical changes would follow." Such equalization would require a massive infusion of funds, and equalization at some lower level would require "leveling down." The state's position was equally untenable. It asked the Court to define constitutional adequacy as minimal adequacy and the funds needed to provide "basic skills." When it came to urban education, the state claimed that its position was to secure "basic skills first." In effect, Wilentz wrote, for the urban poor "basic skills first" always meant "basic skills only."[37]

The tension at work here goes back to *Robinson I*, and it would survive *Abbott II*. The tension is between a constitutional standard or ruling based on funding inequality, on one hand, and substantive educational "adequacy," on the other. The constitutional standard is not "equality," defined as equal funding. There is no requirement that all districts spend at the same level. The standard is "adequacy." However, adequacy has no constant or bright line meaning, and hence it can only be defined relatively—that is, by looking at the education some get in relation to the education that others get. The ELC's powerful legal frame in *Abbott* put the spotlight on social conditions, needs, and resources in the poorest as compared to the richest communities and for the most part left out the middle. Consider Wilentz's language on this point:

As we have noted about the Commissioner's evidence, so we affirm as to plaintiffs': they have not proved what is necessary for a thorough and efficient education. Neither their statistical nor other comparisons informs us of what a district needs in order to have thorough and efficient education: we are left without a standard against which to measure a given districts' efforts. (p. 375)[38]

Wilentz then goes on to say that, "whatever the standard may be," the ELC had proven that certain districts fell below it. Therefore, the Court concluded, the current finance law was unconstitutional "only as applied to poorer urban districts." Poorer urban students had to be "treated differently," for their "needs were dramatically different from those of students in affluent districts" (pp. 366, 375). The state had failed poor urban students, and now the education clause of the state constitution required that the finance law be changed to provide them with access to an adequate education.

This access was to be secured through a four-part rulebook. Any new finance law would have to assure:

1. That funding for regular education in poorer urban districts equaled the level of funding in the property rich districts;

2. That such funding of education in poorer urban districts did not depend on the ability of local school districts to tax;

3. That such funding must be guaranteed and mandated by the state; and

4. That the level of funding in the poorer urban districts was also adequate to provide for the special educational needs of the children there, in order to redress their extreme disadvantage. (pp. 362–363)[39]

A poorer urban district was any district in District Factor Group (DFG) A or B and also classified as "urban." Henceforth, these districts would be known as "special-needs districts" or, later, simply "*Abbott* districts." Property-rich districts were the ones in DFGs I and J. At the time, there were twenty-eight poorer urban districts and 108 wealthy suburban ones. Rule (1), the parity mandate, meant that per pupil spending for regular education, exclusive of categorical state aid or federal aid, had to equal the overall average per pupil spending for regular education in the 108 I and J districts. Rules (2) and (3) meant that it was the state's responsibility to make sure that this happened every year. Rule (4) meant that the state also had to provide additional funds to poorer urban districts, above and beyond the parity mandate, to finance compensatory programs to redress the students' extreme disadvantage. The poor, then, were entitled to "parity plus" (p. 412).

Wilentz's task in his opinion is to justify this "individualizing" of the constitutional standard—this drawing of a line between the poorer urban districts and all other districts—as a matter of state constitutional law. The argument is driven by the sociological approach to constitutional interpretation and the ELC's compensatory vision, which individualizes "adequacy" by linking it to needs and resources available to meet those needs.

In his interpretation of the education clause, Wilentz placed the accent on the Court's long-standing view that educational adequacy was a "continually changing concept." *Robinson I* had so held. In the PSEA, the legislature itself had acknowledged that "the sufficiency of education" hinged "upon the economic, historical, social and cultural context in which that education is delivered" (pp. 367, 369). *Robinson V* held that resource disparities were "plainly relevant" to any inquiry and, indeed, "suggested the inevitability of *Abbott v. Burke*." Some districts could spend more than others, but only after the state assured a constitutionally adequate education in all districts first (pp. 369–370). In *Abbott*,

Wilentz wrote, the ELC's challenge brought "the constitutional obligation into sharp focus as it applies to the urban poor" (pp. 371, 411). By holding that "poorer disadvantaged students must be given a chance to be able to compete with relatively advantaged students," the Court in *Abbott I* had "put a new gloss on the constitutional obligation." Student needs had to be taken into account, and the needs of the poor exceeded the needs of the rich (pp. 370–372).

Wilentz knows that he must defend the controversial line he is drawing. His defense is grounded in the compensatory vision and its view of what race and poverty mean in education. The DFG and "urban" categorizations were reasonable proxies for severe race and class disadvantage. Other districts, poorer rural or suburban ones, for example, might be similar to poorer urban districts in some respects, but they were "not as poor or needy; many were not within DFG A or B, [and] their socioeconomic status is not as compelling." Moreover, "the overwhelming portion of all minorities in the state are educated in . . . the poorer urban districts" (pp. 387–388).

Borrowing liberally from Morheuser's brief, Wilentz states that the urban poor have dire "needs beyond educational needs." They live in "an environment of violence, poverty and despair." They are "isolated from the mainstream of society." They lack not only food, clothing, and shelter, but also "close family and community ties and support," "books in the home," and "helpful role models" (pp. 400–403). They "live in a culture where schools, studying, and homework are secondary . . . While education is largely absent from their lives, we get some idea of what is present from the crime rate, disease rate, drug addiction rate, teenage pregnancy rate, and the unemployment rate." Schools must make up for the material and cultural disadvantages that these children bring with them. "The goal," Wilentz writes, "is to motivate them, to wipe out their disadvantages as much as a school district can, and to give them an educational opportunity that will enable them to use their innate ability" (p. 411).

Money might not help, Wilentz acknowledged. Educational reform would be needed too. But the urban poor were constitutionally entitled to "the same opportunity that money buys for others" (p. 363), "entitled to be treated equally, to begin at the same starting line" (p. 403). "This record," Wilentz concluded,

proves what we all suspect: that if the children in poorer districts went to school today in richer ones, educationally they would be a lot better off. Everything in this record confirms what we know: they need that advantage much more than the other children. And what everyone knows is that—as children—the only reason they do not get that advantage is that they were born in a poor district . . . They face, through no fault of their own, a life of poverty and isolation that most of us cannot begin to understand or appreciate. (p. 412)

The Court's remedial rule book in *Abbott* was odd but intelligible. The Court could not level up all districts to the top, and it would not leave the fate of the urban poor entirely in the hands of elected officials. The Abbott remedy would be costly but not wildly out of reach. For the first year after *Abbott II*, the "parity gap"—that is, the amount of money it would take to equalize per pupil spending between the poorer urban districts and the average level among the 108 wealthiest ones—would have been $400 million. The Court also indicated that the state could phase in any remedy over a period of years.

In one sense, the Court's *Abbott* remedy was an old wine in a new bottle. Proponents of school desegregation had often made arguments for tying the interests of the disadvantaged to the interests of the advantaged. For example, if black children sat next to white children in class, then whatever the dominant white majority did for its kids so too would it have to do for black kids. As one reform attorney put, the *Abbott* remedy was ingenious because it attempted to marry the fate of the urban poor to the interests of the most advantaged students. The Court was saying something very simple: "When it comes to school finance, you may do whatever you like, and do it any way you like, but whatever you do and however you do it, you must do at least this."[40]

The political problem, of course, was that the rest of the state was likely to see this as a shotgun wedding announced by an institution that did not really have a gun. Did the justices really think that minimal compliance with *Abbott* was politically feasible? Would the majority really go along with leapfrogging the poor minority students over most others in order to give them what only the very rich now had? It is impossible to say. However, we do know that judges do not live in a political vacuum, especially if they are New Jersey Supreme Court justices. To the justices, the immediate political context of *Abbott II* must have seemed quite favorable for broader reform, and not merely "minimal compliance." Perhaps the justices reasoned that their landmark decision would add legitimacy to, and place just a few additional policy constraints on, an already redistributive policy initiative that was already well on its way to passage.

Rhetorically, as we have seen, Wilentz's opinion embraces the ELC's compensatory vision and amplifies it with the authority of law. The voice (or "persona") that Wilentz constructs for himself is precisely the voice of the moral reformer. His imagined audience seems to be the state's wealthy, white, complacent suburbanites. It is as if Wilentz wants to pluck them out of their speeding cars and shopping malls, press their faces down on the ghettos, and say: "Look here! Poverty amidst plenty. Shame on you!" The ELC's moral argument would now structure public debate in general and public understandings of Florio's QEA in particular. Now all actors in state education politics would have to reckon with this view. Indifference was no longer an option.

AFTER *ABBOTT II*: PUBLIC REACTIONS AND FLORIO'S QEA

Political events in the month after *Abbott II* proceeded at a furious pace. The Florio administration identified itself with the Court's decision. It backed modifications to the QEA in an effort to conform it to *Abbott II*. The compensatory vision saturated media coverage of the Florio plan. As educational interest groups and wealthier suburban districts woke up to what was at stake, an oppositional language quickly developed. The QEA and *Abbott II* were tightly linked in the public mind. Both threatened the majority with a "Robin Hood plan" that would steal from the rich to give not just to the poor, but to the unworthy poor. The QEA/*Abbott* would level down and dumb down education across the state. Resistance came too late to stop Florio and his merry band of policy technocrats from ramming their tax and education package through the state legislature, but after that they would take a terrible beating in politics.

Governor Florio immediately associated his plan with *Abbott II* and downplayed the substantial differences between his QEA and the Court's rule book. He called the decision "a clear cut victory for the children of this state." In it, he found "reinforcement that [his] plan [was] right and encouragement that it must go forward." Press coverage made the same association. *Abbott II* was "good news for Florio." The Governor's plan would "shift money from affluent to poor school districts."[41]

However, there were some important differences between the QEA and *Abbott II* to be worked out. On one hand, the QEA had not gone far enough to help the poorer urban districts because it had not assured them of "parity plus" with the wealthiest districts; it had not singled out the poorer urban districts for special treatment. To be sure, poorer urban districts would benefit disproportionately from the QEA. But the benefits they got would have followed from the operation of general categories and formulas applicable to all alike. The foundation amounts, representing the Florio advisors' view of the money needed for a "very good education," were the same for all districts, as were the calculations of local ability to pay. So the QEA would have to be modified to somehow conform to the Court's decision. On the other hand, Florio's QEA already made big policy changes that went beyond what the Court required. Most importantly, Florio's QEA shifted the costs for teachers' pension from the state to the local level, but, as it turned out, unexpectedly, the Court had stayed its own hand on that issue.[42]

In response to *Abbott II*, the Florio administration and Democratic legislative leaders adopted two changes to the QEA. Technically, the changes were relatively minor ones. Politically, they only reinforced the association of the QEA with *Abbott II* and the broader sense that Robin Hood was now riding bareback and unimpeded through the Garden State. First, the QEA was amended to designate thirty poorer urban districts as "special-needs districts" (SNDs). These SNDs, or "*Abbott* districts," would have their foundation amount set at 5 percent higher than all other districts. Second, the QEA was amended to impose spending growth caps that would rein in spending increases in the wealthiest school districts. Together, the 5 percent bump for the poor and the limitation of spending increases for the rich might eventually equalize spending at the top and bottom, as required by the Court.[43]

As Florio's package of tax changes and the QEA sped through the legislature, representatives of wealthier school districts and educational interest groups began to voice objections. The mayor of one well-off town happily acknowledged that "government sometimes has to help those who can't help themselves" but added that it "shouldn't take away from others. That's the whole problem with the Florio plan, it's a Robin Hood plan." A school superintendent from another well-off town stated that better-off districts losing state aid faced a "double whammy." They would lose state aid and now faced the new burden of covering the costs for teachers' pensions. Still others bristled at the claim that they were "wealthy" as opposed to hardworking "middle-class" people. In these and other comments, one could discern a racial subtext. The newspaper article reporting these sentiments added that suburban officials "said their frustration is increased because there is no guarantee that the extra money going to the state's poor urban districts will be properly spent."[44]

The teachers' union (the NJEA) and school boards' association (NJSBA) mobilized to fight the shift in the pension costs. Florio had not consulted with the union about this major policy change. In response, as Morheuser put it, "the teachers went absolutely bonkers." After the union failed to block passage of the law, NJEA President Betty Kraemer declared that the shift in pension costs was "an act of war." She vowed to destroy Florio and his Democratic supporters in the legislature at the next election. "I never thought I'd be in bed with the Republicans," she said.[45]

That there was only the barest hint of a legislative process only added fuel to the fires now smoldering around Florio's initiatives. All components of Florio's package were reported out of legislative committees in straight party-line voting. All of them passed the State Senate and State Assembly between June 18 and 22, in close votes. Not a single Republican legislator voted for any of Florio's bills.[46]

The Republican leaders instinctively moved to Reaganite themes. Florio had promised not to raise taxes, and now he was presiding over the largest tax hike in the state's history. The Democrats were "throwing money at problems," and "punishing people for being successful." The QEA "penalized one set of school districts in order to benefit another." The whole process was "outrageous."[47]

On July 3, 1990, the governor signed his QEA into law. As he did, he tried to reassure his critics. The new money for education—some $1.1 billion in new state aid—was not for "flabby, lethargic bureaucracies" or "patronage." It was "for one thing and one thing only—our children." Florio then held the signed bill aloft and declared: "Ladies and gentlemen, a new era."[48]

CONCLUSION: THE DILEMMA OF DIFFERENCE AS A POLITICAL PROBLEM

Thus, as of mid-1990, the ELC, the Court, and the Florio administration stood united behind a redistributive reform program. The wealthy would pay more in taxes, and poor minority students would receive substantially more in the way of educational resources. Unlike the ELC and the Court, the Florio administration was genuinely worried about the need for middle-class support. Reform would not be sustainable, they thought, unless most people benefited. However, the Florio administration's effort to appeal to a majority through elegant policy design, as opposed to a riskier strategy of open public deliberation and debate, would be no match for public understandings shaped by the ELC's compensatory vision and the Court's powerful, policy-specific endorsement of it. It was the ELC's vision and the Court's decision in *Abbott II* that together defined the terms of public discourse.

The normative evaluation of reformers' view is not my concern here. Rather my concern has to do with law, politics, and change—that is, with actually getting from here to there. That concern takes us into a conversation about "the dilemma of difference"—about "how to overcome past hostilities and degradations on the basis of group difference without employing and, in that sense, legitimating [and reinforcing] those very differences."[49] The degrading differences that reformers highlighted between the situations and life prospects of poor minority children and other children were real. They were not fundamentally a product of how reformers framed and projected their challenge. By making that egalitarian vision legal, reformers were bearing witness to injustice and seeking to jolt others into taking notice and taking action. Their success in court was no easy feat.

But there are some difficulties with the compensatory vision. The problem with such portraits of victimization and harm is that they seek to motivate by evoking sympathy and pity. Sympathy is the response we offer to those who are not our equals—to those who are, thank goodness, worse off than us. Victims are not equals. Even if moral argument motivates action and produces material gains, the benefits will be bestowed as a matter of beneficence. Moreover, the same arguments that evoke sympathy can just as easily foster disidentification and resentment. The vision of *Abbott II* in particular rendered poor minority children as the inhabitants of a cultural world radically different from that of the vaunted middle class with its "middle-class values." The eyes-open statement of the raw "facts" of difference (no good role models or books in the home here!) runs the risk of reinforcing the very presuppositions behind "white" disidentification historically tied to racism. As the historian Daryl Michael Scott has noted, pity has a close cousin, whose name is contempt.[50]

As a matter of educational ideology, the compensatory vision also embraces presuppositions that run counter to its own ultimate objectives, for that vision portrays education centrally as a positional good in the competitive race for social mobility and social advantage. Whatever their differences, the ELC and the Kean administration shared this view. In a world of understanding thus created, reformers' objectives were likely to be perceived as a grave threat by middle- and upper-class communities. With education understood as a positional good, the ELC was indeed determined to take something away from the better-off, Morheuser's protestations to the contrary notwithstanding.[51]

In both of these respects—in its accentuation of differences and harms based on race and class and in its acceptance of education as a positional good—the ELC's compensatory vision promised to invite vigorous opposition. Given the content of this vision and its successful translation into law, the practical question is this: How did Morheuser and her colleagues plan to negotiate the predicable, powerful, emotionally laden resistance to this project that would surely follow success in court?

Litigation-oriented reformers, it must be said, can never plan very well. They will rarely be able to control what other actors do in response to their efforts. Unpredictability is predictable. In the New Jersey case, the independent and politically inept actions the Florio administration loom rather large in the story of the subsequent unraveling of reform. Nevertheless, with the benefit of hindsight, we can say that the short answer to the question of how reformers planned to address political resistance can be answered with the word legalism.

The day after *Abbott II* came down, Morheuser lavished praise upon it. She then added an interesting caveat: "We've always understood that the work really begins at this point," she said. "The law books are filled with paper victories that no one has ever enjoyed the benefits of. We can't let that happen."[52] Morheuser meant what she said. It had always been her understanding that political work should not begin until the elite law reformers were armed for battle with just the right court decision. In politics, her work was, indeed, only just beginning.

Reformers spoke in the legal arena for an abstraction they called "the poor urban children." Without some sort of political prong to their effort, the adults in the lives of the poor children (their parents, teachers, or other representatives accountable to adults) could not be seated at the table of politics. They could not be there to see and be seen. They could not be there to look someone else in the eye and assert their claims. They could not be there to give and take.

There was no chance, then, that their actions in politics might come to counterbalance the legal portrait of them as poor, passive, degraded victims.

These reformers overestimated the power of a sympathetic judiciary to produce change and underestimated the need to have live constituents engaged in politics. To their credit, in the upheaval that followed *Abbott II* and the QEA, reformers did eventually use law to leverage action in politics, thereby bringing live constituents onto the political stage. The next chapter examines how *Abbott II* and the QEA defined public debate and structured the organization of education politics and how, in this new context, reformers adroitly turned to politics to rescue their project from defeat.

CHAPTER FIVE

FROM LEGALISM TO POLITICAL ENGAGEMENT: BACKLASH, PERSEVERANCE, AND A CULTURE OF ARGUMENT (WITHOUT END)

P RIOR TO *ABBOTT II*, THE ELC'S COMPENSATORY VISION WAS
in essence a proposal framed and proffered to the courts. The
legal translation of this vision and its acceptance in court did influence the language of public debate and, later, the agendas and decisions of other key political actors and institutions, in addition to the courts. But the judges were the target audience, and the courts were the primary location for the assertion of claims. Now, after *Abbott II*, the discursive universe constituted by this vision and its rendition as law would become deeply embedded in state politics and culture. The vision became constitutional law, and constitutional law in turn structured the enactment of policies that elaborated the vision in the form of more specific concepts and categories. The policies determined the allocation of money for public education. Money and education touch most people deeply—and right where they live. After *Abbott II*, various new interests formed, and preexisting

interests mobilized for action, within the discursive and policy universe of *Ab-bott*. Action and experience in politics would solidify the reality and meaningfulness of the compensatory vision *insofar as* it, and nothing else, constituted a local culture of argument and defined the agenda of contention.

Reformers' success in defining the agenda of contention is not the same thing as their achievement of their ultimate goals. As noted above, no reformers advocating on the behalf of the have-nots can easily control or predict how others will respond to their claims, and this is especially so for legalistic reformers. Legalism as an ideology and strategy accepts and trades on the questionable proposition that law and courts are autonomous from, and morally superior to, ordinary politics. One of the defining features of a legalistic effort is that it will be removed from political domains aside from courts, both before and after judicial decisions. If, as a formal matter, the judiciary has a modicum of institutional independence, then the idea of law's separation from politics is not wholly false. As in New Jersey, the courts may well be the only place within government for the articulation of interests and arguments that have little chance of being heard through other institutional channels. Still, legalism tends to overestimate the powers of courts. We know that if resistance to judicially mandated reform runs high, in the end the courts will be institutionally weak actors.[1]

When we combine the New Jersey reformers' legalistic approach to change with the content of their vision, we can see that their stunning legal victory in *Abbott II* potentially carried within it the seeds of its own destruction. When we add Florio's technocratic approach to his tax and school finance reforms into the mix, it is really a wonder that *Abbott* survived at all. But *Abbott* would not only survive; it eventually flourished. Most accounts of *Abbott* make the Supreme Court the central change agent in this drama. This simplistic view is that reformers kept asking for the Court's intervention, and the Court repeatedly provided it by ordering others to follow its *Abbott II* rule book. Over time, elected officials had no choice but to go along. The law is the law, after all.

The interpretation offered here is different and far more accurate. I explain *Abbott*'s survival and eventual success as a function of two linked factors. First, and foremost, as a massive, popular mobilization against Florio's QEA and *Abbott* seemed destined to consign reformers' project to the dustbin of history, Morheuser and her colleagues made the requisite transition from legalism to a sophisticated realistic approach to law, politics, and change. In this chapter, I describe how this move from legalistic outsiders to political insiders was made and how it mattered in politics. Second, the ELC's political maneuvers both stopped Republican opponents bent on legislative or constitutional overrides of *Abbott* and provided the Court with political contexts in which it could make its ongoing strategic interventions without great fear of serious institutional reprisals. Indeed, without the ELC's turn to politics, it is likely that the Court would have been forced to bow out gracefully by settling for partial reform, just as it had in *Robinson V* and *Mount Laurel III*. The Court is still central to the story, but the point is that the massive redistributive changes wrought by *Abbott* were not produced by the Court acting alone.

In addition to this focus on how the ELC made the move from legalism to political engagement, I will be concerned to show how the vision of *Abbott* shaped the broader organization of education politics throughout the state. By framing politics, the law of *Abbott* gave rise to new identities and interests and provided a new set of constraints and opportunities. Reformers did reasonably well at seizing the opportunity side of what looked to be a rather bad situation in the early 1990s. Their adroit political work eventually allowed them to secure massive material benefits for the state's most disadvantaged communities.

A caveat is in order here. After *Abbott II*, the story gets only denser and more complicated. I will make my way through the welter of details by keeping my eye on the New Jersey reformers and on broader questions about the great virtues and residual defects of their efforts. Among the defects, perhaps the one that looms largest now is the return of the key questions that they repressed about whether New Jersey's urban school systems had or could develop the capacity to turn increased funding into better educational practices and outcomes for poor urban children. While many observers think the jury is still out on that question, it is interesting that, as the twentieth century came to a close, the ELC finally decided to make the problems of urban school reform its own.

THE POLITICS OF BACKLASH: THE UNRAVELING OF REFORM

The backlash against Florio's program was really two intertwined backlashes. A general uprising against the tax hikes framed educational interest groups' more specific objections to the QEA. By the end of the summer of 1990, Florio's "besieged middle class" had the governor himself under siege. By the end of the year, fearing for their political lives, Democratic state legislators moved to amend the QEA by diverting a substantial amount of new state education aid to property tax relief for their middle-class constituents. Florio had no choice but to sign the new law, known as QEA II, in March 1991.

In June 1991, Morheuser petitioned the Supreme Court to strike down the new law. The justices demurred by remanding the case to a lower court for a full trial. In November 1991, the Republican Party won veto-proof majorities in both houses of the state legislature. In 1992, the GOP set out to destroy the QEA and to overturn *Abbott* by constitutional amendment. It was it this point that they were met and blocked by the ELC's political maneuvers.

The ink was not dry on Florio's signature on the QEA when public opinion took a sharp turn against him.[2] In what is surely one of the more bizarre episodes in our age of media politics, "talk radio turned private unhappiness into public tax revolt." A new Trenton-based megawatt radio station (New Jersey 101.5) featured call-in shows on politics and public affairs. In June 1990, talk show hosts began a constant barrage of criticisms of Florio and his program. They "portrayed the Governor as an out-of-touch and imperious bully." At one point, two hosts challenged an angry caller to "do something about it," and he gave out his name and phone number. Overnight, a new statewide antitax organization called "Hands Across New Jersey" was born. Within a week, 5,000 citizens gathered in Trenton to vent their rage. Over the next few months, the radio station functioned as the "nerve center of a statewide tax revolt." The group demanded a repeal of Florio's tax hikes. Its agitation and public demonstrations would continue for the next year or so.[3]

Opposition to the QEA ran parallel to the tax revolt. Florio's claim that the vast majority would see net economic gains from his mix of tax hikes and increased state education aid was wholly lost in the din of the tax revolt and the widely held, *Abbott*-induced view that the central, if not exclusive, goal of the QEA was to help poor urban school districts at the expense of all the rest. Like the antitax forces, opponents of the QEA highlighted the secretive process that produced the legislation, as well as its "Robin Hood" content. Citizens in better-off districts also expressed their fear that money sent to the urban centers would just be wasted.[4]

There were two main overlapping sources of resistance to the QEA. First, education lobbies, led by the NJEA and the NJSBA, vigorously opposed the QEA's shift of teachers' pension costs from the state to the local level. In this regard, they alleged, the QEA was a threat to the quality of education throughout the state. There would be "layoffs, program cuts, a record number of defeated school budgets, and higher taxes." For them, the planned shift in the pension costs had to be reversed, at all costs.[5] Second, personnel from the wealthier districts started mobilizing to oppose the QEA. In August 1990, three separate formations sprang up. School district superintendents spearheaded all three efforts. Soon, a few leaders formed a steering committee bridging the three separate groups.[6]

According to the main leader of this new umbrella group of wealthy districts, many of its participants had been aware of the ELC's litigation as it worked its way up to the Supreme Court, and many "saw *Abbott* as good social policy . . . Many of us believed that more resources should go to the urban centers, and that there should be more reliance on broad-based, statewide taxes." However, all of the wealthier communities agreed that the QEA, as opposed to *Abbott*, needlessly inflicted too much damage on their "lighthouse districts."[7]

By October, the group produced a position paper—indeed, a manifesto of sorts. In a line well written for public consumption, the paper proclaimed that "weak schools should not be made strong by making strong schools weak." If "good districts were forced to dismantle quality programs," the result would be "a leveling down of quality schools throughout the state." The superintendents wanted legislation that "created winners of all children" and that "all New Jerseyans can support." Before long, this group of districts would be called "the Garden State Coalition." It demanded a repeal of the shift in teachers' pension costs and other changes to the QEA that would allow its member districts to maintain high spending.[8]

Thus, whereas before *Abbott* and the QEA the wealthy districts qua districts had not been organized for action in politics, now they were. They had the most to lose, and they were the first to get out of the gate in response. Before too long, the urban districts would do the same, as would middle-income or "foundation aid districts." *Abbott* and the QEA framed the organization of education politics by race and class.

By now, the Florio administration and Democratic legislators were starting to worry. As one Florio aide put it, "we expected to be hit by a Volkswagen, not by a Mack truck." Florio belatedly tried to take his case to the people, but his efforts were transparently reactive and stage managed, and they had no effect on the climate of opinion.[9]

Neither Governor Florio nor state legislators had to face the voters on November 6, 1990. Nevertheless, that election day provided all of the state's politicians with just the sort of data that politicians crave in volatile situations. On that day, U.S. Senator Bill Bradley, New Jersey's enormously popular senior Democrat, very nearly lost his Senate seat to a young political newcomer named Christine Todd Whitman. Whitman's campaign strategy was simple. She associated Bradley with Florio and repeatedly challenged him to take a stand for or against Florio's program. Bradley reminded the voters that he "worked at the federal level" and refused to answer. The day after the election, in an abrupt about-face, Florio announced that "all of his policies—and specifically those touching education—were now subject to negotiation."[10]

Over the next several months, Democratic legislators battled among themselves not over whether to divert money from poorer urban districts to property tax relief but over just how much to divert. If they were to survive the 1991 election, they reasoned, the angry voters would have to perceive them as deeply concerned about middle-class taxpayers, not poor urban children. Senate Democrats seemed to think that an antiurban stance should be combined with vigorous public denunciations of mainstream educational interest groups, especially the NJEA, and "runaway school spending."[11]

In March 1991, the legislature passed a set of amendments to the QEA that, among other things, provided that the state would continue to cover the costs of teachers' pensions for an additional two years, after which the costs would be shifted to the local districts. The new law also lowered the QEA's basic per pupil foundation amounts and placed more stringent limitations on all school districts' spending growth rates. The amended act, know as QEA II, ended up diverting $355 million in planned state education aid to property tax relief and drastically reducing the amounts of aid going to the poor urban districts.[12]

The Democratic legislators' gambit failed. Throughout 1991, GOP leaders built a unified statewide campaign against "Jim Florio Democrats." They promised a rollback of Florio's tax hikes, starting with a reduction of the sales tax from 7 back to 6 percent. Enraged at Florio and Democratic legislators, the NJEA threw its full weight behind Republican challengers to Democratic incumbents. On election day, it was a genuine landslide, with Republicans winning veto-proof majorities in both houses of the legislature. If they could unite, and there was no reason to think that they could not, the Republicans could now govern whether Jim Florio concurred or not. The election did not bode well for the ELC's project, to say the least.[13]

The ELC lawyers had been only lukewarm about Florio's original QEA. To them, it was "only a three-fourths good bill."[14] Florio's advisors prevailed on them to support it as a good start and assured them that it could be modified to do more for the poor (and thereby to comply with *Abbott*) later on. Indeed, absent such modifications in an egalitarian direction, Morheuser believed that she had good grounds to go back to court to challenge the QEA. There was, after all, no real assurance that the measure could meet the Court's "parity plus" mandate within four years.

Now, in the face of an overwhelming backlash, Morheuser and her colleagues seemed truly lost at sea. Cut off and free floating, without organizational clients or any live political constituency, they seemed remarkably impervious to the political realities overtaking reform. While the specific targets of most of the attacks were Florio and his QEA, and not the Court and its *Abbott* decision, backlash rhetoric was typically animated with the strong sense that the whole point of the Florio program was to help the (unworthy) poor at the expense of the (worthy) middle class. And in this milieu, anyone who was not living in poverty was "middle class." With virtually everyone savaging the QEA for going too far, Morheuser relentlessly attacked it for not going far enough. Her grounds were legal, and her approach highly legalistic. She appeared at legislative hearings, waving the Court's decision in *Abbott* around like a bloody shirt. The Court's words were the law, and as such, morally imperative. Defiance was simply immoral discrimination against urban children.[15]

After Democratic legislators ignored her admonitions by amending the QEA, Morheuser made good on her threat to go back to the Supreme Court. In June 1991, she asked the Court to take immediate jurisdiction, strike down the QEA as amended, and declare state funding for teachers' pensions unconstitutional. "This Court," her brief stated, "cannot stand by while another generation of children in poor urban districts, their hopes raised high by inspiring and lofty constitutional pronouncements, sees their hopes dashed on the political rocks below." Not surprisingly, the justices took a glance at their political weather-vanes and decided that they had very well better stand by, at least for a while. Although there were virtually no facts in dispute, and therefore no need to have a trial, in September 1991 the Court remanded Morheuser's challenge to a lower court for a full hearing. It noted that the trial court should consider Morheuser's renewed constitutional challenge to state funding for teacher's pensions, as well as the question of whether the QEA as amended conformed to *Abbott II*. The justices thereby bought themselves some time to watch and wait. They would not be heard from again until July 1994.

Over the course of 1991, Morheuser reported that she turned her attention to what was now the very difficult problem of building political support for *Abbott*. "We had to start over," she said. "It was a year of regrouping and organizing." In the past, other activists, particularly nonlawyers such as Steve Block and Herb Green, had often urged Morheuser to use the lawsuit to build a broad political coalition to support reform. Now their criticisms seemed well founded. Moreover, with *Abbott II* now on the books but also in jeopardy, she had something concrete to offer urban constituents and much less reason to fear close association with urban districts qua districts. So, in 1991, the ELC started cultivating connections with urban district personnel who stood to benefit from *Abbott* and facilitating communications among them. In turn, the urban districts started funneling financial resources to the ELC. Even if mobilized, of course, urban districts and/or urban activists acting alone would have limited power in New Jersey politics. But at least from 1991 on, the ELC could plausibly claim to speak for adults, and, as we shall see in a moment, these adults could make appearances on the political stage.[16]

Riding high on their landslide victory in 1991, in 1992 Republican legislators made good on their promise to repeal Florio's sales tax hike. They also vowed to dismantle the QEA. The QEA was a "grossly expensive, failed social experiment," said the new Senate president. The new chair of the Assembly Education Committee was more graphic: The QEA had to be "bombed, grenaded, destroyed." But an urge to destroy and a good plan of attack are different things.[17]

As he faced the ascendant Republican supermajority, Governor Florio started playing defense, and playing it well. He used budgetary and parliamentary maneuvers to ensure that the Republican legislators could not change the school finance rules for the 1992–1993 school year.[18] Once they were stopped momentarily, the Republicans turned to what they trumpeted as an open and deliberative legislative process. Whereas Florio was the king of the railroad job that had produced the QEA, the Republicans would start by listening (again) to what everyone had to say about the law (before they destroyed it). There would be public hearings around the state. One imagines that what the GOP leaders expected to hear was a strong antigovernment, antitax message, especially from wealthy suburbanites. What they heard instead was a public conversation framed entirely by *Abbott* and, in an odd way, highly constrained by it. When that was not to the Republicans' liking, they introduced resolutions in both houses to amend the constitution so as to overturn *Abbott*. At that point they were met by a new coalition of educational interest groups, with the ELC and its pending litigation at its center.

Legislative hearings provide a good window through which to view interests and arguments. They can tell us who is speaking in a particular policy domain and what they are saying. Republican legislators held five public hearings between April and June 1992. Most witnesses came as representatives of school districts; they were school board members, district superintendents, teachers, and parents. A smattering of activists filled out the picture.[19]

The talk at these hearings is interesting for three reasons. First, it shows that by 1992 the process of people self-identifying as "belonging" to one of the three categories of districts in the tripartite division flowing out of *Abbott* and the QEA was complete. Actors came from "one of the special needs districts," or "one of the urban thirty," or, once just for laughs, "the dirty thirty." Or they were from "one of the I and Js," or from "an ordinary foundation aid [middle-income] district." In one sense this is unremarkable. One would not expect anything else, given a law that uses these categories and makes them determinative of spending for education. Still, we can note that the conversation is not only "only about money" but also fundamentally about relative positions—about one's place in relation to the rest—and not about other things one might talk about when talking about education. The conversation in Kentucky was never anything like this, largely because the Kentucky reformers endorsed a rather different vision of education and successfully sought to have that vision embodied in law.

Second, there was a strange disjunction between witnesses' criticisms of Florio and the QEA, on one hand, and their comments on the Court's decision in *Abbott*, on the other. *Abbott* and the QEA were different things, but they had much in common, too. Indeed, as a matter of practical politics and rational policy, we might say that it would be difficult, if not wrong, to pursue the *Abbott* rule book without having a general tax and finance system that looked something like Florio's original QEA. Yet, witness after witness managed to see a sharp difference between the QEA and *Abbott*.

The QEA had no friends, although critics had disparate objections to it. For witnesses from the urban centers, the problem with the QEA was that it could not deliver that to which they were morally and, now, constitutionally entitled. The compensatory vision and the Abbott rule book were their guide. For witnesses from middle- and high-wealth suburbs, the QEA would level down education across the state and do particular harm to the best "lighthouse" districts. The pension shift, which had been put on hold for two years but was still looming, still weighed heavily on peoples' minds.

The spectrum of views on *Abbott*, as opposed to the QEA, was much different. Interestingly, many representatives from wealthier districts prefaced their attacks on the QEA with heartfelt expressions of concern for the plight of the urban poor and specific endorsements of the Court's decision in *Abbott*. The poor needed and should get a lot more, they said, provided that they themselves did not lose too much. Why couldn't everyone be a winner? Even more conservative citizens from the suburbs and their Republican representatives found themselves in a rhetorical bind. They too expressed concern for the poor and responded to *Abbott* in tones of muted ambivalence, lest they be perceived in public as callous, insensitive, or racially biased. *Abbott*'s moral outlook not only defined the terrain of discussion but also seemed to exercise a certain moral gravitational pull on suggestions about what to do next.

That this was so—and this is the third interesting point about these public hearings—may have had something to do with the fact that school personnel and advocates from the urban centers were an increasing presence as these meetings unfolded. They invoked *Abbott* and its vision again and again. Their Great Society rhetoric about the plight of poor urban children was stirring and stinging, with several witnesses embellishing their remarks with references to the then-recent conflagration in Los Angeles. Actors from the urban centers had moved their bodies in space to enter the lion's den, for no hearings took place in the major cities. They were there to confront their adversaries, look them in the eye, and assert their claims. *Abbott II* provided them with a vision and a set of terms, and gave that vision and set of terms the moral authority of constitutional law.[20]

When the anticipated groundswell of support for further tax cutting via taking education aid away from the cities did not emerge, Republican legislative leaders abruptly shifted gears. In late June, they introduced their resolutions to amend the state constitution so as to overturn *Abbott*. The operative language that would be inserted into the constitution's "thorough and efficient" clause stated that "nothing in this Constitution shall be construed to establish a right to a free public education which would require the provision of state funds to a school district which, when combined with the local share, will exceed 110% of the State average budget per pupil."[21]

The Legislature's education committees then held two more joint public hearings on this proposed constitutional amendment. Opposition to the amendment was vigorous, boisterous, and almost unanimous. The school boards association and the coalition of wealthy districts were both strongly opposed. Personnel and activists from the urban districts attacked it as racist. Unlike the prior batch of five hearings, these two hearings were punctuated with outbursts of protest. Local television news coverage showed panels of mostly white legislators facing rooms packed with angry, mostly minority citizens.[22] The one exception to adamant opposition was the powerful NJEA, which was frankly a little coy about exactly where it stood. It would have to see a specific funding formula ("show us the money"?) before it tipped its hand. Looking back on this period, Morheuser stated that she "listened in amazement" as the NJEA leaders refused to oppose the amendment. "They were single-mindedly focused on the pensions, and only lukewarm about *Abbott* overall."[23]

Although each legislative committee reported the proposed amendment out to its full house for a vote, the intensity of opposition led GOP leaders to table it. It was never voted on in either house.[24]

Meanwhile, behind the scenes of this public battle, the players had opened up various lines of private communication. The Republicans had benefited greatly from the support of the NJEA, and they wanted to secure it again for the 1993 election. However, educational interest groups now feared that general hostility to government and taxes might undercut public support for education funding. The main sticking point for them was the pension issue, and on that front the main threat now came not from Florio but from the ELC and the Court.[25]

The legal threat that the Supreme Court would mandate local funding of pension costs was real, and it took on added urgency just at this moment in July 1992. Morheuser was now back in court conducting a trial in *Abbott*. The Supreme Court had remanded the case to Judge Paul Levy. Trial commenced on July 8 and ended on November 18, 1992. There were two issues: (1) Did the QEA as amended comply with the terms of *Abbott II*?; and (2) Did state funding of teachers' pension costs violate the T & E clause of the state constitution? On the first issue, the technical details were complicated, but the answer was plain as day. If the Court's "parity plus more" remedy was really the law, then the QEA was illegal.[26] On the second issue, Morheuser's claim had more strictly legal merit than it had had when the Court narrowly rejected it in 1990. The Court was careful to leave the door open for another challenge, and it had specifically directed Judge Levy to hear the claim anew. "Legal merit" might not be determinative of the Court's ruling, or it just might be.[27]

At this time, Morheuser and her ELC colleague Steve Block had been involved in some very practical negotiations with the NJEA, the NJSBA, and the Garden State Coalition. An offer for a deal came from the NJEA leadership; as the representative of the urban districts, the ELC accepted it. The quid pro quo was simple. The ELC agreed to withdraw its legal challenge to state funding for the teachers' pensions and to support legislation keeping coverage of pension costs at the state level. In return, the NJEA and "all of the other [education] groups agreed to do nothing further to harm *Abbott*."[28]

The ELC and the NJEA would now anchor a broad coalition of six educational interest groups, plus the leadership of the Garden State Coalition, called the "New Jersey Association for Public Schools" (NJAPS). NJAPS would seek to present a united front in the politics of school finance reform.[29]

Over the second half of 1992, NJAPS in turn formed one point in a triangle involving Republican legislators, on one side, and Governor Florio, on the other. The process involved the ELC and its urban constituents negotiating for position *within* NJAPS and then NJAPS as a whole negotiating with elected officials over the contours of changes to the QEA. Morheuser's starting point within NJAPS was that the group should seek a temporary one-year compromise measure. The Republicans would never go along with everything she wanted, and both the gubernatorial election of 1993 and another appearance before the justices in *Abbott* were still in front of her. The idea of a one-year compromise suited her new coalition partners, provided that the thorn in their side was finally and permanently removed.

For their part, the Republicans had abandoned their proposed constitutional amendment and returned to the ordinary legislative route. All of the players in the game then staked their claims, specified their dollar amounts, and eventually arrived at an omnibus one-year compromise measure that took the school finance debate off the agenda for the 1993 elections.

In the Public School Education Act of 1992, everyone gave some ground, and everyone got something. The big winners were the NJEA and NJSBA. The law provided that the state would permanently retain responsibility for the full costs of teachers' pensions. It gave the poor urban districts yet another significant increase in state education aid, albeit less than they were scheduled to get under the QEA. It also added a small increase in aid to many other districts and provided that no school district would get less state aid than the year before. Finally, the law provided for the establishment of a bipartisan commission to study the finance system and then recommend permanent changes in a report to be issued on November 15, 1993, conveniently right after the election.[30]

The ELC's participation in NJAPS illustrates the kind of interactions and experiences that become possible when reform lawyers get their hands dirty in practical politics. Morheuser had high hopes for NJAPS. For her, the raw quid pro quo was only a starting point for what she foresaw as a political process in which she could win the other groups over to her cause. NJAPS would foster ongoing, face-to-face communications among the ELC and its constituents and the representatives of other groups and communities. In meeting after meeting over a period of roughly two years, Morheuser would make the case that she had been making for so long in court to a new audience. Through her advocacy, she hoped, they would come to know (what she called) "the true meaning of *Abbott*"; they would know "what it means to lose hope" and understand what it would really take for people in the cities "to dream again."[31]

To be sure, as Morheuser well knew, her lofty hopes notwithstanding, she would have to reckon with divergent interests. The only thing on which all the NJAPS groups could agree was that the state should spend an additional $1 billion on education. In this sense, the ELC's old remedy problem simply had a new home. Nevertheless, constant meetings and conversations did produce new understandings and compromises at the margins. Moreover, if there is a basis for trust and if lines of communication are open, then divergent interests can sometimes be modulated so as to defeat a clear common enemy. Although the relevance of NJAPS as a formal alliance faded with the rise of Christine Todd Whitman, its associational patterns reemerged to block the new governor's attempted end run around *Abbott*.[32]

More concretely, Morheuser also hoped that NJAPS could develop and stand behind a new school finance plan that would comply with *Abbott* and that the new Education Funding Review Commission (EFRC) could be the conduit for turning the plan into legislation. Because the Republican Party in the state was increasingly tied to an antitax agenda, the feasibility of this insider strategy obviously turned on the outcome of the 1993 gubernatorial election. If the insider strategy failed in the short term—and it would—then the ELC could still play its hand in the courts, where the wells of sympathy ran deep.

In any event, the ELC's late turn to politics had already saved the day at a crucial turning point in the entire conflict. As we have seen, it had been a two-step process involving, first, the mobilization of urban constituents, and, second, locking horns and cutting deals with other actors. Things in the electoral arena did not unfold as Morheuser wished, but the ELC would remain steadfast and decidedly in the game.

THE ELECTION OF 1993 AND *ABBOTT III* (1994)

By 1993, remarkably, Governor Florio had managed to claw his way back to respectability. Christine Todd Whitman, the clear frontrunner since her near miss against Bill Bradley in 1990, won the Republican nomination and went on to defeat Florio in the general election by a mere percentage point. After running an inept campaign under the pressure of Florio's personal attacks, Whitman actually had to come from behind to beat Florio. She did so on the strength of a late-in-the-campaign promise to secure a 30 percent, across-the-board income tax cut, to be phased in at 10 percent per year from 1995 to 1997. The move reminded enough undecided voters about what they did not like about Florio, and it worked. Although the GOP lost a few legislative seats, it still retained solid majorities in both houses.[33]

In September 1993, just two months before the election, Judge Levy had issued his decision striking down the QEA. Judge Levy also opined that there was really no point in ordering anybody to do anything. Whether there would be a judicial order and what it might say would be up to the Supreme Court.

Whitman had run on a pledge to cut the income tax, and she won. In her inaugural address in January 1994, Whitman pledged that there would be no hedging or backtracking on that promise. In fact, she said, the tax cutting would begin ahead of schedule "with a 5 percent income tax for every family in New Jersey effective January 1, 1994—[or] 17 days ago." The Education Funding Review Commission (EFRC) would take until April 1994 to issue its report. Its blueprint called for the infusion of about $1 billion in additional state education aid. As far as elected officials were concerned, the report was dead on arrival. For the time being, all eyes were trained back on the Supreme Court.[34]

In July 1994, the Supreme Court issued its third decision in *Abbott v. Burke*. Its unanimous per curium opinion was largely a reiteration of its *Abbott II* rule book. After acknowledging that much progress had been made in raising the overall spending in urban districts, the Court reiterated its commitment to "parity spending" and tightened up its definition. Parity meant a "substantial equivalence, approximating 100%," for regular education spending, excluding funding for categorical programs. Progress toward parity had to continue, and in roughly equal annual increments, over the next four years, until parity was achieved for the 1997–1998 school year.[35]

Moreover, the Court wrote, the state had come up far short on the second, "parity plus," prong of the Abbott remedy involving compensatory supplemental programs and services for poorer urban districts. In *Abbott II*, the Court had directed state officials to identify and implement a set of supplemental programs responsive to the special needs of poor urban children. In response, the QEA merely created a new category of aid ("at-risk aid"), tied to poverty rates, and arbitrarily allocated funds into it. There was no assessment of needs and no requirement that local districts actually adopt any specific programs. However, for the Court, much more hinged on supplemental programs than the state seemed to realize. The ultimate goal was "the actual achievement of educational success in the special needs districts." That goal could not be realized unless state officials "identif[ied] and implement[ed] the special supplemental programs and services" that the children needed.[36]

The Court noted that, while it would issue no orders at this point in time, it would now retain jurisdiction. If the state didn't make adequate yearly progress toward parity over each of the next three years, the Court would entertain applications for relief. It set a deadline of September 1, 1996, for the state to have new legislation in place that complied with its Abbott rule book.

Abbott III was another victory for Morheuser and the ELC. Like the new governor, the Court was signaling that it was not backtracking either. It was, in fact, playing the kind of game with the other branches of government that it had often played before—praising, criticizing, poking, prodding, and cajoling for more—without quite risking an immediate confrontation over the complete control of policy. The ELC had asked the Court for a more drastic remedy in the form of a December 1994 deadline for new legislation and a judicial reallocation of funds in the event the legislature failed to act. But with unified Republican government and Governor Whitman's star rapidly rising, the Court wisely gave the whole matter a little breathing space. While the elected officials would have over two years to come up with a new law, it could not have been lost on the governor that she would have to face the Court again before she faced the voters in the November 1997 election. The ELC would have no choice but to spend the next two years in a wait-and-see mode.

THE STRUGGLE CONTINUES: THE ELC, THE COMPREHENSIVE EDUCATIONAL IMPROVEMENT AND FINANCING ACT (CEIFA), AND *ABBOTT IV* (1997)

While Marilyn Morheuser waged her legal and political battles on behalf of poor minority children, she was also engaged in a personal battle against cancer. In the political upheaval over the QEA and *Abbott II*, Morheuser had demonstrated quite a "flair for politics." Once she and her associates moved to create contexts for political action, her human qualities—her drive and charisma, her irrepressible enthusiasm and wry sense of humor, and her ability to empathize with others—served her quite well. Over the course of 1994 and early 1995, however, her illness became increasingly debilitating. On October 22, 1995, Ms. Morheuser died at her home in Newark, New Jersey. She was seventy-one years old.[37]

One month later, the ELC's Board of Directors held a press conference to announce that David Sciarra, a forty-three-year-old cause lawyer with much experience in New Jersey, would be the ELC's new executive director. In an interview, Sciarra stated that his first order of business "was to make sure that the organization didn't close." Over the next few years, he and his colleague Steve Block would work hard to secure financial support from liberal foundations. The ELC's ability to win grants from the foundation world would get a huge boost from the Court's decision in *Abbott IV* (1997) and the remedial process it set up. Sciarra and Block also embarked on what would be a long process of developing the policy research and advocacy capacities needed to render the compensatory vision as a set of more specific programmatic proposals.[38]

When Sciarra took over in late 1995, the outlines of the Whitman administration's response to *Abbott III* were already visible, and for reformers the emerging picture was not pleasing.

Governor Whitman's response to the Court was driven by her unshakable commitment to cutting taxes and her ideological orientation toward education. On education, her views had much in common with former Governor Kean's. Her rhetoric consistently emphasized high standards and accountability through testing and downplayed the significance of resources. Unlike for Kean, however, for Whitman tax cutting took precedence, and therefore she ended up being far more hostile to spending for education in general than Kean had ever been.

It is likely that the governor never had any intention of complying with the Abbott rule book—it would be truly shocking if she did—but her response was never openly defiant. Rather, her sophisticated effort amounted to something along the lines of plausible deniability. Although she clearly was not complying, she could argue that she was. One need only have a proper understanding of the state constitution and the case law to agree with her. As a political matter, in her first year in office, Whitman demonstrated that she would be a formidable opponent. If the Court ended up lacking the stomach for a political fight, Whitman's legal arguments and policy initiatives would give the justices an escape route.[39]

The core idea was simple. The Whitman administration proposed to redefine the meaning of the constitution's thorough and efficient clause through a new (or old) legal argument and new policy initiative, which were mutually reinforcing. Ever since *Robinson I* in 1973, the administration argued, the Court itself had been saying that it focused on money only because it had never been shown a good substantive definition of a constitutionally adequate education. For this same reason, the Court in *Abbott* had latched on to relatively high spending in the wealthiest districts as a constitutional benchmark for the poor. Now, in light of a trend in education policy that was sweeping the nation, the Whitman administration could supply the long-missing core definition of educational adequacy. It would develop rigorous content standards that would specify what all children in New Jersey should "know-and-be-able-to-do." Once the definition of a T & E education was supplied, then the administration could proceed to determine how much it would cost for everyone to offer the requisite opportunity. The legislation that eventually embodied this approach was called the Comprehensive Educational Improvement and Financing Act of 1996 (CEIFA).

The Whitman administration's program began to take shape in February 1995 with a report from Commissioner of Education Leo Klaghotz that sought to justify the turn to content standards as the best general approach. In November, the State Department of Education (SDE) released a second more detailed report, but one still lacking in the crucial details about funding levels and mechanisms. This report indicated that content standards, assessments, and curricular frameworks, all of which were still in development, would be the administration's focal point, and that costs would be calculated by using a model school district and state averages for inputs. At this point, criticisms of Whitman's initiative began to mount. The ELC lawyers took aim at it in light of *Abbott*, of course. They were joined by the mainstream education groups and the Garden State Coalition, all of whom rightly foresaw that a key component of Whitman's effort would be trying to rein in spending in the wealthier suburbs.[40]

In January 1996, Whitman devoted her entire "state of the state" address to education and school finance policy. With the Supreme Court justices seated directly below her, she took aim at the *Abbott* rule book. Money was not the problem in New Jersey, where education spending statewide had increased 400 percent over the past fifteen years. And money was not the solution. She was "committed to changing the way New Jersey defines and measures educational achievement . . . We must stop chasing dollars and start creating scholars. Educational equality will come," she added, "only when we commit ourselves to educational quality for all our children. At the heart of our efforts are core curriculum content standards."[41]

In May, the administration released its final proposal. There were fifty-six standards covering seven core subject areas, with nearly 900 performance indicators. The state would develop assessments (tests) in each area, to be phased in over a five-year period. Unlike previous iterations, this final version contained the analysis of how much it would cost for each district to meet the standards. The per pupil dollar amounts just happened to fall around state average expenditure levels.[42]

The big catch in the whole fabric of the argument, of course, was the lack of any real nexus between the standards and the costs. The state's reasoning about costs not only had no demonstrable relationship to the standards, but was also entirely circular. The standards were not even a curriculum, but rather simply a set of as yet vaguely defined desirable outcomes. The reasoning about costs started with a hypothetical model school district that bore no resemblance to many actual school districts, least of all to poor urban ones. On the basis of this model, it then made certain input-based assumptions (e.g., class sizes capped at twenty-four) and costed out inputs based on state average costs.

However, one key part of the Whitman proposal prevented the argument from collapsing as an obvious sham. Along with the move to content standards, the administration proposed significant changes in the local school budgeting process. The proposed local budget changes at least demonstrated that the administration was serious about its claim that its proposal provided all the money that *any* district really needed to meet the standards. If a district spent at or below the basic per pupil amounts, then no local budget election would take place. Districts would be free to spend above the specified amounts—as the Court had always allowed and as some 300 school districts already did—as long as they went to their local voters to get approval to do so. However, the voters would no longer vote on the entire budget, but only on the "excess amount" above the basic level. In addition, the voters would have to be told, right on the ballot, that the excess amount coming out of their pockets was "constitutionally unnecessary."

Unfortunately for the governor, her plan "was attacked vehemently by all sectors of the public education community, with the wealthy districts leading the charge." Several amendments in the legislative process erased the bright line between the law's basic spending amounts and excess spending over them. The most important changes simply grandfathered in current spending levels in the wealthier districts and did away with any changes in the local school budgeting election process. Voters would continue to vote up or down on the entire budget, from the prior year baseline, just as they had before. Whatever plausibility the administration's claims might have had, they had simply evaporated in the legislative process. The people had spoken, and they had clearly said that, at least when it came to them and their own children, they were determined to spend more on education than Whitman said that they should. If CEIFA stood as passed, the upshot was that the rich would be able to spend as before, while the poor would in effect be limited to the foundation amounts.[43]

Nevertheless, after having secured one extension of the Court's September deadline, on December 20, 1996, Governor Whitman signed CEIFA into law. In January 1997, the ELC returned to the Court. Reformers did not challenge the new content standards per se. Rather they challenged the notion that the standards, without more, provided a full definition of a constitutionally adequate education for all children and attacked the notion that the law's funding amounts had anything at all do with what it would take for children in poor urban districts to meet the new standards.

Notwithstanding the modifications of CEIFA in the legislative process and how they undermined the administration's legal position, knowledgeable observers were not quite sure about how the Court would decide this time. For one thing, as part of its broader strategy, the Whitman administration had inched spending closer to parity over the previous two years. By 1997, the parity gap was down to just 10 percent, or just $250 million. If it wanted to, the Court could say that 90 percent was a good approximation of "parity."[44] For another thing, the Court's great leading liberal light, Chief Justice Robert Wilentz, was no longer there. In July 1996, Wilentz had abruptly announced his retirement due to illness; he died as the result of cancer three weeks later.[45]

But the New Jersey Court was still very much the Wilentz Court, and Justice Alan Handler was still there. Like the U.S. Supreme Court under John Marshall, under Wilentz the New Jersey Court's decisions flowed from certain fixed principles (here, decidedly liberal ones), but the decisions were always modulated in light of astute calculations about the interests of other actors and the immediate political context. By 1997, Whitman was less of star than she had been two years earlier. Some of the negative consequences of her tax and budget policies were now apparent, and it looked as though she would have to struggle to win reelection in November. Moreover, an economic recovery in the state produced unexpected revenue gains. If the justices were to order full parity spending, the money would be there to comply, and it is a safe bet that the justices knew this.[46]

The Court issued its fourth decision in *Abbott v. Burke* in May 1997.[47] In a five to one decision, with Justice Handler writing for the majority, the Court held that while CEIFA "may someday result" in a constitutionally adequate education for all New Jersey children, "the new act is incapable of assuring that opportunity in special needs districts in the foreseeable future" (p. 420). The Court would not depart from the compensatory vision and the Abbott rule book. The compensatory vision would continue to guide the entire legal analysis, this time with some new twists.

The Court not only ordered the state to close the remaining parity spending gap for the 1997–1998 school year and to maintain parity spending for the foreseeable future thereafter. It also took a bold remedial plunge into the murky depths of urban education policy. The compensatory vision had always entailed compensatory programs to wipe out disadvantages and to make the competitive race for educational success a fair one. Now the Court would superintend a judicial process to arrive at the policies and oversee their implementation.

Justice Handler made short work of the Whitman administration's claim that the standards were a solution to the puzzle of adequacy. The standards "themselves do not ensure any substantive level of achievement," Handler wrote (p. 428). Moreover, CEIFA's cookie-cutter approach to deriving the funding levels to meet the standards simply erased the sociological analysis undergirding *Abbott* and the *Abbott* remedies. Following the ELC reformers' lead, the Court had always taken background social conditions and educational needs into view. The "hypothetical model school district" from which the state had derived its dollar figures "rested on the unrealistic assumption that . . . all school districts can be treated alike and in isolation from the realities of the surrounding environments." The model's "insensitivity" to "actual conditions" just would not do, for it "assumed that all children are equally capable of taking advantage of educational opportunity, although the reality of course is that they are not" (p. 431).[48]

The question was whether CEIFA provided poor urban children with an educational opportunity comparable to the one provided to children in the wealthy suburbs, and the answer was clearly "no." It only added insult to injury that a clear majority of the state's citizens had rejected the idea that spending over the basic amounts was "inefficient," or "excessive," or "constitutionally unnecessary" (pp. 429–430).

In *Abbott III*, the Court had made much of its mandate that the state education department should study actual needs in the urban centers and then design compensatory programs well tailored to respond to those needs. With respect to this requirement for "supplemental programs," neither the state nor CEIFA did anything to change the picture the Court had not liked in 1994. Justice Handler's language was rather stern:

We have ordered the state to study the special educational needs of students in the SND's. That has not been done. We have also ordered the state to determine the costs associated with implementing the needed programs. Those studies have not occurred. Without studies of actual needs, it is unclear how a sound program providing for those needs has been accomplished. (p. 438)

Justice Handler then added a new substantive prong to the Court's *Abbott* remedies. Physical facilities for poor urban children had to be "sufficient to enable those students to achieve the substantive standards that now define a thorough and efficient education" (p. 439). The state would be solely responsible for covering the costs of literally billions of dollars in renovations and new school construction.[49]

The Court therefore ordered the case remanded to a trial judge, who would in turn order the commissioner of education to undertake the required studies of compensatory and facilities needs and make a report of findings and proposed solutions. After that, there would be a full adversarial hearing. The trial judge would then make recommendations, which in turn would be reviewed by the Supreme Court (pp. 444–457).

SOME OBSERVATIONS ABOUT OUTCOMES AND AN EPILOGUE, 1998–2009

With *Abbott IV* decided and *Abbott V* on the way, much had been settled, and much remained uncertain.

From reformers' point of view, they had already succeeded beyond their wildest dreams. Even as of the mid-1990s, when they were fighting to rescue

Abbott, they counted it as a great success of their project that, through litigation, they had defined and dominated the political agenda in education policy. Now, with *Abbott IV*, they had completed a process of winning truly massive material benefits for poor urban communities. To be sure, as I have argued, they did not win those benefits through litigation alone—political mobilization, coalition building, and deal making were also required. But to the skeptic of resort to courts to produce change, it must be said that material benefits started flowing immediately after *Abbott II* and never stopped flowing after that. Between 1991–1992 (the first year of the QEA) and 1997–1998 (the first year of full-parity funding), reformers secured an *increase* in state education aid to the poor urban districts of just under $1 billion. With parity spending maintained every year for eleven years after that, and with significant state aid funding supplemental programs in excess of parity aid, we can conclude that the ELC's efforts produced at least $3.5 to 4 billion in state aid to urban districts *that would not have otherwise been forthcoming*. No quibbling about how to calculate spending or how much of the total can be attributed to *Abbott* can undermine the conclusion that massive resources were sought, and massive resources were gained.[50]

But "getting more money in there," as Morheuser often put it, was one thing, and making the money matter was another. *Abbott IV* shifted the ground of the battle to what would be done with enhanced resources—to the nature, costs, and implementation of an array of school reforms, compensatory programs, and facilities improvements—and to what it might mean for these programmatic initiatives to matter or make a difference. The ELC's goals shifted from winning resources to ensuring that resources were used wisely.

Although the ground of the battle had shifted, a certain underlying dynamic would remain much the same. Whitman went on to win reelection in November 1997, albeit narrowly. The Whitman administration begrudgingly accepted parity spending, but it would continue to find creative legal and educational policy arguments to support its strongly held belief that money was not the problem. Even if money were a problem, they thought, parity spending already provided all the money that anyone could want. Thus, for some time to come, reformers would remain in the position of beseeching the courts to order recalcitrant state officials to do that which they were otherwise loathe to do.

For the ELC, it had been long struggle to reach the point where a court order to send money would be obeyed. The court orders to follow would be different in kind and even harder to enforce, for they would be orders to de-sign, fund, and implement educational policies, directed to multilayered, over-burdened, and sometimes simply dysfunctional state and local bureaucracies. Even with good will and decent bureaucratic capacities, this would have been a tall order. With hostile state officials at the helm and generally weak bureau-cratic capacities, the results were fairly predictable: ongoing nasty struggles over the minutia of education policies. After *Abbott V*, which specified com-pensatory programs and facilities improvements, there would be *Abbotts VI, VII, VIII, IX, X*, and so on, all the way to *Abbott XX*—argument seemingly without end. As of this writing, in *Abbott XX* (May 2009), the New Jersey high court has upheld a new statewide finance law—the School Finance Reform Act (SFRA)—and released the state from the *Abbott* parity and supplemental funding remedies. As I briefly discuss below, because SFRA grandfathers in or otherwise preserves many of the reformers' financial and policy gains, the Court's endorsement of the new law is best viewed as but a minor setback, from reformers' perspective.[51]

By 1997, the ELC and its expanded network of urban constituents and political allies knew very well what they were in for and that the courts alone could not save them. One chapter of *Abbott* had closed, and another one—another long one—was just beginning. In addition to setting the policy agenda in education and winning material benefits, reformers regarded the creation of constituen-cies and alliances to support their cause as one of the great successes of their litigation-driven effort. Those constituencies and alliances both provided po-litical support at the level of state policy making, and, later, offered the hope that communities (parent activists, district personnel, policy experts) could be mobilized to support and foster the actual delivery of better education on the ground in the cities.

Abbott IV brought those allies leaping to their feet to give the ELC a standing ovation and thereby helped the ELC mobilize greater political and financial resources. The organization, as such, would continue to make prog-ress in bolstering its political and policy advocacy capacities. Just weeks after *Abbott IV*, the ELC could call a mass meeting—a "Victory Celebration and Briefing"—attended by some 250 people working in urban education from across the state. Although the mood in the room was celebratory and sometime raucous, as speaker after speaker attacked the Whitman administration, ELC Director David Sciarra, who spoke last, was not exactly celebrating. His tone was defiant (he too had harsh words for the Whitman administration) but also a bit somber. Nothing more would be gained, he said, in the absence of political action and struggle.[52]

The ELC's relationship with urban districts qua districts had always been uneasy and ambivalent, and it would remain so. But the point here is that, as this mass meeting demonstrated, political engagement had opened up new possibilities for practical action in the future.

Abbott IV was unprecedented in the history of school finance litigation. The parity remedy was unprecedented, as was the remand order promising judicial oversight of urban policy reform and, potentially, even more money. Because liberal foundations very much like to be where the action is, especially if the cause is well within the ambit of liberal principles, *Abbott IV* positioned the ELC to obtain a new, large infusion of foundation funding. In 1994, the ELC's annual budget was under $350,000. By 2000, largely as the result of grants obtained from various foundations after *Abbott IV*, the ELC's annual budget had quadrupled to around $1.5 million, and by 2008 it was $1.9 million. Much of the money has been used to develop in-house policy research and advocacy capacities, which in turn have leveraged larger networks of talented scholars committed to the ELC's vision.[53] Given the proceedings following *Abbott IV*, all of the expanded resources would be sorely needed.

The Court designated Senior Appellate Judge Michael Patrick King to conduct the remand proceedings. In late 1997, Commissioner of Education Leo Klagholtz submitted two reports to the remand court, one on supplemental needs, and the other on physical facilities. At the heart of the commissioner's proposal was a plan to have something called "whole school reform" (WSR) instituted at every elementary school in the poor urban districts, along with school-based management and budgeting. One implication of this move to WSR was a cognate claim that the urban districts and schools already had all the money that they really needed. The commissioner also recommended full-day kindergarten and a half-day of preschool for four-year-olds, both of which could be had with existing funds. Finally, on facilities, the state hired a firm to conduct a survey and then concluded that $2.7 billion would be needed over the next five years.[54] The ELC attacked the state's methods and conclusions and proposed its own alternative array of programs and interventions, with a price tag of about an additional $800 million, over and above parity spending.[55]

In response, Judge King "charted a middle course." He endorsed the State Department of Education's (SDE's) focus on whole school reform but recommended full-day preschool for all three- and four-year-olds and full-day kindergarten. Judge King arrived at a price tag of an additional $312 million, over and above parity.[56]

The Supreme Court issued its fifth decision in *Abbott v. Burke* in May 1998. With Whitman reelected and the Republicans still in control of the other branches, at this point the Court backed off a bit from its strident tone of just a year before. It accepted the state's and Judge King's template but paired it down considerably. The Court endorsed WSR and full-day kindergarten but reduced the preschool mandate from a full day to a half day of preschool for all three- and four-year-olds. Finally, the Court concluded, the state's response on facilities was good enough. Long-range planning for projects had begun, and the state would have to oversee and fully fund them.[57] Along all of these fronts, the Court required the SDE to write new regulations governing implementation and requests from the districts for more aid.

But the most important point about *Abbott V* was that the Court rejected Judge King's price tag of $312 million. Given WSR and school-based budgeting, the Court could not conclude that existing funds would be insufficient to get the job done. If local school districts thought they needed more money and could demonstrate "particularized needs," then they would be legally entitled to submit proposals to the SDE asking for more money. The commissioner had testified that he would seek more funding if more was needed, and the Court was happy to say that it would now take him at his word.

Thus was educational policy made for the some 300,000 students in the poorer urban districts, and thus were the new battle lines of legal and bureaucratic warfare drawn. One could no doubt write a whole book on *Abbott V* implementation or, perhaps, any one of its disparate major strands. The puzzles and paradoxes of judicially mandated reforms projected through layers of bureaucracy are endlessly fascinating, but they are not the central focus of this book. The new policy initiatives flowed out of the compensatory vision. That vision included winning vastly more resources that could be used to support certain, specific policy interventions. From reformers' point of view, the nature of the fight itself has to count as a success.

From the Whitman administration, there would be only steady, determined bureaucratic diversion and delay. The main goal was not to spend any more money on the urban districts. With the election of Democrat Jim McGreevey as governor in 2001, things got considerably better, but only for a short time. The new governor committed himself to making *Abbott* work and promptly placed several of reformers' old allies in charge at the SDE. Unfortunately, the state's budget crisis and consequent efforts to limit *Abbott* funding once again placed the ELC at loggerheads with state officials.[58]

Through all of this, Sciarra and his colleagues made securing quality preschool programs their highest priority. The gains that they made on the preschool front are truly impressive, and these gains have been fully preserved, even though the Court lifted the parity and supplemental funding remedies in 2009. The progress in preschool education, moreover, seems to be reflected in much improved outcomes in the urban districts on the state's fourth-grade reading and math tests. Progress with whole school reform and facilities renovation and construction has been more halting and uneven.[59]

Many readers will no doubt wonder about the bottom line of academic achievement, as measured by test scores. While improvements are palpable across the poor urban districts at the lowest grade levels, at higher grade levels scores on state tests have been for the most part flat. In addition, there is a fairly wide range of variation in patterns of test score results across the poorer urban districts. It seems that the jury is still out on whether the vastly enhanced resources will produce significant gains in academic achievement as measured by test scores.[60]

A couple of things are clear about the ELC and its ongoing project, however. First, the ELC is now widely regarded as a key player in state education politics, one that is routinely entitled to a seat at the table at the highest levels of government. Second, beginning with *Abbott V*, the ELC started to talk openly and honestly about capacities and conditions for reform at the level of the poorer urban districts and schools. From that point on, it made the problem of good implementation its own.[61]

In January 2008, Democratic Governor Corzine and a Democratic legislature passed a "School Finance Reform Act." The act established a new, weighted school finance formula and abolished the *Abbott* parity and supplemental funding remedies. The state used consultants and expert panels to establish a base per pupil cost at the elementary education level. The formula then adds weights to the per pupil cost for higher grade levels and for at-risk, limited-English-proficiency, and special needs children. In March, the Corzine administration asked the New Jersey high court to find the act constitutional and to hold that the *Abbott* funding remedies were no longer necessary. It pointed out that, increasingly, needy children were more evenly distributed throughout the state. As of 2008, it noted, 49 percent of at-risk students lived in non-*Abbott* districts. Because the new formula used significant weights for at risk students (on a sliding scale of 0.47 to 0.57, depending on the degree of concentration of such students within a district) and for limited-English-proficiency students, it clearly took needs into account. It urged the Court to give the new formula a chance to work. In November, the high court issued a decision preserving the status quo and remanding the case for a full evidentiary hearing.[62]

On May 28, 2009, the New Jersey Supreme Court held that SFRA was constitutional, "to the extent that [the] record permitted its review." In upholding the new law, the Court wrote that it was "choosing to give the benefit of the doubt to the State as it implements a new innovative approach to providing sufficient resources to at-risk pupils wherever they happen to attend public school in New Jersey."[63] It is highly unlikely that the Court's decision marks the end of the line for the ELC and its allies. For one thing, the Court itself left the door slightly ajar with some pointed caveats. Its decision to uphold the new law was premised on the assumption that state officials would fully fund the law's formula. The state's ongoing structural budget crisis will make that requirement difficult to meet. For another thing, the Court made much of the fact that SFRA itself calls for a comprehensive review after three years of operation in order to evaluate how the new formula is actually working.

In any event, the shift from the *Abbott* funding remedies to a statewide, highly needs-based finance law is only a minor setback to the ELC's overall project. As Paul Tractenberg notes in a recent editorial, key elements of *Abbott* remain embedded within SFRA or preserved outside of it. Not only will the preschool reforms won for the poor by ELC continue; they will now be extended to poor children in eighty-four additional relatively poor school districts. Likewise, the school construction program, troubled though it may be, will continue just as before. Finally, the recent setback occurs against the backdrop of twenty years of steadily increasing and greatly enhanced resource and new programs in the *Abbott* districts. Using an inclusive measure of dollars per pupil, but one *not* including federal funds, the state told the Court that the *average* per pupil spending amount in the *Abbott* districts under the first year of SFRA would be $17,325. For the *Abbott* districts, then, enhanced funding levels are grandfathered into the new formula, even though it is likely that funding increases will not quite keep pace with increased costs for the next several years.[64]

CONCLUSION: LAW AND THE POLITICS OF SOCIAL REFORM

What lessons can we draw from this case study about law and the politics of social reform? What did these New Jersey reformers do well, and what might they have done differently and perhaps better? What does this case tell us about the utility of the theoretical approach laid out in Chapter One? That approach has guided my narrative account of this decades-long conflict. My story has been about nature and significance of legal mobilization. It has been about reformers, their vision, and how they translated that vision into law; about their strategic thinking and evasions; about the interplay of legal claiming, on one hand, and the evolution of official legal doctrine and public policies over time, on the other; and, finally, about the influence of legal discourse on public debate and political practice. Because the insights and lessons I seek are practical ones, it is perhaps inevitable that ambiguities and uncertainties abound.

Legalism, Politics, and Social Reform

In the body of research on law and reform dating back to Scheingold (1974), it is almost axiomatic that a legalistic overreliance on courts to bring about change is likely to meet with strong resistance and defeat, and this is especially so if the goal is the redistribution of material resources. In the absence of broader political mobilization and alliances, courts acting alone will lack the power and legitimacy to dictate changes to other institutional actors. The New Jersey case certainly adds another piece of evidence in support of this axiomatic proposition.

The ELC was a liberal, white-led, freestanding, foundation-funded, public interest law firm claiming to speak for poor minority children in the urban centers. For much of the way, its lawyer-leaders bought into legalism and all that it entails about the strategic conduct of litigation-driven reform. They were crusaders in court, not in politics. They chose to represent phantom clients—"the poor children"—in order to enhance their moral authority in court and to obviate the need to answer to anyone else about the conduct of their litigation. Relatedly, they sought to distance themselves from the poorer urban districts, as organizations, also to enhance their chances in court.

Although, eventually, reformers were wildly successful in court, the combination of their legalism and some unforeseen actions of other actors (particular those of the Florio administration), left them at sea when a backlash threatened to undo their legal victory. We then saw how the ELC network deftly turned to politics in 1991–1992. Since then, the ELC reformers' political efforts have been ongoing, complex, and evolving. They have mobilized urban constituents, bargained, compromised, cut deals with other actors, and enhanced their own financial and political resources and policy research capacities.

With respect to law and politics in reform struggles, this analysis raises some questions, but cannot provide definitive answers, for the questions involve counterfactual scenarios. Before 1990, would some other course of strategic action have been both possible and desirable? What impact might a different approach have had on various outcomes? The purported missing component of the New Jersey project before 1990 was political mobilization. Political mobilization would have had two main functions (or benefits). First, an active constituency might have positioned reformers to have greater influence in proceedings and deliberations among elected officials. Second, it might have helped build local community capacities for the effective implementation of education reforms in the event that greater resources were forthcoming.

Along both possible functional lines, reformers' legalism formed a general backdrop to their context-specific "dance with the districts." The dance with the districts loomed large in the eschewal of politics. The school districts offered an obvious, ready-made organizational avenue for broader political mobilization. As we will see, school districts qua districts played just that role in the Kentucky case, as they have in many other states. However, the ELC determined that it was best to hold the urban school districts at arm's length and to neither criticize them nor align itself too closely with them.

Barring engagement and identification with the districts, the ELC might have pursued some other form of political mobilization, such as the formation of a citizens group or coalition or closer coalition-building work with other preexisting advocacy groups. But here we venture closer to pie in the sky. With its minimal resources and fact-heavy case, the ELC might not have been able to manage such political efforts, even if it wanted to. On the other hand, Morheuser stated that she interviewed some 450 to 500 people in preparing her case for trial. Given that subsequent political developments, such as the NJAPS coalition, illustrated possibilities for cross-race and cross-class alliances, perhaps there was some potential for a broader formation much earlier on.

But right away we must also add that, although they proceeded as adherents of legalism, the ELC lawyers also made certain eyes-open, strategic choices. Given certain political realities in the quintessential suburban state, they feared expanding the scope of the conflict prior to winning the right court decision. They very much wanted their finely crafted case to proceed quietly in the rarified, liberal atmosphere of the New Jersey courts. In light of how things turned out, it is hard to say that they were wrong about these things. All that we can say, as ELC Director David Sciarra himself put it in 2002, is that *perhaps* "there was a lost opportunity at the trial phase to put together a broader coalition."[65]

The Kentucky case will show us a rather different pattern of legal and political mobilization, one in which broad-based political work preceded litigation and drove the development of its internal content, and one in which school districts qua districts played an important role.

Legal Translation, the Agenda of Contention, and the Organization of Politics

Paul Tractenberg, Marilyn Morheuser, David Sciarra and their liberal colleagues shared a compensatory vision of education, race, and social equality. At two key points in the conflict, the lawyers showed a striking determination to make their claims (and the law) reflect their reform vision.

Tractenberg's ideological commitments made him uneasy about the prevailing legal theory in school finance cases in the early 1970s. On his view, that theory (wealth neutrality) did not come close to saying and doing what he wanted law to say and do. In response, he did not take a mechanical or instrumental approach to legal doctrine but set out on his own to find an alternative legal theory. Thus, he placed before a basically sympathetic New Jersey

Supreme Court the opportunity to render a favorable decision wholly outside the binding logic of *Rodriguez*. The end result was a vague set of constitutional and statutory norms about educational adequacy, which provided a new set of discursive resources to return to court at a later date.

Morheuser then made use of those norms and categories to translate the compensatory vision into a powerful legal case. She too did so by resisting easy mechanical approaches to existing legal doctrines, opting instead for some creative (and risky) category-and-fact work. Her detailed representations of fact were refracted and given meaning through preexisting, malleable legal norms and categories. Much of this case study has been an account of how this creative legal translation got done.[66]

In the political science literature on law and social change, agenda setting has long been seen as one important function of reform litigation. Certainly, the New Jersey reformers' litigation succeeded in setting the agenda of education politics and policy, as the reformers themselves noted. However, an emphasis on legal mobilization with legal translation at its center takes us beyond mere agenda setting to the very constitution of the terms of debate and the organization of politics.

The more headway reformers made in court, the more their vision came to define the language of public discourse and the content of public policies. Their vision had a particular content, the law embodied that content and gave it authority, and together vision and legal authority created a culture of argument and action. By the early 1990s, when New Jerseyans talked about school finance and education reform, they had to talk about *Abbott* and its compensatory vision. Whether they were supporters, opponents, or in-betweens, people could not avoid talking about things like racial isolation, poverty, and special-needs districts. When they acted, they acted on the basis of identities and interests that were themselves shaped by the law and policy of *Abbott*. Thus, we see that the content of legal arguments and judicial decisions play (or can play) a large role in defining the discursive space within which conflict proceeds and therefore the possibilities for political organization and action.

In Chapter One, I stated that I wanted to bracket the important question of how we should evaluate reformers' particular vision and goals. Whether the vision is morally attractive or worth having is not my concern here. Rather, the theoretical question I want to raise involves how observers and actors might think about the political-strategic implications of law's power to frame politics. In other words, the question is, What are the implications of this sort of analysis for reform practice? One general implication is that, in thinking about options for coordinating legal and political strategies, would-be reformers might be more mindful of the potential role of the content of law in shaping discourse and politics, and might take this into account when thinking about the nature and forms of political action that might support litigation. The idea here is that a vision and its projection through law constitute but a proposal until actors march under its banner and carry it into politics. Particular visions suggest certain contours of conflict, certain practical problems that are likely to emerge, and certain possibilities for action. Consider some speculative remarks about the New Jersey case along these lines.

Reformers' compensatory vision came with certain tensions and paradoxes built in. Its conception of education accepted rather than challenged the view that education is a positional good in the footrace for social mobility, even as it formed the basis for fighting for more resources for the poor so that the contest could be more fair. Its conception of race and poverty painted portraits of cultural deprivation that, at the extreme, rendered poor minority people as devoid of cultural resources or capacities for resistance. They were poor, passive victims. They were objects be pitied but not subjects entitled to mutual recognition and respect. The demands of legal forms—the need to show harm, for example—only heighten the portrayal and projection of what historian Daryl Michael Scott has called "damage imagery."[67]

Criticizing racial liberals like the ELC reformers for endorsing this view might be a worthwhile undertaking from certain political perspectives. However, that is not the point here. Rather, a culturalist legal mobilization approach asks how political mobilization and/or alliances (the forms of political action) might be pursued so as to mitigate or balance against the underlying ideological tensions. In point of fact, the ELC's effort was devoid of any political prong until after *Abbott II*, so we are once again in the realm of counterfactuals. Nevertheless, the ELC's turn to politics provides us with the basis for some observations.

The ELC's halting and uneven mobilization of urban constituents never did approach anything resembling a social movement. However, it did bring new actors onto the political stage and provided them with an ideological vision to champion. It seems to me that the very appearance of those actors in various forums—whether in legislative hearings or backroom negotiations among interest groups or mass meetings to celebrate court victories—undercuts the vision's portrait of its beneficiaries as passive victims who are so traumatized that they cannot possibly speak for themselves. The mobilization of constituents to carry the vision makes them real, concrete, human. While the vision runs a high risk of reinforcing the already prevalent tendency of broader white publics to disidentify with poor minority communities, political mobilization and coalition building at least provided some opportunities for political experiences to cut the other way.

In the Kentucky case study, we will meet a different set of reformers with a rather different general vision of public education. They believed in what I will call a "modern common school vision." Like the New Jersey reformers, the Kentucky reformers too struggled to translate their vision into legal terms. In Kentucky, as in New Jersey, the content of the legal challenge radiated out to frame politics and policies, but in a different way. Compared to the New Jersey reformers, the Kentucky advocates also took a different approach to law and politics. In their effort, political organization preceded and informed legal mobilization and legal translation. But there is more to the Kentucky story than the mere fact that political efforts supported the legal one. In politics, the Kentucky reformers consistently spoke and acted in ways consistent with the common school vision. They proceeded in court *and* marched in politics under the same ideological banner of the common school vision. The case provides a glimpse of what a culturalist approach to law and politics would look like in practice.

PART III

THE COMMON SCHOOL
AND THE QUEST FOR
CONSENSUS

IN 1985, AN ORGANIZATION CALLED THE COUNCIL FOR Better Education, Inc., filed suit in Kentucky challenging the state's school finance arrangements. The Council consisted of sixty-six school districts. The suit claimed, among other things, that the current finance system violated the education clause of the state constitution. The case went to trial in 1987. In 1988, a trial court rendered a decision in favor of plaintiffs, and state defendants appealed to the Kentucky Supreme Court ("the Court").[1]

In *Rose v. Council for Better Education* (1989), the Court used the finance case as the occasion for a rather remarkable decision. After noting that a "child's right an adequate education is a fundamental one under the [state] constitution," it went on to rule that "Kentucky's entire system of common schools is unconstitutional." Its decision, it said, "applies to the entire sweep of the system . . . [It] applies to the statutes creating, implementing, and financing the system and to all regulations pertaining thereto."[2]

Within a year of the Court's decision, the legislature passed an ambitious omnibus measure called the Kentucky Education Reform Act (KERA). KERA sought to change the whole education system, all at once. It included not only a new finance system supported by a large tax increase but also major reforms in the areas of curriculum and testing, state and local school governance, preschool education, and school-based social services. Over the next fifteen years, the school finance changes produced substantially higher education spending in each school district and substantially more spending equality across all districts.

Given Kentucky's history and demographic profile (more on these below), the Court decision and the legislative response to it would seem rather puzzling. Although no one had actually asked it to, the Court struck down every state law and regulation pertaining to education. One would think that if the cry of judicial usurpation of legislative authority would ever be heard, then this would be the case. Yet, there was very little resistance to *Rose v. Council for Better Education*. Moreover, Kentucky had had a long history of animosity to government and taxation. Yet the legislature's response included a $1.3 billion tax increase over two years, when the total state general fund budget was but $9 billion. No backlash against the reform measure and the higher taxes needed to pay for it emerged.[3]

These puzzles dissolve once we place *Council for Better Education* in its immediate political context. Simply put, the Court's decision entered a climate already quite favorable to reform. By 1989, education policy issues had been prominent on the state's political agenda for six years. Public opinion polls measured citizens' increasing receptivity to policy change and higher taxes. Various educational interest groups had mobilized in support of the Council's lawsuit. However, an antitax governor and leading legislators had come to a stalemate over competing education reform programs and taxes. The Court's bold decision broke this institutional logjam and provided the elected officials with cover on the tax question. The Court's decision, then, did not create conditions conducive to reform but rather merely threw a much-needed spark into an already combustible mix of heightened agitation and conflict.

The interesting questions begin here, however. How did the favorable context emerge in the first place? What role did legal mobilization and legal translation play in bringing it about? What were the tenor and content of debate? What ideologies and arguments about education were afoot, and what was their relationship to the litigation?

The Kentucky school finance and education reform effort involved two separate change agent groups. The Council for Better Education, which began forming in 1983, consisted of school districts as represented by school superintendents and board members. It existed solely to prosecute the school finance lawsuit. A second group, the Prichard Committee for Academic Excellence ("Prichard Committee") was a citizens' organization that formed around the same time to lobby for substantive changes in education. At the outset of the Council's court-focused effort, the two groups conferred and then declined to work together. However, by 1987, they joined forces, with each supporting and participating in the other's activities.

These Kentucky reformers created a particular kind of political environment conducive to a particular kind of education reform, and they did so over a period of years through democratic political action that went hand-in-hand with their use of law and courts.

Political action preceded and undergirded the litigation. In turn, the litigation and the court victories it produced expanded the scope of the conflict and shaped the terms of public debate. By 1989, reformers efforts had succeeded in "constitutionalizing" the politics of education reform in the state. The term constitutionalization signals that actors are aware that they have reached a profound historical moment in which fundamental choices about government and politics have to be made. They are aware that they are "making history" and that therefore the situation calls for efforts to rise above narrow self-interests and "politics as usual." I argue that both the political groundwork and the litigation and judicial support were crucial to the creation of this sort of political moment. Without the political mobilization, the constitutional claim and judicial victory would not have had nearly the same impact or meaning. Without the litigation and the constitutional claim, the political mobilization may well have come to very little, if not to nothing.[4]

The reformers in both groups developed and shared a particular ideology about the basic purposes and functions of public education in a democratic polity. Their rhetoric, political action, and, eventually, the content of their legal challenge—all embodied a common school vision of education. The common school tradition emphasizes public education as training for common citizenship and social integration and downplays the economic and social mobility functions of schooling. The original idea of the common school hinged on the desirability and likely integrative consequences of providing a school experience common to all children. Modern and updated iterations of this tradition typically focus most attention on the content of the curriculum, matters of pedagogical style, and the development of a sense of a shared culture or mission in and around schools. The rhetorical emphasis falls on what is (or should be) shared in common by all children through education, whatever their differences.[5]

I will show how the Kentucky reformers embraced this vision and consistently projected it through everything that they said and did, both in politics and in court. As in the New Jersey case study, my account of the Kentucky effort emphasizes four main themes.

The first theme is legal translation. Among observers of school finance litigation, the Kentucky Supreme Court's decision in *Council for Better Education* quickly became Exhibit *A* for the emergence of a new paradigm of educational adequacy litigation. The right at stake was no longer a right to absolute equality of resources but rather to equal access to the resources needed for an adequate education. Interestingly, the Kentucky litigation did not start out as an adequacy case at all. Rather, it began as a case sounding in the legal theory of wealth neutrality.

As the Kentucky reformers' case proceeded to trial there occurred a transformation in the theory and factual substance of the lawsuit, moving away from wealth neutrality to a new case about educational adequacy. The vague, open intellectual space of "educational adequacy" was then filled in with facts and arguments supplied by reformers' common school vision. Like the New Jersey reformers, then, the Kentucky reformers also very much wanted the law to reflect their substantive vision, and they worked hard to accomplish that objective.

The second theme is the Kentucky reformers realistic-cum-culturalistic approach to law, politics, and change. Unlike the New Jersey reformers, the Kentucky advocates were never legalistic. Their litigation effort began with nonlawyers who were quite mindful of the need to mobilize political support for any litigation, long before it was filed. That sensibility itself influenced who they approached to handle the case in court. Their choice was Bert T. Combs, a prominent attorney who had been both a Kentucky high court judge and the state's governor. Combs reinforced the political approach to the case by treating the litigation as just part of a broader political campaign for educational reform. He also argued for turning the case away from wealth neutrality to a broader and highly rhetorical one about educational adequacy. The use of litigation to build and legitimize a broader movement for a particular vision of reform was also aided by the independent political activities of the Prichard Committee.

Realism holds that political mobilization and support are the real engines of change, and that litigation can be useful primarily for its ancillary effects on the alignment of political forces. Culturalism adds a concern with the content of legal arguments and their potential capacity to frame understandings and actions in politics. The Kentucky reformers were self-consciously realistic about law and change. However, in their arguments and actions, they show us what a culturalist approach would look like, for they had an intuitive sense that arguments and actions in all forums should project their substantive vision of education. In other words, it was not just the mere fact of political support for litigation that mattered in Kentucky. It was also that reformers had some awareness of the fact that what they said in court and, by extension, what the courts said, would make a difference in politics.

The third theme is legal translation and the agenda of contention. As in New Jersey, the Kentucky reformers' successful translation of their vision into law defined the language of public debate, structured the organization of education politics, and led directly to certain kinds of policy processes and outcomes. As we shall see, the development and elaboration of the common school vision was primarily the work of the Prichard Committee. But this vision flowed into the litigation in various ways, and the Court's endorsement of it as law made a crucial difference in the conflict. In turn, KERA's multifarious provisions and programs generally reflect and embody this self-same vision.

The fourth theme involves the common school vision and its internal tensions and paradoxes. It is often said that every way of seeing must also be a way of not seeing. When zealous advocates take up the mantle of reform by proclaiming that "we're all in the same boat, we're all in this together," we want to know who is speaking, what entitles them to speak for the whole, and whether certain particular identities, needs, and claims are being repressed in the process. For example, we might ask whether the least advantaged are being well served by the champions of "the common good." Tested against this vantage point, the Kentucky project still comes off looking rather good overall. Nevertheless, the rhetorical emphasis on common values and interests in reformers' project does leave us some lingering questions, as of this writing (2009).

In their project, reformers not only trumpeted a vision of education focused on common goals but also embarked on a quest for a political consensus around this substantive educational agenda. As the 1990s progressed, however, and broad ideals had to be specified and operationalized for use on the ground, the sense of consensus over values and goals naturally faded. This is to be expected, for what is taught and how learning is conceptualized would seem to be inherently controversial. The Kentucky reformers' quest for consensus could not wash away all conflict. For most of the 1990s, it did define the contours of conflict, such that people fought about some things, like curriculum and testing, and not others, like taxes and the finance system. More recently, elected officials have reverted to their old aversion to taxation and spending. After a large influx of funds and rapidly declining inequalities through the late 1990s, funding remained flat thereafter, and inequalities have crept back a bit.

In September 2003, a retooled Council for Better Education filed a new lawsuit. The case stalled in a trial court for a long time. In February 2007, the trial judge dismissed the case, and a few months later the Council decided not to appeal. But while the case was pending, the 2006 legislative session saw the first significant increase in state education funding in five years. The post-KERA era saw the institutionalization of the reform coalition, and, as in New Jersey, it continues to stand watch over education policy.

CHAPTER SIX

THE COMMON SCHOOL IN LAW AND POLITICS: THE DEMOCRATIC ROAD TO *ROSE V. COUNCIL FOR BETTER EDUCATION*

WHEN REFORMERS IN THE UNITED STATES TURN TO law and courts in pursuit of their goals, they inevitably face an objection from the perspective of majoritarian democracy. We entrust legislators to make policies, this argument goes, because they have been chosen by the people, and they are directly accountable to them at the ballot box. As a general matter, judges are not so accountable. Even if they happen to be elected, as they are in Kentucky, judges are supposed to follow the law, not make it. Of course, between following the law and making it up, there lies a vast realm of debates about the nature of legal interpretation and judicial decision making. Before we know whether judges are "following the law," we have to give a theoretical account of what it means to do so, and that account will be controversial. Before we blithely say that courts are a countermajoritarian force in American politics, we should consider whether courts are really just one institutional channel for action, among many channels, neither more nor less inherently democratic than the other ones. But the complications do not easily defeat the force that the objection from democracy tends to have in our politics. As noted in Chapter Two, opponents of change will portray reformers who run to court as engaged in a cynical end run around normal democratic politics. We ought not to be governed by courts, they will say, and when we are, we are not well governed.

From the standpoint of reformers who mobilize the law to bring about change, the judicial legitimacy question is at least in part a practical one. In the New Jersey case, a legalistic belief in courts as a morally superior realm apart from mere politics blended with reformers' strategic calculations about how they could best get from here to there. For the ELC reformers, ideology and strategic assessments led to the conclusion that political mobilization would be counterproductive, at least until the desired court victory was won. In the Kentucky case, the reformers took a realistic approach. The realistic view holds that political mobilization will be required and that litigation itself should be used as a device for fostering it. The Kentucky reformers believed that a demonstration of political support would be needed even to win in court. For them, while law might propose, it would be politics that disposed.

Beyond their realistic view of law and courts as instrumental weapons in a broader political effort, the Kentucky reformers also seemed to grasp that the content of legal arguments could play a role in shaping politics. They wanted their case in court to speak a certain language—to say certain things and not other things. The law had to speak the language of the common school. Reformers also used the same sort of rhetoric in many other political forums and settings, outside the courts. Thus, these reformers acted in ways consistent with their vision, in court and in politics. By speaking and acting under the banner of modern common school ideology, they made their vision progressively more real as the conflict proceeded.

I will argue that this matching of form and content across different institutional settings provided a perfect answer to the objection to reform litigation from majoritarian democracy. In form and content, in law and in politics, these reformers demonstrated that they were engaged in a good-faith democratic effort to change minds and policies. The road to *Rose v. Council for Better Education* was indeed a democratic one.

CONTEXTS FOR ACTION: KENTUCKY'S
POLITICAL CULTURE, HISTORY, AND POLITICS

Kentucky is a poor, predominantly rural state. In 1990, the state's per capita income was $15,000, and 27 percent of its children lived in poverty. The majority of its 3.7 million people lived in rural areas or towns with populations of 25,000 or less. African Americans made up approximately 7 percent of the state's population, the lowest percentage among southern and border states, and most lived in one of Kentucky's two largest cities, Louisville and Lexington. The county school districts encompassing Louisville and Lexington, Jefferson County and Fayette County, respectively, are two of the property-wealthiest districts in the state. Racial discrimination was not much of an issue in the Kentucky school finance conflict.[1]

Observers of Kentucky history and politics typically highlight a series of odd tensions or anomalies. First, Kentucky's political culture is "highly traditionalistic," marked by low levels of political participation and a tendency to defer to politically active elites. Moreover, people are basically conservative and "suspicious of change." They have long been "above all suspicious of taxes of all kinds, for all purposes." Yet, there is also a strange "verve and richness" to state-level politics. Politics in Kentucky has retained its status as sport and spectacle in a way that is no longer the case in most other states.[2]

Second, as its leading political journalist put it, Kentucky "is and always has been a deeply divided state." "From the Appalachian coalfields of eastern Kentucky, through the rolling bluegrass of central Kentucky, to the farmlands and strip mines of western Kentucky, the state is a land of striking contrasts— great beauty and terrible devastation, immense wealth and grinding poverty." Regional divisions find their reflection in "the parochialism, vitality, and influence of [the state's] 120 county governments," and the importance of counties for people as places of origin and identification. Yet divisions and local attachments have not precluded what one observer called a strong sense of "state patriotism." Kentuckians generally do think and talk about themselves as "Kentuckians," especially when it comes to political affairs.[3]

Finally, the grease of Kentucky politics has always been patronage, sometimes doled out through outright graft. Powerful governors build and maintain organizations through patronage, and the lines between public and private can become blurry indeed, as the lawyers, bankers, accountants, and builders who often double as part-time legislators participate in business networks dependent on government largess. Yet, at certain moments, these patronage-driven organizations have backed "high-minded reforms" that cut against the grain of dominant corporate interests.

While these comments on Kentucky politics and culture are admittedly quite general and impressionistic, if there is some truth to them (and obviously I think there is), then they tell us something about the historical constraints that would have to be overcome to secure redistributive change, as well as the cultural symbols and resources that might be mobilized in the process. The generalizations give us some sense of the lay of the land, as it were. The sense of state pride—the felt need to think of Kentucky in general as a special place, not like other places—would be a particular symbolic resource to which the Kentucky education reformers would repeatedly appeal in their quest for consensus.

Three more specific historical-institutional factors shaped the terrain of conflict over school reform in the 1980s and 1990s.

Party Politics and Stable Bifactionalism

As in the rest of the South, from the Civil War until quite recently, party politics in Kentucky was Democratic Party politics. But unlike much of the rest of the South, from the 1930s through the late 1960s, within the Democratic Party in Kentucky there was something approximating two-party competition.

Over this period, two fairly stable factions, each with a distinctive ideological orientation, maintained their identity and vied for control of state government. One faction, headed up by A. B. ("Happy") Chandler, generally took a right-populist stance against government and taxes. The other faction, initially run by Earle Clements, was known as "the Administration faction." It embraced the moderate reformism of the New Deal and mirrored the New Deal Coalition.[4]

Two prominent leaders of the Administration faction, Bert T. Combs and Edward F. Prichard, played central roles in school reform in the 1980s. Combs sat on the state court of appeals (then the state's highest court) from 1951 to 1955 and went on to win election as governor in 1959. As governor, Combs undertook a difficult but successful fight to enact a 3 percent sales tax. Under Combs, state spending for education increased by 62 percent. In the early 1970s, Combs retired from politics and joined the state's largest law firm. He had "an outstanding personal reputation for probity and honesty." Remarkably, Combs had spent much of his life in Kentucky politics and had never once been associated with scandal or corruption. Although little known outside the state, Combs was virtually a "household name" in Kentucky. In 1984, after being pressed by reformers to do so, Combs would agree to serve as lead counsel for the plaintiffs in the school finance case.[5]

Edward F. Prichard Jr. grew up in Kentucky politics. His father was a state legislator and a Chandler supporter. In the mid-1930s, Prichard attended Princeton and then went on to Harvard Law School. After a stint as law clerk to Justice Felix Frankfurter, Prichard served in various New Deal agencies and then returned to Kentucky to launch his political career. However, in 1948, he was caught stuffing ballot boxes and spent five months in federal prison before a pardon came from President Truman. In the late 1950s, Prichard became good friends with Combs and eased into a behind-the-scenes role as the Administration faction's main strategist and speechwriter. Combs called him "Philosopher." By all accounts, Prichard was a highly charismatic, visionary public figure. He embodied all that was large and charming in Kentucky's political traditions. In the early 1980s, Prichard founded a citizen's organization dedicated to educational reform, and it became known simply as "the Prichard Committee."[6]

Political Institutions

Kentucky's late-nineteenth-century constitution reflects a general mistrust of government. It "is a narrow, rambling document designed to curb government rather than guide it, a collection of restrictive statutes rather than an outline of principles." Given Kentucky's patronage-driven politics, governors have traditionally overshadowed and dominated the other branches. However, since the late 1970s, the legislature has increasingly sought ways to challenge governors, especially with respect to the budget process.[7]

Kentucky's judicial system was restructured through constitutional amendment in 1975. This amendment established an intermediate appellate court to handle routine appeals, thereby allowing the high court to control its docket. The 1975 amendment also made judicial elections nonpartisan, and since then electoral accountability has been more form than substance. Over the past two decades, the Supreme Court has decided several separation-of-powers cases brought on by the legislature's new assertiveness. Generally, it has tended to side with the legislature. As we will see, what the Court did with *Council for Better Education* cannot be fully understood apart from this inclination to support the legislature in its conflicts with the executive.[8]

The School Finance System

For most of the 1980s, Kentucky had 180 school districts. Of these, 120 were coextensive with county units. The others were "independent" districts that generally predated the county-based ones. The school finance system that reformers attacked in the mid-1980s can only be described as archaic. Unlike systems in most other states at that time, the Kentucky system distributed the vast majority of state aid for education on a flat-grant basis. In addition, the system was plagued by lax property tax assessment and collection practices, as well as a series of revenue-limitation measures enacted at the state level. As a practical matter, as property values went up, property tax rates had to decline.[9]

The badly outdated school finance system made some sort of policy change more likely. Antitax sentiments and fear of change will eventually bump up against powerful interests that have a stake in the existence of a state education system operating on this side of the Dark Ages. However, the conditions that make some sort of change likely do not determine what kind of change it will be. The direction of reform in Kentucky was shaped by several political actors. The next section turns to these actors, and to what they thought and did over the course of the 1980s. While at first different actors followed different paths, they all shared common school sensibilities about education reform. Eventually, the different paths converged.

LEGAL AND POLITICAL MOBILIZATION AND THE COMMON SCHOOL VISION

The Council for Better Education: Three Men, a "Serrano Suit," and the Lawyer-Politician

School finance reform litigation in Kentucky began with a state-level education administrator named Arnold Guess. As of late 1983, Guess had spent over thirty years working in the state's school system. He had been a district superintendent in two eastern Kentucky counties, and he had held various positions in the State Department of Education (SDE). At this point, Guess was the director of the SDE's Bureau of Administration and Finance. Over the previous decade, he had periodically discussed the possibility of a school finance suit with two of his friends, Kern Alexander and Ted Lavit. Alexander was an education professor specializing in school finance policy. He had grown up in Kentucky, the son of two educators. Lavit was a lawyer and small-town solo practitioner. He and Alexander had been college roommates, and they remained good friends thereafter. All three had closely followed the *Serrano* case in California, and they had often thought about a potential case in Kentucky as their own "*Serrano* suit."[10]

The immediate impetus for the litigation-based reform effort came with the election of 1983. That year, Guess supported the losing candidate for state superintendent of public instruction. When the victorious candidate made it known that he would be fired, Guess resigned and determined to organize a group of school districts to bring a lawsuit. Beginning in early 1984, he targeted local school superintendents, initially focusing on the bottom half of the wealth distribution of school districts. Guess stated that he began by contacting local school superintendents simply because he "knew most of them personally." Alexander and Lavit helped him with this project. Also in early 1984, a newly elected governor, Martha Layne Collins, proposed a tax increase to finance school reforms. However, the legislature refused to go along, and the governor's education package was voted down. Thus, Guess, Alexander, and Lavit's initial effort to form a group of school districts to pursue litigation took place against the backdrop of what would be the first of several failed efforts at reform.[11]

By mid-1984, an initial round of meetings and discussions had produced enough interest to form a steering committee of interested local superintendents and school board members. Participating superintendents agreed to seek an allocation of funds from school boards in their districts to support the proposed litigation.

At the outset, the group's primary reference point for legal strategies and goals was *Serrano v. Priest*. They understood themselves to be pursuing only a limited set of school finance policy reforms that would use increased state resources to equalize local school district tax capacity. Higher and more equal spending across school districts would follow from there. When asked, Guess stated that his initial goal was "power equalization, pure and simple."[12] Guess estimated that to equalize the tax capacity of all Kentucky school districts without leveling down would cost approximately $500 million in additional state revenue each year. As Guess and his colleagues knew, winning that kind of tax increase would be no simple matter. They had already concluded that it could not be won through the political process alone.

There were some vital differences between this Kentucky effort and the *Serrano* case, however. Like *Abbott*, *Serrano* was marked by legalism and legalism's preference for phantom plaintiffs. In the Kentucky case, unlike in *Serrano* and *Abbott*, from the outset there were live (potential) plaintiffs with a political and financial stake in the litigation. The process of planning the litigation was a political process in which nonlawyers went to lawyers for help and then engaged in a dialogue with them about how to proceed. As a group, the Council would become embroiled in political conflict. At the same time, it would have to begin to fashion its own local constitutional and political arguments. It was this political engagement that enabled the content of the legal case to evolve from wealth neutrality to a more robust argument about educational adequacy, defined in relation to the common school vision.[13]

The group's initial meetings and planning sparked opposition and reprisals from potential state defendants, including powerful legislators. Reprisals included state audits of participating local districts and threats of legal action under the theory that the use of local district funds to support litigation was contrary to law.[14]

Given these difficulties, the group decided to ask Bert Combs to serve as lead counsel in the litigation. Combs brought to the case not only the economic resources of the state's largest corporate law firm but also his great wealth "in the political currency of Kentucky—status, reputation, friends, loyalty."[15] In other words, Combs was a good politician as well as a good lawyer. The way he handled the case both helped to build political support for it and moved its content away from the *Serrano* model and toward a more broadly framed and highly rhetorical argument about the adequacy of funding and the overall quality of schools.

Combs began by withholding his support unless additional school districts agreed to join the group. Once he agreed to serve as counsel, Combs advocated a "go-slow approach." In his view, going to court had to be, and had to be perceived to be, a well-justified last resort. Although the case would not actually be filed until November 1985, Combs assigned a young associate (Debra Dawahare) to begin research much earlier. Combs, Dawahare, Lavit, Alexander, and a few others began drafting memoranda and a complaint in November 1984. In May 1985, the group adopted articles of incorporation and the name Council for Better Education. Gaining momentum, the Council now numbered sixty-six school districts.[16]

From the outset, all Council participants were mindful of the need to reassure wealthier school districts and the public generally that they themselves were, as they put it, "anti-Robin Hood." The Council advocated an infusion of funds and leveling up; it had no desire to take resources away from any district. This stance was principled rather than strategic, although it had strategic implications. Given meager levels of spending for education in the state as a whole, these reformers believed, it would be morally wrong to cause resources (whether state or local) to be taken away from any district.[17]

Moreover, Guess and his associates gave life to this anti-Robin Hood view by approaching personnel in every school district in the state in order to ask them to join the group and support the litigation. This is one small example of what it means for an actor to act in ways consistent with the actor's espoused vision. The sense that "we're all in this together" is reinforced when those who would normally be threatened by school finance litigation (the wealthiest districts) are approached and invited to participate as equals in the reform effort. In response to Guess's entreaties, a few wealthier districts did join the Council, and some individual officials from others agreed to provide behind-the-scenes support. According to Guess, approaching every district allowed the Council to make its case for "fair treatment" for the poor and at the same time to offer reassurance on the redistribution issue. As a result, many potential opponents in the school finance conflict were, as Guess put it, "neutralized."[18]

In July 1985, Governor Collins called the legislature into a special session for another pass at education reform. Her second effort was a response to public pressure brought to bear by the Prichard Committee (see below). Although the legislature adopted some modest reforms, in the end it failed to fund them. Once again, elected officials' fear of voter reactions to a tax increase was the major sticking point.

The Council filed suit in state court in November 1985. Plaintiffs named the governor, various other executive officials, the president pro tem of the state

Senate, and the speaker of the House of Representatives as defendants. The complaint alleged that the current school finance system violated the education and equal protection clauses of the state constitution.

With the failure of the legislative route to reform in both 1984 and 1985, Combs could answer critics of the litigation with the claim that "he did not urge the school superintendents to file the suit." As he told the press in early 1986, the superintendents "were reluctant to file the case, but thought they had a duty to do so." As the Council's project got off the ground, another education reform organization was working to bring about change.[19]

The Prichard Committee for Academic Excellence

The Prichard Committee had its origins in an advisory panel appointed by the State Council on Higher Education (a permanent body) in 1980. This permanent body named twenty-eight prominent citizens to this advisory panel, and it asked Edward F. Prichard Jr. to serve as chair. Its task was to assess the state of higher education in Kentucky and to make recommendations for change. Bert Combs was also a member of this advisory panel. Prichard hired Robert F. Sexton to coordinate the panel's activities. Over the next ten years, Sexton became a central player in shaping the educational reform agenda in the state.[20]

In 1981, the Prichard Committee published a report on higher education, calling for higher taxes to fund a set of improvements. Although its activities and recommendations received public attention, elected officials ignored the report. In an interview, Sexton stated that he and Prichard drew two main lessons from this experience. First, a lack of public pressure rendered the group's hard work and reasoned arguments meaningless in Kentucky politics. Any real change would require political organization to overcome resistance to higher taxes. Second, a close study of deficiencies in higher education led the group to notice severe problems with Kentucky's public schools.[21]

In mid-1982, Prichard announced that his advisory panel would reconstitute itself as "a voluntary citizens' group." In 1983, the Prichard Committee expanded its membership from twenty-eight to fifty-eight "citizen volunteers" and announced that it would turn its full attention to elementary and secondary education. Sexton then secured foundation support to fund one full-time staff position (his) and to cover the group's expenses. Sexton and his colleagues consistently used the terms "citizens" and "citizen volunteers" to refer to members who participated in the Committee. This would be a *prominent* citizens group, however—one made up of former governors (including Combs), corporate executives, lawyers, and doctors. Still, Prichard and Sexton consciously sought certain other kinds of representation. Thus, they included several social service providers, leaders from other civic organizations such as the League of Women Voters, and members drawn from different regions of the state. And, Sexton noted, "strong efforts were made to include women and African Americans." Finally, the Prichard Committee consciously *excluded* the leaders of established educational interest groups, such as the teachers' union and the school boards association, to maintain what Sexton called "an outsider's perspective" on the existing system.

Thus, the Prichard Committee became a diverse group of activists with a good deal of social capital. If there was one defect of representation, it was probably on the basis of class. Race and gender came readily to mind within a frame of "we're all in this together," but, perhaps understandably, class did not.[22]

This newly reconstituted Prichard Committee settled on two main projects that would occupy it for the next two years. The first project was the organization of a statewide, electronic town forum on education. The purposes of the town forum were to hear what ordinary citizens had to say about education and to induce the governor to continue to support reform and a tax increase, given her first failed effort in 1984.[23] This organizing effort took place over the course of that year, and it produced a groundswell of public support. Shortly before the event, the *Louisville Courier-Journal* reported that town forums would be held in nearly every school district in the state. The article quoted Sexton extensively. "We are trying to find those people around the state who are really concerned about education and help them get involved in the process . . . We think Kentucky needs a mass movement for better schools and that involvement has to come from the local level." Over 2,000 volunteers had been involved in planning the event.[24]

The town forum took place in November 1984. The program began with a one-hour televised panel discussion involving the governor, the state superintendent of public instruction, and Bert Combs, who appeared as the representative of the Prichard Committee.[25] After the televised segment, citizens offered comments and questions in their local settings. Twenty thousand people attended these forums. In addition, "6,000 individual comments were recorded, 15,000 written statements were handed in, and 200 letters came directly to the Prichard Committee."[26]

This surge of support for change led directly to the governor's willingness to call a special legislative session on education reform in mid-1985. However, the session failed to produce significant policy changes, especially in the area of school finance.

The Prichard Committee's second project involved the production and distribution of a report on Kentucky's public school system entitled *A Path to a Larger Life: Creating Kentucky's Educational Future*. A cross between a citizen's pamphlet and an academic tract, *A Path to a Larger Life* reflects a strong commitment to common school ideals. In both its general outline and specific policy proposals, it foreshadowed the package of reforms eventually adopted by the legislature in 1990.[27]

To produce this report, Sexton orchestrated a remarkable process of group study and deliberation among Prichard Committee members. In 1983, the Committee organized itself into seven subcommittees, with each responsible for studying and making recommendations in a specific educational policy area. Each subcommittee had approximately eight to twelve people and a co-ordinator responsible for communications with Sexton and the larger group. Each met every month for a little over a year. These meetings often took the form of seminars, with conversations focused on the relevance of policy materials to participants' own views and experiences.[28]

If the final product can be taken as indicative, it seems that Sexton and his colleagues were drawn to and made use of what was then but a faint undercurrent in the national education debate. Both the dominant national views and the rush to reform in other states generally embraced the meritocratic, get-tough outlook of *A Nation at Risk*. By contrast, Prichard Committee members gravitated toward the common school themes articulated by Theodore Sizer, John Goodlad, and others. Out of the collisions between these broad academic, common school arguments and their own practical experiences, Prichard Committee members fashioned a brief for comprehensive educational reform in Kentucky.[29]

A Path to a Larger Life runs about 120 pages and contains seven chapters, covering teacher training, curricular reform, school governance, social services, measuring educational outcomes, vocational education, and school finance policy. The talk in the report is always about Kentucky and what Kentuckians share or have in common, and the orientation is always toward the future. Throughout, Kentucky as a whole is compared to other states, and the argument is that it compares unfavorably on virtually every measure of educational performance. Throughout, references to taxes and expenditures are located in a broader common school argument about why more money and more equality in the distribution of resources are needed. The purpose of the chapter on school finance, the report notes, "is to determine the financial mechanisms necessary to implement the improved educational program recommended by the Prichard Committee." Thus, school finance reform is merely a means to otherwise-justified ends.[30]

A Path to a Larger Life is significant in the Kentucky reform effort for three reasons. First, its production involved a political process of group meetings, discussions, and debates. The process itself helped to build and solidify a cadre of influential citizens committed to a particular reform agenda. Second, the Prichard Committee made sure that its report received significant media attention. Third, the report's common school rhetoric and policy recommendations entered the school finance litigation directly in various ways. Sexton presented the Prichard Committee's views at trial, and *A Path to a Larger Life* was accepted into evidence. Thus, the report was part of the record in the case before the Kentucky Supreme Court. More importantly, within the Council for Better Education and among its team of lawyers, Combs increasingly argued for "more of a focus on the quality of schools. We have to make the case for good schools," he said, "as well as adequately financed schools."[31]

As of late 1984, the Prichard Committee leaders had no interest in supporting the school finance reform lawsuit. Although Combs had asked for Prichard and Sexton's support, Sexton noted that:

We just decided that we didn't want to get involved. It was a *finance equity* suit, and we didn't see finance as the central issue. We didn't get involved until 1987 [when] Combs came back and asked me to testify at trial. I testified, and our Committee decided to submit an *amicus* brief . . . In 1984, the legislative prospects were, we thought, good. In 1987, we had a different view of the prospects for reform through legislative action.[32]

Similarly, of the Prichard Committee, Arnold Guess stated, "We knew what they were doing and we approved of it, but they weren't going to court. They weren't getting their feet wet. They were just begging and pleading. There had been various studies over the years, and I'd been involved with some of them, but nothing had been done."[33]

Council for Better Education *Goes to Trial*

As noted above, the Council filed its suit in November 1985, right after Governor Collins's second failed effort to win policy changes from the legislature. The case was assigned to trial court judge Ray Corns. Although named as a party-defendant, Governor Collins responded to the suit with indifference. An independently elected state attorney general also declined to represent other state officials. Legislative leaders stepped forward to defend the state. They retained a private attorney, an old Kentucky politico named William Scent, to handle the case.

Many legislative leaders were angered by the lawsuit. During a regular legislative session in early 1986, the Senate passed a bill banning the expenditure of public funds for "litigation challenging the allocation of such funds." Council members quietly lobbied supporters in the House to oppose this measure, and the bill never made it out of committee there. Legislative hostility led the Council to hold off on prosecuting the case.[34] In May, state defendants moved for summary judgment, arguing that plaintiffs lacked standing and that the case raised a political question. After Corns denied the motion for summary judgment, the latter half of 1986 and the first part of 1987 were taken up with pretrial discovery, mainly in the form of depositions, which, under Kentucky law, could be admitted as evidence at trial.

The case went to trial in August 1987 and lasted but six trial days. Debra Dawahare, Combs's associate, summed up Combs's trial strategy this way: "Keep it simple, keep it quotable, and don't get bogged down in the technicalities."[35] Another strategic device reformers employed along these lines was the commonly used one of "bifurcating the issues," as Alexander put it, between "violation and remedy": "My advice was not to get that remedy problem mixed in while you're determining constitutionality. If you drag all these complex formulas before judges, they'll get nervous." As for constitutional violation, Alexander urged the group to argue that the state constitution was a living document and to use common school rhetoric to inform their claims about the meaning of the education clause.[36]

At trial, Combs and his colleagues ended up emphasizing adequacy far more than equalization. For example, in his opening statement, he told the court, and "the news media," that:

Mr. Combs: We will prove, I think, beyond question, that in these 66 school districts which are plaintiffs . . . that the school system is not efficient, is not adequate, is not sufficient, and does deprive the children in those districts of an opportunity to get an adequate education . . . Now there will be some talk of uniformity. There will be some talk about inequality, but that is not the thrust of plaintiffs' lawsuit. The thrust of this lawsuit is inadequacy . . . I want everybody, particularly the news media, to know that we are not talking about taking money from a district that has money and giving it to [poor districts] . . . We are talking about raising the level in the poor districts and whether it would ever be equal to [rich districts] would remain to be seen. We are not going to be specific in suggesting a solution. I doubt that any one man knows the solution. Now I am hoping that Your Honor is the exception. I am hoping you would have a magic formula of some kind that could correct this situation.

The Court: Hope springs eternal.[37]

Plaintiffs offered the testimony of administrators from poorer school districts and several education policy experts. School superintendents testified about their lack of resources and broken-down physical facilities. Richard Salmon, one of plaintiffs' school finance policy experts, noted that Kentucky was virtually alone in the nation in clinging to a flat-grant system of state aid to education. Sexton, who was qualified as an expert, presented the views of the Prichard Committee. He offered a litany of statistics comparing Kentucky as a whole with other states. Nationally, Kentucky ranked fiftieth in adult literacy, fortieth in teacher–pupil ratio, fortieth in teacher pay, thirty-ninth in high school retention, forty-sixth in percentage of high school graduates going on to college, forty-third in per pupil expenditures, and fortieth in educational expenditures as a percentage of personal income. Reformers offered and the court accepted into evidence the Prichard Committee's report, *A Path to a Larger Life*. Alexander testified about the deficiencies of the school finance system and also offered a discourse on the proper interpretation of the state constitution's education clause.[38]

William Scent, counsel for state defendants, built his case around three basic propositions. First, low spending in poorer districts was in part due to low tax effort. Second, plaintiff districts in particular routinely squandered resources through mismanagement, nepotism, and corruption. Third, the legislature (his "client") had made good-faith efforts to pass reforms, but it was and remained constrained by overwhelming public opposition to tax increases. To the extent that he offered a general theory of his case, Scent appealed to separation-of-powers principles to argue against judicial intervention. Plaintiffs were in effect asking the court to order the legislature to increase taxes; any such decision would itself amount to an unconstitutional judicial intrusion into legislative territory.[39]

Interestingly, the reformers admitted the truth of the first two propositions, and thereby confronted central problems in their case head-on. Kentucky was unusual in that the complaining districts generally did make a lower tax effort, compared to other districts. And mismanagement, nepotism, and corruption were indeed very large problems in more than a few districts. Reformers' responded by offering an explanation that linked the two problems together. Low tax rates were related not only to low levels of education in the first place, but also to a lack of public trust in local schools. In turn, a lack of public concern and attention created the conditions for local officials to get away with mismanagement and corruption. The defendants, Combs told the trial judge, were blaming the victims.

In early 1988, the parties submitted post-trial memoranda and made their closing arguments to the court.

The hard work of democratic action in both law and politics undertaken by reformers between 1984 and 1987 supported political change. Their ideological commitments about education also led them to speak and act in ways that pushed the agenda of debate and the content of the litigation toward common school rhetoric and themes. But how things would turn out also had much to do with official responses. The strange mix of personal style and institutional power struggles characteristic of Kentucky politics would matter a lot too. In addition to being the year that *Council for Better Education* went to trial, 1987 was also a gubernatorial election year. The winner would set his face against higher taxes and alienate leading legislators. As a result, collisions among a small number of actors working from within official institutions within all three branches of government would filter and remake reformers' project into one of profound constitutional moment.

THE POLITICS OF DEADLOCK AND A TRIAL COURT VICTORY

In the election of 1987, as usual, a crowded field of candidates vied for the Democratic nomination for governor. For most of the way the frontrunners were two regulars, former Governor John Y. Brown and then current Lieutenant Governor Steve Besher. For most of the way, Wallace Wilkinson, a forty-five-year-old multimillionaire who had never held elective office, ran fifth in a field of five. Wilkinson had amassed a fortune as the founder and head of a large wholesale textbook company. Between 1984 and 1987, he used his wealth to build a personal political organization.

In the 1987 primary, Wilkinson spent $4.3 million, more money than any other candidate in the race. The cornerstone of his campaign was a "no new taxes" pledge, combined with a proposal for a new state lottery. Wilkinson's campaign was the brainchild of a then-little-known political consultant named James Carville. A particularly effective Wilkinson TV spot showed him standing in the back of flatbed truck speaking to a crowd of supporters: "Do you want higher taxes?" "No!" "Are you for a lottery?" "Yes!" Wilkinson won the Democratic primary and then went on to win the general election by the largest margin of votes in the state's history.[40]

Wilkinson combined old-fashioned conservative populism in the Happy Chandler mold with organizational ideas drawn from his experiences running his many closely held business ventures. He had run as an outsider against government and taxes, and he was used to giving orders and having them followed. As a "brash young governor" who, in Kentucky parlance, "hadn't gone through the chairs," Wilkinson quickly alienated longtime legislative leaders. When some of these legislative leaders floated the idea that a projected budget shortfall and pressing needs warranted new taxes, Wilkinson made it clear that he would stand in their way.[41]

In his January 1988 state of the Commonwealth address, Wilkinson took aim at legislators. He stated that "we cannot tax our way out of our problems, we must work our way out of them." He had not been elected "by the largest margin in Kentucky history to maintain the status quo," he said. Soon, he would submit an austere budget and proposed package of "accountability-based" education reforms. During the legislature's regular session (January through April, 1988), the governor and legislators locked horns at every turn.

Wilkinson stuck to his campaign promise, arguing that "a tax increase would hurt the state's economy." He promised to veto any tax measure. Even though in Kentucky it takes only a simple majority to override a governor's veto, most legislators were unwilling to support a tax increase unless the governor was willing to share public responsibility for it. In turn, legislators buried the governor's educational proposals in committees, and they were never brought to the floor for a vote. As the session ended, legislators were forced to accept the governor's budget, and the governor had been denied even a floor debate on his education plan. Mutual public recriminations followed.[42]

The governor and legislators would remain deadlocked over taxes and competing educational reform agendas until the Court's decision in *Council for Better Education* in June 1989. Even after that, they would continue to do battle. Meanwhile, in 1988, reformers won a court victory at the trial level, with Judge Corns issuing a decision striking down the finance system. Reformers' trial court victory raised the stakes of the interbranch conflict considerably. It threatened the governor and legislators with loss of control over education reform and expanded the scope of the conflict. The trial court's decision also provided additional spaces for the continuation of reformers' democratic efforts to produce a political consensus in support of their particular reform agenda. Now reformers' activities would proceed with added legitimacy, for now "the law" was on their side.

In April 1988, just as the acrimonious legislative session was winding down, Judge Corns heard closing arguments. Combs told the court that "this case is critical for future generations of Kentucky children." He concluded by quoting the Bible. "By their fruits you shall know them," he said, "and this tree is not producing good fruit."[43]

Over the next several months, Corns issued three separate rulings in the case. In his initial decision (May 1988), Corns embraced reformers' interpretation of the state constitution's education clause: "The terms 'efficient,' 'system,' and 'common schools,'" he wrote, were all "terms of art" with "special constitutional import." "Efficient," for example, meant not only "economic efficiency," but also "adequate, uniform, and unitary." Education was a "fundamental right in the Commonwealth," and the current finance system "fail[ed] to provide all of Kentucky's students with substantially equal educational opportunities." Although the legislature had created a system "dependent upon local resources," it had "as a practical matter hampered [local] districts' taxing power." Not only were there unjustified disparities in resources across districts, but Kentucky as a whole compared unfavorably to other states. Kentucky's school system was "one of the most severely deficient in the nation," the judge wrote. Kentucky's children were "suffering from an extreme case of educational malnutrition."[44]

In his second ruling, styled a "supplemental order" (June 1988), Corns appointed a five-member "Select Committee" comprised of "five eminently qualified Kentuckians" to "advise the Court of the most appropriate remedies for . . . correcting deficiencies." Corns named Kern Alexander to serve as the chair of the Select Committee. He also appointed another policy expert affiliated with the reformers and a member of the Prichard Committee.[45]

Corns's Select Committee conducted five public hearings around the state in July. According to Alexander, the Select Committee's initial question was whether to propose specific school finance policy changes or merely to articulate general principles. "We decided," Alexander said, "that we would not propose a specific system with formulas, but that we'd come forward with general guidelines. In terms of strategy, we felt that if we were too specific, then the argument on appeal would be that the court was legislating."[46] The Select Committee's approach undoubtedly took shape in response to legislators' expressions of hostility toward Corns's ruling and evolving remedial process. Corns had retained jurisdiction and had made it clear that his "initial rulings" were not yet "final orders" and therefore not yet subject to appellate review.

In September, the Select Committee submitted a twenty-page report to the court. The report begins by stating nine general principles for a constitutional finance system.[47] It then takes each of the central terms of section 183 of the Kentucky Constitution—efficient, system, and common school—and elaborates them largely in terms of each other, along with terms like adequate, universal, and unitary. In turn, adequacy is discussed through vague talk of student needs and capacities. There is no discussion of school finance policy until the very end, and even here we find only criticisms of the existing system and a call for a "more equitable" distribution of resources. Throughout, the rhetoric of the document appeals to the common school tradition.[48]

In October, Corns issued his final ruling. He again held that the constitution's education clause required "substantial uniformity" in the school system.

He also adopted his Select Committee's statement of general principles and student capacities to be achieved. After noting that there was no constitutional prohibition on local school district spending above some "minimally adequate" level, Corns explicitly endorsed reformers' anti-Robin Hood view: "Since no district is over funded," he wrote, "to take funds away from any district in order to give them to another would have disastrous effects on the entire system." Finally, the court was not claiming "authority to tell the General Assembly *how* the system should be financed"; it was merely striking down the existing finance system.[49]

Reformers' trial court victory generated a great deal of media attention, and that attention reflected reformers' vision and their anti-Robin Hood stance. Both the May and October decisions were front-page news, and reformers were featured prominently in these stories. Reformers sought to trumpet Corns's decision as a landmark. Combs told the press that the decision would have "historic consequences": "This is the first time that a judge in Kentucky has held that education is a fundamental right. It is the first time that a Kentucky court has had the intellectual courage to hold that the Kentucky constitution means what it says[,] that the State is obligated to provide an efficient system of public schools." Other Council for Better Education leaders were careful to emphasize their anti-Robin Hood position. Jack Moreland, a school district superintendent and the president of the Council, stated that the group's "intent never was to take money away from the rich." Arnold Guess stated that "the solution is more revenue." A redistribution of existing resources, he added, would only "redistribute mediocrity."[50]

Corns's decisions and remedial process also expanded the scope of the political conflict in several ways. Important legislative leaders reacted angrily to the Corns rulings. They were especially concerned that the court would use its advisory panel "to dictate policy" to the General Assembly. Although Corns had requested their appearance and participation after he ruled, the legislative leaders said that they would "boycott" the court's remedial process. Now, as it began to look like some sort of change was in the offing, legislative leaders vied for control of what kind of change it would be. They began holding their own hearings on tax and education issues. Thus, because matters of power and turf mean a lot in Kentucky politics, the trial court's decision set legislative leaders off on their own parallel course of exploring the issues and reform options. By

February 1989 (still four months before the Supreme Court's decision), legislative leaders had developed a package of tax and education proposals that went way beyond anything they had considered before.[51]

Within a month after the trial court's May decision, Governor Wilkinson announced that he would not pursue an appeal in the case. He too thought that the existing school finance system was unconstitutional but argued that his own accountability-based program would provide the necessary remedy without the need for new taxes.[52]

Thus, the trial court decisions both amplified and focused the ongoing battle between the governor and legislators. Whereas their fight during the 1988 legislative session had centered on taxes, with education reform positioned as a bargaining chip in that battle, now education itself would become the focal point of the interbranch conflict.

The trial court's intervention also gave rise to a new education coalition composed of representatives of established educational interest groups. The Prichard Committee was an active participant in this new formation of groups and meetings. By January 1989, this coalition too had drafted a report endorsing many of the reforms that the Prichard Committee had been advocating since 1985.[53]

The trial court's opinions embraced reformers' common school rhetoric and attached it to the state constitution's education clause. Later, the Kentucky Supreme Court would adopt this rhetoric along with the trial court's statements about the goals of a constitutional system of public education and the capacities it should cultivate in students. At first blush, this sort of rhetoric strikes one as virtually meaningless. However, if such rhetoric is endorsed by a high court in the sonorous tones of constitutional interpretation and aspiration, and if it is then taken seriously and acted on in politics, then it can channel thought and action in certain directions and not in others. This is what would happen after the Court handed down its decision in *Rose v. Council for Better Education*.

After Corns issued his final order in October, legislators appealed to the Supreme Court for direct review. The Court granted the motion and scheduled oral arguments for December 1988. While the case was pending, the governor and legislators would continue to fight bitterly over education and taxes. In the process, each side would appeal to interest groups and broader publics for support. This effort by elected officials in an interbranch conflict to mobilize supporters is one of the hallmarks of constitutional politics. The dispute between the governor and legislators formed the immediate context for the Court's deliberations and decision in Council for Better Education. Placed in this context, the Court's "activist" decision was in reality quite deferential to legislative authority.

Judge Corns's initial rulings and Select Committee process brought the governor and the Senate president and House speaker together for two meetings in July 1988. Both sides came away trumpeting a "new spirit of compromise." However, follow-up meetings among staff members made it clear that neither side would budge. The governor maintained that no tax increase was needed until his substantive, accountability-based, and very low-cost education reforms were in place, and legislative leaders maintained that higher taxes and broader education reforms would have to be part of the same package. Moreover, the governor would have to share responsibility by publicly supporting new revenue measures.[54]

In mid-August 1988, the governor surprised legislators by announcing that he would call the General Assembly into special session in January. He told the press that he would place before them the same program they had rejected early that year, and that "taxes [would] not be on the agenda." At every opportunity over the course of the fall, he expressed his opposition to new taxes. The legislative leadership and educational interest groups were for a tax hike, and he was against one. Legislative leaders reacted angrily to the governor's announcement and public rhetoric. The governor, they said, was back to his "my way or no way" stance. However, legislative leaders had their own political problem. The chairs of the revenues committees believed that at least $300 million more in state revenue would be needed annually, but they also knew that most legislators would not vote for new taxes unless the governor took the lead in backing them.[55]

The jockeying for position continued throughout the first half of 1989. Wilkinson began the year still threatening to call a special legislative session, now in March. In communications and meetings, he appealed to the new coalition of educational interest groups to support his program. Privately, he assured them that he would support tax increases, but only after the legislature accepted his substantive reforms and they were given a chance to work.

When it became clear in February that the educational groups would side with the legislators, Wilkinson decided that there was no point in calling a special session. He called on legislators to provide him with a list of specific reforms with a price tag and also publicly criticized legislative leaders for "hiding behind" him on the tax issue. He publicly doubted that more than twenty out of one hundred legislators would vote for a tax increase. In mid-April, legislators sent the governor a draft of an educational improvement plan that included some of the governor's ideas as part of broader package of measures. The legislators' estimated price tag was $350 million per year. Over the next six weeks, the governor simply sat on the legislators' proposal and continued to argue for his own.[56]

With the governor and legislative leaders locked in a bitter battle over education, and with the Council's case pending before the Supreme Court, a Bluegrass State Poll showed that fully three-fourths of that state's citizens agreed that schools needed more money, and 56 percent said that "they would be willing to pay more state taxes if they were sure the money would improve education."[57]

CONCLUSION

Over the previous six years, the Kentucky reform groups had done a good deal of hard, democratic political work. Their approach to law, politics, and change had been highly realistic. Indeed, the Prichard Committee, one of two key reform groups, had eschewed litigation altogether in favor of producing grassroots pressure to spur policy change in the legislative arena. It was only after the legislative route was twice tried and twice failed that the Prichard Committee leaders supported and participated in the Council for Better Education's litigation-focused project.

Similarly, the Council itself treated litigation as an instrumental device within a broader political campaign. They never believed that the tax and school finance policy changes that they wanted could be procured by judicial decree alone. The process of bringing the lawsuit to fruition was a political process involving districts qua districts, represented by school superintendents and board members. Combs, in particular, believed that going to court on a matter of social policy had to be, and had to be seen to be, a well-justified last resort—as something that one did only after all else had failed.

The realistic approach meant that reformers' effort in court proceeded alongside of, and interacted in mutually reinforcing ways with, much political activity in several other forums.

The Kentucky reform groups also shared a commitment to a common school vision of education. For them, education was best thought of as preparation for a "larger life" and active citizenship. It was a trust held in common by all for all. They placed the accent on commonalities and downplayed differences and particular disadvantages.

Reformers' common school vision sat rather uneasily beside their initial endorsement of wealth neutrality. To their great credit, reformers intuitively grasped that wealth neutrality did not come close to saying all that they wanted to say. A genuine *"Serrano* suit" would have focused on relative tax capacities and expenditure levels, and nothing more. But the case reformers ended up presenting at trial was predominantly a case about the inadequacy of Kentucky's public education system as a whole, especially in comparison to systems in other states, or to national norms. The argument became a highly rhetorical one about why more money was needed and what might be done with it, statewide, as opposed to one about relative positions or relative inequalities within the state.

This process is best called legal translation. As in New Jersey, a close look at legal framing and trial practice tells us that presentations of facts can drive the evolution of legal categories and norms. However, unlike in New Jersey, where the ELC spun out its framing in *Abbott* from norms and concepts given from *Robinson*, in Kentucky the ideational resources for legal translation came mostly from outside the law altogether. The construction of "constitutional adequacy" as the common school vision in Kentucky was really quite a remarkable fabrication. The Kentucky reformers merely asserted that the Constitution's education clause embodied a right to an adequate education and then filled in the content with facts and policy arguments drawn from their intuitions and modern common school sources.

It seems to be of vital importance that, in both law and in politics, the Kentucky reformers acted in ways consistent with the vision they espoused. Perhaps the most significant behavioral manifestation of the common school vision within the Council was its anti-Robin Hood stance. That position was perfectly consistent with the common school vision itself. The Council leaders not only voiced this position in court and in public, but also acted on it. For example, when Arnold Guess approached every district in the state to seek support for the litigation, he made the common school vision more real by acting in accordance with it.

The common school frame involves not only a certain sort of talk or rhetoric about the purposes and functions of public schools, but also a more detailed ordering of priorities within education policy. Prior to the trial, the Prichard Committee had not only plowed many a political field; it had also worked out a common school agenda in some detail. Its blueprint for reform entered the litigation directly. Moreover, when Prichard Committee members did the hard work of organizing town forums, developing a network of supporters in local school districts across the state, and arriving at their reform program through long hours of study and debate, they made their vision more real by practicing precisely what they were preaching about education.

The reform groups did not self-consciously plan and coordinate the sum total of all of these activities. Still, their projects increasingly converged, thereby opening up a broad two-way street between litigation and political activity, with all of it forwarding the same common school vision. By 1989, all of these efforts created a climate quite favorable for bold reform. The stage was now set for the Supreme Court to weigh in. The Court's decision striking down the entire education system would complete the process of "constitutionalization" surrounding education reform in the state. Its meanings, implications, and impact are the subject of the next chapter.

CHAPTER SEVEN

ROSE V. COUNCIL FOR
BETTER EDUCATION:
KENTUCKY'S
BROWN V. BOARD

THERE IS A DIVIDE IN THE POLITICAL SCIENCE LITERA-
ture on the role of litigation and courts in social policy
conflicts, between research on legal mobilization, on one hand, and on judicial impact, on the other.

Several specific strands of legal mobilization research study actors' engagement in the legal process as component parts of broader social movement or
reform activity. As noted in Chapter One, those who focus on legal mobilization often have a practical intention; they want to understand the interplay of
law and politics in struggles for change so that research might play some role
in informing action. The study of judicial impact typically begins with a court
decision (or set of them in a policy domain) and seeks to trace consequences.
Often, unintended or unanticipated consequences are of the most interest.
Specific strands of this research also have a practical intention, especially when
it comes to judicial interventions in complex social policy processes. Much of
this latter work has been critical of "judicial activism." When they intervene

in social policy disputes, critics argue, courts lack democratic legitimacy and policy-making capacity.[1]

With respect to the literature on legal mobilization, the Kentucky case is interesting for what it tells us about how the content of legal arguments can matter in a broader effort to produce change. One point is fairly commonplace. In Kentucky, legal strategies were not an alternative to political efforts, but rather an instrumentally useful part of engagement in broader democratic politics. The Kentucky case confirms a basic tenet of legal mobilization research: If litigation will have positive effects for reformers, the more important ones are likely to be indirect. But another point—this one about the ideational content of legal and political activities—has received much less attention. By June 1989, reformers had not only been active participants in politics for many years; but when they spoke and acted, in whatever forum, they marched under the common banner of the common school vision. Ideological coherence across institutional settings seemed to make a difference.

The Kentucky case also points up the need for further explorations of the nexus between mobilization and judicial impact. Each is, after all, really just a part of a linked, broader process. The general point to be explored here is the way in which the environment or context for important judicial decisions is in no small part dependent on the nature of the legal and political mobilization that precedes it. At first blush, the Kentucky Supreme Court's decision in *Council for Better Education* looks rather "activist." That is how the decision has generally been perceived, even by political scientists.[2] Viewed in context, the decision was not really activist at all. With respect to courts and judicial impact, what is noteworthy about the Kentucky case is that reformers' broader democratic efforts meant that Kentucky Supreme Court never had to take any remedial plunge at all. Indeed, it would actually reject all hints that there might be judicial management of the legislative process or education policy, even as it struck down the entire public school system. To their credit, the justices recognized that the time was just right for something that would play as a bold stroke. The Court's decision actually did many things: It propped up the legislature in its fight with the governor; it offered up a broad and inspiring rhetorical argument that called on others to seize the moment—to make history—and it issued a "nonremedy" that left it up to others to do the legislating and implementing.

After *Council for Better Education*, there were no legitimacy or capacity questions at all about the Court's decision. Seemingly bold judicial action had a salutary effect, but that result depended on reformers' sustained and ideologically coherent effort to mobilize public support, and on the Court's nuanced sense of both the political situation and its own limits.

The previous chapter told the story of reformers' various legal and political efforts. For the most part, that story ends with the Kentucky Supreme Court's June 1989 decision. The Prichard Committee would continue to expand. It would regard the Kentucky Education Reform Act of 1990 (KERA) as its own baby, as it were, and it would continue to play a large role in the implementation of KERA's many specific reforms. But on school finance policy in particular, neither the Prichard Committee nor the Council for Better Education needed to do much of anything, aside from keeping watch, after the Court put the ball in the legislature's court. Elected officials then took the lead in constructing a comprehensive reform law that soon became a model for the rest of the country.

It remains only to explicate what the Court said and did and to show how the common school vision, now amplified with the authority of state constitutional law, animated both the nature of the legislative process and the substance of the new legislation.

KENTUCKY'S *BROWN V BOARD*: *ROSE V COUNCIL FOR BETTER EDUCATION*

After Judge Corns's October 1988 ruling, the Senate president and House speaker decided to appeal the trial judge's ruling to the state Supreme Court. They instructed their attorney, William Scent, to seek direct review, bypassing the intermediate appellate court. The Supreme Court granted Scent's motion, set up a compressed briefing timetable, and scheduled oral arguments for December.

Scent devoted much of his brief to a recapitulation of the trial testimony and to a litany of procedural issues. For example, he argued at length that plaintiffs lacked standing and that the trial judge had improperly certified the case as a class action. However, when Scent finally reached the core constitutional question, he marshaled a good deal of legal authority for his position. Indeed, viewing the matter abstractly, or out of context, a lawyer might well conclude that the weight of legal authority was decidedly on Scent's side. Unfortunately for Scent, the actual context made the weight of technical-legal authority somewhat beside the point.

As a general frame, Scent hung his hat exclusively on a separation-of-powers argument. Unlike many other state constitutions, Kentucky's contains explicit language about the separation of powers. Scent began with these provisions and then proceeded to a standard two-step separation-of-powers argument. First, what did the state constitution's education clause (Section 183) actually mean? Second, who had primary responsibility for interpreting the education clause, in the first instance?[3]

Scent argued that Section 183 did not mean what reformers' claimed it meant, and, in any event, the Court was duty bound not to answer that question directly, but only at one remove. The Court should bend over backward to defer to the constitutional judgment of the coequal branch of government specifically charged in the Constitution itself with responsibility for the common schools. On the first issue—the meaning of the clause—Scent turned to the constitutional convention and debates that produced the language in 1890–1891. He found that several education clause amendments that included words like uniform and adequate were proposed but voted down. Constitutional intent, to the extent it could be found in what the authors said and did, did not seem to embrace any general right to an equal or adequate education. On the second issue—the idea that courts should judge only at one remove—Scent cited several cases in which Kentucky's highest court had read Section 183 as a grant of plenary power to the legislature over the schools. Even though Scent lost his case, the Court did, in effect, show great deference to legislative authority.[4]

Combs and Dawahare's brief put great weight on the facts. "The evidence at trial," the brief begins, "established beyond question that Kentucky's public school system remains one of the worst in the nation." The brief framed the central constitutional issue as a question about "what 'efficient' means." While this was technically a question of "first impression," it claimed, Kentucky's constitutional history supported its view. But here the best reformers could do was find a few quotes from the 1890–1891 constitutional debates trumpeting the virtues of common schools. Reformers relied heavily on one local case that was not really on point and also on adequacy decisions in school finance cases in other states.[5] In response to Scent's separation-of-powers argument, reformers naturally argued that deference in the past surely implied the power to review and decide today. The situation was dire, and the Court surely had the responsibility to "say the law."

At oral arguments in December 1988, Scent reminded the justices about popular opposition to taxes. He also pointed out that poorer districts, especially from eastern Kentucky, could not be heard to complain, for they generally had low tax rates, compared to the rest of the state. For their part, Combs and Dawahare (who shared the argument for reformers) stuck to their strategy of studiously avoiding all discussions of possible remedies. The trial judge had simply declared the present finance system unconstitutional, and the Court should simply affirm. No one should tell the legislature specifically how to fix things. Combs closed the argument with an appeal to state pride: "Kentucky has become recognized, unfortunately, as the most illiterate state in the nation. Countless young minds throughout our fair state are being wasted."[6]

As we saw in Chapter Six, political events moved rapidly between December 1988 and June 1989. With the help of their litigation and trial court victory, reformers garnered the support of a broad array of educational interest groups and several important legislators. Most players put the annual price tag for reform at around $350 million. As the months passed, Governor Wilkinson was increasingly isolated. By June, the only two remaining party-defendants, Senate President Rose and House Speaker Blandford, were now saying that they had appealed the trial court decision only because they thought that "a case of this magnitude is something that should be decided by the state's highest court." Even their attorney predicted that the Court would rule in favor of reformers because "all of the nonjudicial factors" were in their favor. The immediate political context could not have been more favorable for reformers.[7]

On June 8, 1989, the Kentucky Supreme Court handed down its decision in *Rose v. Council for Better Education*. Writing for the Court, Chief Justice Robert Stephens begins with an interesting introductory passage. The chief justice, it seems, aims to mark out the central features of the Court's opinion. The issue to be decided is "whether the Kentucky General Assembly has complied with its constitutional mandate to 'provide an efficient system of common schools throughout the state.'"[8] In holding that it had not, Stephens wrote, the justices intended neither to criticize the General Assembly nor "to substitute [their] judicial authority for [its] authority and discretion." But "the framers of our constitution," he continued, "intended that each and every child in the state should receive a proper and adequate education, to be provided by the General Assembly" (pp. 189–190). Indeed, "the goal of the framers" of the Kentucky Constitution "is elegantly and movingly stated in the landmark case of *Brown v. Board of Education.*" The chief justice then sets out the famous language from *Brown* about the role of public education in a democratic society. This passage from Brown, Stephens added, would be "the polestar of this opinion" (p. 190).

This introduction neatly captures two related themes at the core of the opinion: (1) judicial deference to legislative power and (2) the "constitutionalization" of broad principles. At the outset, Stephens has staked a claim to judicial modesty. At first glance, this claim seems strange. What kind of deference could there be in a decision that would go on to strike down every statute having anything to do with education? However, as we shall see, the Court in effect did much to clear the path for legislative dominance of the subsequent reform process. Second, by immediately linking local constitutional intent to the U.S. Supreme Court's opinion in *Brown*, Chief Justice Stephens has signaled the kind of project the Court wishes to undertake and the stature it wishes its opinion to have. In interpreting the meaning of the education clause of the Commonwealth's constitution, the Court would elaborate and constitutionalize a set of fundamental principles only loosely tethered to the constitutional past. It would speak the language of constitutional aspiration, leaving it to others to work out particular meanings in the days, years, and decades ahead.

With respect to the evidence presented at trial, Chief Justice Stephens claimed that "an extensive discussion" was "really not necessary." Appellants had not seriously contested the factual accuracy of reformers' evidence. There were significant disparities across districts in financial resources, curricular offerings, student–teacher ratios, and achievement test scores. Moreover, plaintiffs had shown that, judged by national standards, "*all*" Kentucky school districts were "inadequate." Kentucky as a whole, then, had failed to meet the "constitutional standard" (pp. 197–198). The trial court had erred in one respect, however. By retaining jurisdiction and asking legislators to report back to him on their progress, the trial judge had improperly intruded on legislative authority. The courts would not direct the legislature to "enact any specific legislation" or to "raise taxes" (p. 203).

Chief Justice Stephens then turned to the central question in the case: "What is an 'efficient system of common schools?'" In explicating the meaning of this phrase, he generally followed reformers' brief and the trial court's Select Committee report, both of which offered some juicy quotes from the 1890–1991 state constitutional convention. A "brief sojourn into the constitutional debates will give some idea," Chief Justice Stephens wrote, "of the depth of delegates' intention when Section 183 was drafted and eventually made its way into the organic law of this state." A Delegate Beckner, for example, said of "a system of common schools" that " '[i]t is a system of practical equality in which the children of the rich and poor meet upon a perfect level and the only superiority is that of the mind.' " Similarly, another delegate stated: "Common schools make patriots and men who are willing to stand upon common land. The boys of the humble mountain home stand equally high with those of the mansions of the city. There are no distinctions in the common schools, *but all stand upon one level*" (pp. 204–205, emphasis added by the Court).[9]

What, then, would be the Court's definition of an efficient system of common schools? The Court, Stephens wrote, would "not make policy" or "substitute [its] judgment for that of the General Assembly." It would "simply take the plain directive of the Constitution, and, armed with its purpose . . . , decide what our General Assembly must achieve in complying with its solemn constitutional duty" (p. 211).

The crucial passages of the Court's opinion are worth quoting at length:

The system of common schools must be adequately funded to achieve its goals. The system of common schools must be substantially uniform throughout the state. Each child, *every child*, in this Commonwealth must be provided with an equal opportunity to have an adequate education. Equality is the key word here. The children of the poor and the children of the rich . . . must be given the same opportunity and access to an adequate education. . . . In no way does this constitutional requirement act as a limitation on the General Assembly's power to create local school entities and to grant to those entities the authority to supplement the state system. Therefore, if the General Assembly decides to establish local school entities, it may also empower them to enact local revenue initiatives to supplement the uniform, equal educational effort that the General Assembly must provide . . .

The essential, and minimal, characteristics of an "efficient" system of common schools, may be summarized as follows:

1. The establishment, maintenance and funding of common schools in Kentucky is the sole responsibility of the General Assembly.

2. Common schools shall be free to all.

3. Common schools shall be available to all Kentucky children.

4. Common schools shall be substantially uniform throughout the state.

5. Common schools shall provide equal educational opportunities to all Kentucky children, regardless of place of residence or economic circumstances.

6. Common schools shall be monitored by the General Assembly to assure that they are operated with no waste, no duplication, no mismanagement, and with no political influence.

7. The premise for the existence of common schools is that all children in Kentucky have a constitutional right to an adequate education.

8. The General Assembly shall provide funding which is sufficient to provide each child in Kentucky with an adequate education.

9. An adequate education is one which has as its goal the development of the seven capacities recited previously. (pp. 211–213)[10]

Because plaintiffs had shown that the current system did not measure up to these "standards," it was "now up to the General Assembly to re-create, and re-establish a system of common schools." The Court then emphatically stated that it really was wiping the slate clean. The "entire system" was "unconstitutional." Any "[s]tatutes relating to education," it held, "may be reenacted as components of a constitutional system if they combine with other component statutes to form an efficient . . . system" (p. 215). However, the Court would "decline to issue any injunctions, restraining orders, writs of prohibition or writs of mandamus." Not only would the Court not retain jurisdiction, it would not even consider its decision final "until 90 days after the adjournment of the General Assembly, at its regular session in 1990" (p. 216).[11]

The rhetorical quality of the Court's opinion endorses reformers' common school vision. In this, it makes liberal and romantic use of the past—"there are no distinctions in the common schools, but all stand upon one level"—in an opinion that faces the future. It finds no targets of blame for the current state of affairs, but only serious problems in education that demand the attention of citizens and public officials. The Court's language appeals to the common good, and to what "all Kentuckians" (should) share in common. Over the next year or so, the Court's rhetoric was amplified as citizens, journalists, interests groups, and public officials made constant use of it to argue for and legitimize a certain kind of educational reform program.

The Court's decision, as noted, was also quite deferential to legislative power. Not only did it provide cover on the tax issue; by wiping the slate clean, it also altered the existing balance of power in the ongoing fight between the governor and the legislature. Now, in theory, there would have to be some kind of legislative action before the 1990–1991 school year, or else the "entire system" would expire. Wiping the slate clean put the spotlight on the legislature, and its leaders were now ready and well positioned to take control.[12]

A CONSTITUTIONAL POLITICS OF
EDUCATION REFORM: GETTING TO KERA

The process of crafting and passing the Kentucky Education Reform Act of 1990—the process of "getting to KERA"—was both highly agitated and dramatic. It involved two large steps. First, shortly after the Court's opinion, the governor and legislative leaders set up a special task force to draft a comprehensive reform proposal. Second, after the task force completed its work in February 1990, the proposals had to be rendered in statutory form and passed by a legislative body with many rank-and-file members still opposed to, or fearful of, raising taxes. In addition, the governor and legislative leaders would continue to fight about taxes. However, now the issue was not whether there would be a large tax increase but which taxes would be raised and why.

My purpose in this section is not to review these political machinations in great detail, but rather to provide a sense of the tone of public rhetoric and a summary overview of the legislative process. The common school vision continued to frame debate and policy discussions, now with the added power of a Supreme Court opinion that was, as Robert Sexton put it, "treated with acclaim" all around.[13]

Aside from the content of reformers' vision, its translation into law, and how that framed the debate and outcomes, there is another aspect to the politics following the Court's decision that is somewhat elusive but worth remarking upon. Anyone situated before the materials—the newspaper articles, the minutes of some forty-six task force meetings, the statements and actions of various players—would come away with a sense that the people involved felt themselves to be caught up in something historic, something that called them to take extraordinary action and make an extraordinary efforts. They had reached, as the *Courier-Journal* put it, "a crossroads." This quality of "constitutional politics,"

I think, had much to do with reformers' democratic efforts over many years to make their cause the state's cause. The Court's decision certainly emboldened elected officials and undoubtedly placed the issue of education reform at the very top of the state's political agenda.

The day after the decision, Governor Wilkinson held a joint press conference with the Senate president and House speaker. "We have the opportunity to rebuild, to redefine education in Kentucky," he said. "And if we fail, we'll have failed ourselves, our fellow Kentuckians, and our children." The governor indicated that he would now support the "revenue measures" (he was never fond of the word taxes) needed to pay for reform. "Change in the way we approach education in Kentucky . . . " he added, "is no longer a dream. It's the law." The House speaker noted that the Court's decision required "starting from scratch," while the Senate president stated that all the actors were "beyond politics now."[14]

For their part, reformers took care to reiterate their anti-Robin Hood position. For example, on a public television show in June 1989, Combs stated that:

The plaintiffs in this case said in their complaint, and we have said in every motion, every pleading and every argument that we do not want—and will not tolerate— taking money away from one school district and giving it to another. . . . I would advise everybody to put aside any personal gain, ambition, jealousy. . . . I see a lot of good faith and a lot of statesmanship. . . . Once in a great while the Lord above, or maybe the conscience of the people, causes them to rise above political intrigue and envy and selfish advancement.[15]

Newspaper coverage portrayed the Court's decision as historic. The *Louis-ville Courier-Journal*'s immediate editorial response trumpeted a "new beginning" in which the governor and legislators now stood "together as partners in the quest imposed by the Supreme Court in its monumental decision last week." The editorial continued:

Much is at stake in this process. It must not become a process of reductionism. The thrust must be to expand the reach of all schools, particularly in disadvantaged districts, not to diminish their neighbors. In California, funding changes following a similar ruling have limited the ability of schools to offer "extras" such as art, music, and advanced classes. . . . Those are not extras. Even in relatively wealthy districts, Kentucky school children have too few advantages to lose any in the push for equity.[16]

What had already been a fairly constant stream of newspaper articles before the Court's decision became a torrent of coverage. Articles appeared daily, and on many days four, five, and six articles covered education reform.[17]

Public opinion polls revealed the high priority the state's citizens now placed on this issue. A Bluegrass State Poll conducted between July 13 and July 18, 1989, included the following question: "What do you think is the most serious problem or need facing Kentucky?" The largest number of respondents (38 percent) answered that education was, compared to 19 percent who said that it was "jobs and economic development." Sixty-seven percent of those polled said that they would be willing "to pay higher taxes if they were convinced the money would be used to improve the schools." Another Bluegrass State Poll conducted between January 18 and January 24, 1990, "found that an overwhelming majority of Kentuckians [saw] improving public elementary and high school education as highly important and ranked it above seven other major issues facing the legislature." Of the eight issues covered in this poll, education reform "was the only one called 'extremely important' by a majority of respondents." This period between mid-1989 and mid-1990 marked the only time in recent history when another issue had replaced unemployment, jobs, and the economy as the most important one.[18]

Two weeks after the Court's decision, the governor and legislative leaders announced their agreement to set up a twenty-one-member Task Force on Education Reform, consisting of sixteen legislative leaders (eight from each house) and five people appointed by the governor. At another press conference at the end of June 1989, Wilkinson, Rose, and Blandford stated that the Task Force's deliberations would proceed in three steps. First, it would study problems and arrive at a set of substantive changes in education policy and governance. Second, it would gauge the costs of desired policy changes and come up with an overall annual price tag. Third, and only then, it would address the school finance and tax policy questions involved in paying for reform. The three elected officials reiterated their desire to work together. "Kentucky," Wilkinson said, "had the opportunity to remake an entire school system."[19]

The Task Force members decided to divide the body into three committees—curriculum, governance, and finance. Each task force committee then retained a policy consultant from outside the state. Between July 1989 and February 1990, the Task Force and its committees held forty-six public hearings in the process of crafting the sweeping reform law later passed as KERA.

Four general points about the Task Force and its deliberations are worth noting. First, just as in the Prichard Committee's earlier work for *A Path to a Larger Life*, deliberations would be driven by a primary focus on curriculum, pedagogy, and other questions closely related to the point of contact between student and teacher in the classroom. Matters of money would be last, not first, in the order of priority, which moved from curriculum, to governance structures, to school finance policy. The need for new school finance policies and new revenue measures would be justified as a necessary means to otherwise-justified ends.

Second, unlike many other task forces and advisory committees in reform contexts, the Task Force on Education Reform did not include interest group representatives as voting members. Interest groups were not shut out of the process in any way—indeed, they were constantly present and constantly heard from—but none had a seat or a vote. Third, even within the legislative body, we should note that the membership of the Task Force included only sixteen out of 138 legislators. The structure itself was a source of controversy between leaders and rank-and file-legislators. It set up an interesting dynamic in which leaders who were relatively more secure in their positions could appeal over the heads of rank-and-file members directly to the people for support for the Task Force's plan. In the end, leaders also used a good deal of old-fashioned, pork-based vote trading to secure the necessary legislative support.[20]

In the language of political science, this structure, with its denial of voting or vetoing power to interest groups and its limitation of deliberations and policy formation to a small number of legislators, permitted the reasonable aggregation of competing interests. No one could easily pick off pieces of the legislation that they did not like.

Fourth, after legislators put in many long hours of hard work, and after the grind of the actual legislative process in 1990, legislators developed what many participants called a "sense of ownership" of KERA. Indeed, legislators even included within the new law the establishment of a new oversight body housed within the legislative branch. The architects of the new law would have access to feedback about implementation through their own staff. Legislative ownership meant that elected officials would be identified with the new regime and that they would defend it from criticisms thereafter.[21]

The policy consultants that legislators brought in from out of state played important roles in turning a reform vision that was "in the air," as it were, into a reform program and then into legislation. But the determination to go to out of state policy consultants and the process of selecting specific ones were not unrelated to reformers' vision and efforts. Given the presence of education reform on Kentucky's political agenda for five years, legislative leaders and staff had already developed good contacts with national organizations concerned with education issues, such as the Education Commission of the States, the National Conference of State Legislatures, and the Center for Policy Research on Education. The Prichard Committee was also well connected to those national policy reform circles. Given the national attention generated by the Court's unusual decision, nationally recognized policy experts were, in turn, rather intrigued by the idea that a new education system could be built from the ground up.

As a result, and not surprisingly, the policy experts who packed their bags for long stays in Kentucky over the next six months generally shared reformers' modern common school outlook. Like the Prichard Committee members and the Council's experts, they were quite willing to talk in sweeping rhetorical language about a new regime of teaching and learning for "all children," about local, broadly defined "communities" that could arrive at and pursue "common goals" and "learning outcomes," about teaching students "in a setting where they are taken seriously and personally."[22]

The Task Force's Curriculum Committee retained David Hornbeck as its policy consultant. Hornbeck, a noted lawyer, theologian, and education reformer, shared reformers' common school vision and married it to the latest thinking (a cynic might say "fads and fashions") in the education school world. During his first visit with Kentucky legislators, he surprised them by talking earnestly about broad philosophical questions. He wanted to know "whether we believe all children can learn; whether we can successfully teach all types of children, and what it is we want children to learn."[23]

Hornbeck forcefully advocated what was then a new concept, "performance-based" or "outcome-based" education. The approach is widely embraced and familiar enough now. It requires the articulation of learning goals—what students "should know and be able to do"—and the development of assessment mechanisms to determine whether the schools are succeeding. But Hornbeck and the legislators put a particular common school spin on standards, outcomes, and accountability. For Hornbeck, this approach also required that assessment practices go beyond standardized tests to include more "authentic" assessments of skills and performances requiring the use of knowledge and demonstrations of competence (e.g., writing and problem solving of various sorts; portfolios of "best work"; group exercises requiring "performance").

For Hornbeck, the success of outcome-based education depended on a structure of meaningful rewards and sanctions *for teachers and schools*. Assessment devices tied to rewards and sanctions would bring reform down to the classroom, for, as Hornbeck put it, "what is tested will be what is taught" and "actions must have consequences." Hence, much of the Curriculum Committee process involved debate over Hornbeck's advocacy of rewards and sanctions for schools, based on new "performance assessments." Moreover, if teachers and other school personnel were to be held accountable, Hornbeck also claimed, then they must have decision-making authority about teaching methods and instructional materials. Hence he proposed "school-based decision making" in the form of school counsels.[24]

Hornbeck's ideas dovetailed enough with what the governor had been advocating all along so as to allow the governor to claim that this was his program too. It also helped that Hornbeck and the Curriculum Committee used and sought to build on the work of the Governor's Council on School Performance Standards, which the governor had established by executive order back in February 1989.[25]

Of course, everything depends on the content of the goals, the process through which the goals are translated into "measurable outcomes," the assessment devices used to determine success, and the infrastructure to help teachers and schools adjust to what purports to be a new regime.

With respect to the content of principles and goals, the Curriculum Committee gravitated to common school themes. For example, the potential for competitiveness across different kinds of communities in a system focused on outcomes, rewards, and sanctions was muted by the plan's two main features: First, the school, and not the student, teacher, or district, would be the relevant unit of analysis; and, second, each school would be placed in competition with itself. Rewards and sanctions would hinge on a school's level of internal improvement, measured against a baseline of its own prior performance and not on its level of achievement compared to any other school.

The Curriculum Committee also endorsed a further effort to define and measure performance across "a broad curriculum" in seven separate subject areas. This was decidedly not a narrow, basic-skills approach to achievement. The committee also embraced the novel idea of an "ungraded primary program," replacing what had been grades K–3. An ungraded primary program reflects the common school tradition because its purpose is to allow all students to experience success in their early years, proceeding at their own rate. Here, the competitive race implied by grade levels and grading does not even begin until the fifth year of formal schooling (fourth grade). Finally, the Committee, following Hornbeck's lead, argued that early childhood education and social service provision at all levels were vital parts of this overall reform program.[26]

The Governance Committee's wide-ranging discussions and proposals strongly reflected the "good government" side of the reformers' project. The messiness and (often) sheer incompetence of local (democratic) school governance as it actually existed in Kentucky was traded in for governance structures that would select and empower education professionals and other elites. At the end of its deliberations, the Governance Committee proposed a complete restructuring of school administration, from top to bottom. Its remarkable recommendations included:

- A reconstituted State Board of Education. The current arrangement allowed the governor to appoint State Board members. The Committee proposed making the State Board the joint creature of the executive and legislative branches.

- The replacement of the elected state superintendent of public instruction with an appointed commissioner of education. The new commissioner would take over on January 1, 1991.

- The complete abolition of all positions at the existing State Department of Education, effective June 30, 1991.

- School-based decision making in all schools by 1996–1997, unless the State Department of Education granted a waiver.

- Severe restrictions on political activities or the appearance of nepotism at the district level. For example, school board members, district superintendents, and school principals would all be precluded from holding their positions if they had immediate relatives working in the district. Teachers would be precluded from participating in school board elections or politics.

- The establishment of an Office of Educational Accountability located with the Legislative Research Commission (a body made up of legislative leaders and legislative staff).

All of these changes were enacted as part of KERA.[27]

The Task Force's Finance Committee hired John Augenblick as its outside policy consultant. Augenblick worked closely with Tom Willis, a staff member at the legislature's research office. Augenblick and Willis engaged in a complicated set of deliberations and negotiations with leading legislators. The policy experts, it turned out, were far more concerned with producing more equality than were leading legislators. Augenblick informed me that he and Willis "attempted to place an absolute limit on the amount of money that a district could spend over others." Legislators rejected the very idea of limiting expenditures in any district. Augenblick and Willis argued that sufficient increases in spending in poorer districts and overall equity required some caps on how high the best-off districts could go. In the end, a compromise produced very liberal limits on any district's superior spending in relation to others.

Legislators were also interested in another question that Augenblick had spent some time thinking about. He called this "the hold harmless" question. Politics goes better if all districts gain at least some state aid, but what is a gain for political feasibility is a loss for greater equality. Augenblick's concerns eventually resulted in KERA containing a rule that created a range of state aid *increases* for all districts for two years. No district would get less than an 8 percent increase in year one, and none would get less than another 5 percent increase in year two. Most districts saw larger state aid increases. The fact that all districts gained state aid is, itself, reflective of the common school orientation. Several other features of the school finance system, which will be discussed in more detail shortly, would embody common school ideals.[28]

As the work of the Task Force proceeded, Wilkinson and legislators continued to find things to fight about. As late as December 1989, the governor was still hinting that he might veto tax measures. When it looked like the governor might again stand against a tax hike, legislators and reformers invoked the Court's decision and threatened to go back to court for help. Surprisingly, after that, Wilkinson proposed a tax package with power and "progressivity" beyond anything leading legislators were willing to do. Wilkinson's populism had many faces. Nevertheless, when the Task Force finally wrapped up its work in February 1990, another round of meetings between the governor and legislators produced agreement on Task Force's plan for a total revision of the education system and on its conclusion that an increase in state revenues of about $500 million per year would be needed to fund it. After a few more weeks of conflict over the nature of tax policy changes, the governor relented and accepted the legislative program. Some changes to the state income tax code and a 1 percent sales tax increase (which Wilkinson had opposed) would anchor a $1.3 billion tax increase over the next two years.[29]

In March, with only a few weeks left in the legislative session, the Kentucky Education Reform Act was introduced as House Bill 940. It took approximately 300 pages to articulate all of the substantive policy changes and planned processes, and the entire bill ran 900 pages because every single education law had to be reenacted. With the governor now supporting the legislature's proposed sales tax increases, the remainder of the legislative process involved parliamentary maneuvers in which leaders sought to fend off hostile amendments and, as the House Speaker put it, engaged in much "swapping of brick and mortar for votes." The House passed KERA as a package by a vote of fifty-eight to forty-two. A week later, the Senate passed a slightly different version by a vote of thirty to eight. The next day, after an impassioned speech by the House majority leader, the House voted again and accepted the Senate's version of the bill. The measure included the tax hike of $1.3 billion over two years. On April 11, Governor Wilkinson signed KERA into law.[30]

THE KENTUCKY EDUCATION REFORM ACT: DEVELOPMENTS AND CONSEQUENCES, 1991–2009

As passed, KERA purported to change everything at once. It quickly became the leading national example of what education policy specialists were soon calling "systemic reform." KERA contained three basic sections tracking the nature and order of priority of the Task Force's three committees. Part 1 addresses curriculum in the form of a statement of "seven capacities" to be fostered and six basic "learning goals." It also endorsed a broad set of reforms related to professional development for teachers and administrators, site-based management, and the school-based provision of social services. These changes included a half day of preschool for all at-risk four-year-olds. Part 2 addressed a plethora of governance issues, noted above. Part 3 set up a new school finance system styled "Support Educational Excellence in Kentucky," or SEEK.

In this section, I describe the new school finance system and review some research tracing out its financial consequences. I also offer some brief remarks about other aspects of KERA's implementation.

SEEK embodied the common school vision in several ways.[31] It had (and has) three basic components, or, as its architects put it, "three tiers"—the foundation, tier I, and tier II. First, SEEK set up a basic foundation aid plan with a required local tax effort. State aid would close any gaps between locally generated revenues and the per pupil foundation amount. Thus, for the first time in Kentucky history, state aid would flow to local districts in inverse relation to local district wealth.[32]

Second, on top of this foundation plan, there would be tier I, a "wealth-equalized" option for local districts to tax and spend above the foundation amount. Here, a local district could decide to levy a tax that would result in an increase of its revenues by 15 percent above the base amount. For this level of revenue above the base, the state would provide aid to ensure a yield at a local tax base of 150 percent of the state average tax base. In other words, each district could act as if its own tax base was 150 percent of the state average tax base, until revenues reached the base amount plus 15 percent.

Third, tier II permitted local districts leeway to tax and spend above the base and tier I. For this part of the finance plan, districts would foot the entire bill. Most importantly, the ability to outspend other districts was limited by a liberal cap of no more than 30 percent over the base plus tier I.

SEEK's logical structure and actual operation reflect the common school vision in two basic ways. First, although it allows local leeway for a few wealthier districts to spend more than most others, it ties the degree of this local leeway to the level of a common, generally applicable foundation amount. At least in theory, everyone has a material interest in the level of the common base. Second, over its first six years (1990–1991 to 1995–1996), every district in the state received substantial increases in state aid, and every district saw increases in overall education expenditures. In addition, because property poorer districts got and spent relatively more money, SEEK produced not only absolute gains for all but also gains in the overall equality of the system.

School finance experts Picus, Odden, and Fermanich conducted in-depth analyses of the Kentucky finance system for the Kentucky Department of

Education in 2000. They constructed several data sets using various ways of counting dollars, and then they applied the full panoply of commonly used school finance statistics. Among other things, Picus and colleagues show that, on all ways of counting dollars, the coefficient of variation was lower in 1999–2000 than it was in 1990–1991. In addition, in 1999–2000, the coefficient of variation for all expenditure measures was at or below the generally accepted benchmark level of 0.1 for an equitable system. Their analysis shows a precipitous decline in relative inequality to 1996–1997 and then slight increases in relative inequality thereafter. Still, in 1999–2000, healthy gains in relative equality remained, against the 1990–1991 baseline.[33]

Similarly, Flanagan and Murray use various school finance statistics to measure the degree of relative equality in the Kentucky school finance system between 1987 and 1997. "Across all measures," they write, "inequality in educational resources has fallen sharply . . . since the passage of KERA."[34] Doug Reed conducted his own evaluation using students as his unit of analysis and various school finance statistics. Reed calculated the Gini coefficient, a standard measure of relative inequality in a distribution, for eight states experiencing school finance litigation (five with favorable court decisions and three with unfavorable ones). Out of all the states in Reed's analysis, Kentucky showed the sharpest drop in relative inequality.[35]

Over the first six years of implementation, anecdotal evidence supported this favorable assessment of school finance policy changes. In Powell County, a school district "on the western edge of Appalachia," a local tax increase brought about an additional $1.3 million increase in state aid, a reporter noted. "A year after [KERA]," she continued, "many students in Powell County are finishing their first year in a school with a librarian, counselor, full-time art classes, aides assigned to assist potential dropouts, and watertight roofs—all luxuries for a county where property taxes generate just $116,000 per year."[36] In Rockcastle County, another poor district in Appalachia, per pupil spending rose from $2,836 in 1989–1990 to $3,737 in 1991–1992. Local administrators told a reporter that they "felt like tycoons."[37] For much of the litigation, the president of the Council for Better Education was Jack Moreland, a district superintendent from Eastern Kentucky. In Moreland's district, "where poor white children from public housing and modest cottages make up most of the student population and 70 percent of the students are eligible for school lunches," total state and local revenues increased from $2.9 million in 1989–1990 to $4.6

million in 1993–1994. For this district, the new money meant new computer equipment and two new preschools, among other things.[38]

Beginning around 1997, observers and advocates began to worry again about declining overall financial support for education in Kentucky. The equity gains remained, but now the threat was that the system might treat everyone equally badly. By 2000, the General Assembly had increased the foundation base amount from $2,305 (in 1990–1991) to about $2,900 (for 2000–2001), but that increase was not quite enough even to keep pace with inflation. Thus, those tracking finance and equity trends uniformly presented a picture of wonderful progress through 1996–1997, and flat funding and a little backsliding on equality thereafter.[39]

In 2003, the Council for Better Education, which now included virtually every school district in the state, filed a new legal challenge to the state's funding system under *Rose v. Council for Better Education*. Resistance from legislators and a lack of financial resources to support the litigation delayed prosecution of the case for several years. With the case pending, the 2006 legislative session produced the first significant increases in state education funding (about $250 million) in the past five years. In February 2007, a trial judge dismissed this new case. The Council for Better Education then decided not to appeal.[40]

Through it all, the basic terms of public discourse have continued to reflect the common school vision. Discussions of goals, objectives, and current problems still reflect reformers' ideological outlook. Now, the heady days of high-minded reform and their embodiment in legal norms serve as cultural resources for ongoing conflicts, in new contexts.

A SUCCESS STORY?

The Kentucky reform effort, then, is indeed a success story. The criteria for success in this account are fairly straightforward. In this case, legal and political mobilization went hand in hand and converged toward a particular vision of educational reform. This effort shaped the terms of public debate and set the state's political agenda. It produced legal victories transforming state constitutional doctrine. In turn, legal and political mobilization and court victories combined to bring about various policy changes under the umbrella of KERA. And, finally, among these policy reforms was a new school finance system that has increased the absolute level of resources for education and significantly reduced the degree of relative resource inequality across school districts.

One might object that this picture of "success" is incomplete. One might make two sorts of claims along these lines. First, as any of the Kentucky reformers would agree, the ultimate goal of their efforts was to change consciousness, behaviors, and routine practices at the school district, school, and classroom levels. If these changes are of the right sort, then they should produce better educational experiences and outcomes. Both steps in this chain are problematic and would need to be carefully investigated before we could make an unequivocal claim for "success."[41] We have good reason to suspect that changes in educational practices closer to the ground are likely to be uneven, And, even if achieved, these changes may or may not in fact produce "better educational experiences and outcomes" for children.

This book is not centrally concerned with policy implementation issues. I have relied on school finance researchers to gauge finance policy changes and outcomes, and finance is only one of several important domains to examine. On the school finance front, the Kentucky effort succeeded, and did so beyond all reasonable expectations.

Otherwise, KERA is nothing if not multifaceted and complex. It includes evolving and contested elements of centralization (e.g., curricular reforms, testing, and accountability) and decentralization (e.g., school-site councils comprised of parents, teachers, and administrators). It was brought about by outside, bottom-up pressures, but many of its reforms were imposed on schools from the top down. It contained a host of educational policy components, and, just as in New Jersey, researchers have studied and debated the design, implementation, and consequences of virtually all of these.[42] My own survey of this body of research on KERA's implementation revealed strong evidence of significantly changed teaching practices, functioning local school site councils at almost all schools, significant improvements in the provision of preschool education (e.g., a half day of preschool for over 30,000 at-risk four-year-olds, representing 77 percent of those eligible under the program and 30 percent of all four-year-olds), and clear, respectable (but not earth-shattering) gains in student achievement. For example, over the 1990s, Kentucky realized modest gains in scores on the National Assessment of Student Progress, or NAEP, a fairly reliable indicator when it comes to measuring improved performance over time.[43]

On the issue of whether the common school vision is an attractive one, I once again fall back on the claim that my purpose is not normative evaluation. Rather, the focus here has been on understanding the nature of legal mobilization and its relationship to politics in reform struggles. Here, the Kentucky case has some valuable lessons to teach us.

CONCLUSION: LESSONS FOR LEGAL MOBILIZATION THEORY

In Chapter 1, I claimed that legal mobilization theory could be more attentive to the details and significance of legal translation and to the ideational dimensions of the nexus between legal and political strategies. I argued that the culturalist view of law itself counseled greater concern with the ideological content of claims making in law. Speaking one way rather than another within law is likely to have great consequences for reformers, both with respect to their internal mobilization of support, and in their relations with other groups and actors.

In the Kentucky reform project, litigation began with a few individuals who made use of a leading school finance case from California. To their credit, they understood that flesh-and-blood clients (officials representing local school districts) and political support would be crucial ingredients of success, even in court. Perhaps because he had been a successful politician, Mr. Combs knew that initiating reform litigation is a little like engaging in civil disobedience. It should be, and should be widely perceived to be, a well-justified last resort.

With respect to legal translation, what began as a "*Serrano* suit" focused upon *relative* tax capacity and educational expenditures was quickly transformed into an "adequacy" suit. Law review writing on school finance litigation makes much of the distinction between "equity" and "adequacy" framing in school finance cases.[44] But the important translation point—one that only a mobilization approach can comprehend—is that reformers elaborated on and rendered "adequacy" in terms of the rhetoric and modern policy frame of the common school. This common school frame structured the Council for Better Education's arguments about legal meaning, its presentation of evidence in court, and its public rhetoric. Perhaps the most significant manifestation of common school ideology within the litigation was the Council's anti-Robin Hood stance, a stance perfectly consistent with the common school vision itself.

Leaders of the Council not only voiced this position in court and in public; they also acted in ways consistent with it—for example, by approaching every school district in the state to seek support for the legal challenge.

As noted in Chapter 6, the common school frame involves not only a certain sort of talk or rhetoric about the purposes and functions of public schools, but also a more detailed ordering of priorities within education policy. Aside from the effort to present finance policy as a means to otherwise justified ends, the reformers' case in court was long on rhetoric and short on policy details. Given the increasingly favorable political climate as the conflict evolved, this vagueness was a virtue.

The creation of this favorable political context depended, as it often does, on the existence of a broader political effort outside court. But I think there is much more to this story than the mere fact of political mobilization. The success of this effort in changing the political climate and bringing about results, I would argue, also had much to do with the high degree of ideological coherence between the legal and political components of the reform project as a whole. The legal mobilization approach allowed us to trace the convergence between the values and activities of the Council for Better Education, on one hand, and the Prichard Committee for Academic Excellence, on the other. It was the Prichard Committee that plowed the political fields and worked out the common school reform agenda in more detail. Moreover, when Prichard Committee members did the hard work of organizing town forums, developing a network of supporters in local school districts across the state, and arriving at their reform program through long hours of study and debate, they made their vision more real by practicing precisely what they were preaching about democracy and education. After its effort to bring about reform through normal political channels failed, the Prichard Committee decided to support the Council's legal challenge to the state's school finance system. This opened up a two-way street between political advocacy and litigation, with the common school frame increasingly animating both prongs of the reform effort.

The claim here is that there was something causally significant about the fact that "everything was working in one direction," both strategically and ideologically, from reformers' side of things. In this case, ideological coherence between the legal and political prongs of the reform effort seemed to facilitate winning desired changes, and in two basic ways. First, coherence, and a shared sense of meaning and purpose, played a role in allowing reform groups to include and motivate their own members, in mobilizing new constituents, and in informing the thinking and activities of reform lawyers.

Second, it seems that legal/political ideological coherence made litigation-backed reform more "legitimate" in the eyes of broader publics. This is a proposition linking coherence to success that has received scant theoretical attention. As noted above, one problem when reformers rely on law and courts, as they often must, is that broader audiences view their project as a cynical end run around (more) legitimate democratic politics. Reformers, this argument goes, are just going to the courts to win policies that they could never win in the legislative arena.

A focus on "coherence" as I have described it in the Kentucky case calls for a researcher's observations and judgments not only about reformers' extrajudicial strategies and tactics, but also about the content of their arguments and the quality of their practices and actions, in different kinds of institutional settings. Indeed, many of the dilemmas of legal mobilization arise from the disjunctions and tensions between courts and other differently constituted institutional channels for politics. When the legal and political components of a reform project fit together well, and when rhetoric is backed by consistent action along both the legal and political dimensions, then perhaps reformers are more likely to demonstrate their good faith about democratic politics as well as their deep commitment to the vision they seek to have embodied in law. At least in the Kentucky case, it seems, just this sort of good faith and commitment had persuasive power in politics. No one objected to judicially mandated reform on legitimacy grounds. Moreover, no one had any occasion to worry about judicial capacity because reformers' democratic efforts meant that the courts never had to take any remedial plunge.

Reformers' common school vision and democratic political mobilization framed the politics of school reform in Kentucky and brought about sweeping policy changes that few would have thought possible, given the degree of hostility toward government and taxation in the state's political culture.

Nothing in this discussion so far speaks directly to the issue of reformers' consciousness about these matters or to the question whether and in what sense they made choices about them. In the Kentucky case, two separate groups worked for a time on independent projects. Even after they formed an alliance in 1987, it seems that more was done through intuitions and practical judgments about what would work and much less through overall planning or conscious design than my constructed narrative account might imply. Whatever one concludes from these materials about actual consciousness, I think it fair to say that the Kentucky effort is what culturalism in practice might look like. In the Kentucky case, those who pursued litigation shared a sense that the law had to speak a certain language and that that same vision had to animate political argument and action in other forums.

There are, it should be noted here, two important and analytically distinct alternative explanations for Kentucky's surprising landmark education reform law.[45] Each of these alternative explanations is relevant not only for understanding the Kentucky case, but also for its implications for the broader contrasts I have drawn between Kentucky and New Jersey. First, in Kentucky, the education and school finance system was so archaic that modernization in some form had to take place. As a result, no one had much of a stake in defending the status quo. That was not true of the New Jersey system. Second, in Kentucky the perceived beneficiaries of reform were poor white children, whereas in New Jersey the perceived beneficiaries were poor minority children. Race, one might say, makes all the difference. These potential objections to a heroic portrayal of the Kentucky reformers' efforts as a great success story or, as in much policy literature, a "miracle," have considerable force.

Nevertheless, under an interpretive approach, we must also acknowledge that the analytically distinct are in reality entangled. In understanding the Kentucky case, there is no good way to separate the causal influence of the particular local context and the racial identity of beneficiaries, on one side, and the reformers' and their impressive, ideologically coherent forms of legal and political mobilization, on the other side. Notwithstanding the important contextual factors conducive to change, I think we can say that the Kentucky reformers had obstacles enough to overcome. It is not necessary to reckon up the precise role of all the factors at work in the production of sweeping reform in order to maintain that legal and political mobilization, properly understood, played a significant part.[46]

In the conclusion, I shall return to each of these alternative considerations as each relates to the contrasts between Kentucky and New Jersey.

PART IV

CONCLUSION

CONCLUSION

LEGAL TRANSLATION

Michael Katz once wrote that "[h]istorians and other social scientists who offer interpretive accounts of social issues always face a 'last chapter' problem." Readers expect them to offer "clear lessons" and "unambiguous recommendations." However, interpretive accounts, with their emphasis on context, complexity, and contingency, inevitably disappoint these expectations.[1] Rather than offering sharp hypotheses and causal arguments, interpretive accounts often bank on the dynamic interaction between loosely specified "frameworks" and close empirical investigation.

This study began with a theoretical framework about legal mobilization and the politics of reform in the United States. To some well-established propositions and conceptual tools, I added a particular focus on legal translation—what it is, how it actually gets done, and why it matters. Understanding legal translation and its significance, I have argued, requires attending not only to myriad contexts for social action—for example, the historical evolution of legal norms and institutions in particular jurisdictions, or local geographies of power, or cultural traditions—but also to the ideological starting points from which the "carrying over" proceeds. It requires an attempt to understand the thinking of actors at a given time in a given place and an attempt to handle the ethereal stuff of ideologies and discourses.

Out of the many factors impinging on the process of legal translation, I have highlighted two ideological ones as particularly salient and useful for purposes of analysis. Would-be change agents will have, first, an ideological orientation toward their cause, and, second, an ideological orientation toward law, politics, and change. Both of these orientations shape the contours and processes of legal translation. Legal translation should be viewed as a practical activity at the core of legal mobilization, which is in turn a broader process requiring material resources and, often, at least some measure of judicial support. As a consequence of their legal ideologies, actors may embrace different ideas about the lawyer–client relationship, different ideas about combining litigation with other forms of political organizing and action, and different ideas about what courts can and cannot do for them.

Legal translation matters, for speaking one way rather than another within law is likely to have significant political implications. For example, as we have seen, the specific content and connotations of a legal claim may help mobilize some people, neutralize others, and countermobilize still others (or it may have some specific combination of these three effects). Particular legal claims present courts with opportunities for decision and often shape the content of judicial opinions. In turn, judicial opinions can play a powerful role in shaping and defining the language of public debate and the agenda of contention in politics. In short, legal translation matters because law can and often does frame politics. Law certainly framed politics in just these ways in the New Jersey and Kentucky school finance conflicts.

TWO WORLDS OF SCHOOL FINANCE REFORM

The New Jersey and Kentucky reform projects arose out of different soil and pursued quite different visions of education. In both cases, reform lawyers and their compatriots were determined to frame legal challenges that reflected their respective substantive visions. In neither case was the process of legal translation regarded by them as easy, automatic, or mechanical. In both cases, the state's highest court eventually embraced reformers' vision as state constitutional law. In both cases, the content of legal claims and their projection and amplification in court played a large role in framing the language of public debate, defining interests, and shaping policy processes and outcomes.

In New Jersey in the early 1970s, Professor Tractenberg studied the Coons team's legal theory of wealth neutrality and found it wanting in light of his compensatory vision of schooling and social justice. In response, he found legal materials to craft a novel legal theory about a state constitutional right to "the best possible" education. In the *Robinson* cases, reformers did not get everything they wanted from the courts, and they got even less of what they wanted from politics. Still, *Robinson* left a rich legacy of legal norms, and it had other important feedback effects. Indeed, the establishment of the ELC itself was in part of result of the school finance reform litigation.

We saw that Marilyn Morheuser and her colleagues thought long and hard about their next legal challenge before opting for a risky fact-driven approach to remaking the law so that it would reflect their vision. As *Abbott v. Burke* worked its way through the courts under the guiding light of compensatory justice, *Robinson's* endorsement of "minimum adequacy" was transformed into *Abbott's* insistence on taking "relative needs" into account.

In Kentucky, what began as a *Serrano* suit about the equalization of relative tax capacities quickly became infused with common school themes and rhetoric. Former Governor Combs, Kern Alexander, and several other Kentucky reformers shared a sense that their case in court should reinforce their vision of education. We charted the dropping out of wealth neutrality as the Council's litigation proceeded through trial and appellate decision. In the end, the case was transformed from one about just school finance into one about education writ large. As in New Jersey, "law" proved to be quite a malleable resource for claims making. In Kentucky, legal norms were not so much reconfigured as suddenly invented through the infusion of common school political rhetoric and policy discourse.

Although the two cases are similar in that in each law framed politics according to reformers' respective educational ideologies, they diverge when it comes to reformers' respective ideological orientations toward law, politics, and change.

The New Jersey reformers embraced legalism until after their victory in *Abbott II* and the rise of a powerful backlash that threatened to overturn it. Right through 1992, they relied exclusively on law and courts, happily opted for phantom clients, and carefully prevented other advocacy groups from having anything to say about the substance of their litigation. Thus, they passed up possible opportunities to mobilize constituents and to form alliances. They believed that everything hinged on winning the right kind of court ruling and seemed to believe that judicial edicts were moral imperatives that everyone else would (or at least should) follow. Moreover, to protect their chances in court, they evaded rather than confronted questions about administrative capacities and political corruption in poorer urban school districts. In other words, they made a strategic choice not to talk about something at the very core of their struggle for better education for disadvantaged children. Given their litigation-related reasons for this evasion and eventual success in winning vast material resources, it is hard to second-guess them on this strategic evasion. However, we can say that their evasion left it to others to define and discuss administrative competence (with the implication that more money would just be wasted) and, perhaps left some genuine problems festering for many years.[2]

Although I have suggested that the New Jersey reformers probably should have taken the risk of greater engagement in politics, and that they probably should have confronted rather than evaded administrative problems in the urban districts, one could still plausibly conclude that they made wise strategic choices. One could conclude that broader political efforts and more honesty were either not feasible or inadvisable, and that court victories really did have to come first in order to create the conditions for a broader politics of reform in the 1990s and into this century.

Thus, the New Jersey reformers embraced legalism, but it is not quite right to say that they were captured or captivated by it. Rather, it makes more sense to say that legalism was for them a general lens refracting what in many instances were eyes-open strategic calculations and choices. After *Abbott II*, political realities quickly brought the ELC network around to a more realistic approach. From then on, litigation proceeded hand-in-hand with a constantly shifting series of alliances, deals, and tacit political collaborations with other actors. Law was still their central weapon, but now the arena was all of politics. They won vast resources for the most disadvantaged children, along with a modestly promising array of compensatory programs.

In Kentucky, reformers' thinking about law, politics, and change was always self-consciously realistic. Broader political efforts preceded and then ran hand-in-hand with litigation. Both the plaintiff group of school districts and the Prichard Committee engaged in lobbying for about two years before the litigation was filed. Moreover, the Council's leaders treated the litigation process itself as political one. Here, there were flesh-and-blood clients (mainly school district superintendents and board members) situated in organizational milieus. They held a direct political and financial stake in the litigation, and they played a role in shaping its content.

In the Kentucky case, it was not just the combination of political with legal activities that mattered but also the fact that, in everything they said and did, reformers projected the same ideological vision of education reform. Although they were self-consciously realistic about law and politics, in effect what they actually did offers us a good model of what it would mean to take a culturalist approach to law, politics, and change. They sought to spark democratic political mobilization, left no institutional channel for politics untouched, and marched everywhere under the same banner of the common school. What they sought to do, in short, was to remake the state's entire political culture with respect to education. To a large extent, they succeeded.

Although my focus has not been on courts as such, the comparative analysis of two litigation-centered reform efforts does leave us with some observations and questions to ponder about the role of the judiciary. The differences in the content and nature of the judicial interventions in these two cases should not lead us to overlook an important commonality. Both cases vindicate the idea that, in the United States, courts are often vital, and not merely incidental, forums for the articulation, development, and projection of novel moral and political claims. While we might agree with Gerald Rosenberg when he argues that courts acting alone are weak agents of change, we must immediately add that legal mobilization can play a big part in fostering political support in the first place and in defining a favorable context for impact.[3]

Finally, the two case studies present stark differences with respect to judicial remedies and forms of judicial intervention. In New Jersey, reformers made sociological arguments well tailored to their state's particular legal history and culture. Moreover, they consistently asked the courts to provide the kind of specific policy mandates and administrative oversight that would be unthinkable in many other state systems. Professor Tractenberg asked the *Robinson I* court to require that other state officials provide all children with "the best possible education," defined as some (as yet unspecified) outcomes. Although perhaps not with an entirely straight face, Marilyn Morheuser asked the *Abbott II* court to require other state officials to fund all districts at the level of the highest spending districts—in one of the highest-spending states in the nation.

Although the New Jersey high court never went quite as far or quite as fast as the reformers wished, it often went quite far and fast indeed. In *Robinson IV*, the court threatened to reallocate state school aid itself, if the other branches failed to act; after *Robinson V*, it actually ordered the schools closed for nine days in July. In *Abbott II*, facing a tough remedy problem, the court crafted its own set of funding rules just for the poor urban districts. In *Abbott IV*, frustrated with the slow pace of compliance, the court plunged into overseeing the design and implementation of compensatory urban education policies. It has been an active policy maker and administrative overseer in urban education ever since.

In Kentucky, by contrast, reformers never sought to have the courts impose specific education policies or to take on the role of administrators. Sexton and his Prichard Committee colleagues were uninterested in litigation until after the legislative route to their goals failed not once but twice. Within the litigation, even when judges seemed to be inviting policy proposals, as Judge Corns did with his "Select Committee," reformers self-consciously refrained from offering any. Their reluctance to urge the courts to make policy, it seems, stemmed not from any pure, high-minded love for majoritarian democracy, but rather from their strategic calculations. As they perceived politics in their state, stronger judicial policy interventions would be widely perceived as illegitimate.

In the end, the high court's opinion in *Counsel for Better Education* offered nothing in the way of policy rules or mandates. There was nothing particularly binding there, even in the way or broad principles. Indeed, once we place the decision in its political context, the pretense of "bold judicial activism" melts away. The court's decision was in reality highly deferential to legislative authority. It thus represented a newer, softer, more collaborative form of judicial participation in the policy process.[4]

SOME COMPETING CONSIDERATIONS

In viewing the contrasts I have drawn between the New Jersey and Kentucky reform efforts, it might be said that I have given too little explanatory weight to structural conditions and constraints and too much to individual agency and choice. In Kentucky, the school finance and education systems were simply archaic, giving many elites a strong material interest in some form of change and leaving virtually no one with a strong interest in defending the status quo. In New Jersey, by contrast, the existing system worked very well for many very well-off people. Moreover, to overplay agency and choice in these two cases is to badly underplay the centrality of race and racism in American politics and policy. In New Jersey, no effort to bring about changes in education benefiting the have-nots could possibly avoid the terrain of racialized conflict, and therefore no effort could avoid running the risk of reinforcing race/class divisions. In Kentucky, by contrast, questions about poverty and equal educational opportunity were not racialized because virtually all minority children lived in two large, urban, and decidedly property-wealthy school districts. On this view, it is quite possible to see both legal framing and political mobilization as derivative phenomena, easily explained by broader structural conditions and constraints.[5]

I do not mean to deny the importance of these basic social facts about the respective finance systems and the contours of race and poverty in the two states. They surely did shape and constrain the range of plausible arguments and actions. However, the important questions concern the range of choices actors had about legal frames and political strategies, the choices they in fact made, and the difference it made that they chose one way rather than another. The issue of alternative, plausible courses of action might be pursued in two ways. First, we can ask the perfectly empirical question of what choices the particular actors in these cases in fact considered and made, taking their values and goals as given. Second, we can go on to ask about a broader range of choices that some hypothetical group of reformers might have, but that the actual reformers did not consider, given roughly similar values and goals.

The Kentucky reformers seemed to have had a wider range of options, compared to the New Jersey reformers. The structural conditions in the state were far more conducive to a relatively smooth, and perhaps even sweeping, reform process. Those conditions also made the common school frame both more likely to arise and more likely to gain acceptance. However, the "educational adequacy" argument, with adequacy rendered in common school terms, was far from inevitable. The many discussions of the Kentucky litigation and reform law have overlooked the internal transformation of the litigation, from its initial conception as a *Serrano* case (with all of the virtues and defects of wealth neutrality as a legal theory) to the broadly framed common school argument. Although there was no one decision point that marked this transformation, the actors involved were highly concerned about questions of leveling, Robin Hood, and the proper role of courts. The *Serrano* path was ready made and well lit, but the Kentucky reformers took a different route.

Moreover, for some hypothetical group of Kentucky reformers, it would have made perfect sense to see and talk about poor white children in Appalachia in precisely the same way that the New Jersey reformers saw and talked about poor minority children in the New Jersey ghettos. Appalachia was, after all, one of the birthplaces of culture of poverty and compensatory arguments in the early 1960s. It would have been plausible to highlight the uniquely severe deprivations of rural poverty and the special educational need arising from them. Interestingly, I found no evidence that the actual Kentucky reformers ever considered such a frame.[6]

In New Jersey, structural constraints loomed larger. It is true that no effort on behalf of the have-nots could have avoided the treacherous political and cultural terrain of racialized poverty; surely, the interest of the urban minority poor would have to be a large part of any such effort, and surely better off communities would not easily accept policy changes. Still, the New Jersey reformers contemplated and made many important choices. The New Jersey high court's opinion in *Robinson I* was largely a result of one such choice about legal framing, and that opinion had profound and long-lasting effects on subsequent politics and policy. In framing *Abbott*, Morheuser and her colleagues explicitly considered two other kinds of legal challenges, aside from the one they actually pursued. One of these rejected alternatives was a traditional school finance case focused on tax burdens, expenditures per pupil, and the entire distribution of school districts. Such a traditional case might have been supported through a political coalition of poor and working-class districts qua districts. Such a coalition might have bridged the sharp race and class divides in the state. This alternative effort would face hard going in New Jersey, but the notion is not absurd.[7]

While we cannot really know about roads not taken, we do know that the New Jersey reformers viewed themselves as the champions of the urban minority poor and viewed the courts as their oasis. Their values and goals shaped their thinking, choices, and actions. Their compensatory legal frame was not inevitable, and it mattered quite a bit in its own right. For example, when Governor Florio and his advisors crafted a reform law that sought to channel educational resources to broader swatch of the have-nots via universal policy categories, and thus to channel fewer resources to the minority poor than reformers desired, the effort was widely understood through the lens of reformers' (and the courts') compensatory frame. The frame did explicitly reference, confront, and reinforce racial divisions, of course. Whether that is a good or bad thing depends mostly on one's political perspective.

SCHOOL FINANCE REFORM LITIGATION AND RESEARCH

The New Jersey and Kentucky school finance cases are but two of tens of ongoing conflicts nationwide. Decades of litigation have given rise to vast and varied bodies of scholarship on this topic, from normative and conceptual law review writing, to studies of judicial decision making and impact, to technical policy analysis and evaluation. Although I have drawn on some of this work, it has not been my purpose to join in on these policy-domain specific conversations. However, at this point, it does make sense to ask about what a focus on legal mobilization and legal translation has to offer to scholars doing law and policy research on school finance litigation.[8] I discern three broad strands of current research that might benefit from putting legal mobilization and translation on their radar screens.

The first and most common kind of work has been done by law professors and typically appears in law reviews and edited volumes. What stands out most in this type of work is the conceptual distinction between "equity" and "adequacy" cases, and what is made of it. Equity and adequacy cases are said to be *the* "competing paradigms" in school finance challenges and court decisions.[9] As Minorini and Sugarman put it, "equity cases are about getting worse treatment than someone else," whereas "adequacy cases are about getting worse treatment than one is entitled to with reference to some absolute standard."[10] Much law review writing goes on to personify these abstract, conceptual notions of equity and adequacy. Once brought to life, the two competitors are then made to square off against each other as if they were parties on opposite sides of a lawsuit.[11]

The personification of concepts tends to work an erasure of the actual persons, organizations, and ideologies driving reform struggles. They become simply, generically, and interchangeably "plaintiffs," "advocates," and "reform lawyers." Reading these pieces, one is reminded of John T. Noonan's celebrated discussions of "persons" and "masks" of the law, and his call for recognition of the ethical significance of the "stripping" and "skeletonization" of conflict in much legal thought and judicial opinion writing.[12]

A focus on legal mobilization and legal translation demonstrates that there is a good deal more to equity and adequacy than these conceptual discussions allow. Equity and adequacy take on specific meanings in light of broader educational visions and differently conceived political projects. Meanings can and do shift over time, as would-be change agents learn from their efforts and as courts and other actors react to them. In New Jersey, a minimum adequacy frame after *Robinson* became the nation's premier example of an attempt to take on relative inequalities. In Kentucky, what began as an equity suit a la *Serrano* soon became the nation's premier adequacy suit. In both cases, equity and adequacy depended on the location of distributional and other educational policy questions within broader ideological frames about education and inequality.

A second and more diverse strand of work on school finance litigation seeks to explain judicial decision making and/or impact. Here, scholars have naturally treated state-by-state litigation across the nation as a quasi-laboratory for social scientific research. Why is it that some courts intervene, while others stay out? When courts do intervene, does it make any real difference? If so, how and why?

On the first question about the determinants (or correlates) of favorable court decisions, researchers have investigated a large number of variables: Is it something about a given state's constitutional texts or the intentions of constitutional framers?; or the type of legal argument advanced by plaintiffs (equity or adequacy)?; or the distributional features of the finance systems under attack?; or the racial identity of plaintiffs or plaintiff-districts?; or the nature of reform coalitions?; or the method of selecting state judges?; or the judges' role orientations or policy preferences? From the standpoint of political science, the central findings of this research are not surprising. Framers' intentions and constitutional texts seem to have little to do with judicial outcomes, and the values and policy preferences of judges seem to matter a lot. The role of race and racial identity seems more controversial and not well understood.[13]

On the second and third questions—when courts intervene, does it matter and, if so, how and why?—several researchers have compared school finance outcomes in states with decisions finding constitutional violations to such outcomes in states in which courts declined to intervene. Some scholars explicitly cast this research as an examination of Gerald Rosenberg's thesis that courts generally lack the power to produce social change.[14] Two careful studies show positive financial consequences from judicial interventions and thereby call into question Rosenberg's more sweeping claims about judicial weakness. Murray, Evans, and Schwab used econometric modeling to show that favorable court decisions correlate with both increased state spending for education and the equalization of educational resources within states.[15] Similarly, Doug Reed's *On Equal Terms* includes an empirical analysis of school finance outcomes in eight states, five with interventionist court decisions and three in which courts rejected challenges. He too concluded that Rosenberg underestimated the ability of court's to shift policy outcomes.[16]

While these studies of judicial decision making and impact are often useful for gaining a more panoramic view of school finance litigation, as a general matter they have neglected legal mobilization and legal translation as significant factors or variables. Some important work in political science has shown how the study of legal mobilization and support structures can explain not only the fate of reform struggles but also judicial responses to legal challenges and/or the impact of judicial participation in policy processes.[17] The present study adds a focus on reform ideologies and legal translation processes to the mix of social scientific research on school finance litigation. Although the focus has not been on courts per se, it is reasonably clear that, once we understand the mobilization of the law in the New Jersey and Kentucky cases, we can understand much about judicial behavior and impact that would be otherwise inexplicable. Legal mobilization and translation are important explanatory factors.

The third strand of work on school finance litigation consists of recent neoconservative attacks on it.[18] While their specific questions and analyses vary, what binds these neoconservatives together is their commitment to two central claims. First, they argue, the key policy remedy for what ails public education is the introduction of markets or marketlike mechanisms. Research has failed to reveal much of a connection, if any, between increased spending and gains in student achievement. Gains in student achievement, which must be rendered in measurable terms (mainly test scores), are the central goal of education. Under current bureaucratic arrangements, spending more money is likely to be either to be futile or perverse.[19]

Second, this view holds, courts are politically illegitimate and institutionally incompetent actors in school finance policy, compared to the other branches of government. Neither the intentions of state constitutional framers nor state constitutional provisions provide a sound basis for judicial forays into school finance policy. School finance cases are "essentially political rather than legal events" in which "self-interested actors" (teachers unions, bureaucrats, elite liberal reformers, and the foundations backing them) engage in a quest for more and more educational spending. When they win, they turn "classroom failure into courtroom success."[20]

Moreover, "educational adequacy" is a hopelessly vague idea. It has no discernable meaning in the decided cases because "[d]efining a generality with more generalities does not make a generality more precise." No case yet yields "judicially manageable standards." When the courts intervene, they act as naked power organs. Indeed, judicial interventions pose a serious threat to "the traditional constitutional order" and the "core institutions of democratic governance." Judicial legitimacy will decline, thereby impeding the ability of courts to do what they should be doing.[21]

Taken as a whole, the neoconservative view offers important insights and much food for thought. Everyone agrees that there is no easy and unproblematic linkage between increased spending and better educational outcomes, whatever the ideologically laden vision of "better outcomes" might be. Analyses of policy design and bureaucratic incentive structures encourage everyone to think more seriously about the political and organizational changes that might be needed to make money matter more. In addition, as I have argued, legal and court processes are best viewed primarily in political terms. The courts are not some otherworldly realm of reasoned deliberation and wisdom set apart from the inevitable clash of ideologies and interests.

At the same time, a focus on legal mobilization and translation allows us to raise some questions about the neoconservative critique. For one thing, it counsels considerable skepticism about the neoconservatives' wholly skeptical view of law, politics, and courts. From the standpoint of legal mobilization theory, their view is theoretically naïve and empirically undefended. Moreover, it does prodigious rhetorical work for them in their public advocacy for their own vision and strongly desired policy changes, and against more school spending under the banner of other agendas.

The neoconservatives cast reformers as liberal elites and self-interested bureaucrats *invariably* engaged in an antidemocratic end run around normal democratic processes. Their tone and eye for detail tell us that something rather nefarious is going on. The judges, in turn, are cast as well-meaning generalists easily duped by reformers' sob stories.[22]

It is true that many perceive judicial interventions in social policy conflicts as illegitimate intrusions on the democratic process. However, as political scientists and even a few constitutional theorists have long argued, the judiciary can just as easily (and almost as plausibly) be viewed simply as an additional channel for democratic politics in a complex constitutional democracy. After the rise of the modern administrative state, the judiciary has in fact often been a place for minority interests or viewpoints to go when they have no place else to go. That the courthouse doors are open may well enhance rather than detract from the functionality of complex system of democratic representation. In addition, both the substance and rippling consequences of judicial decisions may be democracy enhancing as well.[23]

When it comes to nature and capacities of courts, as compared to other governmental institutions, the neoconservatives make the old mistake of comparing, on the one hand, the messy realities of litigation and judicially managed policy reform with, on the other hand, abstract and idealized assertions about "normal" democratic politics and policy making. Indeed, their accounts of the separation of powers and democratic governance often read like they come right out of high school civics textbooks. Perhaps they have not noticed that in the modern administrative state each branch of government routinely performs some tasks and functions traditionally thought to be at the core of all of the others. Comparative institutional analysis can be quite valuable, of course, but only if a given institution's actual processes and performances are compared with other institutions' actual processes and performances.[24] Prior to judicial interventions in New Jersey and Kentucky, the normal, wholesome democratic process does not come off looking all that good.

Indeed, for empiricists, the neoconservative critics can be strangely impervious to certain empirical questions. We should remember that the claim that a given set of reformers who turn to the courts are involved in a cynical end-run around the democratic process is in large part an empirical claim. It may be true, as it arguably was of the New Jersey reformers until the early 1990s. Or it may be false, as it was of the Kentucky reformers. Or, one imagines, the truth might lie somewhere in between. But the claim is not true by definition. We should also remember that the question as to whether an observer and actors in the world have the same values and goals is an empirical one. However, the neoconservatives often assume that everyone subscribes to their ideological position about education's goals and valued outcomes, and that therefore the only policy questions are technical ones about how to get from here to (a supposedly agreed on) there. It is then much easier to cast finance reformers in the role of self-interested actors who are in bad faith, as opposed to being people who happen to disagree with them on normative grounds about education.[25]

LEGAL TRANSLATION AND LEGAL MOBILIZATION THEORY: FINAL THOUGHTS

Unlike legal and policy scholars who study school finance litigation, students of legal mobilization in reform conflicts and/or social movements have long understood that legal norms and institutions coexist in complex, interdependent relationships with politics and culture. Starting with Scheingold's *The Politics of Rights*, much inquiry has proceeded under the steam of a realist approach to law and politics. Many political scientists and sociolegal scholars have explicated the distortions and myths of legalism and highlighted the potential utility of rights claiming and litigation as ancillary tactics in broader struggles. Over the past generation, scholars have embraced a culturalist reconceptualization of law and how it can matter in social reform conflicts. They have often connected this reconceptualization of law to broader theorizing about social movements or reform struggles.

My argument has been that legal translation matters a great deal in broader processes of legal and political mobilization. It has not been that legal translation is all that matters. Much else, such as the particular array of organizations seeking change, the broader distribution of material resources and social capital, and the particular features of specific times, places, and institutions, obviously matters too. Nothing follows inexorably from legal framing choices, or from ideologically consistent reformist arguments and actions across legal and political settings, or from official endorsement of particular legal frames.

A legal claim that is not much believed in or cared about for its substance may provide reform groups with the strategic leverage needed to carry on their real fight elsewhere. In addition, the confrontational quality of legal challenges in an adversary system—the simple fact of standing up to those in power—may be symbolically important for a movement, quite apart from the content of the claim. Finally, in some instances, closed courthouse doors may induce advocates to explore new modes of organization and action in politics.[26]

My implicit theoretical claim has been that legal translation choices and processes could be better understood and more fruitfully investigated. Toward that end, I have offered one possible framework for understanding and investigating legal translation and how it matters. This framework should be of interest to a range of scholars studying reform litigation, cause lawyering, and law and social movements.

In the language of social movement scholars, legal framing options and choices within legal doctrines and court processes should be conceptualized as a species of political opportunity. The range of possible framing options is likely to vary from conflict to conflict, time to time, place to place, and policy area to policy area. In some contemporary and ongoing struggles, observers and activists alike have engaged in vigorous debates over the legalization of grievances and disputes generally, and over the particular virtues and defects of alternative possible legal frames. Struggles for women's rights, and particularly for abortion rights and reproductive freedom, and struggles for gay rights, and particularly for the right to gay marriage, come readily to mind.[27] In other reformist efforts—for example, the denser and more difficult terrain of "institutional reform litigation," the translation and framing questions seem seldom to get asked.[28] In either case, what the present study urges is (1) a rethinking of legal framing inquiries in terms of the translation of ideologies, both substantive and legal; and (2) attention to the resulting *ideological* articulation (or resonance or dissonance) of legal frames with a broader set of reform or social movement activities. This ideological articulation concerns not only the meaning of legal claims and strategies within reform or movement organizations but also the interplay of legal discourses with broader cultural logics that maintain or challenge the status quo.[29]

The approach taken in this book also implicitly endorses the importance of more mindfulness about certain boundary tensions. One conceptual distinction I have been concerned to maintain involves the separation of change agents' values and goals, on one hand, and their strategic thinking and choices, on the other. What movement groups or reformers are trying to accomplish is one thing, and how they think that they can best get from here to there is another. These two modes of thought and action often run together in practice, and they can and do shift over time. Nevertheless, the conceptual distinction not only enhances clarity about analytically distinct questions, it also reminds the researcher to be careful about substituting her or his own values and goals for those of agents in the world.

Another related conceptual distinction implicit in the present study involves the divide between observer and observed and, particularly, ideological conceptions of law, politics and change held on both sides of this divide. Since the early 1970s, much inquiry into law, politics, and social change has evidenced a practical intention flowing out of observers' sympathy with radical or liberal reform goals. Often, observers and critics study such efforts with the hope that research might inform practice. This posture requires and has yielded much sympathetic observation—for example, understanding social action in consideration of the actors' own values and understandings—and also much criticism. There must be some ground or standpoint from which to apprehend and to criticize.

A broad view of the historical development of legal mobilization and cause lawyering research reveals a historical trajectory of sorts in the perspectives of these observer/critics, moving from legalism to realism, and then from realism to culturalism. From the early 1970s on, observers grounded their criticisms of legalistic reform practice in a political frame of reference informed centrally by legal realism. More recent culturalist analyses accept much of the realist frame— e.g., judges routinely engage in value choices and policy making—but add a focus on law's content and discursive and cultural power. Interestingly, culturalist research has uncovered a good deal of legal realism in the thinking and practice of many would-be change agents. These change agents seem to understand the limits of legalism. Their projects might still fail, of course, for various reasons, but pure legalism seems increasingly to be a thing of the past.[30]

When they have found this realism-in-action, culturalist observer/critics have characterized it as a sophisticated or savvy advance over legalism. A culturalist approach with a focus on legal translation presents the possibility of taking the next step in this historical trajectory of development between observer-critics who study law, politics, and reform, on one hand, and would-be change agents who contemplate the role of law and courts in their efforts, on the other. This next step would entail explicitly thinking about the culturalist legal mobilization perspective as an observer standpoint for critical evaluations of realist-informed practices in the world. In other words, culturalism might play the same role in relation to realism that realism has historically played in relation to legalism.

What, then, would culturalism mean if it were brought to bear in critical evaluations of realist-informed practice? This general question only yields more specific questions. Given that would-be change agents often understand that legal tactics work best as ancillary ones in broader political efforts, are they also mindful of the potential power of competing legal discourses? How do they actually understand their legal framing options? What choices do they make about legal framing, and why? Might they have thought differently about legal discourses and legal framing, in the context of their goals, resources, and other strategies and tactics? When a social movement can be said to be in existence, how do the various organizations and projects occupying the field think about the division of labor within the movement and the determination of some formations to resort to legal strategies and tactics?

The predominant view of law and politics among movement and reformist actors in the United States today seems to be realistic. Political projects viewing law realistically, or instrumentally, may often reach for some readymade legal tools. That might make sense in the context of a given larger battle, or it might not.

In both the New Jersey and Kentucky cases, we saw how actors resisted picking up the readymade tools (the existing or obvious legal theories) in order to make the substance of their legal claims reflect their substantive ideological visions. They creatively mobilized the law and ultimately succeeded in changing minds and policies about education and inequality.

ACKNOWLEDGMENTS

IT HAS TAKEN ME AN UNUSUALLY LONG TIME TO COMPLETE this book. It is therefore a great pleasure, finally, to have the opportunity to thank some of the people and institutions that have helped me along the way, even if many debts will have to go unmentioned. I hope those left out will forgive me.

I thank the Spencer Foundation in Chicago for supporting this project not once but twice, and for introducing me to the world of educational research. I thank R. Shep Melnick, my mentor and dissertation advisor at Brandeis, for his intellectual guidance. I have been fortunate to teach at several wonderful institutions over the course of my academic career. I thank my former colleagues in the Department of Political Science at Rutgers-New Brunswick (faculty and graduate students alike), especially Susan Lawrence and Milton Heumann. Milt and Susan gave me much support and, by their example, much inspiration. I thank my former colleagues in the Department of Political Science at the City College of New York for their good cheer and decency, and also my new colleagues and friends in the Department of Political Science, Economics and Philosophy at the College of Staten Island, for creating an intellectual environment that is both serious and warm.

I thank the following people in the law and society community for useful feedback on my work and/or advice and support: Rose Corrigan, Charles Epp, Howard Erlanger, Beth Harris, Michael McCann, Brian Pinaire, Doug Reed, Stuart Scheingold, Larry Solan, and Amy Ruth Tobol. Over many years, Michael McCann was incredibly generous with his time, encouragement, and critical insights. More recently, Stuart Scheingold provided helpful comments and some much-needed, honest advice. As reviewers for Stanford University Press, Doug Reed and Malcolm Feeley offered valuable comments and criticisms. Two old friends, Kevin McMahon and Elizabeth Bussiere, each read significant portions of the manuscript and also provided valuable feedback. In addition, both Kevin and Liz have taught me much about the true meaning of academic integrity.

I also thank my many students whose zest for life, love of learning, and understanding of the concept of solidarity, gave me something to believe in; thanks especially to Brandon Bolin, Lisa Gonzalo, Seth Shelton, Tamara Toles, and Joblin Younger. I also thank M. Adrienne Jones, a teacher and kindred spirit at City College, for her friendship and ready supply of "positive energy."

Many reformers studied in this book were generous with their time, assistance and insights. In New Jersey, I would particularly like to thank Steve Block, Herb Green, Ernest Reock, and Paul Tractenberg. Professor Tractenberg read an earlier version of the manuscript and provided useful comments. In Kentucky, I would particularly like to thank Debra Dawahare of the law firm of Wyatt, Tarrant, and Combs, and Robert Sexton and Cindy Heine of the Prichard Committee for Academic Excellence. They provided access to documents, many thoughtful observations, and a glimpse of what Kentucky charm means.

I owe a special debt of gratitude to Julia Burch, editor and writing coach extraordinaire, for her hard work, bulldozing critiques, and incredible kindness. Without Julie's help, I would not have been able to finish this book. I also thank Kate Wahl at Stanford University Press for great suggestions that improved the manuscript and Margaret Pinette for painstaking copyediting.

I acknowledge the struggles and sacrifices of my late parents, Jack and Kay Paris, and I thank my six siblings, Jim, Frank, David, Tom, Cathy, and Mary, and their spouses and many children, for the constant and quiet goodness that marks our family. I thank Bernice and Richard Higer, Nancy Higer and Matt

Sakkas, and Bruce Higer for welcoming me into their family with open arms and for providing constant love and support. And, finally, I thank Amy Higer and our two delightful children, Teddy and Anna Higer-Paris. Best friend, wonderful mother, ardent comrade, committed teacher—day in and day out—Amy makes my world a beautiful place. I dedicate this book to her.

ABBREVIATIONS USED IN NOTES

CJ	*Louisville Courier-Journal*
EW	*Education Week*
HL	*Lexington Herald-Leader*
NYT	*New York Times*
SL	*Newark Star-Ledger*

NOTES

NOTES TO INTRODUCTION

1. Kozol (1991).

2. To ask these questions is not to answer them, of course. School finance policy questions are complicated, and current arrangements have been defended on a variety of grounds. I provide a review of the normative and empirical policy debates in Chapter Three.

3. For overviews of school finance reform litigation, see West and Peterson (2007). An appendix in West and Peterson provides a comprehensive review of litigation through 2005. See also Hanushek (2006); Koski and Reich (2006); Koski (2004); McUsic (1999, 2004); Hochschild and Scovronick (2003); Schrag (2003); Heise and Ryan (2002); Reed (2001), Ladd and Hansen (1999); Ladd, Chalk, and Hansen (1999); Ryan (1999a,b); Gittell (1998); and Enrich (1995). The best single source of current state-by-state information is the website of the Advocacy Center for Children's Educational Success with Standards (ACCESS), maintained by New York State's Campaign for Fiscal Equity and Teacher's College: www.schoolfunding.info. ACCESS reports that, between 1989 and 2007, plaintiffs won final court victories in no fewer than twenty states, while defendants won such victories in eleven states.

4. My conception of ideology is liberal and nonpejorative. An ideology is simply a set of culturally conditioned beliefs, "a symbolic framework in terms of which to formulate, think about, and react to political problems . . ." (Scheingold 2004: 14, quoting Geertz). Here, ideology runs back to individuals, albeit individuals situated in social milieus. It is simply a specific set of values, beliefs, and preferences, held by some specified social actors, about something in particular. Ideology in this sense is an inevitable fact of life for all human beings—it is the natural result of our "emotion-laden and partial response to the world and to others in it," and it gives "any thinking person a sense of direction" (Shklar 1986: 4). Social actors may be more or less aware, or unaware, of what the observer interprets to be their ideological orientation. My use of the term *ideology* also signals that I

seek to examine ideas and beliefs that are "rough and ready" for action in politics and not highly elaborated or formally defended. For a brief discussion of the essentially contested concept of ideology, see Eagleton (1991). Below, in separating out two senses of ideology (substantive and legal), I draw on Milner (1986).

5. In January 2008, the New Jersey Legislature passed and Democratic Governor John Corzine signed new school finance measure called the School Finance Reform Act (SFRA). This law established a new statewide weighted school funding formula. The governor then moved the New Jersey Supreme Court for an order terminating the *Abbott* remedies of parity and supplemental funding for the poorer urban districts. The state argued that these *Abbott* remedies were no longer needed because the new formula provided enhanced funding for all districts with large numbers of poor and limited-English-proficiency students. In May 2009, the New Jersey high court upheld the new finance law and ended the Abbott parity and supplemental funding remedies. I provide a more detailed summary of these recent developments and what they might mean in Chapter Five.

6. For an account of the national "educational adequacy movement" that places the Kentucky experience at its center, see Schrag (2003, especially Chapter 2).

7. See, for example, Scheingold (1974, 2004), Milner (1986), McCann (1994), Silverstein (1996), Harris (1998), Schultz (1998), and Schneider (2000). This research tradition also encompasses a growing body of work on "cause lawyering." See Sarat and Scheingold (1998, 2001, 2004, 2006) and Hilbink (2004). Related inquiries on law and social reform include Handler (1978), Olson (1984), Lawrence (1990), Rosenberg (1991), and Epp (1998).

NOTES TO CHAPTER ONE

1. Scheingold (1974; second edition: 2004: 4, 9).

2. The best early elaboration of the mainstream political science approach to law and courts is probably Martin Shapiro's brief for "political jurisprudence" (1964). For a review of studies of interest group litigation conducted within the framework of mainstream political science, see O'Connor (1980). For a review of vast and varied bodies of mainstream research on the impact of judicial decisions, see Cannon and Johnson (1999).

3. I use the term *realism* to evoke "legal realism," the jurisprudential source of this view. The quote "how law and politics actually work" is taken from Scheingold's new preface to the second edition of *The Politics of Rights* (2004: xx). All citations after this point are to the second edition. This discussion of Scheingold draws on my review essay on the second edition of Scheingold book (M. Paris 2006). I am grateful to the editors of *Law and Social Inquiry* for permission to reproduce parts of this review essay in this chapter.

4. Shklar (1964; second edition, 1986: 1–3, 8). Early on, Scheingold acknowledged that the "entire first section" of *The Politics of Rights*—that is, Chapters 2 through 5—relied heavily on Shklar (Scheingold 2004: 13, nt. 1).

5. Scheingold (2004: 78–79, and, generally, Chapters 3–5).

6. Scheingold (2004: 5). This is a rendition of the myth of rights cued to Scheingold's practical intentions and immediate social context. This was a context marked by the so-called rights revolution and the prevalence and stature of social reform litigation. Of course, the prototype for the operation of the myth of rights at this historical moment was the NAACP's legal strategy attacking Jim Crow. For discussions of the NAACP "prototype" of planned, affirmative social reform litigation, see Bell (1976), Olson (1981), Tushnet (1987), and Wasby (1995).

7. Scheingold (2004: 84).

8. Scheingold (2004: 131 [first quote]; 85 [second quote]; see also 95–96; 151, 203–204; and, generally, Chapters 9–11).

9. Scheingold's conception of law and politics drew on American legal realism and its diffusion through political science in the form of "political jurisprudence." On legal realism, see G. E. White

(1972; 1973), Purcell (1973), and Stumpf (1998). On political jurisprudence, see Shapiro (1964; 1992). Scheingold's reliance on legal realism in the mid-1970s could hardly have been otherwise because all of the intellectual resources for critical reflection on his topic were realist informed.

10. As Malcolm Feeley has noted, we can mark the origins of perspectives seeing "law as constitutive" (culturalism) and "decentering law" (legal meanings in society) with Scheingold's work. See his Foreword to the second edition of *The Politics of Rights* (2004).

11. Tamanaha (1997: 58).

12. For a discussion of this "gap problem" in judicial impact studies, see Feeley's (1992) review of Rosenberg's *The Hollow Hope* (1991).

13. This discussion of these two examples of realist scholarship on law and reform does no justice to either of them. Handler's book broke new ground in three ways: (1) To Scheingold's focus on litigation's mobilizing potential, Handler added a number of more mundane indirect benefits, such as gaining media attention, garnering financial support from foundations, and leveraging bargaining in other forums; (2) Handler was the first to highlight the details and importance of the attorney–client relationship in reform struggles, and the larger questions of representation, participation, and accountability included therein; (3) Handler also distinguished between policy goals and organizational goals and noted that these might or might not be in synch. Rosenberg's impressive book has been widely reviewed and debated. See McCann (1992), Feeley (1992), and Schultz (1998).

14. McCann (1994; 1998a; 1998b).

15. Tamanaha (1997: 58) (first quote), Gillman (2001: 493) (second quote). See also Geertz (1973), Bohman (1991: Chapter 3), Emirbayer and Mische (1998).

16. CLS scholars were radical critics. They argued that legal discourses played a large role in constituting and legitimating existing political arrangements. Law produced ideology, in the pejorative sense of the term. CLS scholars focused much of their attention on challenging ideological constructs about law itself. See Unger (1983), Gordon (1984; 1988), Tushnet (1984), and Kelman (1987). CLS's negative portrayal of rights called forth a number of responses from within the legal academy developing a more nuanced and contingent conception of rights. See Sparer (1984), Schneider (1986), Minow (1987), Crenshaw (1988), and Williams (1991: 147–165). For key developments in law and society research focused on "disputes," see *Law and Society Review, 1980–81*. For work in political science bridging realism and culturalism, see Zemans (1982), Olson (1984), Milner (1986), and Brigham (1987). For a work in sociology marking a major shift in the study of social movements, see McAdam (1982).

17. McCann (1992; 1994: 292) criticized Rosenberg (1991) for making sweeping claims about the disutility of litigation without actually studying the change agents and what (they thought) they were up to. As McCann used *standpoint shift* and, as I use it here, the term does not imply any privileged ground for the apprehension of truth.

18. McCann (1994: 7, 286–287; 1998a: 81).

19. McCann used a four-stage model of social movement activity and then examined the role of things legal at each stage. He argued that legal mobilization played one kind of role in (a) the movement building stage, another kind of role in (b) processes of policy formation and change, and still another kind in (c) the implementation stage. Finally, conflict and policy change leave (d) a legacy of new law, policy, and experiences, which might later have new feedback effects. As for the broader contexts for movements, McCann's account included developments in the political economy, the historical evolution of antidiscrimination law, and many other evolving features of the polity (1994: 7, 92–137).

20. McCann (1994: 60–61, 90–91, 130–31, 140–45, 288–96). McCann argued that the utility of legal strategies was at its maximum at the first, movement-building stage of conflict but diminished steadily as conflict proceeded to policy change and implementation.

21. As J. B. White puts it, "law is a language into which other languages must be continuously translated" (1996: 55). He views law as a branch of rhetoric in which speakers must look outside themselves in disciplined ways. They must face the past insofar as it is embodied in authoritative legal materials. They must face adversaries who will challenge their interpretations, and they must face the present social context and problems at hand. Out of these tensions, White suggests, speakers give new life to old texts and new meanings emerge. For White, this process is essentially "literary and compositional" (1990: xiv, 21, 79–80, 89). White's view has been criticized by sociolegal scholars as an overly idealistic or romantic one. See Brigham (1987: 25–28), Tushnet (1990), Levinson (1991), and Binder and Weisberg (2000: Chapter 4). While I generally agree with White's critics, I do think that a political reinterpretation of his key notion of legal translation can enrich legal mobilization theory by incorporating more attention to the narrative, rhetorical, and performative dimensions of legal claims and arguments.

22. Amsterdam and Bruner (2000: 165–66 [first quote], 110 [second quote]).

23. In developing this typology, I have drawn on an insightful review essay on the cause lawyering literature by Thomas Hilbink (2004).

24. Hilbink's essay contains some pertinent commentary. He states that his term *lawyering* encompasses not merely "what lawyers *do* . . . , but also how lawyers *conceive of what they do*." He notes that "one could videotape two lawyers arguing in court, and those two lawyers might appear to be doing the same thing. However . . . , the way those two lawyers think about what they are doing, and how their actions as lawyers fit into a larger set of beliefs and relationships necessitate distinctions that may not be immediately obvious" (2004: 662, n. 6). Later, Hilbink also notes that many of the authors working on cause lawyering have highlighted the issue of whether lawyer's professed beliefs in professionalism and law ("the myth of rights") "is deeply held or simply strategic" (2004: 676, n. 25).

25. McCann (1994). See also Amsterdam and Bruner (2000) and Feeley and Rubin (1998: Chapter 6).

26. Elizabeth Schneider's discussion of feminist lawyering offers a good example of what culturalism might mean in practice. Writing about her own experience as a feminist activist and lawyer, Schneider states that "we asserted rights not simply to advance legal argument or to win a case but to express the politics, vision, and demands of a social movement, and to assist in the political self-definition of that movement. We understood that winning legal rights would not be meaningful without political organizing and education to ensure enforcement of those rights. Lawmaking could be constitutive and creative; it could have political meaning independent of its success in the courts" (2000: 30).

27. As John Brigham noted in the 1980s, realist studies in political science tended to leave "doctrine and impact separated." Brigham was right to urge us not to separate doctrine and impact, however much commitments to positive social science made that option attractive. The implication of the insight for legal mobilization theory is simply that actors might try to be cognizant of the fact that ideas in law will help shape "the language of politics," and thereby "contribute to the association of what is possible with the authority of the state" (1987: 196).

28. Narratives, as Peter Brooks has noted, "are never innocent, but always presentational" (1996: 17).

29. Feagin, Orum, and Sjoberg (1991: 21, quoting Schama [1989: xvi]).

30. Feagin, Orum, and Sjoberg (1991); Brooks (1996: 14, 19) ("enchainment of events"). McCann (1996) cites Feagin et al. It might be useful to compare my narrative case study approach with McCann's different case study approach in *Rights at Work*. While McCann's approach was an interpretive one, he also had what he called some "conventional social scientific commitments." He wanted to offer an empirically grounded "generalizable framework" (1994: 14). Obviously, I think McCann

succeeded. Nevertheless, it is worth noticing that McCann's goal of producing a general theoretical framework plays a rather large role in structuring his presentation of his research. McCann studied twenty-four cases of pay equity conflict, involving different degrees of legal mobilization. None of the cases are presented in narrative form, from some "start" to some "finish." Rather, the cases are broken apart and recompiled in order to provide data under McCann's general theory about how rights work at different temporal stages of conflict. As a result, the reader is unable to understand the agents and the choices they made in anything approximating the fullness of space and time. What is a great gain for social science (the generalizable framework) entails some loss for understanding agents and actions in context.

31. Bellow and Minow, Introduction (1996: 29).

32. Jerome Bruner has suggested that interpretive accounts might be judged by criteria internal to interpretivism. "Verisimilitude," he claims, is not the same as "truth." Indeed, for Bruner, verisimilitude actually depends on an author getting a reader to suspend disbelief. The story will be true simply by virtue of "seeming to be so." Although I think Bruner overstates his point a bit, I also think there is something to this notion of how interpretive accounts might be judged (Bruner 1996: 121–122, and, generally, Chapter 5).

33. McCann discussed this point in a 1998 essay (1998b). See also Calavita (2001).

34. McCann (1998b: 326). As Feeley and Rubin note in a related context, "judgments about the success or failure of judicial action clearly depend on one's underlying values. This does not foreclose thoughtful analysis and debate, but it precludes the easy characterization of specific results as successful or unsuccessful" (1998: 366, and, generally, Chapter 9).

NOTES TO CHAPTER TWO

1. Hochschild and Scovronick (2003: 19–21, 54).

2. Increases in education spending measured in real dollars: *National Center for Education Statistics (NCES), Fast Facts* (2002). Overall spending on public elementary and secondary education in real dollars increased 30 percent over the course of the 1980s and an additional 25 percent over the 1990s: *NCES, The Condition of Education* (2004).

3. Hochschild and Scovronick (2003: 20).

4. Hochschild and Scovronick (2003: 10). In his explication of "the American Creed," Gunner Myrdal saw education as central: "Education has always been the great hope for individual and society. In the American Creed it has been the main ground upon which 'equality of opportunity for the individual' and 'free outlet for ability' could be based. Education has also been considered the best way—and the way most compatible with American individualistic ideals—to improve society" (1972 edition: lxxii, quoted in Kirp [1982: 32]). See also Tyack and Cuban (1995: 1–6).

5. Hochschild and Scovronick (2003: 4, 20).

6. Odden and Picus (1992); Guthrie, Garms, and Pierce (1988).

7. Odden and Picus (1992: 6–7); Ladd and Hansen (1999: 30–31) (internal citations omitted).

8. Ladd and Hansen (1999: 28). Geographically tiny New Jersey has over 600 districts, 211 of which are K–12. Kentucky now has 176 districts, down from 180 in 1985 when the school finance litigation was filed.

9. *Edgewood v. Kirby* (1989: at 393).

10. My description of state school finance policies relies on Yinger (2004b); Gold, Smith and Lawton (1995); and Odden and Picus (1992).

11. On the issue of full state assumption, see McUsic (1999: 112–115). McUsic argues that full state assumption would be problematic at best.

12. This paragraph relies on Coons, Clune, and Sugarman (1970). Quotes in the paragraph are taken from Ladd and Hansen (1999: 74–75).

13. A description of the systems in place in all fifty states as of 2002–2003 can be found in Yinger (2004b, Appendix B: 331–351). The ACCESS website includes a page for each state with summaries of each state's finance system. See www.schoolfunding.info.

14. The apt phrase *nested inequalities* is taken from Hochschild and Scovronick (2003: 21–26, 52–63).

15. For an account of the connections between the suburbanization of American politics and educational inequalities, see Gittell (2005) and also Jackson (1985).

16. For a discussion of the economics of school systems, property values, and housing markets, see McUsic (1999: 98) and Hanushek (1991: 445–448).

17. In 1998–1999, New Jersey, the highest-spending state, provided an average per pupil expenditure of $10,700. Massachusetts, another high-spending state, provided $8,750. However, California spent only $6,500 per pupil, and Utah, the lowest-spending state, provided a little under $4,500 (Hochschild and Scovronick [2003: 22]). A more recent and comprehensive account of inequalities across states in spending and certain educational outcomes can be found in Liu (2006). Liu shows that for 2001–2002, after adjusting spending for differential costs and needs, the top ten spending states spent an average of $7,861 per pupil, whereas the bottom ten spending states spent $5,292 (2006: 1–2). On interstate disparities, see also Ladd and Hansen (1999: 30–31) and Evans, Murray, and Schwab (1999).

18. Texas: *Edgewood v. Kirby* (1989, at 392, cited in Minorini and Sugarman (1999b: 56]). Illinois: "A+ Illinois" website: www.aplusillinois.org. This advocacy group reports that "46 Illinois school districts with about 45,000 students spent less than $6,000 per student, while 18 districts with over 48,000 students were able to spend over $14,000 per student." New Jersey: *Abbott v. Burke* (1990). See also Education Trust (2005).

19. Education Trust (2005: 7).

20. Carr and Furhman (1999: 137). For a discussion of political constraints on reform, see Augenblick (1998).

21. West and Peterson (2007); Briffault (2007); Dunn and Derthick (2007); Koski and Reich (2006); McUsic (2004); Minorini and Sugarman (1999a, b); Ryan (1999a, b); Enrich (1995); Underwood (1995); and Clune (1992).

22. On this point, see Kirp (1982: 39).

23. *Brown* (1954) could be read to say that every child had a federal constitutional right to "equal educational opportunity." Where the states had determined to provide public education, the *Brown* Court had written, it had to be made available to all "on equal terms." In other cases, the Court found other "fundamental rights," like the right to vote and the right to travel, to be implied in the due process or equal protection clauses of the Fourteenth Amendment. Still other cases seemed to say that wealth, like race, was a suspect basis for governments to use in allocating important opportunities or benefits. The era was thus rife with intellectual and legal resources for a federal constitutional challenge to state school finance systems. For examples, see *Baker v. Carr* (1962); *Reynolds v. Sims* (1964); *Harper v. Va. Board of Elections* (1966); *Griffin v. Illinois* (1956); *Gideon v. Wainwright* (1963); *Douglas v. California* (1963); *Shapiro v. Thompson* (1969); *Boddie v. Connecticut* (1971); and *Hobson v. Hanson* (1967), affirmed sub. nom. *Smuck v. Hanson* (1969). In this context, policy intellectuals and reform-oriented lawyers developed several new briefs for school finance litigation. See Wise (1968) and Coons et al. (1970). For discussions of this formative period, see Elmore and McLaughlin (1982), Guthrie (1983), and Minorini and Sugarman (1999a, b).

24. *McInnis v. Shapiro* (1968), affirmed sub. nom. *McInnis v. Ogilvie* (1969). See also *Burruss v. Wilkerson* (1970). The cases are discussed in Elmore and McLaughlin (1982) and Tractenberg (1997).

25. Elmore and McLaughlin (1982: 32, quoting a 1980 interview with John Coons). Observers agree that the Coons team's theory made finance reform litigation viable at a time when it otherwise would not have been. See Elmore and McLaughlin (1982) and Guthrie (1983). See also Minorini and Sugarman (1999b: 38).

26. In a footnote, the California high court also cited to "equivalent" equal protection language in the state constitution as a *possible* additional basis for its ruling (*Serrano I*, 1249, note 11). *Serrano I* was nevertheless almost wholly an argument about equal protection under the U.S. Constitution. Later, after the U.S. Supreme Court rejected this theory completely in *Rodriguez* (1973), the California Supreme Court dredged up this footnote and "reaffirmed" its original holding under the equal protection provisions of its own state constitution (*Serrano II, 1976*).

27. Elmore and McLaughlin (1982: 53). These authors provide an account of the national mobilizing and publicity impact of *Serrano I*.

28. The phase "best possible education" is taken from Professor Tractenberg's comments in response to an earlier draft of this manuscript.

29. Between 1969 and 1981, Ford funneled some $30 million into school finance research and litigation reform projects nationwide. See *Education Week* (hereinafter cited as *EW*): April 26, 1989. See also Guthrie (1983).

30. A complete, state-by-state listing of litigation and outcomes from 1971 through February 2005 can be found in the appendix to West and Peterson (2007: 345–358). See also Briffault (2007), Ryan (1999a: 266–269, nn. 73–84), and Minorini and Sugarman (1999a, b). Some of the early victories—particularly the Washington and West Virginia cases—foreshadowed the turn to "adequacy" arguments in the 1990s.

31. See, for example, West and Peterson (2007: 7) and Schrag (2003).

32. Minorini and Sugarman (1999a: 196).

33. Michael Rebell, a leading reform attorney, has noted this connection between the standards movement and the rise in the number of lawsuits winning in court, as have many conservative critics, who charge that advocates have "turned classroom failure into courtroom success." See Rebell (2007a: 21), and compare West and Peterson (2007), Heise (2007), and Lindseth (2006).

34. ACCESS website: www.schoolfunding.info.

35. Recently, two edited volumes, Hanushek (2006) and West and Peterson (2007), bring together points 2 and 3 ("money is not the problem" and "courts should stay out of this policy domain") in a concerted attack on judicial interventions in finance policy.

36. Briffault (1990a, b). This discussion of local control draws principally on Briffault.

37. On the purported link between localism and participation in education, see also McDermott (1999) and McUsic (1999).

38. The economic efficiency argument for local control traces its roots to Tiebout (1956). Briffault (1990a, b) goes through the arguments and empirical evidence about local unit size and efficiency in great detail.

39. The research tradition that grounds these claims traces its roots to James Coleman's famous report, *Equal Educational Opportunity* (Coleman et al. 1966). See also Coleman (1969), and Jencks (1972). The Coleman report ushered in what is known as "production-function" research, which in turn gives rise to the cost–quality debate. For many years thereafter, scholars reanalyzed the Coleman report's data and debated its findings. In the 1970s and 1980s, scholars went on to pursue literally hundreds of production-function studies, producing a large body of research. As Peter Schrag has recently noted, the Coleman report casts a rather long shadow in American education (2003: Chapter 4). Schrag's discussion offers an insightful and accessible guide to the cost-quality debate. See also Ladd and Hansen (1999: 141–42) and sources cited therein.

40. For discussions of Hanushek's work, see, in addition to Schrag (2003: Chapter 4), Hanushek (2006) and Ladd and Hansen, eds. (1999: 142).

41. See, for example, Ferguson (1991), Ferguson and Ladd (1996), and Burtless (1996). In Tennessee, an actual experiment varying class size in the early grades (K–3) purported to find that small class size (thirteen to seventeen students) over four years yielded positive and enduring achievement gains. See Ladd and Hansen (1999) for a review of this research. Ladd and Hansen conclude that skepticism about the linkage between resources and measureable outcomes was, but no longer is, the consensus among scholars working in this arcane field. They note that no new consensus has emerged, however.

42. See Rothstein (1998).

43. Reformers have not had great difficulty in meeting the production-function objection, although it is something that they have had to spend time and money contesting. For a good example of how finance reformers have responded to Hanushek's view, see Rebell and Wardenski (2004). The authors note that Hanushek has testified against reformers in twelve school finance cases, and that courts have ultimately rejected his testimony in fully nine of these (2004: 45, n. 101).

44. In the school finance area, for example, Matthew Springer and James Guthrie (2007) claim that "contemporary adequacy research and lawsuits are increasingly guided by narrowly self-interested plaintiffs seeking to bypass the conventional competitive political process and procure private gain at public expense" (2007: 117). For this "end run" claim, see also Dunn and Derthick (2007: 339–340) and Stern (2006). A classic statement of the "lack of capacity" critique of the role of courts in social policy disputes is Horowitz (1977). For a thoughtful example of the conservative argument for judicial restraint in the school finance context, see Dunn and Derthick (2007). For the contrary view of the role of courts in school finance conflicts, see Rebell (2007a, b).

45. See Rebell (2007a, b) and Block and Rebell (1982).

46. See Introduction, n. 4, above.

47. Hochschild and Scovronick (2003); Labaree (1997); D. Paris (1995); and Tyack and Cuban (1995).

48. Hochschild and Scovronick (2003: 2).

49. On the footrace metaphor as problematic, see also Jencks (1988: 528) and Hirsch (1977: 5–6, 27–31). For a recent elaboration of Hirsch's view and how it can be invoked to advocate for "equity" understood as a fairer footrace, see Koski and Reich (2006).

50. Labaree (1997: 1, and generally, Introduction). As Labaree is well aware, his case turns on the existence of a substantial disjunction between credentials and what they are commonly thought to signal or represent. Labaree argues that what elite credentials really signal is a kind of cultural capital—learning how to walk the walk and talk the talk—as much as or more than actual knowledge or skills. This issue and how Labaree addresses it is beyond the scope of the present inquiry.

51. Labaree (1997: 22–26).

52. Labaree (1997: 26, 26–34).

53. The classic source lampooning meritocracy, and making the more serious point that even a true meritocracy might well be a very ugly place, is Michael Young's brilliant satire, *The Rise of the Meritocracy* (1958).

54. For Labaree, the view that has lost the most ground is democratic equality. Political theorist David Paris developed a similar tripartite framework for tackling competing "themes and theories" in public education (1995). Paris also argued that the common school tradition has been given short shrift lately (1995: 49–50, 62, 194–203).

55. Jencks (1988).

56. Writing about the Kentucky reformers' ideology as they expressed it may be taken to signal my endorsement of it. It does not. When some defined groups are being wronged or discriminated

against by other groups, then "setting one group off against another" might be just the right thing to do. "We are all in this together" can be an inspiring and effective approach, or it can be a cover for some interests to prevail over others. The point to note is that it would have been possible for a reform project in Kentucky to make claims on behalf of poor whites in rural Appalachia in just the same way the New Jersey reformers made "culture of poverty" claims on behalf of poor minority children in the cities. This book offers a study of how substantive visions and legal ideologies matter and get played out through legal and political channels. It attempts to neither endorse nor condemn the normative visions of education uncovered.

NOTES TO INTRODUCTION TO PART II

1. The Court's decision in *Abbott II* (1990) came after a prior procedural decision in *Abbott I* (1985), which remanded the case to an administrative law judge for trial. Quotes from *Abbott II* (1990: 362–363, 403). Parts of this New Jersey case study draw on a section of a previously published book chapter, Paris and McMahon (1998), in Schultz (1998). I am grateful to David A. Schultz for permission to republish parts of this book chapter here. Just before this book went to press, I became aware of a recently published history of the *Robinson* and *Abbott* cases authored by political journalist, Deborah Yaffe (2007). Yaffe's book covers some of the same ground that I cover here and sometimes in far greater factual detail. While I draw on this work occasionally, it will not be possible to highlight every instance in which our accounts converge and diverge.

2. In January 2008, the state passed a new finance law, the School Finance Reform Act (SFRA). SFRA provoked yet another return to court. This time, the state asked the high court to declare that the Abbott remedies of parity and supplemental funding were "no longer necessary," and reformers cross-moved for a declaration that they were. In November 2008, the high court remanded the case for a full evidentiary hearing. After receipt of a special master's report, the New Jersey Supreme Court granted the state's motion and ruled that SFRA should be given a chance to operate. See *Abbott v. Burke* (2009) (*Abbott XX*). I review these developments in more detail in Chapter Five.

3. Interview with Marilyn Morheuser (hereinafter "Morheuser Interview").

4. Minow (1990: 20). Minow is careful to note the other horn of the dilemma—that the stigma of difference can be re-created by ignoring it as well as by focusing on it, as in the view that public policy must always be "color blind." The compensatory vision made the problem of education "a problem *about* a disadvantaged minority" (not about "us") and highlighted the marks on certain children as inhabitants of a decidedly different and deficient cultural environment (not "our culture") (Connell 1993: 23). See also Scott (1997).

NOTES TO CHAPTER THREE

1. Cohen (2003: 6–7). I have drawn on Cohen's masterful historical account for this chapter's introductory sections and particularly on her view that the postwar American settlement had plausibly promised more freedom and equality, even though it ended up producing segmented, homogeneous suburbs that fostered a privatized, narrow conception of the public good.

2. Salmore and Salmore (1993: 1); Cohen (2003: 197). See also Gittell (2005).

3. Salmore and Salmore (1993: 201) (number of municipalities and municipalities per square mile); *Abbott v. Burke*, Office of Administrative Law, Decision by Administrative Law Judge Steven Lefelt (1988: 131) (number of school districts) [hereinafter "Lefelt Decision"].

4. Cohen (2003: 232). As Cohen notes, despite long having one of the highest per capita incomes in the country, New Jersey voters have long been hostile to state level taxes. In the 1990s, New Jersey still relied more heavily on local property taxes than any other state with both sales and income taxes. See Cohen (2003: 232–234) and Salmore and Salmore (1993: 239–258).

5. Cohen (2003: Chapter 1).

6. Cohen (2003: 197).

7. Sternlieb and Hughes (1986: 39), in Pomper, ed., (1986); and Salmore and Salmore (1993: 5).

8. On the rebellions in New Jersey in 1967, see the *Report* of the National Advisory Commission on Civil Disorders [popularly known as the Kerner Commission Report] (1968: 56–84).

9. Cohen (2003: 212) (Newark, 1940–1970). Over this same period, Newark lost total population, declining from a peak of 422,000 in the 1930s. In the 1980s Newark lost 16 percent of its population, dropping below 300,000 for the first time in the twentieth century (Sternlieb and Hughes, in Pomper 1986: 29; and Salmore and Salmore 1993: 5).

10. Population data for 2000 from "New Jersey Quickfacts" from the U.S. Census Bureau, State and County Quickfacts. http://quickfacts.census.gov/qfd/states/34000.html (visited June 1, 2006). The concentrations of racial minorities in New Jersey's other cities are similar: As of 2000, blacks and Hispanics comprised 56 percent of Jersey City's population of 239,000, 83 percent of Paterson's population of 150,000, 69 percent of Elizabeth's population of 123,000, 54 percent of Trenton's population of 85,000, 92 percent of Camden's population of 80,000, and 95 percent of East Orange's population of 69,000.

11. 1970 figures from Brief of Amici Curiae, Newark Chapter of the NAACP, on Appeal to the Supreme Court of New Jersey (1972: 79) (copy on file with author); 2000 figures from the Education Law Center (2004b), www.edlawcenter.org/ELCPublic/elcnews_040522_MinorityEnrollments.htm [visited September 11, 2004]).

12. Poverty figures are based on the percentage of students eligible for free and reduced-price lunches under federal law (data from the Education Law Center (2004c), www.edlawcenter.org/ELCPublic/elcnews_040522_PovertyEnrollments.htm [visited September 11, 2004]).

13. On this constitutional revision process generally, see Salmore and Salmore (1993: 121–126). The 1947 constitution made the office of the governor "among the strongest in the nation." The governor is the only state official in New Jersey elected statewide, a trait New Jersey shares with only two other states, and he or she has substantial formal powers. Since the 1960s, New Jersey governors have exercised the office's powers and have come to play the leading role in setting the agenda in state politics (Salmore and Salmore 1993: 128–130).

14. Historian G. Edward White associates sociological jurisprudence with progressivism and the Progressive Era. For White, progressives of various stripes generally shared the assumption that society was in a constant state of flux and change and that progress, especially "moral progress," depended on impartial and enlightened government by experts. Sociological jurisprudence was a theory about law, the nature of judicial decision making, and the proper role of courts that fit with this more general outlook on society, change, and the political role of governing elites (White 1972: 1002–1004). On sociological jurisprudence and legal realism, see also Purcell (1973).

15. On Vanderbilt and sociological jurisprudence in New Jersey, I rely principally on Tarr and Porter (1988: 64–66; 184–236). For quotes on Vanderbilt and judicial restraint, see Tarr and Porter (1988: 193–194). See also Lehne (1978: 43).

16. The origins of *Robinson* are recounted in Lehne (1978: 26–29) and Yaffe (2007: 9–30).

17. Tractenberg (1997: 23, nn. 79, 80).

18. Tractenberg (1974); Interviews with Paul Tractenberg (hereinafter "Tractenberg Interviews").

19. *New Jersey Constitution*, Article VIII, Sec. 4, para. 1.

20. Tractenberg Interviews; Tractenberg (1997: 23–24).

21. *Robinson v. Cahill* (1972: 280). On the trial, see Lehne (1978: 38–40) and Yaffe (2007: 25–30).

22. *Robinson v. Cahill*, 62 N.J. 473; 303 A.2d 273, at 277. Further citations in the text are to page numbers in the *Atlantic Reporter*. We cannot know the Court's motives for this doctrinal choice.

We do know that *Robinson* proceeded in the shadow of the U.S. Supreme Court's deliberations and decision in *Rodriguez*. In *Robinson I*, issued on April 3, the New Jersey Court felt constrained to note that it had prepared its opinion in the case before the U.S. Supreme Court had issued *Rodriguez* on March 21. Whatever the Court's actual motives, we also know that Tractenberg's elaborated argument under the state education clause was there and available for the Court to accept or to conveniently use, as the case may be.

23. *Landis v. Ashworth* (1895), quoted in *Robinson I* (294–295). Tractenberg's brief on appeal in *Robinson* cited *Landis* on nine separate pages and discussed it at length (brief on file with author).

24. In his brief, Tractenberg had asked the Court to take it upon itself to define the constitutional mandate in terms of "output standards." The amount of money needed in a given place would then be the amount of money needed to get desired results. Needless to say, the Court declined this invitation and instead asked the legislative branch to give the matter some thought.

25. The Court's lack of clarity, I would add, can be either a great virtue or terrible defect, depending on one's broader perspective about law and the proper role of courts in a constitutional democracy. Critics of judicial activism would no doubt marvel at the audacity of a court that could strike down an entire, complex school finance system because it did not provide "what the Constitution commands," and then in the very next breath say that it really had no idea of what the content of that command could be. Those more sanguine about court interventions to protect minority interests excluded from ordinary politics might see no contradiction in this. The Court did well by setting the agenda; it was merely calling the rest of the state polity to the seminar table for a hard look at the neglected problem of equal educational opportunity.

26. *Robinson v. Cahill* (1973) [*Robinson II*].

27. Lehne (1978: 19).

28. Governor Byrne's plan would have guaranteed every school district a tax base per pupil equal to twice the statewide average local tax base. This would have increased the state's share of total education spending from 30 to 50 percent. For the details, see Lehne (1978: 107–115).

29. *Robinson v. Cahill* (1975: 3) [*Robinson III*]; *Robinson v. Cahill* (1975: 197–198) [*Robinson IV*].

30. The PSEA's finance provisions and formulas, like most school finance arrangements, were rather complicated. The law established three basic kinds of state aid to education: equalization aid, minimum aid, and categorical aid. Only the first type would cut strongly against unequal tax bases, tax rates, and educational spending levels. These provisions are reviewed in great detail in *Robinson v. Cahill* (1976) [*Robinson V*] and in the Lefelt Decision (1988: 44–93). See also Reock (1993).

31. In 1981, the TPAF accounted for $350 million in state aid. By 1990, that figure was $1 billion. See Corcoran and Scovronick (1998).

32. Lehne (1978: 149).

33. *Robinson v. Cahill*, 69 N.J. 449, 355 A.2d 129 (1976) [*Robinsion V*]. Further citations in the text to page numbers in the *Atlantic Reporter*.

34. See *Robinson v. Cahill* (1976: 459) [*Robinson VI*].

35. Interview with Steven Eisdorfer (hereinafter "Eisdorfer Interview").

36. Between 1973 and 1977, the Ford Foundation provided a total of $1,725,000 to the ELC (Yaffe 2007: 88–90). Foundation funding can be seen as a mixed blessing for reformers. Reformers' independent resource base was clearly crucial in *Abbott v. Burke*. As we will see, *Abbott* was truly a massive case. It is hard to imagine any other political formation in the state with the resources and inclinations to do what the ELC would do in *Abbott*. On the other hand, as Joel Handler (1978) noted, foundation-funded, free-standing public interest law centers make it easier for legalistic lawyers to adopt a go-it-alone approach to litigation and reform.

37. Lehne (1978: 100–101).

38. Goertz (1978). Reock's 1979 study was commissioned by the state legislature's Joint Committee on Public Schools. For the Reock Study, See *Newark Star-Ledger* (hereinafter cited as *SL*): October 5, 1979. These reports garnered media attention: See also *SL*: April 30, 1978; and July 26, 1979.

39. Interview with Herbert T. Green (hereinafter Green Interview). Both Green and MacInnis would continue to be strong players in state education politics, and both have been part of the ELC's work. Schoolwatch later became the Public Education Institute, which Green continued to direct over the next three decades. MacInnis would return to the state legislature—this time as a state senator—in the mid 1990s. There he emerged as the leading critic of the Whitman administration's response to *Abbott*. Later still, Governor James McGreevey would tap him to head up the State Department of Education's oversight of the implementation of *Abbott* in poorer urban school districts.

40. Tom Corcoran joined the State Department of Education in 1976 as its new director of evaluation. He later became chief of staff to the education commissioner. His proposal to develop a set of program and content standards was defeated in favor of purely procedural model—"essentially," he stated, the State Department of Education ended up "requiring local districts to plan to plan" (Interview with Thomas Corcoran, hereinafter "Corcoran Interview"). He met Tractenberg and Green through Schoolwatch's participation at state board of education meetings and became friendly with them. After leaving the department of education in 1979, Corcoran happily agreed to support the *Abbott* litigation. In 1990, he became Governor Florio's chief education policy advisor and thereafter had a more ambivalent relationship to the ELC and *Abbott* (Corcoran Interview).

41. Under the PSEA, much of the infusion of new state money for education had gone to taxpayers, not education (Lefelt Decision 1988: 113).

42. Eisdorfer Interview. The next several paragraphs rely on this interview.

43. The Office of Public Advocate was created in 1974. It functioned as a public interest law firm lodged within state government. The office played a central role in the *Mount Laurel* litigation (see below) challenging exclusionary zoning policies throughout New Jersey. It also supported the ELC's efforts in *Abbott* with substantial resources. In 1994, Governor Whitman eliminated the office.

44. Morheuser Interview. On Morheuser's background and career, see also *New York Times* [hereinafter cited as *NYT*]: June 24, 1990; July 22, 1994; and October 24, 1995; Dougherty (2004: 93–95); and Yaffe (2007: 59–85).

45. In interviewing several participants in the New Jersey reform effort, it was clear to me that they shared something akin to movement culture but here without the social movement part. They had a common way of looking at big questions. Their language and outlook reflected the liberal integrationism of the 1960s and the efforts of many liberals to confront the dilemmas and limits of that view. With respect to race, poverty, and education, we can find the ELC reformers' vision fully elaborated in Kenneth Clarke's powerful polemic *Dark Ghetto* (1965). Both Tractenberg's and Morheuser's formative political experiences took place in that milieu. Both liberally used the kind of rhetoric that we find in the Kerner Commission Report. American had become "two nations, two societies."

46. Quotes from *Abbott II* (1990).

47. These sorts of comparisons across poor cities and rich suburbs have been common in political discourse since the early 1960s. They were repopularized by Jonathan Kozol's widely noted *Savage Inequalities* (1991). Interestingly, in writing his book, Kozol drew inspiration and evidence from his good friend Marilyn Morheuser (See *NYT*: July 22, 1994). The compensatory vision and comparative method are familiar enough. Morheuser's insight was to refigure the doctrinal legacy of *Robinson* and the PSEA in light of them.

48. In the Kentucky case, we will see just this sort of political mobilization standing behind the particular common school vision pursued through law and courts. In looking at the New Jersey case, we can ask counterfactual questions, but of course we cannot answer them. It may well be that the legalistic approach was the best possible one, all things considered.

49. Eisdofer in particular expressed the view that the litigation had to be kept separate and apart from politics. In response to a question about the possibility of mobilizing political support, he stated that "the courts are going to be a countermajoritarian prospect in any event. We wouldn't be there if we had any hope of succeeding in politics. We go to court because we don't" (Eisdorfer Interview).

50. Morheuser Interview. Yaffe (2007) finds and tracks the lives of all "plaintiff-children" in *Abbott*. As noted in Chapter One, the details of the attorney--client relationship, and the difficult questions of participation, representation, and accountability involved, have long been a central concern for scholars interested in law and social change. See, especially, Handler (1978) and Olson (1984). In his typology of kinds of cause lawyers, Hilbink (2004) notes that lawyers' recruitment of phantom plaintiffs is characteristic of the legalistic approach, which he calls "elite vanguard lawyering." In this pattern, the lawyer's client is not really a person or a group but the lawyer's own conception of the cause. The lawyer, and not the client, will be in charge.

51. Bierbaum (1985), Anyon (1997), Lefelt Decision (1988: 274–376), and Yaffe (2007: 89, 99, 103, 120, 127, 332). Bierbaum's magazine exposé describes the "nearly perpetual state of turmoil" in the Newark School District in the early 1980s brought about by political struggles for power and jobs among political factions. Anyon's book is a portrait of what was actually happening in some schools in Newark in the early 1990s, based on extensive participant observation, interviewing, and document analysis. A racial liberal herself, Anyon is careful to link the conditions she reports to broader structural forces in the political economy. The Lefelt Decision contains an extensive examination of administrative practices in the four districts from which the ELC drew plaintiff-children. He found that there were indeed significant administrative problems. Yaffe's book documents perceived administrative problems in the urban districts, as well as the ELC's awareness and strategic evasion of these problems.

52. Morheuser knew how the state would attempt to respond to her planned lawsuit because she had already seen the state's response to a separate school finance lawsuit filed by the Newark Board of Education in April 1980. The Newark district's case was styled *Sharif v. Byrne* (Complaint, Amended Complaint, and Answer on file with author). The state's answer to this complaint hammered away at administrative problems in Newark. The ELC filed its complaint ten months later, in February 1981. Although based in Newark (the state's largest city and school district), the ELC was so concerned about administrative problems there that it did not even want any "plaintiff-children" from Newark.

After the ELC filed *Abbott*, the Newark Board of Education moved its trial court to consolidate the two cases. Morheuser strenuously resisted the Newark Board's effort. The trial court granted the consolidation motion in June of 1981, and Morheuser appealed. Her brief on appeal provides some insight into her legalistic thinking about the ELC's relationship to urban school districts qua districts, and its stance on the administrative capacity issue. Morheuser argued that the Newark Board and its lawyer had legal conflict of interest. The interest of the Board and the district and the interest of the poor children were not the same. "*Abbott* plaintiffs," she wrote, "are solely children." They [read "the ELC"] "legitimately fear that their interests will go unrepresented and, worse still, that positions injurious to their interests will be argued in their names." Further, she wrote, in response to the state's defense in the Newark case, "*Abbott* plaintiffs . . . *must necessarily remain agnostic on the issue of conduct of local school boards*, since the Constitution places the responsibility for providing educational resources and opportunity squarely on the State" (The ELC's Brief in Support of Motion for Leave to Appeal [undated], emphasis added) (Copy on file with author). While the ELC's appeal was pending, Steve Eisdorfer helped to persuade the Newark officials to withdraw their lawsuit altogether and to support the ELC's effort in *Abbott* (Eisdorfer Interview).

53. My claims about Morheuser's strategic thinking in this paragraph are derived from interviews with several of her fellow reformers and especially from interviews and many conversations with Herbert Green and Steve Block. Block was a longtime research and policy person at the ELC.

Both Green and Block reported that during the 1980s they urged Morheuser to take a different, more candid approach to the issue of administrative capacities and practices in poor urban districts. Both Green and Block were nonlawyers, and consequently they had less power and authority than did Morheuser and the other lawyers. Yaffe (2007: 103) comes to the same conclusion about Morheuser's approach.

54. Green Interview. Green also stated that Morheuser had to spend much of her working life in and around urban school districts to put together the truly massive factual case that she presented at trial in *Abbott*. He stated that he observed her at countless meetings and public events. In his view, she was a charismatic figure who, although she was white, "easily connected" with black groups and audiences. He stated that he thought that her rapport with the black community stemmed in part from the religious foundations of her political work and that she often used religious terms and imagery in her work in the urban centers.

55. Both ALJ Lefelt (1988) and the New Jersey Supreme Court (1990) would eventually hold that gross mismanagement was confined to a few districts and that, in any event, mismanagement could not account for all that much money.

56. I mean to say here that this issue of administrative practices in urban districts presented the ELC reformers with a difficult moral and strategic dilemma and not that I have any easy answer to it. It may well be that more candor in politics would have jeopardized their chances in court. Moreover, given their independence and aloofness from politics, it is not at all clear that the ELC could have done anything about administrative practices, even if it had the will to do so. These issues are both intractable and varied across districts. But what is at issue here is, perhaps, a question of rhetoric (there could have been more candor and more commentary from the ELC); and the difference that rhetoric can make is establishing broader public support for reform. The ELC won, but it has never been able to convince broader publics that the money is being well spent. The Kentucky case will provide a sense of how that might have been done.

57. *SL*: February 6, 1981.

58. Complaint in *Abbott v. Burke* (copy on file with author).

59. In the November 1981 gubernatorial election, Kean beat Florio (a U.S. Representative from the Camden area) by a mere 2,000 votes (Salmore and Salmore 1993: 25, 49). Kean's grandfather served as a U.S. Senator. His father served in the U.S. House of Representatives for twenty years (1938–1958) (Kean 1988: 208–239).

60. Kean (1988: 215, 235). See also *NYT*: June 26, 1990, where Cooperman is quoted as stating that *Abbott* seeks "more money to do the same things that haven't worked."

61. Jencks (1988). For a more recent version, see Thernstrom and Thernstrom (2003).

62. For the content of Kean's "excellence reforms," see Salmore and Salmore (1993: 168–169), Corcoran and Green (1989), and *NYT*: October 5, 1989. On Kean's easy reelection in 1985, see *NYT*: November 6, 1985, and November 7, 1985.

63. The state's legal response included the usual appeal to "local control" as a constitutional interest supporting the existing school finance system. However, given the rejection of that idea in *Robinson*, and given that Kean and Cooperman doggedly pursued their own highly "state centralizing" reform program, the state's local control arguments rang rather hollow throughout the *Abbott* litigation. On the state's increasing regulatory attention to urban districts, see Kanige (1987), Lefelt Decision (1988: 274–351, 395–414), and Dolan (1992).

64. Judge Long's ruling is unpublished. The transcripts are quoted in the briefs on appeal from her order, which she issued from the bench (on file with author).

65. *Abbott v. Burke* (1984).

66. Like Governor Kean, Wilentz was a scion of a prominent New Jersey political family. His father, David Wilentz, was a well-known lawyer and political power broker in New Jersey politics.

Wilentz himself had served two terms in the lower house of the state legislature (1965–1969). He served as chief justice until his untimely death from cancer in 1996. On his background and other work on the Court, see *NYT*: July 24, 1996; *SL*: July 24, 1996. Handler was a scholarly judge who published in law reviews from time to time.

67. The *Mount Laurel* saga runs parallel to and shares many features in common with the New Jersey school finance litigation. See Dwyer, Kirp, and Rosenthal (1995).

68. *Abbott v. Burke*, 100 N.J. 296, 495 A.2d 376 [*Abbott I*] (1985). Further citations to page numbers in the *Atlantic Reporter*.

69. The Court also noted that OAL should assign the matter to a judge with "special qualifications commensurate with the case itself" (p. 394). The OAL had been created in 1978 to "systematize the work of hearing examiners assigned to investigate complaints against state agencies. Administrative judges make recommendations to agency heads, who can accept or reject them. A complainant dissatisfied with the final agency determination can appeal to court" (Salmore and Salmore 1993: 185).

70. See *SL*: July 24, 1985; *NYT*: September 1, 1985; Morheuser Interview.

NOTES TO CHAPTER FOUR

1. Lefelt Decision (1988: 3–13). Further citations to Lefelt Decision in the text by page numbers.

2. Sherman (1988); Corcoran Interview ("exactly when and by how much").

3. Noticing this internal logic narrowing the challenge down to one about poorer urban districts is important for two reasons. First, within the case, it helps to explain why the New Jersey Supreme Court in *Abbott II* (1990) singled out only certain districts for funding and compensatory program remedies. The odd remedy that the Court came up with was not one that the ELC ever asked for or even imagined. It was the Court's doing. Second, the narrowing of the case was a consequence of the ELC's compensatory "race and poverty" frame. As we will see, that legal frame had particular consequences for public debates and the broader organization of politics.

4. The SDE's original purpose was to have a rough-and-ready way to compare the performance of similar or "comparable" school districts. DFGs were formed out of a composite measure of several aggregate statistics (Lefelt Decision 1988: 24, 426).

5. The creative use of their adversaries' DFG constructs was but one instance of the ELC's varied appeal to the authority of existing law and policy to make its case. In this instance, the fact that the state already classifies and categorizes districts with an elaborate set of measures on SES obviates the need for the ELC to do the work of constructing and defending the categorical boundaries for itself. The other main instance of this larger phenomenon was the ELC's brilliant use of state statutory and regulatory norms (see below). McCann (1994) explores a similar pattern for pay equity activists. Through legal challenges, they appropriated employers' "job evaluation studies" and turned them to their own uses.

6. The discussion here glosses over a number of arcane battles over numbers and statistics and what they mean. For example, five different ways of categorizing and counting expenditures were actually in play.

7. Most graphically, the state at one point asserted that comparing wealthy suburban South Orange/ Maplewood to poor urban Jersey City was like "comparing oranges to *rotten* apples" (p. 362).

8. The state used Professor Eric Hanushek as one of its expert witnesses. Hanushek's testimony covered the cost–quality literature and its main findings and implications. His New Jersey–specific research was directed mainly to showing that, under the PSEA, local fiscal capacity explained only about 20 percent of variations in district spending. The state also called Professor Herbert Walberg. Walberg conducted a cost–quality study using data for all New Jersey school districts. He used district-level data on socioeconomic status (SES) to develop a model that produced a set of predictions about

what district-level test scores should be. Then, using district level aggregate test scores for the state's minimum basic skills test for 1983–1984, he compared actual scores with his (SES-only) predicted scores. The difference between the predicted scores and actual scores purported to isolate the value added by schooling. Walberg concluded that "there was no support for the contention that districts with higher per student expenditures achieve higher achievement scores than districts of comparable [SES] with lower per student expenditures" (p. 349–350).

9. In East Orange, state audits conducted in the early 1980s revealed loose accounting practices and fiscal improprieties (p. 285). In Jersey City, Lefelt found that urban politicians had turned the school district into an instrument of patronage politics, to the great detriment of educators and children (pp. 306–314, 333). Nevertheless, Lefelt would go on to find that East Orange and Jersey City were aberrational (pp. 341–342).

10. *NYT*: August 26, 1988; *SL*: August 26, 1988a, b.

11. See Sherman (1988).

12. *Abbott v. Burke*, Decision of Commissioner of Education (1989). The existing system, Cooperman concluded, was perfectly constitutional. The ALJ had misconstrued the constitutional standard. There was "no mandate . . . that all children receive the same educational programs and services" (pp. 629–630). Moreover, to attribute shortcomings to a lack of money and to discount the role of mismanagement was "to deny logic and enthrone naivete" (pp. 672–673). In the urban districts, "a blanket infusion of monies without change of budgeting and management behavior would not increase student achievement" (p. 841). Cooperman's decision runs 233 pages, numbered from pp. 608–841.

13. *SL*: April 14, 1989.

14. *Abbott v. Burke*, Brief on Behalf of Plaintiff-Petitioners (1989) (hereinafter "Abbott II Brief") (copy on file with author); quotes from pp. 5, 43, 85, 185. Filing her brief in *Abbott* gave Morheuser another opportunity to garner some media attention (*SL*: June 25, 1989).

15. The budget numbers are reviewed in Corcoran and Scovronick (1994). An abridged version of this paper was published as Corcoran and Scovronick, in Gittell (1998). Here I rely also on an interview with Corcoran.

16. *Abbott II Brief*. The brief was crystal clear about the idea that the constitutional standard for poor urban children could be found in the wealthiest districts: "Suburban districts do not consider their greater educational opportunities frills. Nor do plaintiffs . . . Attempts to fix a standard of adequacy other than in terms of what the most advantaged schools provide are doomed to endless debate and failure" (pp. 184–185).

17. Morheuser Interview. Obviously, Morheuser did not describe her approach to remedy in the way that I characterize it here. She did say that she knew what the proposed remedy would cost and that she did not want the focus to be on that point in court or in politics. In fact, during the interview, Morheuser jokingly noted that, at oral argument in September 1989, the Supreme Court justices thrice asked her how much her remedy would cost. Although she knew the answer, she said, each time she "evaded the question." As we will see, the Court would be left to work out a solution to the remedy problem on its own.

18. Morheuser Interview.

19. Within a year after Morheuser submitted her brief in *Abbott II*, the Florio administration would secure an overall tax increase in the amount of $2.8 billion, the largest tax hike in the state's history. Of that amount, $1.6 billion was slated to go to state education aid. Even with this huge infusion of funds, the policy architects could not avoid reshuffling existing state aid categories and allocations, thereby making local taxpayers in better-off districts pay more taxes to maintain level funding.

20. *Abbott II Brief*. For this reason, policy elites within the Florio administration suspected that the Supreme Court would also forbid state funding of teachers' pensions. Their Quality Educa-

tion Act would shift costs for the pensions from the state to the local level. The money thereby freed up could then be distributed to local districts in an inverse relationship to the level of local district wealth, or through the "wealth-equalizing" formula. In the end, the Supreme Court did not strike down state funding for teachers' pensions. However, the Court did indicated that it might well strike down state funding of the pensions at some future date.

21. For a discussion of the NJEA's organizational capacities, resources, and outlook around 1990, see Fromm (1993).

22. *Abbott v. Burke*, Brief on Behalf of Defendants-Respondents (1989), pp. 198–199 (copy on file with author).

23. *NYT*: September 3, 1989; Corcoran and Green (1989); Sinding (1989). See also *EW*: May 16, 1990.

24. Salmore and Salmore (1993: 62–68) (Florio "saw no need to raise taxes"); Kehler (1992) (Florio and the NJEA); *NYT*: September 3, 1989.

25. Kehler (1992) ("Florio's plucky story"); Judis (1990) ("good government technocrat").

26. *NYT*: November 5, 1989 (election results).

27. The Florio administration initially planned to secure the sales tax hike in 1990 and then seek the income tax increase and school finance reform law in 1991. Had that course been followed, perhaps the Court could have provided Florio with some cover. However, Democratic legislative leaders balked at the prospect of voting for a tax increase twice in two consecutive years leading up to an election. In these discussions, Florio came to see the wisdom in a "get it all done once and get it all done quick" approach. Interview with Margaret Goertz ("Goertz Interview"). Goertz's husband worked with the state's treasury department, and he was in on these conversations (Corcoran Interview; Kehler 1992: 46; Corcoran and Scovronick 1994).

28. Corcoran Interview.

29. Corcoran Interview; Corcoran and Scrovonick (1994).

30. The QEA is described in all of its intricate detail in Goertz and Goertz (1990).

31. Corcoran Interview. Corcoran and Scovonick (1994).

32. Excerpts from Florio's first inaugural address reprinted in *New Jersey Legislative Manual, 1990*; *SL*: March 4, 1990.

33. *NYT*: March 5, 1990; May 14, 1990.

34. Morheuser's initial response to the QEA after she finally saw it at the end of May was highly critical. The day before *Abbott II* came down, she told a legislative committee that the QEA was "deeply flawed" and "should be rejected" (*SL*: June 5, 1990; Sherman 1990).

35. See Dwyer, Kirp, and Rosenthal (1995).

36. *Abbott v. Burke*, 119 N.J. 287; 575 A.2d 359 (N.J. 1990) [*Abbott II*]. Further citations in the text are to pages in the *Atlantic Reporter*.

37. Later in his opinion, Wilentz attacked the callousness of the state's position in that it asked the poor to accept that which the rich would never accept. Wilentz wrote that "[i]f absolute equality were the constitutional mandate, and 'basic skills' sufficient to achieve that mandate, there would be little short of a revolution in the suburban districts when parents learned that basic skills is what their children were entitled to, limited to, and no more" (pp. 397–398). Ironically, in 1996, the rhetorical ploy would later have its parallel in reality when the Whitman administration proposed to limit spending in wealthier districts. There followed something a "little short of a revolution" in the suburban districts. Fortunately for the ELC, by then it had formed a political alliance with these wealthy districts and other educational interest groups.

38. This ambiguity between resource inequality (and the "parity plus mandate") and substantive educational adequacy would also be at the center of the Whitman administration's response to the Court.

39. The Court does not refer to its *Abbott* remedy as a rule book. "Rule book" is my characterization. I use it because the *Abbott* mandates would function as something like a rule book to which claimants could point, over and over again, even if the "rules" would not actually be followed for another eight years or so.

40. Eisdorfer Interview.

41. *NYT*: June 6, 1990a (Florio quotes), June 6 1990b (Florio plan shifts money from rich to poor).

42. The Court had invalidated "minimum aid," as expected, but not state funding of teachers' pensions. Still, the Court made clear that it was troubled by the "counterequalizing" nature of state funding and that it was not "foreclosing the possibility that [it] may be constitutionally infirm" (*Abbott II*, pp. 407–408). This threat of future judicial invalidation of state funding for teachers' pension would later provide the ELC with a key bargaining chip in politics.

43. The 5 percent increase for the SNDs was an arbitrarily chosen number. It had no necessary relationship to the Court's parity mandate or its notion that even more money would be needed to fund supplemental compensatory programs. Because outcomes under the QEA were unpredictable, there was no sure way to tell whether the Court's parity mandate would be achieved (Goertz and Goertz 1990: 107–109).

44. *SL*: June 17, 1990. This article then goes on to quote State Senator John Dorsey of wealthy Morris County. With *Abbott II*, he said, the Court was "requiring working class people residing in middle-income communities who drive around in Fords to buy Mercedes for people in the poorest cities because they don't have cars."

45. Morheuser Interview; *NYT*: June 22, 1990 ("in bed with Republicans"), Fromm (1993) ("act of war"), Salmore and Salmore (1993: 254).

46. *NYT*: June 22, 1990.

47. *UPI News Service*, June 20, 1990 (quoting Republican State Senator Gerald Cardinale of Bergen County—"punishing people for being successul"); *UPI News Service*, June 21, 1990 (quoting Republican Assembly members Dale Farragher of Monmouth County—"throwing money"—and Joseph Kyrillos of Camden County—"outrageous"); *NYT*: June 22, 1990 (quoting Republican Senator Robert E. Littell of Sussex County—"penalize one set of school districts").

48. *SL*: July 4, 1990.

49. Minow (1990: 20).

50. Scott (1997). There is another dimension to the ELC and Court stance that is harder to put one's finger on. It has to do with rhetorical style or tone. The voice embraced by both Morheuser and the Court is the voice of the moral reformer. Here there is an affinity between a sermonizing rhetorical style and the content of the compensatory vision itself. Victimization is particularly shameful when the victimized are poor pitiful children. Both style and substance tend to moralize the debate. The claimants set themselves up as morally pure and righteous and cast all opposition in the role of immoral opponents to simple justice. That kind of rhetorical stance is likely to produce powerful, emotionally charged responses from various actors.

51. Of course, in America, education is fundamentally about the competitive race to get ahead. The point here is that it is not only about that, and, thus, there are other ways of talking about it. The Kentucky case study will make this point clearer. More importantly, my point is not that the New Jersey reformers should have struggled to fashion some other frame, but that, *given this frame*, political mobilization and engagement would be particularly important to realize change.

52. *NYT*: June 24, 1990 (quoting Morheuser on *Abbott II*).

NOTES TO CHAPTER FIVE

1. The now classic statement of this view is Rosenberg (1991).

2. A *Star-Ledger*/Eagleton Institute poll conducted in early July 1990 "found that 80 percent gave the governor negative ratings on his tax policy and 65 percent similar marks on the budget. Three quarters could not cite anything positive Florio had done since he took office" (quoted in Salmore and Salmore 1993: 254).

3. For a lively account of the tax revolt and "Hands," as the group came to be called, see Kehler (1992: 46, quotes at 47). See also Judis (1990); Shure (1994); *NYT*: November 2, 1991; *SL*: February 17, 1991, April 25, 1991.

4. *NYT*: July 11, 1990, September 17, 1990; Corcoran Interview.

5. *SL*: July 29, 1990; *NYT*: September 2, 1990. Of course, the NJEA's and NJSBA's real concern was with what the shift in responsibility for pension costs would mean at the bargaining table.

6. The first and largest of the three groups was based in Monmouth County in the southern part of the state where antitax and anti-Florio sentiments ran high. A second group was based in wealthy Morris County; and a third, with a more dispersed membership, was called together by the superintendent of schools in Princeton. Meetings drew hundreds of participants, with about 100 school districts represented (Interview with Mark C. Smith ["Smith Interview"]). Smith was the superintendent of schools in Westfield, a well-off suburb. He was instrumental in setting up a steering committee to merge the three groups into the broader organization that became the Garden State Coalition (*NYT*: September 1, 1990).

7. Smith Interview.

8. Smith Interview; *SL*: October 26, 1990.

9. Judis (1990: 31, quoting unnamed Florio aide); *NYT*: August 9, 1990.

10. Although Bradley's margin of victory in 1984 had been 64 to 38 percent, and although he outspent Whitman twelve to one, he beat the unknown and inexperienced Whitman by a mere three percentage points. On the election: *SL*: November 7, 1990, November 8, 1990a; Ryan (1997). On Florio's about-face: *SL*: November 8, 1990b; *EW*: November 21, 1990.

11. The Senate Democrats were led by State Senate President John Lynch. He was blunt about what he wanted to do: "We are skimming some money that otherwise would have been distributed to the state's urban centers in the form of school aid and using it to reduce municipal tax rates everywhere," he said (*NYT*: January 8, 1991; *SL*: January 11, 1991).

12. Under the original QEA, thirty poorer urban districts were to receive an overall increase in state aid of $526 million. Under QEA II, they would get an increase of $287 million. However, because of the way spending growth limits and aid allocation rules under the QEA II worked, they saw an increase of only $44 million for general education spending (Goertz 1993).

13. The NJEA endorsed forty-six Republicans and three Democrats (Fromm [1993]; *EW*: October 23, 1991). In the State Assembly, where the Democrats held a slight edge of forty-three to thirty-seven going into the election, the Republicans came out with a fifty-eight to twenty-two majority. In the State Senate, where the Democrats margin was twenty-three to seventeen going in, the Republicans came away with a twenty-seven to thirteen edge. Generally, only those Democrats representing urban constituencies were returned (*SL*: November 6 1991a, b, c).

14. Eisdorfer Interview.

15. *NYT*: September 2, 1990 (Morheuser "is already dissatisfied with the law and threatening to go back to court unless certain amendments are tacked on"); *EW*: October 10, 1990 ("Morheuser threatened to bring the issue back to court if amendments are not made . . . "); *NYT*: November 1, 1990 (Morheuser threatens return to court if QEA is modified); see also: *EW*: November 21, 1990; *SL*: December 15, 1990, January 11, 1991, January 13, 1991.

16. Morheuser Interview.

17. *EW*: January 22, 1992 (quoting Republican Senate Present Donald DiFrancesco); *NYT*: August 5, 1992; New Jersey Office of Legislative Services, Hearing Transcript (April 6, 1992a, p. 12) (comments of Assemblyman John Rocco) (copy on file with author).

18. Florio solved this immediate budget crisis by coming up with a budget trick involving a revaluation of all state pension funds. The move, which experts regarded as actuarially sound, saved the state a whopping $1 billion (*EW*: March 25, 1992, April 8, 1992). The pension revaluation and the resumption of a phase out of state aid to the wealthiest districts produced the absolute greenest year for the poor urban districts between 1991 and 1997–1998—an increase of general education aid to the thirty special-needs districts for the 1992–1993 school year of $239 million, with their total share of all state aid increasing from 37 to 41 percent. Thus, even with a vigorous backlash and ongoing efforts to undo reform, we should not overlook the facts that *Abbott II* produced material benefits for urban school districts and that those benefits started flowing right away (Reock 1996); Goertz 1994a: 9–10).

19. Hearings were held in 1992 on April 6 (Trenton), April 23 (Union), May 6 (Cherry Hill), May 22 (Cherry Hill), and June 9 (Hankensack). Overall, about fifty witnesses testified (New Jersey Office of Legislative Services 1992a; transcripts on file with author).

20. For example, Richard Porth, a school board member from Trenton, quoted *Abbott's* rule book and attacked the QEA as incapable of meeting it. He asked legislators for "reflection upon the Los Angeles riots" and "the great divisions between rich and poor in America" (May 6, Transcript pp. 29–33). Eugene Campbell, the superintendent of schools in Newark, defied legislators "to drive through the streets of Newark or Camden, and then drive through Summit or Saddle River and tell me that all students start at the same level." He went on to talk about what he himself witnessed in Newark in the summer of 1967 and during the rioting in Los Angeles (June 9, Transcript, pp. 19–31). Houston Stevens, a member of the Newark parent–teacher organization, stated that urban advocates wanted "leveling up," not "leveling down." "The whole state," he said, "was endangered by the twin evils of crushing poverty and separation by race and class . . . If we are to avoid the anger and frustration borne of unequal treatment . . . that led to recent events in Los Angeles . . . , New Jersey must fund equal and excellent education for all" (June 9, Transcript, pp. 232–236). In his testimony, Paul Tractenberg also asked the legislators to "back away from the details of funding formulas" to consider "what the real problem is." The real problem had to do with "race and social class and cities and justice," as the "episode on the West Coast has made so graphically clear" (May 6, Transcript, pp. 21–23).

21. *Senate Concurrent Resolution No. 64* and *Assembly Concurrent Resolution No. 7*, Introduced June 18, 1992 (copy on file with author) (*SL*: June 24, 1992). Article IX of the New Jersey Constitution governs the amendment process. It provides two distinct and relatively difficult paths to amendment. If the Republicans wanted their amendment on the ballot for the November 1992 election, they had until August 2 to secure passage by three-fifths vote in each house.

22. The public hearings were held on June 26 and July 9 (New Jersey Office of Legislative Services 1992b; transcripts on file with author). During the July 9 hearing, the Republican legislator chairing the hearing twice interrupted the proceeding to admonish those in the audience to come to order. This was a public hearing, he said, "not a demonstration."

23. Morheuser Interview; July 9 Hearing (Transcript, pp. 17–21).

24. *SL*: June 30, 1992; *EW*: August 5, 1992.

25. According to Mark Smith, president of the Garden State Coalition at the time, a leading Republican senator had approached him in the hope of getting his group's support for the GOP's plan to rescind the QEA as well. Aside from the pension issue, Smith said, those active in his group were much less hostile to "equity" than the senator had initially surmised (Smith Interview).

26. The parity gap, or amount of money needed to equalize per pupil for regular education across rich and poor districts, was at this time about $450, or a little higher than it had been in 1990. Everyone was now spending significantly more money for education, but the gap had not narrowed (*SL*: July 9, 1992; Bird 1992a).

27. The ELC's renewed challenge on the pension issue is an idiosyncratic yet crucial part of the story because it gave the ELC a key bargaining chip to use as leverage in its political negotiations with mainstream education interest groups. Democrats had put the pension cost shift on hold for two years, but, as of July 1992, it was still scheduled to go into effect for the 1993–1994 school year. Morheuser had always viewed the pension shift as essential for freeing up the state aid needed to help the urban centers. In the face of her first attack on state funding, the Court's rationale for not striking down state coverage vaguely pointed to "administrative considerations." However, Florio's original QEA had dealt squarely with these "administrative considerations." It showed that the administration of the fund could actually be left entirely with the state. The state could simply send the local districts a bill for their share of the costs—see, no administrative problem at all. Morheuser made precisely this argument before Judge Levy. She also pointed out that, overall, the I and J districts got a hefty $355 per pupil more out of state funding for pensions, compared the poorer urban districts. As legal matter, then, state funding for teachers' pension was just like the minimum aid that the Court had already struck down.

28. Morheuser Interview; Smith Interview; Interview with Steve Block ("Block Interview"). On July 16, 1992, the ELC held a joint press conference with the NJEA to announce the deal. It was, as the *Star-Ledger* noted, "a major departure from Morheuser's long-held stance against state-funded teacher pensions" (*SL*: July 17, 1992).

29. The other NJAPS member groups were the NJSBA, the New Jersey Association of School Administrators, the New Jersey Association of Principles and Supervisors, the New Jersey Association of School Business Officials, and the New Jersey Parent–Teacher Association. The Garden State Coalition did not have formal status or a vote within NJAPS, but its leading members played vital roles through the other organizations.

30. Under the compromise measure, the ELC settled for an increase of $115 million in regular education aid for poor urban districts. The bipartisan commission would be called "the Education Funding Review Commission" (Morheuser Interview; Smith Interview; Bird 1992b; *NYT*: August 30, 1992; *SL*: September 24, 1992, December 14, 1992, December 18, 1992, December 21, 1992, and January 15, 1993).

31. Morheuser Interview.

32. Consider two illustrations of how NJAPS provided the ELC with contexts for practical political activity: (1) In an interview, Mark Smith, the leader of the Garden State Coalition, reported that many in his group changed their positions a bit as the result of intense interactions with Morheuser. The school personnel in this group were certainly more liberal than citizens in their districts. They were open to hearing Morheuser's arguments and inclined to be moved by them. As a result, Smith said, "we ended up agreeing that we should lose some state aid." (2) NJAPS controlled three out of fifteen seats on the Education Funding Review Commission (EFRC) established by the 1992 compromise legislation. Morheuser cut an interesting little deal within NJAPS in the debate over which of the six constituent NJAPS groups would get the seats. She agreed that the ELC would not vie for a seat, provided that the other groups participated in a three-day weekend "retreat" on *Abbott* and urban education reform. The former nun turned lawyer then presided over the retreat. Participants reported that the event was marked by many intense discussions among people from different organizations and kinds of communities (Morheuser Interview, Smith Interview, Goertz Interview).

33. *NYT*: February 28, 1993, September 23, 1993; Ryan (1997) (discussion of 1993 campaign); Whitman defeated Florio by a mere 26,000 votes out of millions cast. The Republicans were left with a twenty-four to sixteen majority in the State Senate and a fifty-three to twenty-seven edge in the Assembly (Barr 1994).

34. Office of Legislative Services, *New Jersey Legislative Manual 1994* (1994: 487–1992) (excerpts from Whitman's inaugural address), *NYT*: January 19, 1994; *SL*: April 14, 1994.

35. *Abbott v. Burke*, 136 N.J. 144, 643 A.2d 575 (1994) [Abbott III]. The Court noted that the special-needs districts had already received a substantial infusion of funds (some $700 million, the Court said), and that the parity gap—that is, the total amount of money needed to bring the poorer urban districts' regular education budgets up to the average per pupil amount among the wealthiest districts—had narrowed by 10 percent. Expressed as a percentage, that gap had shifted from 75 to 85 percent. Still, as Morheuser's brief noted, the amount of money that would be needed to close the gap immediately remained a hefty $447 million (or about the same in absolute terms as in 1990), and ten special-needs districts were still spending $2,000 per pupil below the average I and J district amount.

36. The Court's emphasis on the parity plus prong of the *Abbott* rule book may have owed something to the record that Morheuser made at the remand trial before Judge Levy in 1992. The groundwork for what would later become central to the case—the *Abbott V* remedies concerning specific compensatory programs—was being laid here. Morheuser had delivered another masterful courtroom performance. By 1992, the state had taken over the operation of two large urban New Jersey school districts—Jersey City in 1989 and Paterson in 1991. State takeover provided yet another opportunity for Morheuser to use the state's activities and turn them to her advantage. She produced Dr. Elena Scambio, the state superintendent of schools for Jersey City, to testify about students' needs and the money it would really take to respond to those needs. Scambio's lengthy testimony emphasized the multiple risk factors her students had, their "unreadiness" to learn on entering school, and the current inadequacy of the resources available to her district (Levy Decision 1993, pp. 24–27; unpublished opinion, copy on file with author).

37. In his study of the NAACP's legal strategy to overturn *Plessy*, legal scholar Mark Tushnet uses the phrase "a flair for politics" in an effort to capture the human qualities that made Thurgood Marshall a truly great reform lawyer (1987: xiv). The phase seems perfectly appropriate for Morheuser as well. See also *NYT*: October 24, 1995; and Yaffe (2007).

38. Interviews with David Sciarra ("Sciarra Interviews"). Over the course of 1996, Steve Block spent much of his time convening a group of school leaders and education policy experts to produce a report/advocacy document titled *Wiping Out Disadvantages: The Programs and Services Needed to Supplement Regular Education for Poor School Children* (Education Law Center, 1996). The title itself came from a line in *Abbott II*. The effort helped set the agenda on the Court's parity plus remedial prong when reformers returned to Court a few months later (Block Interviews).

39. The day after *Abbott III* came down, Whitman was downright genteel: Yes (of course) she would comply and, no (absolutely not), she would not rethink her promised income tax cuts. Note the language Whitman used to promise "compliance": "The Department of Education in conjunction with my office, legislative leadership, and the public, will craft a new funding formula . . . that will be submitted to the Legislature in time to comply with the timetable established by the Court." In other words, something would be submitted, and on time (*SL*: July 13, 1994). Whitman's popularity grew immensely over the course of 1994, especially after the national Republican landslide in the November election of that year (*NYT*: March 9, 1994, March 17, 1994, and July 1, 1994).

40. *EW*: March 5, 1995; *SL*: November 22, 1995, December 1, 1995; Tractenberg (1997: 60–62); Reed (2001: 150–154).

41. New Jersey Office of Legislative Services, 1996 (Excerpts from Governor Whitman's "state of the state" address).

42. For the policy details on CEIFA, see Tractenberg (1997: 60–64); Reed (2001: 150–54); *SL*: May 18, 1996.

43. Tractenberg (1997: 60) (Whitman plan attacked "vehemently"). Just as the Court had inadvertently intimated in *Abbott II*, the idea that the rich would be forced to get by on significantly less money was met by "little short of a revolution" in the wealthier districts. In February 1996, the

Garden State Coalition organized a mass indoor rally in the wealthy suburb of Livingston that drew 1,000 people. Later that year, it oversaw a process whereby legislators received 10,000 letters objecting to the Whitman administration's proposal (Reed 2001: 150–154).

44. Whereas Whitman's first budget (prior to *Abbott III*) had sent the poorer urban districts a paltry increase in state aid of $28 million, the next two (after *Abbott III*) increased aid by $100 million and $57 million, respectively (Reock 1999). On the parity gap, see also *Abbott v. Burke* (1997: 443–444, n. 25) [*Abbott IV*].

45. Governor Whitman quickly nominated her attorney general, Deborah Poritz, to serve as the new chief justice. Because Poritz had worked on the development of CEIFA, she recused herself from participation in *Abbott IV*.

46. *SL*: May 15, 1997 (noting unexpected revenue windfall of between $200 and $600 million).

47. *Abbott v. Burke*, 149 N.J. 145, 693 A.2d 417 (1997). Further citations in the text to page numbers in the *Atlantic Reporter*.

48. Justice Handler went through the state's model in some detail and picked it apart. The model school district contained one elementary school with 500 students, one middle school with 675 students, one high school with 900 students, and a central office. Assumptions about the number of teachers, class sizes, textbooks, administrative staff, and so on, followed. Actual costs were then pegged to statewide averages, presumably on the theory that average costs in the nation's highest-spending state had to be good enough. Where the new standards fit into this picture was something of a mystery. Justice Handler nicely picked out one small detail and made it tell the whole story. The state's model assumed that one security guard was sufficient for its imagined 900-student high school. Trenton High School had 3,000 students. Therefore, according to the model, Trenton High School needed money to cover the costs of employing exactly and only 3.3 security guards. However, at that moment, Trenton High School as it actually existed employed twenty security guards (pp. 430–432).

49. The facilities question had been lurking around in the case since Lefelt's trial decision. No one disagreed with the basic conclusion that physical plants in the poorer urban districts were in a bad state of disrepair. The Court's determination to add facilities to its list of judicially supervised remedial mandates was probably a function of legal mobilization, which was in turn part of the ELC's broader pattern of forming alliances and working more closely with other groups since 1991. On the facilities front, the ELC worked with a reformer named Joan Ponessa, a researcher at the Public Affairs Research Institute of New Jersey, located in Princeton. Using state and local data, Ponessa wrote up detailed analyses of facilities problems and needs (1997). Ponessa's work was presented to the Court in *Abbott IV* by the League of Women Voters via an amicus brief. Ponessa later joined the staff of the ELC.

50. The year-to-year breakdown of the amounts of state aid *increases* prior to *Abbott IV* is as follows: 1991–1992, $187 million, of which only $44 million was available as general education aid; 1992–1993, $239 million—includes both general aid and at-risk categorical aid; 1993–1994, $115 million, plus a $50 million fund for capital improvements; 1994–1995, $28 million; 1995–1996, $100 million; 1996–1997, $57 million; 1997–1998, $250 million, per *Abbott IV*. The total here is thus $984 million (Reock 1999). Using state data, Reock constructed charts following the course of spending and local tax rates in the poorer urban districts, compared to other types of districts, for the period from 1990–1991 through 1999–2000. Whereas as of 1990 the poorer urban districts taxed at the highest rates and spent less on regular education than all other types of districts, by 1999 they taxed at the lowest rates and spent significantly more than all but the I and J Districts, with whom they had reached "parity." By 2002, the average per pupil amount for regular education in poorer urban districts was $10,110, and the average total per pupil expenditures was over $14,500. Parity funding was then maintained every year between 1997–1998 and 2008–2009 (Sciarra Interviews). In addition, the state has

funded supplemental programs at increasing rates (reaching over $700 million per year by 2008), over a period when all other state education aid for other districts has been essentially frozen (Reock Certification 2008; copy on file with author). In 1992–1993, the poor urban districts received 41 percent of all state aid to education. By 2006–2007, Yaffe reports, "the *Abbott* districts, which enrolled 23 percent of New Jersey's public school students, were getting 57.6 percent of the state's school aid" (2007: 329).

There are many other outcomes and consequences of this effort that one could take up, from various perspectives. For example, one might wonder about the financial impact on non-*Abbott* and non-wealthy school districts, districts in which approximately 60 percent of the state's public school students are educated. On this last question, see Lauver, Ritter, and Goertz (2001) (showing that middle-income districts did get squeezed). More broadly, we could wonder about the role of the litigation in facilitating Republican dominance of state government for eight years or in fostering the state's current, severe budget woes. The policy outcomes in which I am interested begin with the standpoint of the ELC reformers and their ultimate goals.

51. *Abbott v. Burke VI* (2000) (state has failed properly to implement the preschool program in accordance with *Abbott V*); *Abbott v. Burke VII* (2000) (state must fully fund school renovations and construction in the Abbott districts); *Abbott v. Burke VIII* (2002) (clarifying procedures for disputes between ELC and school districts over preschool plans and further clarifying substantive standards for preschool education); *Abbott v. Burke IX* (2002) (memorializing bargain between ELC and the McGreevey administration, freezing for one year further implementation and funding increases for supplemental programs but maintaining parity spending and increasing preschool spending by $150 million); *Abbott v. Burke X* (2003) (mediation agreement for future procedures between ELC and McGreevey administration and "maintenance budget order" granting state's motion for a one-year continuation of a freeze on additional funds for supplemental programs); *Abbott v. Burke XI* (2003) (order memorializing maintenance budget order); *Abbott v. Burke XII* (2004) (SDE's motion for minor modifications of the Court's preschool order in *Abbott VI* granted); *Abbott v. Burke XIII* (2004) (ordering mediation on SDE's motion for modifications of order issued in *Abbott* X); *Abbott v. Burke XIV* (2005) (plaintiffs motion for relief respecting funding and implementation for school construction in Abbott districts granted to a limited extent); *Abbott v. Burke XV* (2006) (state's motion for "maintenance," or "flat" budgets for *Abbott* districts granted, provided parity funding and preschool funding are maintained); *Abbott v. Burke XVI* (2006) (clarification of 2006 maintenance budget order); *Abbott v. Burke XVII* (2007) (plaintiffs' motion for enforcement of prior court orders denied without prejudice as premature; *Abbott v. Burke XVIII* (2008) (plaintiffs' motion for enforcement of prior court orders denied without prejudice as premature); *Abbott v. Burke XIX* (2008) (state's motion to be released from the *Abbott* parity and supplemental funding remedies and for a declaration that the SFRA of 2008 is constitutional remanded to a special master for a full evidentiary hearing); *Abbott v. Burke XX* (2009) (state's motion to be released from the *Abbott* parity and supplemental funding remedies and for a declaration that the SFRA of 2008 is constitutional granted). Electronic copies of the *Abbott* decision can be found at: www.edlawcenter.org/ELCPublic/AbbottvBurke/AbbottDecisions.htm.

52. The meeting, which I attended and observed, took place on June 24, 1997, at the headquarters of the state bar association in New Brunswick, New Jersey.

53. ELC 1994 Annual Statement (copy on file with author), Sciarra Interviews, and Seidenstein (2008). The ELC's in-house policy expertise and its linkages with larger research and policy evaluation communities runs along three basic lines: early childhood education; district and school-level curricular reforms (including "whole school reform," or WSR) and general "indicators" of progress; and physical facilities planning and construction. The focus of litigation after *Abbott V* has been mainly bureaucratic agencies and regulations specifying and implementing the Court's *Abbott V* ruling.

54. WSR is an umbrella term for several organizational and curricular restructuring models implemented at the school level, most often at the elementary school level. The best-known examples are Robert Slavin's "Success for All" program and James Comer's School Development Program. What all WSR models have in common is the aggregation of all funding streams coming into a school so that all resources can be focused on the new mission and educational technologies. The blending of all funding streams was what made it possible for the commissioner to argue that existing resources were sufficient. Of the various WSR models, the commissioner was most smitten with Success for All, which features focused and scripted instruction in math and reading, with ongoing assessments. See Erlichson, Goertz, and Turnbull (1999), and Erlichson and Goertz (2001). I rely also on interviews with David Sciarra.

55. Among other things, the ELC proposed full-day preschool for all three- and four-year-olds, full-day kindergarten, class sizes of fifteen through third grade, and an array of school-based, on-site health care and social service programs.

56. Reed (2001: 252) (King "charted a middle course"). Judge King's recommendations contain a detailed review of the proceedings on remand. His report is included as an appendix to the Supreme Court's decision in *Abbott V* (1998).

57. After *Abbott V*, under pressure from the courts and facing a statewide need for facilities construction, in July 2000 the legislature passed the "Educational Facilities Construction and Financing Act," which provided for the expenditure through bonds of some $8 billion statewide, with much of the money going to renovations and new schools in the *Abbott* districts. Implementation has been tortuous and slow. See Education Law Center (2004a). Since 2004, given the state's severe budget deficits, money has run out for the statewide school construction program. Reformers have returned to court to seek orders for the continuation of construction projects in the *Abbott* districts. Yaffe reports that, by mid-2006, "the *Abbott* districts had seen forty new schools and 37 additions and major renovations." However, hundreds of planned projects had been put on hold (2007: 328).

58. A good review of the politics and practical difficulties surrounding *Abbott V* implementation can be found in Greif (2004). See also Yaffe (2007: 281–303, 322–334).

59. In response to a question about his concerns and strategic priorities in the wake of *Abbott V*, David Sciarra stated that: "We made preschool our top priority right away. This is where we'd spend our time . . . The mandates here are fairly clear. We had great success in court here. Whole School Reform and School Management Teams are much more complicated and harder to get a handle on. Preschool was clearer, and we view it as very important, so we prioritized that" (Sciarra Interview). Preschool for three- and four-year-olds in the urban districts expanded considerably over the period from 1999–2000 and 2005–2006, going from 19,000 children served to over 40,000, which represents the enrollment of 78 percent of those eligible. Moreover, as the result of the ELC's determination to fight first and hardest on the preschool front, the quality of the programs and expenditures per pupil are quite high. Preschoolers are almost uniformly taught by college graduates who are certified as early childhood teachers. Per pupil spending for preschool was $10,361 in 2004–2005. These preschool program gains were preserved in the SFRA of 2008 because the state's costing-out of per pupil expenses for the preschool program was based on the actual operation of the preschool program in the *Abbott* districts. This was not true for SFRA's calculations of per pupil expenditures for K–12 education, or for the weights attached to funding for at-risk and limited English proficiency students (Sciarra Interview, 2009). On fourth grade language arts and math tests, children in the *Abbott* districts have made impressive gains, compared to the rates of increasing scores in other districts. See Education Law Center (2006) and NIEER Study (2005). "NIEER" is the National Institute for Early Education Research, housed at Rutgers University, New Brunswick, New Jersey. A recent longitudinal study by NIEER (2007) shows that children who attended *Abbott* preschool programs for two years outperformed those who attended for only one year or those who did not attend at all, through the end of kindergarten.

60. For an in-depth discussion of test score results, see ELC (2006). Perusal of the ELC's website here (press releases; lists of coalition partners) evidences a strong program to mobilize advocates and citizens to both help local educators and to hold them accountable under *reasonable* standards and benchmarks for progress. On test scores, see also Goertz and Weirs (2007), Yaffe (2007: 323–325), *SL*: October 29, 2004; *North Jersey Media Group*: June 23, 2003; *Trenton Times*: June 22, 2003.

61. In a 2002 interview, Sciarra stated that whole school reform was "a complete mess" and "school-based budgeting" was a "complete disaster." He stated

> We have a state committed to parity funding, at least for now, and we have over $300 million annually in supplemental aid, on top of parity, and also about $100 million in the forced use of local budget surpluses. And all of this with no record of assessment on what the money did, the use of the funds, and what the funds produced. We have no budgeting protocol, or tracking of programs, never mind the question of educational results. We need some serious re-thinking, first on whole school reform models, and then on ongoing assessments . . . Look, the time has come to ask what the money is doing, and how it can be made to matter.

62. An at-risk student is defined as one eligible under federal law for a free or reduced-price lunch. On the recent legislation and litigation, see *NYT*: December 21, 2007, January 8, 2008, May 29, 2009; *SL*: September 22, 2008, November 19, 2008.

63. *Abbott v. Burke* (2009) [*Abbott XX*], Slip Opinion, p. 40.

64. *Abbott XX*, p. 44, n. 14. This paragraph relies on Tractenberg (2009) and a telephone interview with David Sciarra (2009). Sciarra gave two reasons for the Court's decision to give SFRA a chance to operate. First and foremost, he said, reformers' success over the past ten years in steering ever-increasing amounts and percentages of state aid to the *Abbott* districts (while state aid to all other districts remained flat) made the status quo "politically unsustainable." Second, he said, the Court likely grew weary of having to address disputes between the ELC and the urban districts, on one hand, and state officials, on the other, on a yearly basis.

65. Sciarra Interview (2002).

66. Watching Tractenberg and Morheuser at work, we have to wonder whether their legalism and their dogged determination to make law say what they wanted it to say were not part and parcel of the same complex of views about law and social reform. A more realistic instrumental approach to legal doctrine might have led Tractenberg to pursue wealth neutrality as a serviceable device to get some more money for the have-nots. The same sort of thing could be said of Morheuser as she contemplated her options for framing *Abbott*. Instrumentalism might have led her to take one of the paths of lesser resistance, instead of the path she actually took. Ideally, reform lawyers would combine the creativity that we saw here with an awareness of the need for political mobilization.

67. Scott (1997).

NOTES TO INTRODUCTION TO PART III

1. The Kentucky Constitution's education clause states that: "The General Assembly shall, by appropriate legislation, provide for an efficient system of common schools throughout the state" (*Kentucky Constitution*, Section 183). In 1985, there were a total of 180 school districts in Kentucky. Today there are 174. This case study draws on my earlier article on the Kentucky case (Paris 2001). I am grateful to *Law and Social Inquiry* for permission to reproduce parts of this article.

2. *Rose v. Council for Better Education* (1989: 212, 215–216).

3. Miller (1994: 127) (tax increase and state budget); Kentucky Department of Education (1995); Flanagan and Murray, in Yinger (2004a); Reed (2001: Chapter 2) (level of resources and changes in resource inequality).

4. Constitutional scholar Bruce Ackerman has developed the notion of "constitutional politics" (1991). I borrow some language from Ackerman here.

5. See Katznelson and Weir (1985: 208); D. Paris (1995: 62). For examples of common school perspectives on education, see Goodlad (1984) and Sizer (1984).

NOTES TO CHAPTER SIX

1. Miller (1994: 10–11, 72); Dove (1991: 83–84). Kentucky's basic demographic portrait had not changed much by 2000. The population increased to slightly over 4 million, but the rate of increase was slower than that for the nation as a whole. The percentage of children living in poverty had declined somewhat, to 22 percent. African Americans still made up but a little over 7 percent of the state population. Data from U.S. Census, Fast Facts: http://quickfacts.census.gov/qfd/states/21000.html.

2. Landy (1978: 197) ("anomalies" and "verve and richness"); Miller (1994: 3) ("traditionalistic political culture"); and Pearce (1987: 2) ("suspicious of change and taxes").

3. Landy (1978: 201, 216); Pearce (1987). This paragraph and the next draw on these two sources.

4. Chandler, a charismatic Southern conservative, was famous for his tirades against government and taxes. He was elected governor in 1935 and moved on the U.S. Senate in 1939. In 1945, he left the Senate to become commissioner of professional baseball. He was again elected governor of Kentucky in 1955. Earle Clements was elected governor in 1947. Clements, "more than any other previous Kentucky governor, shared the view of the national Democratic Party" (Pearce 1987: Chapter 2, 45–48; Landy 1978: 210).

5. Pearce (1987: 64–65, 120-21) (Combs's term as governor); Landy (1978: 201, 206) ("reputation for honesty" and "household name"). See also Combs (1991). Combs was born in eastern Kentucky in 1911. He received his law degree from the University of Kentucky in 1937. In 1967, a few years after his term as governor, President Johnson appointed him to the Sixth Circuit Court of Appeals. In 1970, Combs resigned from the federal appellate court to run for governor but lost. He then became a partner in the state's largest corporate law firm, Wyatt, Tarrant, and Combs.

6. Dove (1991: 10); Schlesinger (1985).

7. Pearce (1987: 15) (constitution as "rambling document"); Miller (1994). The Kentucky Constitution of 1891 was the state's fourth. Efforts at wholesale revision have failed since 1891, but the constitution has been amended piecemeal thirty-two times since then. See Miller (1994).

8. Miller (1994: 101; 154–161) (citing and describing several separation of powers cases).

9. In *Russman v. Luckett* (1965), the state's highest court held that the state constitution required that property be assessed at "100% of fair cash value." In response, in 1966 the legislature passed a revenue-limitation measure, known as the Rollback Law, pegged to 1965 tax yields. In 1979, the legislature passed House Bill 44, a property tax revolt measure limiting revenue growth for school districts to 4 percent per year. Higher revenue yield was subject to voter recall. The history of Kentucky's school finance system is reviewed in great detail in the Court's decision in *Council for Better Education*.

10. Interview with Arnold Guess ("Guess Interview"); Interview with Kern Alexander ("Alexander Interview"); Interview with Ted Lavit ("Lavit Interview"); Dove (1991). Lavit is not what one would expect in a reform-oriented lawyer. A Republican and ardent social conservative, Lavit rightly saw no contradiction between his political values and what he called "the philosophy of *Serrano*." In its pure form, the wealth neutrality theory of *Serrano* leaves it to local communities to determine much about the content of education. What it equalized was simply local tax capacity and local choice.

11. Guess Interview. The substance of the governor's education proposals included more standardized testing of students and competency testing for teachers. The ideological orientation toward education was consistent with the "excellence movement" sweeping the nation in the early 1980s. Miller (1994: 240) (Governor Collins's proposals); *Lexington Herald-Leader* (hereinafter cited as *HL*): January 4, 1984; *Louisville Courier-Journal* (hereinafter cited as *CJ*): July 10, 1984.

12. As noted in Chapter Two, the Coons team's preferred policy mechanism for realizing the legal theory of wealth neutrality was "power equalization." See Coons, Clune, and Sugarman (1970).

13. I should say here that the Council was not at this point and never would be marked by high levels of ongoing participation. As an organization, it existed solely to prosecute the legal action. It met every few months, with approximately twenty to thirty people attending each meeting. The Prichard Committee successfully pursued broader political mobilization. Still, the Council quickly developed a network of contacts and supporters reaching into many school districts. This network proved useful for developing the capacity for political action—e.g., for distributing information, keeping the lawyers apprised of developments in other organizations in education, and bringing some pressure to bear in the legislative arena in certain instances (Guess Interview; Interview with Jack Moreland ["Moreland Interview"]). On the legalism of the *Serrano* lawyers, see Elmore and McLaughlin (1982: 42–45).

14. Guess Interview; Alexander Interview; Moreland Interview; Dove (1991: 89).

15. Alexander Interview ("political currency"); Guess Interview. Alexander stated that because Lavit was a Republican in a heavily Democratic state, "we needed a prominent attorney to carry the ball here . . . ," and "Combs was the logical choice." He noted that Guess "knew [Combs], I mean on a personal basis, and in Kentucky that means something." Guess stated that he first met Combs in eastern Kentucky in 1954. For Combs's own account of his involvement in the case, see Combs (1991). Combs died in a car accident in December 1991.

16. Interview with Debra Dawahare ("Dawahare Interview") ("go-slow approach"). Combs's approach treated litigation the way that left activists often treat civil disobedience—it should not be undertaken until one has exhausted alternative forms of political action. In December 1984, Combs gave a speech before a meeting of the Kentucky School Superintendents Association. He noted that his willingness to serve as counsel in the planned lawsuit turned on the degree of political support. He would represent the plaintiffs in a school equity suit on a pro bono basis, "if enough school district leaders seek the action." He added that "I do not think you should do this unless you have substantial political support" (*Louisville Times*, December 4, 1984). For this paragraph, I also rely on my review of the files on the case at Combs's law firm, Wyatt, Tarrant, and Combs (hereinafter cited as Combs Files). Copies of documents from Combs Files cited below are on file with author.

17. The Council's early planning memoranda reflect a concern about the strategic implications of the leveling up versus leveling down problem. By the time of the Supreme Court's decision in the case, talk of leveling of any sort, up or down, had faded into the background of a much broader debate about substantive educational policy changes and the dollars needed to pay for them (Combs Files).

18. Guess Interview. Dove also documents the anti-Robin Hood stance of the Council for Better Education (1991: 89, 115).

19. The complaint was modeled on the complaint in *Serrano*. It reflected the influence of *Serrano* on reformers' thinking, right down to the use of the seven richest and seven poorest school districts for purposes of comparison. As of 1983–1984, the complaint noted, the highest-spending district in the state spent $4,109 per pupil, while the lowest-spending district spent $1,641. The average-per-pupil expenditure among the seven highest-spending districts was $2,726, while the average among the seven lowest was $1,748 (Complaint, *Council for Better Education et al. v. Martha Layne Collins* [copy on file with author]). On Combs's comments about litigation as a last resort, see also *CJ*: January 19, 1986.

20. Interviews with Robert F. Sexton ("Sexton Interviews"); *CJ*: May 27, 1980. Sexton grew up in Louisville. He did his undergraduate work at Yale in the mid-1960s and then went on to receive a PhD in history at the University of Washington in 1970. Through the 1970s, he taught for a few years at the University of Kentucky and then moved into university administration. Within a few years after 1980, his work heading up the Prichard Committee would become his vocation.

21. Sexton Interviews; *HL*: June 8, 1982.

22. Sexton Interviews. *CJ*: June 6, 1982; *HL*: September 8, 1983.

23. Sexton reported that Governor Collins was not pleased to have been in the position of advocating a tax increase in early 1984 and then failing to get legislators to go along. She was now on record as in favor of higher taxes, and she had nothing to show for it. Sexton stated that it "was clear that she felt she had been burnt and wouldn't risk it again." Once this large, statewide forum was in place, Sexton added, "we went to the governor and we said, 'we'd like you to lead it'" (Sexton Interview; *HL*: September 19, 1984).

24. *CJ*: November 11, 1984.

25. Combs was filling in for Prichard, who had fallen ill that week. At this point, Combs had not yet made a public commitment to represent the Council for Better Education, although his private files indicate that he fully intended to, provided that the legislative route to reform failed. Prichard's health had been failing for some time. He died in December 1984 (*CJ*: November 17, 1984; Sexton Interviews).

26. *CJ*: November 17, 1984; Adams (1993a) (data on participation, letters, comments).

27. Prichard Committee (1989). *A Path to a Larger Life* was initially released in 1985. In early 1989, while *Council for Better Education* was pending, the Prichard Committee rereleased the report in book form. The 1989 version was published by the University of Kentucky Press. All citations are to the 1989 edition.

28. The seven subcommittees were (1) teaching and teacher education, (2) high school reform, (3) administration and leadership, (4) vocational education, (5) school effectiveness (effective schools research), (6) children and youth services, and (7) school finance policy. My comments here rely on interviews with Sexton and an interview with Cindy Heine ("Heine Interview"), deputy executive director of the Prichard Committee. I also reviewed four of the seven separate files for these subcommittees, for the period 1983 through 1985.

29. National Commission on Excellence in Education (1983). See also Sizer (1984); Goodlad (1984). For a discussion of the "excellence movement" of the early 1980s, see Toch (1991). For help with discerning broader ideological tendencies in education in the 1980s, I have relied on D. Paris (1995).

30. Prichard Committee (1989: 99) (school finance quote). Reflecting its broader endorsement of modern common school ideology, the content and rhetorical tone of the Report emphasizes arriving at shared goals for education and treats education as training for common citizenship. For example, a chapter on goals and curriculum took issue with the "'work harder' message . . . of several of the leading national education reports of recent years." "By itself," the report proclaimed, "more rigor is not enough" (1989: 21). Underlying its statement of goals, the report continued, "is the belief that the pursuit of 'excellence' must also include the pursuit of 'equality'" (1989: 24–27). A chapter on administration and governance attacked what it portrayed as rampant political corruption in local school districts, especially in eastern Kentucky. However, the report noted that mismanagement and corruption were "the symptoms of the disease rather than the disease itself" (1989: 45). Another chapter on social services in schools made the case for preschool programs and counseling and support services, such as teenage pregnancy prevention and in-school day care: "National reports claim that the 'nation is at risk,' but these reports have not always, in our view, concentrated on the most relevant reasons for this risk," the report stated. The nation was experiencing "a poverty boom," and children were "getting the brunt of it" (1989: 49–51). The facts of poverty and its consequences "show that the lives and problems of all children, not just our own and our neighbors, affect all Kentuckians" (1989, 53).

31. Sexton Interview; Guess Interview (quoting Combs).

32. Sexton Interview.

33. Guess Interview.

34. The minutes of a February 1986 meeting of the Council for Better Education note "a general consensus . . . that while the General Assembly is meeting, the Council should make every effort not to draw attention to the suit" (Combs Files).

35. Dawahare Interview. See also Dove (1991: 95).

36. Alexander Interview. "We argued," Alexander continued, "for reinterpreting 'efficient' in light of broader common school themes . . . I have always looked to Horace Mann and his use of 'efficient.' We need to see it in a broader light today, but this is the origin of it." After the trial court ruled in plaintiffs' favor, Alexander would get to write his views about "an efficient system of common schools" into the record, in the form of an advisory report to the trial judge.

37. *Council for Better Education v. Martha Layne Collins*, Trial Transcript, 4 August 1987, day 1, 3–6, in Combs Files (hereinafter Trial Transcript).

38. Salmon Testimony. Trial Transcript, Day 1, pp. 101–142. Salmon, an education professor at Virginia Polytechnical Institute, also reviewed the history of the Kentucky school finance system and the state's long history of hostility to general revenue measures. He noted that fully 94 percent of all state aid was distributed on a flat-grant basis (Alexander Testimony, Trial Transcript, Day 2, pp. 127–199, and Day 6, pp. 4–26, 52–69; Sexton Testimony, Trial Transcript, Day 1, pp. 35–99).

39. Scent's efforts often backfired. For example, to support his charge that plaintiff districts routinely squandered resources, Scent compared five plaintiff districts from eastern Kentucky with one fairly high-wealth but low-tax-effort district from the Lexington area. This one district (Woodford County) spent just a few hundred dollars more per pupil than the five poorer districts but produced much better results. The better results, however, could be easily attributed to the much higher SES of the student populations. Scent produced the school superintendent from Woodford County to support this strategy. On cross-examination, Combs asked the witness whether his own district was adequately funded. The witness answered: "Absolutely not. I don't think there is a district in Kentucky that is adequately funded" (Trial Transcript, day 3, 102–103. Similarly, Scent produced the chairs of the House and Senate revenue committees (Rep. Joe Clarke and Sen. Michael Moloney, respectively) to testify about the difficulties legislators faced in raising taxes. Comb's cross-examinations maneuvered the legislators into acknowledging that the General Assembly had authorized a number of reforms as necessary but then simply failed to fund them (Trial Transcript, day 3, 24 [Rep. Clarke], and 49 [Sen. Moloney]).

40. Wilkinson's campaign and the 1987 election are covered in detail in Miller and Jewell (1990: 67–125). On Wilkinson's background, see Kentucky Historical Society (1988).

41. Alexander Interview ("brash" and "hadn't gone through the chairs"); *CJ*: December 12, 1987.

42. See *CJ*: January 22, 1988 (quoting Wilkinson's address), January 30, 1988, February 5, 1988, March 19, 1988, March 24, 1988b.

43. *CJ*: April 19, 1988.

44. *The Council for Better Education, et al. v. Wallace Wilkinson*, Findings of Fact, Conclusions of Law, and Judgment, Franklin Circuit Court, Division I, Civil Action No. 85-CI-1759 [unpublished opinions on file with author], pp. 10–15. Wilkinson had been substituted in for former Governor Collins as the main party-defendant. Throughout the litigation, he remained indifferent to it, neither opposing nor supporting it. After Corns ruled, Wilkinson decided not to appeal to the Supreme Court. The appeal was taken and prosecuted by President of the Senate John "Eck" Rose and Speaker of the House Donald Blandford.

45. *CJ*: June 7, 1988, *HL*: June 25, 1988. The other two members of the Select Committee were the state superintendent of public instruction and a partner in Combs's law firm active in Republican Party politics.

46. Alexander Interview.

47. The Select Committee Report was later published as Alexander et al. (1989). Further page citations to page numbers in this reprinted version. Many of the report's nine principles for a constitutional finance system go beyond finance to education in general. Of these nine principles, two (numbers 5 and 7) embody legal constraints derived from the legal theory of wealth neutrality. They were:

(5) The school shall be financed with tax resources which are distributed in such a manner as to ensure that the quality of a child's education will not be dependent on the fiscal ability of the local school districts;

(7) The schools shall be financed in a manner which will prevent the quality of a child's education from being dependent upon the vagaries of local tax effort[.]

The two principles were accepted and restated by Corns in his final order in slightly modified form. In its decision in *Council for Better Education*, the Kentucky Supreme Court also listed nine principles of a constitutional system. In the Supreme Court's version, however, the two principles reflecting wealth neutrality are omitted in favor of more general language about "equal educational opportunity" and an "adequate education." Wealth neutrality dropped out of the case as it proceeded.

48. For example, "common schools," the Report says, "were created as institutions where all children, regardless of economic or social condition, could obtain public instruction free of charge . . . This enlightened [common school] philosophy generally followed the ideas of eminent thinkers of the time who sought to build a republican government on the foundation of a more literate and homogeneous mass of people." The common school "presumes a system of 'practical equality,' where a 'perfect level' of education is offered to all" (p. 147). As we will see, the Kentucky Supreme Court would pick up and restate much of this rhetoric.

49. *The Council for Better Education, et al. v. Wallace Wilkinson*, Findings of Fact, Conclusions of Law, and Judgment, Franklin Circuit Court, Division I, Civil Action No. 85-CI-1759 [unpublished opinions on file with author], October, pp. 2–3, 6, 12.

50. *CJ*: June 1, 1988 (first Combs quote), May 29, 1988 (Moreland quote), June 3, 1988 (Guess quote), October 15, 1988; *HL*: October 15, 1988.

51. In June 1988, Senate President Rose and House Speaker Blandford issued a Joint Statement in which they attacked the court's ruling and the judge's appointment of a select committee. The judge had all but ordered the legislature to raise taxes, and this was an improper intrusion on legislative authority. They would appeal in order to defend the separation of powers (Joint Statement of Rose and Blandford, June 24, 1988 [unpublished; copy on file with author]). See also *HL*: June 25, 1988 ("dictate policy" and "boycott").

52. *HL*: June 4, 1988, June 27, 1988.

53. Sexton Interview; *CJ*: February 8, 1989.

54. *CJ*: July 7, 1988, July 15, 1988 ("new spirit of compromise"); *HL*: July 18, 1988. The fear of elected officials about raising taxes had deep roots in the state's political history. Wilkinson's efforts dovetailed with the contemporary national mood—recall that mid-1988 was right around the time of George H. W. Bush's "read my lips" pledge before the presidential election of that year. But locally most elected officials were thinking about what they actually referred to as "the bloodbath of 1968." The topic was not student demonstrations or urban riots, but rather what happened after the last significant increase in a broad-based, statewide tax in Kentucky. The last significant increase had come under a Republican governor (Louie Nunn) in 1968, and it involved an increase in the sales tax from 3 to 5 percent. In the legislative elections of 1969, there was a 50 percent turnover in the House and 24 percent turnover in the Senate. *CJ*: June 18, 1989 ("bloodbath of '68"), August 27, 1989.

55. *CJ*: August 20, 1988, August 23, 1988, September 9, 1988, October 16, 1988, November 14, 1988, January 14, 1989.

56. Sexton Interview; *CJ*: February 2, 1989, February 15, 1989, February 25, 1989, March 5, 1989, March 7, 1989, March 29, 1989, April 6, 1989, April 13, 1989, May 4, 1989. Sexton participated

as the Prichard Committee's representative in the coalition of education groups and attended its meetings with the governor. Another fascinating wrinkle in the whole story is the role of *The Louisville Courier-Journal* itself as an active participant in the conflict. The paper had the largest circulation in the state, and it embraced an old style of political engagement and argumentation in its reporting and editorial policy. Over and over again, it openly supported and trumpeted the views of the Prichard Committee; and over and over again, it attacked the governor's views. Dove (1991) remarks upon the paper's position. Its advocacy role was so glaring that I decided to interview the paper's editor and vice president about the paper's perspective and stance (Interview with David Hawpe). Hawpe stated that: "Most of us around here are tax and spend Democrats. We absolutely felt that we needed more money for schools and we pursued that." When it came to writing news stories, Hawpe said, his paper sought to be fair and balanced. When it came to editorials, however, "the gloves could and should come off." Of Governor Wilkinson, Hawpe stated that "he was an entrepreneur and that was his mindset . . . So, yes, we took a clear position. [When] he talked about schools, he always thought of economic preparation and job training. We had a broader vision, a vision of education as preparation for life." The paper published stinging editorials critical of the governor and supportive of reformers on February 5, February 9, February 19, and March 5, 1989.

57. *CJ*: April 30, 1989. This poll was conducted between April 13 and April 19, 1989, and it surveyed 817 respondents.

NOTES TO CHAPTER SEVEN

1. Horowitz (1977), Melnick (1994), Sandler and Schoenbrod (2003). Applications of the standard criticism of "judicial activism" in the school finance context can be found in Hanushek (2006) and West and Peterson (2007). In the conclusion, I refer to these accounts as "the neoconservative attack on school finance litigation" and discuss its virtues and defects in light of the present study.

2. For example, Doug Reed's valuable book (2001) on courts and school finance policy explains the way the Kentucky reform process went entirely as a function of the Court's sweeping decision. The Court's opinion is important, of course, but it could not have had the meaning and impact that it did without reformers' efforts.

3. The separation-of-powers language is contained in Sections 27 and 28 of the current Constitution. Again, the education clause states: "The General Assembly shall, by appropriate legislation, provide for an efficient system of common schools throughout the state" (*Kentucky Constitution*, Section 183).

4. Scent cited and discussed: *Prouse v. Board of Education* (1909) ("The whole subject of common school education is confided to the judgment of the General Assembly by the Constitution."); *Elliott v. Garner* (1924) ("The constitution requires the General Assembly to provide an efficient system of common schools throughout the state; and how it shall best accomplish this object is purely a matter of legislative discretion"); and *Commonwealth v. Griffin* (1930) ("framers gave lawmakers wide latitude to the Legislature. What the system is, or is to be, is left wholly to the discretion of the Legislature") (*Rose v. Council*, Brief for Appellants 1988, pp. 88–90 [copy on file with author]).

5. *Rose v. Council*, Brief for Appellees (1988, p. 1, 39) (copy on file with author). The one local case was *Wooley v. Spalding* (1956). *Wooley* involved the discriminatory nature of a local school board's decision to close a high school.

6. *CJ*: December 8, 1988; *HL*: December 8, 1988.

7. *CJ*: June 3, 1989.

8. *Rose v. Council for Better Education*, 790 S.W2d 186 (1989), at 189. Further citations to *Southwest Reporter* by page number in the text.

9. The Court cites *Official Report* (1890: Vol 3: 4460, 4531). This convention lasted approximately eight months. The records of the proceedings are over 6,000 pages long. Of everyone seeking

to make use of the convention's processes and deliberations, William Scent did the most to locate statements and proposals in their actual historical context. The Court itself was not very serious about its assertions about the "intent of the framers." As the Court's opinion reaches its rhetorical climax, talk of actual "intent" shifts to claims about the broad "purpose" of the education clause itself. The Court's real approach to precedent can also be seen in how it handled local cases. Here, we bump into a fascinating little tangent about racism and Kentucky's legal history.

Stephens quoted language from four Kentucky cases on Section 183 without bothering to discuss the facts or issues. He simply set forth language supportive of his current claim that this section embodied some substantive standard that was not being met, adding his own restatements and embellishments. The only case Stephens discussed in any detail was *Wooley v. Spalding* (1956). It is not surprising that the chief justice is less than careful in his treatment of four out of the five cases he cites in a section styled "local precedents." His effort here is the usual one—to create the illusion of legal authority for what is a clear departure from prior law. My claim is that the Court's authority really comes from the fit between its rhetoric and what it "does" with respect to the legislature, on one hand, and the immediate, *reformer-created* political context, on the other. In only one case in the state's history had the state's highest court *struck down* a state statute because it violated section 183. However, the Court in *Rose v. Council for Better Education* did not rely on it, and it is instructive to consider why it did not.

In *Trustees of Graded Free Colored Common Schools v. Trustees of Graded Free White Common Schools* (1918), a state statute permitted local taxes on corporations but provided that they could be used to support only the white schools. The Court of Appeals (the highest court) held that state law already, and quite appropriately, provided for "the sequestering of all revenues from the property of white people in the support of white schools." To now deny "colored schools" the benefits of taxes on corporations, in addition to confining them to the already "bare revenue arising from the property of colored people" would leave them with "no system at all." This "everlasting ruin of the colored schools," the court held, would "render the poorest and most helpless of our citizenship, those who are and have always been the state's special object of protection and care, a hopeless burden and menacing danger, instead of an efficient and helpful contingent." Thus, the court struck down the statute.

Reformers had cited this case in their posttrial brief to the trial judge, with an effort to cleanse it of what they called its "archaic racial distinctions." However, they abandoned reliance upon the case in the brief on appeal, and there is no citation to it there. In *Rose v. Council for Better Education*, the Kentucky Supreme Court relegated it to an inconsequential footnote, which, in its entirety, read as follows: "The Court did, in fact, address the constitutionality of a statute under the mandate of Section 183 in *Trustees of Graded Free Colored Common Schools v. Trustees of Graded Free White Common Schools* [1918]." Thus, according to Chief Justice Stephens, the Court in *Trustees* had "addressed" the constitutionality of a law under Section 183, and that was it. For reformers on appeal and for the Court itself, it seems, although the case was directly on point, a direct confrontation with it (and the necessary "explaining away" of the "archaic racial distinctions") threatened to undermine the larger fiction that the Court was sifting some historical intent or purpose out of the past. I am merely pointing out that there are reasons to be skeptical about the Court's own assertions about historical intent and purpose. I do not wish to open up the theoretical issues involved in a claim that the Court is not really "following the law" because then I would have to give my own account of what it means to follow the law and why my view is a correct or plausible one. The issue is important, but not for my purposes.

10. Earlier in the opinion, the court had adopted a version of the trial court's Select Committee's list of "seven capacities" that a common school system should foster in all students, including such things as "sufficient oral and written communication skills to enable students to function in a complex and rapidly changing civilization," and "sufficient self-knowledge and knowledge of his or her mental and physical wellness," and the like (pp. 211–212).

11. Four other justices joined Chief Justice Stephens's opinion for the Court. Of these, two issued concurring opinions. Two justices dissented. However, one of the dissenting justices (Justice Vance) did so because he thought that the Court had not gone far enough to ensure equality in resources across districts. Only one justice (Justice Leibson) would have ruled in favor of appellants.

12. As noted above, plaintiffs had not asked for this sweeping declaration, and although there was evidence about education in general in the case, very little in the record supported the conclusion that every statute touching education should be struck down. As Combs put it right after the decision, "we asked for a thimble full, and we got a bucket full" (quoted in Miller 1994: 167–168).

13. Sexton Interviews.

14. *NYT*: June 9, 1989 [AP Wire Service] (Wilkinson quotes); *CJ*: June 9, 1989a (Wilkinson quotes), June 9, 1989b (quoting House Speaker Blandford and Senate President Rose).

15. *CJ*: June 12, 1989.

16. *CJ*: June 11, 1989.

17. The *Courier-Journal* continued to blend reporting and advocacy. Over the latter half of 1989 and into 1990, it opened its pages wide to various interested actors, such as the Prichard Committee, the state teachers' union, and the state school boards association, to allow them to project their views. It also ran a series of unusually long articles, styled "Kentucky at the Crossroads," on the history of tax and education policies and contemporary proposals. The *Lexington-Herald Leader* soon followed suit with its own twelve-part series of articles, styled "Cheating Our Children."

18. *CJ*: August 6, 1989, February 4, 1990. See also Miller (1994: 68–70).

19. *CJ*: June 28, 1989. The establishment and use of such extraordinary, "just for this occasion" lawmaking bodies is another hallmark of Bruce Ackerman's "constitutional politics" (Ackerman 1991). The paradigm case is the 1787 Constitutional Convention itself. But Ackerman also ingeniously treats the Committee of Fifteen in Congress after the Civil War as such a quasi-legal, higher lawmaking body. I don't want to take the analogy too far, but it does seem that extraordinary bodies invested with grave responsibilities and authority are a marker that something very important is going on. The records of the forty-six meetings of the Task Force and its committees consist of typed notes styled "minutes" and cassette tapes. I cite these below as "Task Force Minutes" (copies of all minutes on file with author). No transcripts of the proceedings were made. I base my observations on a review of all notes and interviews with several participants.

20. Of the sixteen members of the Task Force from the General Assembly, fourteen were Democrats, and only two were Republicans. In the House overall, there were seventy-one Democrats and twenty-one Republicans. In the Senate, there were thirty Democrats and eight Republicans. The creeping realignment in favor of the Republican Party throughout the South came last to Kentucky, and its impact was felt least when it came to state elective office. In the last five to ten years, the Republican Party has achieved competitiveness.

21. As the 1990s progressed, and goals and outcomes were specified and made concrete, opposition to KERA would arise, especially among social conservatives who objected to the "liberal humanism" in the curricular goals and assessment mechanisms. School site-based management, a new ungraded primary program eliminating grades for grades K–3 (which the state later largely abandoned), and antinepotism provisions were all also controversial. "Legislative ownership" would matter in reformers' efforts to fend off these attacks on KERA. Well into the 1990s, many legislators felt that the reform measure was "their baby" (Sexton Interviews). See also *EW*: May 18, 1994, March 13, 1996.

22. An important player in the Task Force's processes and deliberations was Frank Newman, who was then the president of the Education Commission of the States. Newman attended and presided over two planning session in July 1989, and he returned in February 1990 to help put all the separate pieces together in one package. Interview with Frank Newman ("Newman Interview"). The

quotes in the text are taken from Newman's notes from an all-day meeting on July 27, 1989 (Task Force Minutes).

23. Task Force Minutes, Committee on Curriculum, August 21, 1989.

24. Task Force Minutes, Committee on Curriculum, September 12, 1989.

25. In February 1989, in the midst of his fight with legislators, Wilkinson used an executive order to set up a Council on School Performance Standards. He charged it with the task of defining desired outcomes and designing tests to measure performance. The legislative process after the Court's decision retained the form of this move but shifted the content and mechanisms in the direction of the common school (see the discussion in the text below). KERA would recognize and continue the work of this body by delegating to it the tasks of defining outcomes, designing assessments, including "authentic" ones involving the qualitative evaluation of performances, and fashioning a system of sanctions and rewards running to schools (KERA [passed as *House Bill 940*], Sections 2 through 11).

26. Over the course of the 1990s, the state was forced to revise its testing and accountability system substantially. It now uses a more traditional system, relying mainly on standardized tests. In 2004, the legislature also abolished monetary rewards for high-performing schools. The ungraded primary system also failed to take root. See Hess (2007), Weston and Sexton (2007), Flanagan and Murray (2004: 199-201), Pankatz and Petrosko, eds. (2000), and Steffy (1993).

27. For the important governance policy changes in KERA, see House Bill 940, Sections 52, 56–66, 71, 73, 75–79, 89–92. For a summary, see Kentucky Legislative Research Commission (1997).

28. Interview with John Augenblick ("Augenblick Interview"), Interview with Tom Willis ("Willis Interview").

29. For details of the politics and competing tax proposals, see *CJ*: February 11, 1990, February 24, 1990a,b, March 8, 1990, March 9, 1990, March 10, 1990, March 11, 1990, March 29, 1990. I also rely here on an interview with State Senator Michael Moloney, then the chair of the State Senate's Revenue and Appropriations Committee.

30. *CJ*: March 22, 1990, April 12, 1990.

31. The account of the structure of SEEK that follows is based on House Bill 940, Sections 93–115; Adams (1993b); Kentucky Legislative Research Commission (1997); Augenblick Interview; and Willis Interview.

32. The provisions of SEEK are specified in House Bill 940, Sections 93–115. Compared to the old system, SEEK increased the base amount by several hundred dollars, although at $2,305 per pupil for 1990–1991, it still remained low compared to most other states. By 1995–1996, the base amount had been raised to $2,570. Under this basic foundation component of SEEK, each district was required to levy a tax rate of 30 cents per $100 of property value. This represented a mandatory tax hike for forty-seven districts (out of a total of 178 districts), many of them poorer districts that had been failing to make much of a local tax effort.

33. Picus, Odden, and Fermanich (2001).

34. Flanagan and Murray (2004: 202–206). The authors also note total real revenues for districts spending at the fifth and ninety-fifth percentile of districts in 1989–1990 compared to 1997–1998. In 1989–1990, the districts spending at the fifth percentile had total revenues of $4,300 per child, and the districts spending at the ninety-fifth percentile had total revenues of $6,586. In 1997–1998, districts spending at the fifth percentile had total revenues of $5,208, and the districts spending at the ninety-fifth percentile had total revenues of $7,301.

35. Reed (2001: 29, and generally, Chapter 2). Other school finance research supports the picture painted by Picus et al., Flanagan and Murray, and Reed, respectively. Jacob Adams (2000) found that education funding increased 19 percent in real dollars over the first three years of KERA/SEEK. By 1997, the range—the difference in education spending between the highest-spending district and the

lowest-spending one—had narrowed by 22 percent since the start of KERA. The restricted range—the difference in education spending between the district at the ninety-fifth percentile of spending and the district at the fifth percentile—showed a 77 percent difference in spending in 1989–1990, but only a 38 percent difference in 1997.

Kentucky's Legislative Research Commission (1996) reported that, during the period between 1989-90, the last year before KERA, and 1995-96, total state and local spending for education increased from just over $2 billion to $3.1 billion, or over 50%. Over this same period, out of a total increase in state and local revenues of $1.143 billion, increased state aid represented $767.3 million and increased local revenues accounted for $375.9 million. Total state aid increased by 49.1%, while local effort increased by 84.6%. Kentucky Legislative Research Commission (1996: 98, 100-102).

36. *EW*: April 10, 1991.

37. Stanfield (1991).

38. Moreland Interview; *NYT*: March 26, 1996.

39. Odden and Picus (2001). The homepage of the Prichard Committee's website contains direct links to press releases, reports, and inflation-adjusted charts on education spending from 1989–1990 through 2006. The data also show a replay of something that emerged in New Jersey in the 1980s in that health and pension benefit costs have risen far faster than all other costs, and hence have eaten up larger and larger shares of each education dollar. See www.prichardcommittee.org/index.html.

40. A litigation update can found at the website of the Advocacy Center for Children's Educational Success with Standards (ACCESS), at: www.schoolfunding.info/news/litigation/3-1-06 litupdate.php3. See also the Prichard Committee's website for commentary on recent legislative sessions: /www.prichardcommittee.org.

41. Here, we would have to specify and defend the relevant criteria and measures for improved educational experiences and outcomes. Most analyses focus on student achievement measured in various ways, most commonly by standardized achievement tests. There are many other outcome measures as well. But the Kentucky reformers pursued a broader vision, and an evaluation from their standpoint should take this fact into account. See Minow (1991).

42. See Weston and Sexton (2007), Hess (2007), Pankatz and Petrosko (2000), and Foster (1999). Of these sources, Weston and Sexton's account provides the best brief survey of implementation and trends across KERA's various component parts.

43. NAEP results are summarized in Kentucky Department of Education (2000: 51). See also the Newsletter of the Prichard Committee, Winter 2006, available at www.prichardcommittee.org/index.html, and Weston and Sexton (2007). Weston and Sexton summarize and compare NAEP results from, on one hand, 1990 and 1992 and, on the other hand, 2005 and 2007.

44. See, for example, Enrich (1995), McUsic (1999), and Koski and Reich (2006).

45. I am grateful to Doug Reed for critical comments that helped clarify these issues.

46. Another point along these lines might be that, in Kentucky, reformers' educational ideology was a mainstream, nonthreatening one, carried forward in many instances by political elites. The New Jersey reformers' educational ideology, by contrast, was explicitly redistributivist. Thus, in Kentucky, the very moderation of reformers' ideological orientation, quite apart from legal and political mobilization, helps explain the eventual general acceptance of their program. The analytical distinction between vision and goals, on one hand, and strategies and tactics, on the other hand, is an important one, I think. However, to conclude that it is really the moderate, nonthreatening content of the vision, and not strategies and tactics, that is really doing the causal work here, one would have to conclude that the litigation effort was unimportant or incidental to the overall reform struggle. That notion seems obviously wrong. The most that one can say is that broader structural factors made the common school vision more likely to arise and more likely to be accepted. But this just leads us back to thinking about the important structural conditions and constraints and the question whether I have given them their due in the overall analysis.

1. Katz (1995: 7).

2. In response to an earlier draft manuscript of this book, Rutgers Law Professor and New Jersey reformer Paul Tractenberg objected that I had "too casually" accepted charges that many poor urban school districts in New Jersey suffered from administrative mismanagement and corruption. Indeed, he opined that he thought that such problems were no more characteristic of poor urban districts than other districts in the state. I think he is wrong about this. See the sources cited above in Chapter 3, note 51; and see Chapter 5, note 61. But given the racially charged nature of this question—reformers rightly see some racial animus in the charges of mismanagement and corruption commonly leveled at urban districts—it is important once again to be clear about my point. My point is not that the fundamental problems in poor urban districts were really mismanagement and corruption. Although they were and are real, they are best viewed exactly the way the Kentucky reformers viewed them in rural eastern Kentucky. These problems are symptoms, not unchangeable causal forces. That is, lack of administrative capacity and some measure of outright corruption follow from the deeper problems of extreme concentrated poverty and the public disengagement and cynicism that arise from mismanagement and corruption in a school district. It was the problems of political organizing against these social conditions and practices that the New Jersey reform effort left untouched for a long time.

3. As many scholars have argued, given the fragmentation and complexity of the American polity, it is the institutional features of courts that make it possible for them to hear and to air moral and political claims that would otherwise have a very hard time finding a place. For an insightful elaboration of how and why courts can function this way, see Mather (1995, 1998).

4. For a recent analysis of "older" (harder, command-and-control) and "newer" (softer, collaborative) forms of judicial intervention in the context of institutional reform litigation, see Sabel and Simon (2004). Sabel and Simon make a good case in favor of the new forms and against the older ones. On the other hand, from the standpoint of reformers in some cases, rules or mandates have the advantage of setting out clear goals or benchmarks against which subsequence official behavior can be measured. In his EdD dissertation comparing policies and outcomes in New Jersey and Kentucky, New Jersey activist Steve Block argued that judicial mandates were to be preferred, if the goal was greater material benefits for the least advantaged (Block 2004).

5. Again, I thank Doug Reed for his insightful comments on these points.

6. I would note that school district support for a lawsuit was initially strongest in the eastern and poorer parts of the state, and that as reform took off some particularly important organizing efforts took place there. See Hunter (1999).

7. In many other states, most notably Texas, school finance litigation has been supported by just these kinds of cross-race, cross-class coalitions. In Texas, state-level school finance litigation was initially backed by the same activists and organizations that brought the *Rodriguez* case in the late 1960s. The effort was part of a broader struggle by and for Mexican Americans for basic civil rights and equal educational opportunity. In the early 1980s, reformers' effort to recruit school districts to back a lawsuit in the state court stalled. Reformers believed that the identification of their cause as one by and for Mexican Americans impeded their ability to win broader support from poorer white districts qua districts, even though these districts had a strong material interest in finance reform. In response, they set up a spin-off organization with additional (and more mainstream) attorneys and proceeded to garner cross-race and cross-class support for the suit that eventually resulted in the *Edgewood* cases. In Texas, many poorer African American students live in school districts within Houston and Dallas, with most of these districts are at the very top of the property-wealth distribution. I base these comments on Texas on interviews with several Texas activists and attorneys and my own research on the case. See also Lavine (1997) and Farr and Trachtenberg (1999).

8. Obviously, an exhaustive review is beyond my scope here. A selection of some prominent examples of research will have to suffice.

9. Briffault (2007), Koski and Reich (2006), Verstegen (2004), Heise and Ryan (2002), Ladd and Hansen, eds. (1999), McUsic (1999), Minorini and Sugarman (1999a,b), Enrich (1995), Heise (1995), Underwood (1995), and Clune (1992, 1994).

10. Minorini and Sugarman (1999a: 47).

11. For example, in a much-cited law review piece, Peter Enrich urged "the advocates of a fairer distribution of educational resources to leave equality behind." Equality arguments, he said, ran into insurmountable difficulties when it came time to implement court decisions and rhetorically threatened deeply held American values with the specter of Robin Hood (1995: 159–161, 165). Law professor Molly McUsic made a similar argument in favor of "the adequacy paradigm" over the "the equity paradigm." McUsic added that adequacy cases allowed litigation to reflect "advances in education policy," thereby enhancing the role of "educators and experts" in the litigation and policy reform process (1999: 115-119). Later still, law professor William Koski and political scientist Rob Reich published a competing brief for "bringing equity back in." The adequacy enthusiasts, they argued, had failed to understand that education is really mostly a private, positional good. The thing that matters is relative position, and reformers should therefore be fighting for relative equality (2006: 545).

12. Noonan (1976). For Noonan the refraction of persons and events through the forms of legal concepts and rules was both necessary and good. He wrote to remind his legal brethren of what might be lost in translation. Not all law review writing on school finance litigation ignores the persons and organizations backing reform. See Koski (2004) (comparing reform efforts and judicial outcomes in Wisconsin and Ohio), Hunter (1999) (describing the Kentucky reform effort), and Farr and Trachtenberg (1999) (describing the Texas reform effort). However, none of this work focuses on the substantive and legal ideologies in play or on the process of legal translation.

13. Studies exploring the determinants of judicial decision making in school finance cases include Koski (2004), Edwards and Ahern (2004), Lundberg (2000), Swenson (2000), and Ryan (1999a). Ryan called attention to the racial identity of the beneficiaries of reform as an important topic. See also Ryan (1999b, 1999c). Reed (2001) also examines the significance of race in school finance conflicts, in relation to mass public opinion and interest group activity.

14. Important impact studies include Reed (2001); Bosworth (2001); Evans, Murray, and Schwab (1999); and Murray, Evans, and Schwab (1998).

15. Murray, Evans, and Schwab (1998). On this analysis, the California experience, which was characterized by leveling down, clearly emerges as an outlier.

16. Reed (2001: Chapter 2).

17. See Lawrence (1990), McCann (1994), and Epp (1998).

18. Hanushek (2006), West and Peterson (2007). See also Greene (2005: Chapter 1) and Thernstrom and Thernstrom (2003: Chapter 8). For an old but still useful explication of neoconservativism, see Steinfels (1979).

19. West and Peterson (2007: 1), Hanushek (2007: 80). Other neoconservative authors typically point out that there are numerous examples of low-spending but high-performing school districts, as well as high-spending but low-performing ones. Evers and Clopton (2006), Walberg (2006). The neoconservative vision of education also typically favors a focus on "core" academic subjects and a preference for traditional methods of instruction. See Thernstrom and Thernstrom (2003).

20. Dunn and Derthick (2007: 322) ("lawsuits as political rather than legal events"), Hanushek (2006: xvii), Koret Task Force on K–12 Education, in Hanushek (2006: 346) ("self-interested parties"), and West and Peterson (2007: 8) ("classroom failure into courtroom success"). See also Springer and Guthrie (2007: 117). For a historical analysis belaboring the obvious point that neither framers' intentions nor constitutional texts (read literally) support judicial interventions, see Eastman (2007).

21. Dunn and Derthick (2007: 331) ("defining a generality") and (322, 327, 339) (lack of judicially manageable standards, threat to constitutional order and core institutions of democratic governance); Heise (2007: 270) (grave concerns about judicial legitimacy).

22. For example, Springer and Guthrie state that "contemporary adequacy research and lawsuits are increasingly guided by narrowly self-interested plaintiffs seeking to by-pass the competitive political process and procure private gain at public expense" (2007: 117). Dunn and Derthick delight in letting us in on the dirty little secret that school finance lawyers actually know that finance lawsuits are "political rather than legal events." Listen as they tell about what one of them observed at an advocates' conference: "Beyond speaking of standard litigation tactics . . . , they spoke also of success at spinning the media, hiring public relations firms, and hiring a lobbying firm to work with the legislature, all standard political tactics . . . They spoke of the utility of lawsuits as a tactic of agenda setting" (2007: 324). The only thing surprising here is that the authors think that all of this is surprising.

23. See, for example, Cavanaugh and Sarat (1980), Ely (1980), and Feeley (1992).

24. For a good example of the high school civics textbook view of democracy, see the Koret Task Force Policy Statement, in Hanushek (2006: 336-337). For important theoretical commentary on the role of courts in the modern administrative state, see Shapiro (1964: Chapter 1), and Feeley and Rubin (1999).

25. For an example of neoconservative critic who criticizes school finance reformers by covertly substituting his own ideological values and sense of desired outcomes for reformers' actual ones, see Hess (2007).

26. Struggles for environmental protection and justice often seem to make good use of instrumental invocations of legal claims, such as statutory requirements for environmental impact statements. See Handler (1978), and Marshall (2006). On the civil rights movement's use of federal courts to make symbolic statements by standing up to those in power, see Poletta (2000). Marshall (2006) also notes the symbolic importance of "confrontation" that is almost inherent in a legal challenge. McCann and Silverstein (1998) have shown how blocked legal opportunities or merely tepid judicial support can encourage political innovation and mobilization.

27. Feminist critics of various stripes, from Ruth Bader Ginsburg (1985) to Catherine MacKinnon (1987), have questioned whether the right to abortion or, more broadly, to reproductive freedom, might not have been better cast as a matter of equality and the equal protection of the laws, as opposed to the individual autonomy and due process of law. For example, the history we read in *Roe* is the history of religious, medical, and legal (read "male") views of the fetus and not, say, the history of men subordinating women through the control of their sexuality and reproductive capacities and powers. The same kind of tension between autonomy and equality frames reappears in struggles for gay rights. For example, in *Bowers v. Hardwick* (1986) the underlying facts certainly lent themselves to an equal protection challenge based not only on the unequal application of a facially neutral "sodomy law," but also on the particular targeting of Michael Hardwick for humiliation and degradation by state officials, based on his identity. However, the ACLU lawyers handling his case plausibly thought that an autonomy claim grounded in *Griswold* and *Roe* had a much better chance for success in the federal courts. See Irons (1988: 381–403). For treatments of debates over gay marriage and alternative possible legal frames and their relation to reform practices and politics, see Rubenstein (1997), Grestmann (2004), and Levitsky (2006).

28. See Sabel and Simon (2004).

29. It seems to me that there has been a tendency to neglect the problem of legal framing "within" official legal doctrines and courts in many current studies of legal mobilization and cause lawyering and/or law and social movements. I think this tendency is a consequence of deeper theoretical commitments to a culturalist understanding of law and the corollary notion that researchers

should decenter their inquiries into law and legal meaning. Decentering law counsels a turn away from "the hierarchy of formal institutions and doctrines" to "the way law is shaped and reshaped by relationships of citizens apart from the direct involvement of courts" (Scheingold 2004: xxii [first quote] and McCann 1998b: 326 [second quote]). Culturalism and decentering together hold that law is a key medium of symbolic power operative *in* society. To understand its role in conflicts involving subordinated groups, it must be studied where it operates. See Marshal and Barclay (2003). This makes perfect sense. However, a problem with decentered approaches—one that I think the focus on legal translation helps correct—is the sense that the space for egalitarian reconstructions of meaning exist in social locations outside of courts, and not so much at "the center" (within official law and courts). The center is generally cast as the realm of constraint. Decentered approaches to legal meanings certainly acknowledge that official legal frames vary and that would-be change agents sometimes have and make choices about how to frame legal challenges. But consciousness, agency, and choice about legal framing have not been taken to be important problems worthy of close study in their own right. For one fascinating attempt to bridge the social movement literature with political organizing and legal claiming in education reform efforts, see Oakes et al. (2008).

30. See, for example, Olson (1984), Milner (1986), McCann (1994), Silverstein (1996), McCann and Silverstein (1998), Southworth (1998), and various studies contained in Sarat and Scheingold, eds. (1998, 2001, 2004, 2006). A recent *Harvard Law Review* article by Orly Lobel (2007) goes as far as to claim that an a priori privileging of "extralegal activism" has become the new orthodoxy. Lobel overstates his case. He does so because he is for the most part reading texts produced by other critical (and often clinical) law professors, as opposed to social practices themselves. A preference for extralegal activism and a strong bias against litigation may well have become the orthodoxy in certain critical circles in the legal academy, but not in the worlds of activism. Still, Lobel's insightful piece offers a useful catalogue of what all is now routinely said to be wrong with litigation and a discussion of why various forms of social action might be situated on more equal footing, at least a priori.

REFERENCES

Ackerman, Bruce. 1991. *We the People: Foundations*. Cambridge, MA: The Belknap Press of Harvard University Press.

Adams, Jacob. 1993a. "The Prichard Committee for Academic Excellence: Credible Advocacy for Kentucky Schools," *Consortium for Policy Research in Education* (December).

———. 1993b. "School Finance Reform and Systemic Change: Reconstituting Kentucky's Public Schools," *Journal of Education Finance*, 18: 318.

———. 2000. "Resource Equity and Educational Adequacy," in Pankratz and Petrosko, eds., *All Children Can Learn*, San Francisco, CA: Jossey-Bass.

Advocacy Center for Children's Educational Success with Standards (ACCESS). Website: www.schoolfunding.info.

Alexander, Kern, et al. 1989. "Constitutional Intent: 'System,' 'Common,' and 'Efficient,' as Terms of Art (Report By the Select Committee Members to Judge Ray Corns, September 15, 1988)," *Journal of Education Finance*, 15: 142.

Amsterdam, Anthony G., and Jerome Bruner. 2000. *Minding the Law*. Cambridge, MA: Harvard University Press.

Anyon, Jean. 1997. *Ghetto Schooling*. New York: Teacher's College Press.

Augenblick. John. 1998. "The Role of State Legislatures in School Finance Reform: Looking Backward and Looking Ahead," in Gittell, ed., *Strategies for School Equity.*

Barr, Stephen. 1994. "The State of the State," *New Jersey Reporter* (Jan/Feb).

Bell, Derek. 1976. "Serving Two Masters: Integration Ideals and Client Interests in School Desegregation Litigation," *Yale Law Journal*, 85: 470.

Bellow, Gary, and Martha Minow, eds. 1996. *Law Stories.* Ann Arbor: University of Michigan Press.

Bierbaum, Martin. 1985. "Schools for Scandal," *The New Jersey Reporter* (October): 34.

Binder, Guyora, and Robert Weisberg. 2000. *Literary Criticisms of Law.* Princeton, NJ: Princeton University Press.

Bird, Kathleen. 1992a. "Adversary's Expert Boosts School Funding Plaintiffs," *New Jersey Law Journal* (July 13): 3.

———. 1992b. "Judges, Legislators Weigh School-Funding Plans," *New Jersey Law Journal* (November 30): 7.

Block, Arthur, and Michael A. Rebell. 1982. *Educational Policymaking and the Courts: An Empirical Study of Judicial Activism.* Chicago, IL: University of Chicago Press.

Block, Steve. 2004. "Comparing the Adequacy of New Jersey and Kentucky Court Mandates, Statutes and Regulations to Remedy Unconstitutional Public Education." Dissertation, Department of Education Administration, Seton Hall University.

Bohman, James. 1991. *New Philosophy of Social Science: Problems of Indeterminacy.* Cambridge, MA: The MIT Press.

Bosworth, Matthew. 2001. *Courts as Catalysts: State Supreme Courts and Public School Finance Equity.* Albany: State University of New York Press.

Briffault, Richard. 1990a. "Our Localism: Part I: The Structure of Local Government Law," *Columbia Law Review.* 90: 1.

———. 1990b. "Our Localism: Part II: Localism and Legal Theory," *Columbia Law Review.* 90: 346.

———. 2007. "Adding Adequacy to Equity," in West and Peterson, eds. *School Money Trials: The Legal Pursuit of Adequacy.*

Brigham, John. 1987. *The Cult of the Court.* Philadelphia: Temple University Press.

Brooks, Peter. 1996. "The Law as Narrative and Rhetoric," In Peter Brooks and Paul Gewirtz, eds., *Law's Stories: Narrative and Rhetoric in Law.*

Brooks, Peter, and Paul Gewirtz, eds. 1996. *Law's Stories: Narrative and Rhetoric in Law*. New Haven, CT: Yale University Press.

Bruner, Jerome. 1996. *The Culture of Education*. Cambridge, MA: Harvard University Press.

Burtless, ed. 1996. *Does Money Matter? The Effects of School Resources on Student Achievement and Adult Success*. Washington, DC: Brookings Institution.

Calavita, Kity. 2001. "Blue Jeans, Rape, and the 'De-Constitutive' Power of Law," *Law and Society Review* 35: 89–116.

Cannon, Bradley C., and Charles A. Johnson. 1999. *Judicial Policies: Implementation and Impact*, Second Edition. Washington, DC: Congressional Quarterly Press.

Carr, Melissa C., and Susan H. Furhman. 1999. "The Politics of School Finance in the 1990's," in Ladd, Chalk, and Hansen, eds., *Equity and Adequacy in Education Finance*.

Cavanaugh, Ralph, and Austin Sarat. 1980. "Thinking about Courts: Toward and beyond a Jurisprudence of Judicial Competence," *Law and Society Review* 14: 371.

Clark, Kenneth, 1965. *Dark Ghetto: Dilemmas of Social Power*. New York: Harper and Row.

Clune, William H. 1992. "New Answers to Hard Questions Posed by *Rodriguez*: Ending Separation of School Finance and Educational Policy by Bridging the Gap between Wrong and Remedy," *Connecticut Law Review* 24:721

———. 1994. "The Shift from Equity to Adequacy in School Finance," *Educational Policy* 8:376.

Cohen, Lizabeth. 2003. *A Consumer's Republic: The Politics of Mass Consumption in Postwar America*. New York: Vintage Books.

Coleman, James, et al. 1966. *Equality of Educational Opportunity*. Washington, D.C: Government Printing Office.

———. 1969. "The Concept of Equal Educational Opportunity," in Harvard Educational Review Editorial Board, ed., *Equal Educational Opportunity*, 9–24. Cambridge, MA: Harvard University Press.

Combs, Bert T. 1991. "Creative Constitutional Law: The Kentucky School Reform Law," *Harvard Journal on Legislation* 28: 367.

Connell, R. W. 1993. *Schools and Social Justice*. Philadelphia, PA: Temple University Press.

Coons, John E., William H. Clune III, and Stephen Sugarman. 1970. *Private Wealth and Public Education*. Cambridge, MA: Harvard University Press.

Corcoran, Thomas, and Herbert T. Green. 1989. "Educating New Jersey: The Unfinished Business of School Reform," *New Jersey Reporter*: 32 (October), pp. 32–36.

Corcoran, Thomas, and Nathan Scrovonick. 1994. "More Than Equal: New Jersey's Quality Education Act," Unpublished manuscript on file with Author.

———. 1998. "More Than Equal: New Jersey's Quality Education Act," in Gittell, *Strategies for School Equity*.

Crenshaw, Kimberle W. 1988. "Race, Reform, and Retrenchment: Transformation and Legitimation in Antidiscrimination Law," *Harvard Law Review* 101: 1331.

Dolan, Margaret. 1992. "State Takeover of a Local School District in New Jersey: A Case Study," *Consortium for Policy Research in Education (CPRE)*, Research Report Series TC-008.

Dougherty, Jack. 2004. *More Than One Struggle: The Evolution of Black School Reform in Milwaukee*. Chapel Hill: University of North Carolina Press.

Dove, Ronald. 1991. "Acorns in a Mountain Pool: The Role of Litigation, Law and Lawyers in Kentucky Education Reform," *Journal of Education Finance* 17: 83.

Dunn, Joshua, and Martha Derthick. 2007. "Adequacy Litigation and the Separation of Powers," in West and Peterson, eds., *School Money Trials*, pp. 322–344.

Dwyer, John P., David L. Kirp, and Larry A. Rosenthal. 1995. *Our Town: Race, Housing, and the Soul of Suburbia*. New Brunswick, NJ: Rutgers University Press.

Eagleton, Terry. 1991. *Ideology: An Introduction*. London, England: Verso.

Eastman, John C. 2007. "Reinterpreting the Education Clauses in State Constitutions," in West and Peterson, eds., *School Money Trials*.

Education Law Center. 1996. *Wiping Out Disadvantages: The Programs and Services Needed to Supplement Regular Education for Poor School Children* (Steve Block, principal author). Newark, NJ: Education Law Center.

———. 2004a. *Breaking Ground: Rebuilding New Jersey's Urban School: The Abbott School Construction Program* (Joan Ponessa, principal author). Available at www.edlawcenter.org/ELCPublic/AbbottSchoolFacilities/ AbbottSchoolConstructionProgram.htm.

———. 2004b. *Minority Enrollments in Abbott Districts*. Available at: www .edlawcenter.org/ELCPublic/elcnews_040522_MinorityEnrollments.htm.

———. 2004c. *Poverty Enrollments in Abbott Districts*. Available at: www .edlawcenter.org/ELCPublic/elcnews_040522_PovertyEnrollments.htm.

———. 2006. *The Abbott Districts in 2005–06: Progress and Challenges*, A Report of the Abbott Indicators Project (Arain Applewhite and Lesley Hirsch, Authors). Available in PDF format at: http://edlawcenter.org/index.htm.

Education Trust. 2005. *The Funding Gap 2005*. Retrieved on July 16, 2009, from: www.edtrust.org.

Edwards, Yohance C., and Jennifer Ahern. 2004. "Note: Unequal Treatment in State Supreme Courts: Minority and City Schools in Education Finance Reform Litigation," *New York University Law Review* 79: 326.

Elmore, Richard F., and Milbrey W. McLaughlin. 1982. *Reform and Retrenchment: The Politics of California School Finance Reform*. Cambridge, MA: Ballinger.

Ely, John Hart. 1980. *Democracy and Distrust: A Theory of Judicial Review*. Cambridge, MA: Harvard University Press.

Emirbayer, Mustafa, and Ann Mische, "What Is Agency?" 1998. *American Journal of Sociology* 103: 962.

Enrich, Peter. 1995. "Leaving Equality Behind: New Directions in School Finance Litigation," *Vanderbilt Law Review* 48: 101.

Epp, Charles R. 1998. *The Rights Revolution: Lawyers, Activists, and Supreme Courts in Comparative Perspective*. Chicago, IL: The University of Chicago Press.

Epstein, Lee, ed. 1995. *Contemplating Courts*. Washington, DC: Congressional Quarterly Press.

Erlichson, Bari Anhault, and Margaret Goertz. 2001. *Implementing Whole School Reform in New Jersey: Year Two*. New Brunswick, NJ: Department of Public Policy and Governmental Services, Rutgers University.

Erlichson, Bari Anhault, Margaret Goertz, and Barbara Turnbull. 1999. *Implementing Whole School Reform in New Jersey: Year One in the First Cohort Schools*. New Brunswick, NJ: Department of Public Policy and Governmental Services, Rutgers University.

Evans, William N., Sheila Murray, and Robert M. Schwab. 1999. "The Impact of Court-Mandated School Finance Reform," in Ladd, Chalk, and Hansen, eds., *Equity and Adequacy in Education Finance*.

Evers, Williamson M., and Paul Clopton. 2006. "High-Spending, Low-Performing School Districts," in Hanushek, ed., *Courting Failure*.

Farr, Steven J., and Mark Trachtenberg. 1999. "The *Edgewood* Drama: An Epic Quest for Educational Equity," *Yale Journal of Law and Policy* 17: 607.

Feagin, Joe R., Anthony N. Orum, and Gideon Sjoberg, eds. 1991. *A Case for the Case Study*. Chapel Hill: University of North Carolina Press.

Feeley, Malcolm M. 1992. "Review: Hollow Hopes, Flypaper, and Metaphors," *Law and Social Inquiry* 17: 745.

———. 2004. "Foreword" to Stuart A. Scheingold, *The Politics of Rights: Lawyers, Public Policy, and Political Change. Second Edition*. Ann Arbor: University of Michigan Press.

Feeley, Malcolm M., and Edward L. Rubin. 1999. *Judicial Policy Making and the Modern State: How the Courts Reformed America's Prisons*. New York: Cambridge University Press.

Ferguson, Ronald F. 1991. "Paying for Public Education: New Evidence on How and Why Money Matters," *Harvard Journal on Legislation* 28: 465.

Ferguson, Ronald F., and Helen Ladd. 1996. "Economics of School Reform: Three Promising Models," in Ladd, ed., *Holding Schools Accountable*.

Finifter, Ada W., ed. 1993. *Political Science: The State of the Discipline*. Washington, DC: American Political Science Association.

Flanagan, Ann E., and Sheila Murray. 2004. "A Decade of Reform: The Impact of School Reform in Kentucky," in Yinger, ed., *Helping Children Left Behind*.

Foster, Jack. 1999. *Redesigning Public Education: The Kentucky Experience*. Lexington, KY: Diversified Services.

Fromm, Steven. 1993. "The ABC's of Clout," *New Jersey Reporter*: 26 (September).

Gambitta, Richard A. L, Marilyn L. May, and James C. Foster, eds. 1981. *Governing through Courts*. New York: Sage Publications.

Garth, Bryant G., and Austin Sarat, eds. 1998. *How Does Law Matter?* Evanston, IL: Northwestern University Press.

Geertz, Clifford. 1973. *The Interpretation of Cultures: Selected Essays*. New York: Basic Books.

Gillman, Howard. 2001. "Review: What's Law Got to Do with It? Judicial Behavioralists Test the 'Legal Model' of Judicial Decision Making," *Law and Social Inquiry* 26: 465.

Ginsburg, Ruth Bader. 1985. "Some Thoughts on Autonomy and Equality in Relation to *Roe v. Wade*," *North Carolina Law Review* 63: 375.

Gittell, Marilyn J., ed., 1998. *Strategies for School Equity: Creating Productive Schools in a Just Society*. New Haven, CT: Yale University Press.

———. 2005. "The Politics of Equity in Urban School Reform," in Petrovich and Wells, eds., *Bringing Equity Back In*.

Goertz, Margaret. 1978. *Money and Education: Where Did the 400 Million Dollars Go?* Princeton, NJ: Educational Testing Service.

———. 1993. "School Finance in New Jersey: The Saga Continues," *Journal of Education Finance* 18: 346.

———. 1994. "The Equity Impact of the Quality Education Act in New Jersey," Paper Presented at the Annual Meeting of the Education Finance Association, Nashville, TN.

Goertz, Margaret, and Robert Goertz. 1990. "The Quality Education Act of 1990: New Jersey Responds to *Abbott v. Burke,*" *Journal of Education Finance* 6: 104.

Goertz, Margaret, and Michael Weirs. 2007. "Assessing Success in School Finance Litigation: The Case of New Jersey," Paper Prepared for the Symposium on Equal Educational Opportunity: What Now?, Teacher's College, Columbia University.

Gold, Steven D., David M. Smith, and Stephen B Lawton, eds. 1995. *Public School Finance Programs in the United States and Canada, 1993–94, Volume 1.* Albany: Nelson A. Rockefeller Institute of Government, SUNY.

Goodlad, John. 1984. *A Place Called School: Prospects for the Future.* New York: McGraw-Hill.

Gordon, Robert W. 1984. "Critical Legal Histories," *Stanford Law Review* 36: 57.

———. 1988. "Law and Ideology," *Tikkun* 3: 14.

Greene, Jay P. 2005. *Education Myths: What Special Interest Groups Want You to Believe about Our Schools and Why It Isn't So.* Oxford, UK: Rowman and Littlefield Publishers.

Greif, Alexandra. 2004. "Politics, Practicalities, and Priorities: New Jersey's Experience Implementing the *Abbott V* Mandate," *Yale Journal of Law and Policy* 22: 615.

Grestmann, Evan. 2004. *Same-Sex Marriage and the Constitution.* New York: Cambridge University Press.

Guthrie, James W. 1983. "United States School Finance Policy," *Education Policy and Analysis* 5: 207.

Guthrie, James, Walter Garms, and Larry Pierce. 1983. *School Finance and Education Policy.* New York: Longman Publishing Co.

Handler, Joel F. 1978. *Social Movements and the Legal System.* New York: Academic Press.

Hanushek, Eric A. 1991. When School Finance "Reform" May Not Be Good Policy. *Harvard Journal of Legislation* 28: 423.

———, ed. 2006. *Courting Failure: How School Finance Lawsuits Exploit Judges' Good Intentions and Harm Our Children.* Palo Alto, CA: Education Next Books, Hoover Institution Press.

————. 2007. "The Alchemy of 'Costing Out' an Adequate Education," in West and Peterson, eds., *School Money Trials.*

Harris, Beth. 1998. "The Dynamics of Legal Leverage: Defending the Right-to-Home," in Sarat and Ewick, eds., *Law, Politics, and Society.*

Harvard Educational Review Editorial Board, ed. 1969. *Equal Educational Opportunity.* Cambridge, MA: Harvard University Press.

Heise, Michael. 1995. "State Constitutions, School Finance Litigation, and the 'Third Wave': From Equity to Adequacy," *Temple Law Review* 68: 1151.

————. 2007. "Adequacy Litigation in an Age of Accountability," in West and Peterson, eds., *School Money Trials.*

Hess, Frederick M. 2007. "Adequacy Judgments and School Reform," in West and Peterson, eds., *School Money Trials*, pp. 159–194.

Heubert, Jay P., ed. 1999. *Law and School Reform: Six Strategies for Promoting Educational Equity.* New Haven, CT: Yale University Press.

Hiese, Michael, and James E. Ryan. 2002. "The Political Economy of School Choice," *Yale Law Journal* 111: 2043.

Hilbink, Thomas M. 2004. "You Know the Type . . . : Categories of Cause Lawyering," *Law and Social Inquiry* 29: 657.

Hirsch, Fred. 1977. *Social Limits to Growth.* London: Routledge and Kagan Paul.

Hochschild, Jennifer, and Nathan Scovronick. 2003. *The American Dream and Public Schools.* New York: Oxford University Press.

Horowitz, Donald. 1977. *The Courts and Social Policy.* Washington, DC: The Brookings Institution.

Hunter, Molly. 1999. "All Eyes Forward: Public Engagement and Educational Reform in Kentucky," *Journal of Law and Education* 28: 485.

Irons, Peter. 1988. *The Courage of Their Convictions: Sixteen Americans Who Fought Their Way to the Supreme Court.* New York: The Free Press.

Jackson, Kenneth. 1985. *Crabgrass Frontier: The Suburbanization of the United States.* New York: Oxford University Press.

Jencks, Christopher. 1972. *Inequality: A Reassessment of the Effect of Family and Schooling in America.* New York: Harper/Colophon Books.

————. 1988. Whom Must We Treat Equally for Educational Opportunity to Be Equal? *Ethics* 98: 518.

Judis, John B. 1990. "A Taxing Governor," *The New Republic*, October 15, 1990: 31.

Kanige, Jeffrey. 1987. "Showdown over Schools: The State's Intervention Plan," *New Jersey Reporter* (September).

Katz, Michael. 1995. *Improving Poor People: The Welfare State, the "Underclass," and Urban Schools as History.* Princeton, NJ: Princeton University Press.

Katznelson, Ira, and Margaret Weir. 1985. *Schooling for All: Class, Race, and the Decline of the Democratic Ideal.* New York: Basic Books.

Kean, Thomas H. 1988. *The Politics of Inclusion.* New York: The Free Press.

Kehler, David. 1992. "The Trenton Tea Party: The Story of New Jersey's Tax Revolt," *Policy Review*: 46.

Kelman, Mark. 1987. *Critical Legal Studies.* Cambridge, MA: Harvard University Press.

Kentucky Department of Education. 1995. *The Kentucky Education Reform Act: The First Five Years.* Frankfort: Author.

———. 2000. *Results Matter: A Decade of Difference in Kentucky's Public Schools, 1990–2000.* Frankfort, KY: Author.

Kentucky Historical Society. 1988. "Governor Wallace Wilkinson." *The Register of the Kentucky Historical Society.* Lexington: Author.

Kentucky Legislative Research Commission. 1996. *Annual Report.* Office of Educational Accountability, Lexington, Kentucky.

———. 1997. *A Citizens Guide.* Lexington, KY: Office of Educational Accountability.

Kirp, David. 1982. *Just School: The Idea of Racial Equality in American Education.* Berkeley: University of California Press.

Koret Task Force on K–12 Education. 2006. "Funding for Performance," in Hanushek, ed., *Courting Failure.*

Koski, William S. 2004. "The Politics of Judicial Decision-Making in Educational Policy Reform Litigation," *Hastings Law Journal* 55: 1077.

Koski, William S., and Rob Reich. 2006. "What 'Adequate' Isn't: The Retreat from Equity in Educational Law and Policy," *Emory Law Journal* 56: 545.

Kozol, Jonathan. 1991. *Savage Inequalities.* New York: Basic Books.

Labaree, David. 1997. *How to Succeed in School without Really Learning: The Credentials Race in American Education.* New Haven, CT: Yale University Press.

Ladd, Helen F., ed. 1996. *Holding Schools Accountable: Performance-Based Reform in Education.* Washington, DC: The Brookings Institution.

Ladd, Helen F., and Janet S. Hansen, eds. 1999. *Making Money Matter: Financing America's Schools.* Commission on Behavioral and Social Sciences and Education, National Research Council, Washington, DC: National Academy Press.

Ladd, Helen F., Rosemary Chalk, and Janet Hansen, eds. 1999. *Equity and Adequacy in Education Finance: Issues and Perspectives.* Commission on Behavioral and Social Sciences and Education, National Research Council, Washington, DC: National Academy Press.

Landy, Marc. 1978. "Kentucky," in Alan Rosenthal and Maureen Moakley, eds., *The Political Life of the American States.*

Lauver, Sherri C., Gary W. Ritter, and Margaret Goertz. 2001. "Caught in the Middle: The Fate of Non-Urban Districts in the Wake of New Jersey's School Finance Litigation," *Journal of Education Finance* 26: 281.

Lavine, Richard. 1997. "School Finance Reform in Texas, 1983–1995," in Robert H. Wilson, ed., *Public Policy and Community.*

Law and Society Review. 1980–81.

Lawrence, Susan E. 1990. *The Poor in Court: The Legal Services Program and Supreme Court Decision Making.* Princeton, NJ: Princeton University Press.

Lehne, Richard. 1978. *Quest for Justice: The Politics of School Finance Reform.* New York: Longman.

Levinson, Sanford. 1991. Conversing about Justice [Book Review]. *Yale Law Journal* 100: 1855.

Levitsky, Sandra R. 2006. "To Lead with Law: Reassessing the Influence of Legal Advocacy Organizations in Social Movements," in Sarat and Scheingold, eds., *Cause Lawyers and Social Movements.*

Lindseth, Alfred A. 2006. "The Legal Backdrop to Adequacy," in Hanushek, ed., *Courting Failure.*

Liu, Goodwin. 2006. "Interstate Inequality in Educational Opportunity," *New York University Law Review* 81: 2044.

Lobel, Orly. 2007. "The Paradoxes of Extralegal Activism: Critical Legal Consciousness and Transformative Politics," *Harvard Law Review* 120: 937.

Lundberg, Paula J. 2000. "State Courts and School Funding: A Fifty-State Analysis," *Albany Law Review* 63: 1101.

MacKinnon, Catherine A. 1987. *Feminism Unmodified: Discourses on Life and Law.* Cambridge, MA: Harvard University Press.

Marshall, Anna-Maria. 2006. "Social Movement Strategies and the Participatory Potential of Litigation," in Sarat and Scheingold, eds., *Cause Lawyers and Social Movments.*

Marshall, Anna-Maria, and Scott Barclay. 2003. "In Their Own Words: How Ordinary People Construct the Legal World,' *Law and Social Inquiry* 28: 617.

Mather, Lynn. 1995. The Fired Football Coach (Or, How Trial Courts Make Public Policy). In Lee Epstein, ed., *Contemplating Courts.*

———. 1998. "Theorizing about Trial Courts: Lawyers, Policymaking, and To-bacco Litigation," *Law and Social Inquiry* 23: 897.

McAdam, Doug. 1982. *Political Process and the Development of Black Insurgency, 1930–1970*. Chicago: University of Chicago Press.

McCann, Michael W. 1992. "Review: Reform Litigation on Trial," *Law and Social Inquiry* 17: 715.

———. 1994. *Rights at Work: Pay Equity and the Politics of Legal Mobilization*. Chicago: University of Chicago Press.

———. 1998a. "How Does Law Matter for Social Movements?" in Bryant G. Garth and Austin Sarat, eds. *How Does Law Matter?* Evanston, IL: North-western University Press.

———. 1998b. "Law and Political Struggles for Social Change: Puzzles, Paradoxes, and Promises for Future Research," in David A. Schultz, ed., *Leveraging the Law: Using Courts to Achieve Social Change*. New York: Peter Lang Publishing.

McCann, Michael W., and Helena Silverstein. 1998. "Rethinking Law's 'Allure-ments': A Relational Analysis of Social Movement Lawyers in the United States," in Scheingold and Sarat, eds., *Cause Lawyering*.

McDermott, Katherine. 1999. *Controlling Public Education*. Lawrence: Kansas University Press.

McUsic, Molly S. 1999. "The Law's Role in the Distribution of Education: The Promise and Pitfalls of School Finance Litigation," in Jay P. Heubert, ed., *Law and School Reform*.

———. 2004. "Symposium: *Brown* at Fifty: The Future of *Brown v. Board of Education*: Economic Integration of the Public Schools," *Harvard Law Review* 117: 1334.

Melnick, R. Shep. 1994. *Between the Lines: Interpreting Welfare Rights*. Washington, DC: The Brookings Institution.

Miller, Penny M. 1994. *Kentucky Politics and Government: Do We Stand United?* Lincoln: University of Nebraska Press.

Miller, Penny M., and Malcolm E. Jewell. 1990. *Political Parties and Primaries in Kentucky*. Lexington: University of Kentucky Press.

Milner, Neal. 1986. "Dilemmas of Legal Mobilization: Ideologies and Strategies of Mental Patient Liberation Groups," *Law and Policy* 8: 105.

Minorini, Paul A., and Stephen Sugarman. 1999a. "Educational Adequacy and the Courts: The Promise and Problems of Moving to a New Paradigm," in Ladd, Chalk, and Hansen, eds., *Equity and Adequacy in Education Finance*.

———. 1999b. "School Finance Litigation in the Name of Educational Equity: Its Evolution, Impact, and Future," in Ladd, Chalk, and Hansen, eds., *Equity and Adequacy in Education Finance.*

Minow, Martha. 1987. Interpreting Rights: An Essay for Robert Cover. *Yale Law Journal* 96: 1860.

———. 1990. *Making All the Difference: Inclusion, Exclusion, and American Law.* Ithaca, NY: Cornell University Press.

———. 1991. "School Finance: Does Money Matter?" *Harvard Journal on Legislation* 28: 395.

Murray, Sheila E., William N. Evans, and Robert M. Schwab. 1998. "Education–Finance Reform and the Distribution of Educational Resources," *American Economic Review* 88: 789.

Myrdal, Gunner, with Richard Sterner and Arnold Rose. 1972 edition. *An American Dilemma: The Negro Problem and American Democracy.* New York: Pantheon.

National Advisory Commission on Civil Disorders. 1968. *Report* [Kerner Commission Report]. New York: Bantam Books.

National Center for Education Statistics (NCES). 2002. *Fast Facts.* Retrieved on July 16, 2009, from: http://nces.ed.gov/fastfacts/display.asp?id=66.

———. 2004. *The Condition of Education*, Indicator 35. Retrieved in September 2006 from: http://nces.ed.gov/programs/coe/204/section6/indicator35.asp.

National Commission on Excellence in Education. 1983. *A Nation at Risk.* Washington, D.C.: U.S. Department of Education.

National Institute for Early Education Research (NIEER). 2005. *The State of Preschool.* Available at www.nieer.org.

———. 2007. *Abbott Preschool Longitudinal Effects Study* [APPLES]. Available at www.startingat3.org/news/Sa3news_070618_NIEERBenefitsStudy.htm.

New Jersey Office of Legislative Services. 1990. *New Jersey Legislative Manual, 1990.* Trenton, NJ.

———. 1992a. *Committee Meeting Before the Senate Education Committee and Assembly Education Committee: Quality Education Act of 1990.* Hearings Recorded and Transcribed by the Hearing Unit.

———. 1992b. *Public Hearing before Senate Education Committee and Assembly Education Committee*, Senate Concurrent Resolution No. 64 and Assembly Concurrent Resolution No. 7 (Proposed constitutional amendment to define the system of free public schools which must be provided by the Legislature). Hearings recorded and transcribed by the Hearing Unit.

———. 1994. *New Jersey Legislative Manual, 1994.* Trenton, NJ: Author.

———. 1996. *New Jersey Legislative Manual, 1996.* Trenton, NJ: Author.

Noonan, John T. 1976. *Persons and Masks of the Law: Cardozo, Holmes, Jefferson, and Wythe as Makers of the Masks.* Berkeley: University of California Press.

Oakes, Jeannie, John Rodgers, Gary Blasi, and Martin Lipton. 2008. "Grassroots Organizing, Social Movements, and the Right to High-Quality Education," *Stanford Journal of Civil Rights and Civil Liberties* 4: 339.

O'Connor, Karen. 1980. *Women's Organization's Use of the Courts.* Lexington, MA: Lexington Books.

Odden, Allan R., and Lawrence O. Picus. 1992. *School Finance: A Policy Perspective.* New York: McGraw-Hill.

Odden, Allan, and Lawrence O. Picus. 2001. *Assessing SEEK from an Adequacy Perspective,* Report Prepared for the Kentucky Department of Education. Available at: www.schoolfunding.info/states/ky/4-4-03CostingOut.php3.

Official Report of the Proceedings and Debates in the Convention to Adopt, Amend or Change the Constitution of the State of Kentucky. 1890-1891. Vols. 1-4. Frankfort, Kentucky.

Olson, Susan. 1981. "The Political Evolution of Interest Group Litigation," in Gambitta, May, and Foster, eds., *Governing through Courts.*

———. 1984. *Clients and Lawyers: Securing the Rights of Disabled Persons.* Greenwood, CT: Greenwood Press.

Pankatz, Roger S., and Joseph M. Petrosko. 2000. *All Children Can Learn: Lessons from the Kentucky Experience.* San Francisco, CA: Jossey-Bass.

Paris, David C. 1995. *Ideology and Educational Reform: Themes and Theories in Public Education.* Boulder, CO: Westview Press.

Paris, Michael. 2001. "Legal Mobilization and the Politics of Reform: Lessons from School Finance Litigation in Kentucky, 1984–1995," *Law and Social Inquiry* 26: 631.

———. 2006. "Review: The Politics of Rights: Then and Now," *Law and Social Inquiry* 31: 999.

Paris, Michael, and Kevin J. McMahon. 1998. "The Politics of Rights Revisited: Rosenberg, McCann, and the New Institutionalism," in Schultz, ed., *Leveraging the Law.*

Pearce, John Ed. 1987. *Divide and Dissent: Kentucky Politics, 1930–1963.* Lexington: The University Press of Kentucky.

Petrovich, Janice, and Amy Stuart Wells, eds. 2005. *Bringing Equity Back In: Research for a New Era in American Education Policy.* New York: Teachers College Press.

Picus, Lawrence O., Allan Odden, and Mark Fermanich. 2001. *Assessing the Equity of Kentucky's SEEK Formula: A Ten-Year Analysis.* A Report Prepared for the Kentucky Department of Education. Available at: www.education.ky.gov/cgi-bin/MsmFind.exe?QUERY=Picus&submit=Search.

Poletta, Francesca. 2000. "The Structural Context of Novel Rights Claims: Southern Civil Rights Organizing, 1961–1966," *Law and Society Review* 34: 367.

Pomper, Gerald R., ed. 1986. *The Political State of New Jersey.* New Brunswick, NJ: Rutgers University Press.

Ponessa, Joan. 1997. "A Crisis for School Districts: More Students, New Programs, and No Extra Room," Princeton, NJ: Public Affairs Research Institute.

Prichard Committee for Academic Excellence. 1989. *A Path to a Larger Life: Creating Kentucky's Educational Future.* Lexington: University of Kentucky Press.

Purcell, Edward A. Jr. 1973. *The Crisis of Democratic Theory: Scientific Naturalism and the Problem of Value.* Lexington: University of Kentucky Press.

Rebell, Michael A. 2007a. "Ensuring Successful Remedies in Educational Adequacy Litigations," Paper Prepared for the Symposium on Equal Educational Opportunity: What Now?, Teacher's College, Columbia University.

———. 2007b. "Poverty, Meaningful Educational Opportunity, and the Necessary Role of the Courts," *North Carolina Law Review* 85: 1467.

Rebell, Michael A., and Joseph J. Wardenski. 2004. *Of Course Money Matters: Why the Arguments to the Contrary Never Added Up.* New York: The Campaign for Fiscal Equity.

Reed, Douglas S. 2001. *On Equal Terms: The Constitutional Politics of Educational Opportunity.* Princeton, NJ: Princeton University Press.

Reock , Ernest. 1993. *State Aid for Schools in New Jersey, 1976–1993.* New Brunswick, NJ: Center for Government Services, Rutgers University.

———. 1996. *State Aid for Schools in New Jersey, 1976–1996.* New Brunswick, NJ: Center for Government Services, Rutgers University.

———. 1999. *State Aid for Schools in New Jersey, 1976–1999.* New Brunswick, NJ: Center for Government Services, Rutgers University.

Rosenberg, Gerald N. 1991. *The Hollow Hope: Can Courts Bring about Social Change?* Chicago, IL: University of Chicago Press.

Rosenthal, Alan, and Maureen Moakley, eds. 1978. *The Political Life of the American States.* New York: Praeger.

Rothstein, Richard. 1998. *The Way We Were? The Myths and Realities of America's Student Achievement*. New York: Century Foundation Press.

Rubenstein, William B. 1997. "Divided We Litigate: Addressing Disputes among Group Members and Lawyers in Civil Rights Campaigns," *Yale Law Journal* 106: 1623.

Ryan, Alan. 1997. "Review: Conservatives, Nasty and Nice," *New York Review of Books* (June 26): 27.

Ryan, James E. 1999a. "The Influence of Race on School Finance Reform," *Michigan Law Review* 98: 432.

———. 1999b. "Schools, Race, Money," *Yale Law Journal* 109: 249.

———. 1999c. "*Sheff*, Segregation, and School Finance Litigation," *New York University Law Review* 74: 529.

Sabel, Charles F., and William H. Simon. 2004. "Destabilization Rights: How Public Law Litigation Succeeds," *Harvard Law Review* 117: 1015.

Salmore, Barbara G., and Stephen A. Salmore. 1993. *New Jersey Politics and Government: Suburban Politics Comes of Age*. Lincoln: University of Nebraska Press.

Sandler, Ross, and David Schoenbrod. 2003. *Democracy by Decree: What Happens When Courts Run Government*. New Haven, CT: Yale University Press.

Sarat, Austin, and Patricia Ewick, eds. 1998. *Studies in Law, Politics, and Society, An Annual*, New York: Sage Publications.

Sarat, Austin, and Thomas Kearns, eds. 1996. *The Rhetoric of Law*. Ann Arbor: The University of Michigan Press.

Sarat, Austin, and Stuart Scheingold, eds. 1998. *Cause Lawyering: Political Commitments and Professional Responsibilities*. New York: Oxford University Press.

———. 2001. *Cause Lawyering and the State in a Global Era*. New York: Oxford University Press.

———. 2004. *The Worlds Cause Lawyers Make: Structure and Agency in Legal Practice*. Stanford, CA: Stanford University Press.

———. 2006. *Cause Lawyers and Social Movements*. Stanford, CA: Stanford University Press.

Schama, Simon. 1989. *Citizens: A Chronicle of the French Revolution*. New York: Alfred A. Knopf.

Scheingold, Stuart A. 1974. *The Politics of Rights: Lawyers, Public Policy, and Political Change*. New Haven, CT: Yale University Press.

———. 2004. *The Politics of Rights: Lawyers, Public Policy, and Political Change. Second Edition*. Ann Arbor: The University of Michigan Press.

Schlesinger, Arthur Jr. 1985. "Pritch: A New Deal Memoir," *New York Review of Books* (March 28): 21.

Schneider, Elizabeth. 1986. "The Dialectic of Rights and Politics: Perspectives from the Women's Rights Movement," *New York University Law Review* 61: 589.

———. 2000. *Battered Women and Feminist Lawmaking*. New Haven, CT: Yale University Press.

Schrag, Peter. 2003. *Final Test: The Battle for Adequacy in America's Schools*. New York: W. W. Norton Co.

Schultz, David A., ed. 1998. *Leveraging the Law: Using Courts to Achieve Social Change*. New York: Peter Lang Publishing.

Scott, Daryl Michael. 1997. *Contempt and Pity: Social Policy and the Image of the Damaged Black Psyche, 1880–1996*. Chapel Hill: The University of North Carolina Press.

Seidenstein, Robert G. 2008. "Education Law Effort Expanding Nationally," *New Jersey Lawyer* (June 9).

Shapiro, Martin. 1964. *Law and Politics in the Supreme Court: New Approaches to Political Jurisprudence*. New York: The Free Press.

———. 1993. "Public Law and Judicial Politics," in Finifter, ed., *Political Science*.

Sherman, Rori. 1988. "In New Jersey, Who Is Really the Boss? Jury Still Out," *The National Law Journal* (December 19).

———. 1990. "The N.J. Robin Hood Solution," *National Law Journal* (May 28).

Shklar, Judith N. 1964. *Legalism: Law, Morals, and Political Trials*. Cambridge, MA: Harvard University Press.

———. 1986. *Legalism: Law, Morals, and Political Trials,* 2nd ed. Cambridge, MA: Harvard University Press.

Shure, John. 1994. "Gunning for Florio," *The New Jersey Reporter* (March/April): 36.

Silverstein, Helena. 1996. *Unleashing Rights: Legal Meaning and the Animal Rights Movement*. Ann Arbor: The University of Michigan Press.

Sinding, Rick, 1989. "Editorial," *New Jersey Reporter* (May): 2.

Sizer, Theodore. 1984. *Horace's Compromise: The Dilemma of the American High School*. Boston, MA: Houghton Mifflin.

Southworth, Ann. 1998. "Lawyers and the Politics of Rights in Civil Rights and Poverty Practice," Paper Presented at the Annual Meeting of the Law and Society Association, Boulder, Colorado.

Sparer, Edward. 1984. "Fundamental Human Rights, Legal Entitlements, and the Social Struggle: A Friendly Critique of the Critical Legal Studies Movement," *Stanford Law Review* 36: 509.

Springer, Matthew, and James W. Guthrie. 2007. "The Politicization of the School Finance Legal Process," in West and Peterson, eds., *School Money Trials*.

Stanfield, Rochelle. 1991. "Equity and Excellence," *National Journal* (November 11): 2860.

Steffy, Betty E. 1993. *The Kentucky Education Reform: Lessons for America*. Lancaster, PA: Technomic Publishing Co.

Steinfels, Peter. 1979. *The Neo-Conservatives*. New York: Simon and Schuster.

Stern, Sol. 2006. "*Campaign for Fiscal Equity v. New York*: The March of Folly," in Hanushek, *Courting Failure*.

Sternlieb, George, and James W. Hughes. 1986. "Demographic and Economic Dynamics," in Gerald Pomper, ed., *The Political State of New Jersey*, p. 39.

Stumpf, Harry P. 1998. *American Judicial Politics,* Second Edition. Upper Saddle River, NJ: Prentice-Hall.

Swenson, Karen. 2000. "School Finance Reform Litigation: Why Are Some State Supreme Courts Activist and Others Are Restrained," *Albany Law Review* 63: 1147.

Tamanaha, Brian Z. 1997. *Realistic Socio-Legal Theory*. New York: Oxford University Press.

Tarr, Alan G., and Mary Cornelia Porter. 1988. *State Supreme Courts in State and Nation*. New Haven, CT: Yale University Press.

Thernstrom, Abigail, and Stephan Thernstrom. 2003. *No Excuses: Closing the Racial Gap in Learning*. Cambridge, MA: Harvard University Press.

Tiebout, Charles M. 1956. "A Pure Theory of Local Expenditures," *Journal of Political Economy* 54: 416.

Toch, Thomas. 1991. *In the Name of Excellence: The Struggle to Reform the Nation's Schools, Why It Is Failing, and What Should Be Done about It*. New York: Oxford University Press.

Tractenberg, Paul. 1974. "*Robinson v. Cahill*: The 'Thorough and Efficient' Clause," *Law and Contemporary Problems* 38: 312.

———. 1997. "A Tale of Two States: A Comparative Study of School Finance and Educational Reform in California and New Jersey," Unpublished Manuscript.

———. 2009. "Moving Education Equity to the Next Level," available at: website: www.edlawcenter.org/test/ELCPublic/elcnews_090608_TractenbergOpEd.htm.

Tushnet, Mark. 1984. "An Essay on Rights," *Texas Law Review* 62: 1363.

———. 1987. *The NAACP's Legal Strategy against Segregated Education, 1925–1950*. Chapel Hill: University of North Carolina Press.

————. 1990. "Review: Translation As Argument," *William and Mary Law Review* 32: 105.

Tyack, David, and Larry Cuban. 1995. *Tinkering toward Utopia: A Century of Public School Reform.* Cambridge, MA: Harvard University Press.

Underwood, Julie K. 1995. "School Finance Adequacy as Vertical Equity," *University of Michigan Journal of Law Reform* 28: 493.

Unger, Roberto M. 1983. *The Critical Legal Studies Movement.* Cambridge, MA: Harvard University Press.

United States Census Bureau. 2002. *New Jersey Quickfacts.* Available online at: www.quickfacts.census.gov/qfd/states/3400.html.

Verstegen, Deborah A. 2004. "The Law of Financing Education: Towards a Theory of Adequacy: The Continuing Saga of Equal Educational Opportunity in the Context of State Constitutional Challenges to State School Finance Systems," *St. Louis University Public Law Review* 23: 499.

Walberg, Herbert J. 2006. "High-Poverty, High-Performance Schools," in Hanushek, ed., *Courting Failure.*

Wasby, Stephen L. 1995. *Race Relations Litigation in an Age of Complexity.* Charlottesville: University of Virginia Press.

West, Martin R., and Paul E. Peterson, eds. 2007. *School Money Trials: The Legal Pursuit of Educational Adequacy.* Washington, DC: The Brookings Institution Press.

Weston, Susan Perkins, and Robert F. Sexton. 2007. "Substantial but Not Yet Sufficient: Kentucky's Effort to Build Proficiency for Each and Every Child." Paper Prepared for the Symposium on "Equal Educational Opportunity: What Now?" Teacher's College, Columbia University, New York.

White, G. Edward. 1972. "From Sociological Jurisprudence to Realism: Jurisprudence and Social Change in Early Twentieth-Century America," *Virginia Law Review* 58: 999.

————. 1973. "The Evolution of Reasoned Elaboration: Jurisprudential Criticism and Social Change," *Virginia Law Review* 59: 279.

White, James Boyd. 1990. *Justice As Translation: An Essay in Cultural and Legal Criticism.* Chicago, IL: The University of Chicago Press.

————. 1996. "Imagining the Law," in Austin Sarat and Thomas Kearns, eds., *The Rhetoric of Law.* Ann Arbor: The University of Michigan Press.

Williams, Patricia. 1991. *The Alchemy of Race and Rights.* Cambridge, MA: Harvard University Press.

Wilson, Robert H., ed. 1997. *Public Policy and Community: Activism and Governance in Texas.* Austin: University of Texas Press.

Wise, Arthur. 1968. *Rich Schools, Poor Schools: The Promise of Equal Educational Opportunity*. Chicago, IL: University of Chicago Press.

Yaffe, Deborah. 2007. *Other People's Children: The Battle for Justice and Equality in New Jersey's Schools*. New Brunswick, NJ: Rutgers University Press.

Yinger, John, ed. 2004a. *Helping Children Left Behind: State Aid and the Pursuit of Educational Equity*. Cambridge, MA: The MIT Press.

Yinger, John. 2004b. "State Aid and the Pursuit of Educational Equity: An Overview," in John Yinger, ed., *Helping Children Left Behind: State Aid and the Pursuit of Educational Equity*. Cambridge, MA: The MIT Press.

Young, Michael. 1958. *The Rise of the Meritocracy, 1870–2033: An Essay on Education and Equality*. London: Thames and Hudson.

Zemans, Frances Kahn. 1983. "Legal Mobilization: The Neglected Role of the Law in the Political System," *American Political Science Review* 77: 690.

NEWSPAPER ARTICLES CITED

General References

April 26, 1989: "The Movement: Not Policy's Engine, but It's 'on the Train,'" *Education Week* (Nancy Mathis).

New Jersey Case Study

Newark Star-Ledger, or Star-Ledger

1978, April 30: "Study Finds Wide Gap in School Aid Formula" (Robert Braun).

1979, July 26: "School Aid Revise Could Add $53 Million" (Robert Braun).

1979, October 5: "Council Told Gap Is Growing Wider between Rich and Poor" (Vincent Zarate).

1981, February 6: "Suit Challenging the T & E Law Filed on Behalf of Poor, Minorities" (Robert Braun).

1985, July 24: "State Top Court Rules on Steps for Challenge of New Jersey School Aid Formula" (Robert G. Seiderstein).

1988, August 26a: "School Funding Formula Ruled Inequitable and Unworkable" (Matthew Reilly).

1988, August 26b: "Reactions Reflective of District" (Anthony Shannon).

1989, April 14: "State Board Affirms Funding Formula" (Matthew Reilly).

1989, June 25: "Legal Brief Brands School Funding Formula Racially, Economically Biased" (Kathy Barrett Carter).

1990, March 4: "Governor Aims at Policy Shift on Education" (Robert Braun).

1990, June 5: "Suit Lawyer Urges Rejection of Florio School Plan" (Matthew Reilly).

1990, June 17: "Suburbs Expect Tax Wallop from School Funding" (P. L. Wycoff).

1990, July 4: "Florio Signs School Aid Bill and Vows Safeguards" (Robert Schwanberg).

1990, July 29: "Teachers, School Boards Worried from Fallout over Pension Switch" (Bill Gannon).

1990, October 26: "School Chiefs Say Funding Law Threatens the Best" (Robert Braun).

1990, November 7: "Bradley Narrowly Edges Whitman as Voters Vent Anger over Taxes" (David Wald).

1990, November 8a: "Ellis Admits Florio's School Plan May Require Modifications to Work" (Robert Braun).

1990, November 8b: "Republicans See Vindication, Urge Tax Rollback" (Vincent Zarate).

1990, December 15: "School Aid Lawyer Promises Fight on Teacher Pension Plan" (Matthew Reilly).

1991, January 11: "Education Figure Rips Proposed Aid Shift" (Matthew Reilly).

1991, January 13: "Court Fight Vowed over School Funding System" (Matthew Reilly).

1991, February 17: "Partisan Politics Fractures Unity of Hands across New Jersey" (David Wald).

1991, April 25: "Founder Leaves Anti-Tax Group, Cites Hoopla over Political Plans" (David Wald).

1991, November 6a: "Assembly Edge Is 58–22" (Anthony F. Shannon).

1991, November 6b: "Dems Are Reduced to Urban Faithful" (David Wald).

1991, November 6c: "Senate Margin 27–13" (David Wald).

1992, January 28: "Teacher Pension Changes May Yield More State Aid" (Matthew Reilly).

1992, June 24: "School Fund Overhaul on Fast Track" (Matthew Reilly).

1992, June 30: "GOP Makes Strides on Capping State Aid to City School Districts" (Matthew Reilly).

1992, July 9: "School Aid Formula Defended, Faulted as Court Battle Begins" (Kathy Barrettt Carter).

1992, July 17: "Lawyer Fights School Funding Law Drops Teacher Pension Issue."

1992, September 24: "Republican Leaders Unveil Blueprint for Changing School Aid Formulas" (Matthew Reilly).

1992, December 14: "Key Parties Hammer Out School Funding Accord" (Matthew Reilly).

1992, December 18: "Legislature Votes School Aid, Study to Find Fund Formula" (Matthew Reilly).

1992, December 21: "Urban Officials Hail School Funding Formula" (Matthew Reilly).

1993, January 15: "School Accord Boosts State Aid by $291 Million" (Matthew Reilly).

1993, October 22: "School Funding a Tough Task to Tackle" (Matthew Reilly).

1994, April 8: "Whitman Panel Presents School Funding Law That Resembles Florio's QEA" (Matthew Reilly).

1994, April 14: "Panel Urges Big School Aid Hike but Plan Gets Chilly Reception" (Matthew Reilly).

July 13, 1994: "Whitman Stands by Her Promise to Cut Income Taxes by 30 Percent" (Joe Donahue).

1995, November 22: "Overhaul Juggles School Funding" (Donna Luesner).

1995, December 1: "Law Center Chief Raps New School Funding Proposal" (Nick Chiles).

1996, May 18: "State Submits Its Figures on Per Pupil Costs" (Robert Schwanberg).

1996, July 24: "Wilentz Dies after Battle with Cancer" (Kathy Barrentt Carter).

1997, May 15: "The Judging Will Put an End to the Fudging" (John McLaughlin).

2004, October 29: "Reading and Writing Scores Rise in Needy School Districts" (John Mooney).

2008, September 22: "State Suit Puts Abbott System in the Balance" (John Mooney).

2008, November 19: "Justices Block Bid to Change Abbott Funding" (*Star-Ledger* staff).

The New York Times

1985, September 1: "Key Issues in Limbo as School Begins" (Priscilla Van Tassel).

1985, November 6: "Kean Is Easy Victor in Jersey" (Joseph F. Sullivan).

1985, November 7: "Referendum: A Man Whose Popularity Cuts Across All Lines" (Joesph F. Sullivan).

1988, August 26: "Jersey Funds for Schools Found Flawed" (Joseph F. Sullivan).

1989, September 3: "As Schools Open, Kean's Legacy Is Assessed" (Priscilla Van Tassel).

1989, October 5: "New Jersey Seizes School District in Jersey City, Citing Total Failure" (Robert Hanly).

1989, November 5: "Kean's Successor to Face Lean Times" (Robert Hanly).

1990, March 5: "New Jersey Schools: Rich, Poor, Unequal" (Robert Hanly).

1990, May 14: "Florio Shifts Policy from School Testing to More Aid to Poor" (Robert Hanly).

1990, June 6a: "Good News for Florio" (Peter Kerr).

1990, June 6b: "New Jersey Ruling to Lift Aid for Poor Districts" (Joesph F. Sullivan).

1990, June 22: "Florio School-Aid Package Gains Final Approval" (Peter Kerr).

1990, June 24: "About New Jersey" (Anthony Depalma).

1990, June 26: "Cooperman Is Back at Center of Storm on School Testing" (Priscilla Van Tassel).

1990, July 11: Op-Ed: "Is the Florio Plan Stiff Medicine or Poison?" Pro: "It's the Only Cure" (Stephen D. Dnistrian and Moureen Muenster); Con: "It Will Murder the Middle Class" (David Sacks).

1990, August 9: "Florio to Talk Directly to Citizens on Tax Increases" (Wayne King).

1990, September 1: "New Jersey's Wealthy School Districts Gird for Battle on Aid" (Robert Hanly).

1990, September 2: "Schools Preparing for Changes in Financing" (Priscilla Van Tassel).

1990, September 17: "New School Aid in '91? Toms River Isn't Cheering" (Robert Hanly).

1990, November 1: "School Officials Vent Anger over New Jersey Financing Law" (Robert Hanly).

1991, January 8: "Democrats Urge Big Shift in Florio Plan" (Peter Kerr).

1991, November 2: " 'Hands' in '91: Where Did the Crowds Go?" (Wayne King).

1992, August 5: "Republicans Halt for a Breath as They Undo Florio's Efforts" (Jerry Grey).

1992, August 30: "Trenton GOP Shifting School Aid to Suburbs" (Wayne King).

1993, February 28: "Florio Gains in Popularity, New Poll Says" (Jerry Grey).

1993, September 23: "Florio Attacks Whitman's Tax Cut Proposal" (Jerry Grey).

1994, January 19: "Little Warning Given of Tax Cut in Whitman Speech" (Jerry Grey).

1994, March 9: "Whitman Maintains High Profile, Sunny Side Up" (Iver Peterson).

1994, March 17: "Whitman's Goal: Cut Taxes without Wounding Voters" (Jerry Grey).

1994, July 1: "Victory over Doubters" (Iver Peterson).

1994, July 22: "At the Bar" (Kimberly McLarin).

1995, October 24: "Marilyn Morheuser Dies at 71; Fought for Parity in Education" (Wolfgang Saxon).

1996, July 24: "Robert Wilentz, 69, New Jersey Chief Justice, Dies; Court Aided Women and the Poor" (David Stout).

2007, December 21: "With Little Time Left, Trenton Lawmakers Weigh New Formula for School Financing" (David W. Chen).

2008, January 8: "New Jersey Revamps State Aid to Schools" (David W. Chen).

2009, May 29: "Court Backs New Jersey Aid Revision: Less Focus on Poorest Schools," (Winnie Hu).

Education Week

1990, May 16: "Cooperman Legacy: Gutsy Reform, Unsolved Problems" (Lynn Olson).

1990, October 10: "New Jersey Educators Seek Use of Urban Schools, Huge Funding Increases" (Jonathan Weismann).

1990, November 21: "Florio to Consider Changing Unpopular Finance Law" (Jonathan Weismann).

1991, October 23: "Shifts in Education Politics Seen in N.J. Election Battle" (Jonathan Weismann).

1992, January 22: "Florio Offers Olive Branch to Republicans, Taxpayers" (Karen Diegmueller).

1992, March 25: "Republicans in N.J. Assembly Unveil Funding Plan" (Karen Diegmueller).

1992, April 8: "Florio Outflanks Republicans in School Aid Debate" (Karen Diegmueller).

1992, August 5: "N.J. Lawmakers Sidetrack Constitutional Amendments" (Karen Diegmueller).

1995, March 5: "N.J. to Debate Standards before Revisiting School Finance Issue" (Mark Walsh).

Other Papers:

1990, June 20: *UPI News Service.*

1990, June 21: *UPI News Service.*

2003, June 22: *"Abbott* Reforms Are Producing Strong Gains," Robert E. Slavin, *Trenton Times* [Op Ed piece].

2003, June 23: Davis, Maria "Student Scores Show Progress, but Critics Question Price," Maria Davis, *North Jersey Media Group/NorthJersey.com.*

Kentucky Case Study

The Lousiville Times

1984, December 4: "Chance That School Leaders Will File Equity Suit Increases" (staff)

The Lousiville Courier-Journal

1980, May 27: "Group Asks What the Future Holds for Education" (staff).

1982, June 6: "Education Panel Plans to Keep Going" (staff).

1984, July 10: "Prichard Panel Lists Preliminary Proposals for Reforming Schools" (staff).

1984, November 11: "Forums' Planners Want Mass Movement for Better Schools" (staff).

1984, November 17: "Educational Forums Are Considered Successful" (staff).

1986, January 19: "Combs Calls School Finance Suit the Best Way to Settle Issue" (staff).

1987, December 12: "Legislators Intensify Sparring with Wilkinson" (Scott Thurm).

1988, January 22: "Budget Woes Demand Common Sacrifice, Governor Asserts" (Bob Johnson).

1988, January 30: "Wilkinson's Opposition Means Chances for New Taxes Almost Nil, Lawmakers Say" (staff).

1988, February 5: "Unveiling of Wilkinson's Education Plan Delayed" (Carol Marie Cropper).

1988, March 19: "Canceling of Panel's Meeting May Kill Governor's School Bill" (Carol Marie Cropper).

1988, March 24b: "Senators Urge End to Confrontations between Governor and Legislators" (John Voskuhl).

1988, April 19: "Arguments Finished in Poor Districts' Case" (Al Cross).

1988, May 29: "Ruling Expected Citing Disparity between Rich and Poor Systems" (Fran Ellers and Carol Marie Cropper).

1988, June 1: "School Finance System Struck Down, Opening Way for Vast Changes" (Carol Marie Cropper).

1988, June 3: "Metro Area Districts Reflect Kentucky's Have, Have-Not System" (Larry Bleiberg).

1988, June 7: "Alexander to Lead Panel on Financing for Schools" (Carol Marie Cropper).

1988, July 7: "Wilkinson, Legislative Leaders Seek School Accord" (Al Cross and Carol Marie Cropper).

1988, July 15: "Wilkinson, Legislators Healing Split on Education" (Tom Loftus).

1988, August 20: "Wilkinson to Call Special Session on Education for January" (staff).

1988, August 23: "Wilkinson Says Session Won't Deal with Taxes" (staff).

1988, September 9: "Wilkinson Stumps for Lottery, Education Reforms, in Elizabethtown" (David Cazares).

1988, October 15: "Judge Orders State to Find More Money for Schools" (Carol Marie Cropper).

1988, October 16: "Impact of School Finance Case Up to Governor, Combs Says" (Carol Marie Cropper).

1988, November 14: "Officials Hoping for Thaw in Education Freeze" (Carol Marie Cropper).

1988, December 8: "Skeptical State Supreme Court Hears School Finance Arguments" (Carol Marie Cropper).

1989, January 14: "Wilkinson Announces Warren Plant, Baits Education Foes" (Tim Roberts).

1989, February 2: "School Session Likely to Be Limited by Wilkinson" (Tom Loftus).

1989, February 8: "Wilkinson Meets with Educators, Says He's Open to Their Ideas" (Tom Loftus and Carol Marie Cropper).

1989, February 15: "Special Session Is Put on Hold by Wilkinson" (Carol Marie Cropper).

1989, February 25: "Tax Increase for Education Lacks Support, Governor Says" (Tom Loftus).

1989, March 5: "News" (Bob Johnson).

1989, March 7: "Education Leaders Unsure of Whether Wilkinson Will Take Tax Initiative" (Carol Marie Cropper).

1989, March 29: "Wilkinson, Lawmakers Say Education Talk Helped" (John Voskuhl).

1989, April 6: "Wilkinson Says He'll Consider a House Education Plan" (Richard Wilson).

1989, April 13: "Legislators Agree on a $350 Million School Plan" (Tom Loftus).

1989, April 30: "News" (Dick Kaukas).

1989, May 4: "Governor to Take His Time with Review of Education Package from Democrats" (Mark R. Chellgren).

1989, June 3: "Many Think High Court Will Back Corns on Fair School Funding" (Tom Loftus).

1989, June 9a: "Independents Emerge as a Political Issue" (Larry Bleiberg).

1989, June 9b: "News" (Tom Loftus).

1989, June 11: "Editorial" (staff).

1989, June 12: "Combs Says Ruling Won't Spell Trouble for Wealthier Schools" (Tom Loftus).

1989, June 18: "Run, Dick, See Your Legislator Cower in Fear of Mr. Tax" (Robert T. Garrett).

1989, June 28: "News" (Michael Jennings).

1989, August 6: "Most Say They'd Support Higher Taxes for Schools" (Dick Kaukas).

1989, August 27: "State's Tax System Creates Crisis: It's Obsolete, Inadequate, and Unfair" (Tom Loftus).

1990, February 2: "Bluegrass State Poll: Public Ranks School Reform as Top Issue" (Rick McDonough).

1990, February 11: "Education Task Force Quickens Pace as Clock Ticks" (Michael Jennings).

1990, February 24a: "School Reforms Get 'Qualified' Approval" (Patrick Howington).

1990, February 24b: "School Plan Seeks Big Jump in State Spending for Schools" (Michael Jennings).

1900, March 8: "Education Plan Ready for Legislative Action" (Michael Jennings).

1990, March 9: "Mammoth School-Reform Bill to Begin Journey Through Legislature Today" (Michael Jennings).

1990, March 10: "Criticism Begins Quickly as School Bill Is Introduced" (Michael Jennings).

1990, March 11: "News" (Al Cross and Tom Loftus).

1990, March 22: "House Passes Reform Bill after Heated Debate" (Patrick Howington, Michael Jennings, and Richard Wilson).

1990, March 29: "School-Reform Bill Gets Senate Approval" (Michael Jennings and Patrick Howington).

1990, April 12: "News" (Michael Jennings).

Lexington Herald-Leader

1982, June 8: "Building from the Blueprint: Watching Out for Excellence" (staff).

1983, September 8: "Prichard Committee Changing Its Focus" (staff).

1984, January 4: "Laying the Foundation for Education Reform" (staff).

1984, September 19: "Collins Endorses Education Forums" (staff).

1988, June 4: "Wilkinson Lauds Ruling on School Funding" (Todd Pack).

1988, June 25: "Legislators to Boycott Judge's Committee" (Mary Ann Roser).

1988, June 27: "Wilkinson Says That Legislators Critical of School Ruling Have Wrong Attitude" (Todd Pack).

1988, July 18: "Prichard Panel Sees Ray of Hope" (Mary Ann Roser).

1988, October 15: "Judge Orders Boost in School Funding" (Mary Ann Roser).

1988, December 8: "Justice Says School Finance Ruling Vague" (Mary Ann Roser).

The New York Times

1989, June 9: "Kentucky High Court Says State Must Redesign Its School System" (AP Wire).

1996, March 26: "Revamped Kentucky Schools Are a Study in Pros and Cons"

Education Week

1991, April 10: "After First Year, Kentucky Reforms Called 'On the Move'" (Lonie Harp).

1994, May 18: "The Plot Thickens" (Lonie Harp).

1996, March 13: "Kentucky Judge Upholds Statewide Testing System" (News Summary).

CASES CITED

Abbott v. Burke, Office of Administrative Law, Docket Number EDU 5581-85 (Decision by Administrative Law Judge Steven Lefelt). [Lefelt Decision]

Abbott v. Burke, OAL Docket Number EDU 5518-85 (Decision of Commissioner of Education Saul Cooperman).

Abbott v. Burke, 477 A.2d 1278 (New Jersey Sup. Ct., App. Div., 1984).

Abbott v. Burke, 100 N.J. 296, 495 A.2d 376 (1985) [Abbott I].

Abbott v. Burke, 119 N.J. 287; 575 A.2d 359 (1990) [Abbott II].

Abbott v. Burke, Docket No. 91-C-00150. Superior Court of the New Jersey, Chancery Division, Mercer County. Unpublished Decision by the Hon. Paul Levy (1993).

Abbott v. Burke, 136 N.J. 144, 643 A.2d 575 (1994) [Abbott III].

Abbott v. Burke, 149 N.J. 145, 693 A.2d 417 (1997) [Abbott IV].

Abbott v. Burke, 153 N.J. 480, 710 A.2d 450 (1998) [Abbott V].

Abbott v. Burke, 163 N.J. 95, 748 A.2d 82 (2000) [Abbott VI].

Abbott v. Burke, 164 N.J. 84, 751 A.2d 1032 (2000) [Abbott VII].

Abbott v. Burke, 170 N.J. 537, 790 A.2d 602 (2002) [Abbott VIII].

Abbott v. Burke, 172 N.J. 294, 798 A.2d 842 (2002) [Abbott IX].

Abbott v. Burke, 177 N.J. 587, 832 A2d 891 (2003) [Abbott X]

Abbott v. Burke, 177 N.J. 596, 832 A2d 609 (2003) [Abbott XI]

Abbott v. Burke, 180 N.J. 444, 852 A2d 185 (2004) [Abbott XII]

Abbott v. Burke, 182 N.J. 153, 862 A2d 538 (2004) [Abbott XIII]

Abbott v. Burke, 185 N.J. 612, 889 A2d 1063 (2005) [Abbott XIV]

Abbott v. Burke, 187 N.J. 191, 901 A2d 299 (2006) [Abbott XV]

Abbott v. Burke, 196 N.J. 348, 953 A2d 1198 (2006) [Abbott XVI]

Abbott v. Burke, 193 N.J. 34, 935 A2d 1152 (2007) [Abbott XVII]

Abbott v. Burke, 196 N.J. 451, 956 A2d 923 (2008) [Abbott XVIII]

Abbott v. Burke, 196 N.J. 544, 960 A2d 360 (2008) [Abbott XIX]

Abbott v. Burke, Slip Opinion, May 29, 2009 [Abbott XX] (available at: website: www.edlawcenter.org/ELCPublic/AbbottvBurke

Baker v. Carr, 369 U.S. 186 (1962).

Boddie v. Connecticut, 401 U.S. 371 (1971).

Bowers v. Hardwick, 478 U.S. 186 (1986).

Brown v. Board of Education, 347 U.S. 483 (1954).

Burruss v. Wilkinson, 310 F. Supp. 572, aff'd 397 U.S. 44 (1970).

Commonwealth v. Griffin, 105 S.W.2d 1063 (Ky. Ct. of App., 1930).

Council for Better Education, et al. v. Wallace Wilkinson. Findings of Fact, Conclusions of Law, and Judgment, Franklin Circuit Court, Division I, Civil Action No. 85-CI-1759 (1988).

Douglas v. California, 372 U.S. 353 (1963).

Edgewood v. Kirby, 777 S.W. 391 (Tx. S. Ct., 1989).

Elliott v. Garner, 130 S.W. 307 (Ky. Ct. of App., 1910).

Gideon v. Wainwright, 372 U.S. 335 (1963).

Griffin v. Illinois, 351 U.S. 12 (1956).

Griswold v. Connecticut, 381 U.S. 479 (1965).

Harper v. Va. Board of Elections, 383 U.S. 663 (1966).

Hills Development Corp. v. Township of Bernards, 510 A.2d 621 (N.J. 1986) [Mount Laurel III].

Hobson v. Hansen, 265 F. Supp. 902 (D.D.C., 1967), aff'd as modified, *Smuck v. Hansen*, 408 F2d 175 (D.C. Cir., 1969).

Landis v. Ashworth, 57 N.J.L. 509 (NJ Sup. Ct., 1895).

McInnis v. Shapiro, 293 F. Supp. 327 (N.D. Ill., 1968), aff'd mem. sub nom. *McInnis v. Olgilvie*, 394 U.S. 322 (1969).

Plessy v. Ferguson, 163 U.S. 537 (1896).

Prouse v. Board of Education, 120 S.W. 307 (Ky. Ct. of App., 1909).

Reynolds v. Sims, 377 U.S. 533 (1964).

Robinson v. Cahill, 118 N.J. Super. 223, 287 A.2d 187 (1972) [Botter Decsion].

Robinson v. Cahill, 62 N.J. 473, 303 A.2d 273 (1973) [Robinson I].

Robinson v. Cahill, 63 N.J. 196, 306 A.2d 65 (1973) [Robinson II].

Robinson v. Cahill, 67 N.J. 335, 335 A.2d 6 (1975) [Robinson III].

Robinson v. Cahill, 67 N.J. 333; 339 A.2d 193 (1975) [Robinson IV].

Robinson v. Cahill, 69 N.J. 449, 355 A.2d 129 (1976) [Robinsion V].

Robinson v. Cahill, 70 N.J. 155, 358 A.2d 457 (1976) [Robinson VI].

Roe v. Wade, 410 U.S. 113 (1973).

Rose v. Council for Better Eduction, 790 S.W2d 186 (Ky. S. Ct.) (1989).

Russman v. Luckett, 391 S.W.2d 694 (Ky. Ct. of App.) (1965).

San Antonio Independent School District v. Rodriguez, 411 U.S. 1 (1973).

Serrano v. Preist, 487 P.2d 1241 (Cal. S. Ct.) (1971) [Serrano I].

Serrano v. Preist, 557 P.2d 929 (Cal. S. Ct.) (1976) [Serrano II].

Shapiro v. Thompson, 394 U.S. 618 (1969).

Southern Burlington County N.A.A.C.P. v. Township of Mount Laurel, 336 A.2d 713 (N.J. 1975) [Mount Laurel I].

Southern Burlington County N.A.A.C.P. v. Township of Mount Laurel, 456 A.2d 390 (N.J. 1983) [Mount Laurel II].

Trustees of Graded Free Common Schools v. Trustees of Graded Free White Common Schools, 203 S.W. 520 (Ky. Ct. of App.) (1918).

Wooley v. Spalding, 295 S.W.2d 563 (Ky. Ct. of App.) (1956).

INTERVIEWS

New Jersey Case Study

Block, Steve. November 1995, November 1996, and September 2002.

Corcoran, Thomas. September 1994.

Eisdorfer, Stephen. September 1994.

Florio, James. September 1994.

Goertz, Margaret. September 1994.

Green, Herbert. September 1994.

Morheuser, Marilyn. June 1994.

Reock, Ernest. September 1998.

Sciarra, David. September 2002, September 2006, and July 2009.

Smith, Mark. September 1994.

Strickland, Lynn. September 2002.

Tractenberg, Paul. June 1994 and November 1995.

Kentucky Case Study

Adams-Rodgers, Lois. July 1996.

Alexander, Kern. June 1995.

Augenblick, John. September 1995.

Dawahare, Debra. March 1995.

Guess, Arnold. August 1995.

Hawpe, David. July 1996.

Heine, Cindy. June 1996 and September 2006.

Lavit, Ted. March 1995.

Moloney, Michael. July 1995.

Moreland, Jack. June 1995.

Newman, Frank. June 1995.

Sexton, Robert, June 1995 and June 1996.

Willis, Tom. June 1995.

INDEX